A Small Greek World

PREVIOUS BOOKS BY IRAD MALKIN

Greek and Roman Networks in the Mediterranean (ed. with Christy Constantakopoulou,
and Katerina Panagopoulou)

Mediterranean Paradigms and Classical Antiquity (ed.)

Ethnicity and Identity in Ancient Greece

Ancient Perceptions of Greek Ethnicity (ed.)

The Returns of Odysseus: Colonization and Ethnicity

Myth and Territory in the Spartan Mediterranean

Leaders and Masses in the Roman World: Studies in Honor of Zvi Yavetz (ed. with
Z.W. Rubinsohn)

Leaders and Leadership in Jewish and World History (ed. with Zeev Tzahor)

La France et la Méditerranée (ed.)

Mediterranean Cities: Historical Perspectives (ed. with R.L. Hohlfelder)

Religion and Colonization in Ancient Greece

A Small Greek World

Networks in the Ancient Mediterranean

IRAD MALKIN

OXFORD
UNIVERSITY PRESS

OXFORD
UNIVERSITY PRESS

Oxford University Press is a department of the University of Oxford.
It furthers the University's objective of excellence in research,
scholarship, and education by publishing worldwide.

Oxford   New York
Auckland   Cape Town   Dar es Salaam   Hong Kong   Karachi
Kuala Lumpur   Madrid   Melbourne   Mexico City   Nairobi
New Delhi   Shanghai   Taipei   Toronto

With offices in
Argentina   Austria   Brazil   Chile   Czech Republic   France   Greece
Guatemala   Hungary   Italy   Japan   Poland   Portugal   Singapore
South Korea   Switzerland   Thailand   Turkey   Ukraine   Vietnam

Oxford is a registered trademark of Oxford University Press
in the UK and certain other countries.

Published in the United States of America by
Oxford University Press
198 Madison Avenue, New York, NY 10016

© Oxford University Press 2011

First issued as an Oxford University Press paperback, 2013

Library of Congress Cataloging-in-Publication Data
Malkin, Irad.
A small Greek world : networks in the Ancient Mediterranean / Irad Malkin.
    p.   cm. — (Greeks overseas)
ISBN 978-0-19-973481-8 (hardcover); 978-0-19-931572-7 (paperback)
1. Greece—Civilization—To 146 BC 2. Mediterranean Region—Civilization—Greek influences.
3. Greeks—Mediterranean Region—History. 4. Greeks—Colonization—Mediterranean Region.
5. Greece—Colonies—Mediterranean Region. 6. Network Theory—Networks—Small Worlds.
I. Title. II. Series.
DF222.2.M35   2012
938—dc22   2010049158

GREEKS OVERSEAS

Series Editors
Carla Antonaccio and Nino Luraghi

This series presents a forum for new interpretations of Greek settlement in the ancient Mediterranean in its cultural and political aspects. Focusing on the period from the Iron Age until the advent of Alexander, it seeks to undermine the divide between colonial and metropolitan Greeks. It welcomes new scholarly work from archaeological, historical, and literary perspectives and invites interventions on the history of scholarship on the Greeks in the Mediterranean.

A Small Greek World Networks in the Ancient Mediterranean
Irad Malkin

Italy's Lost Greece Magna Graecia and the Making of Modern Archaeology
Giovanna Ceserani

The Invention of Greek Ethnography From Homer to Herodotus
Joseph E. Skinner

Dan Daor
Forever my friend

Series Editors' Foreword

This series is dedicated to reconceptualizing the emergence of Greek communities all around the Mediterranean during the late Iron Age and the Archaic period. The series publishes contributions that encompass archaeological and literary perspectives, applying new methods and theoretical approaches and bringing together old and new evidence, with a special but not exclusive emphasis on the cultural and historical implications of recent archaeological research. While the main focus is on the Archaic period down to the beginning of the fifth century, we do not exclude the fourth century, especially as regards the western Mediterranean. Our aim is to provide a common forum for the convergence of various experiences and traditions in order to articulate new paradigms for the interpretation of the Greek expansion in the ancient Mediterranean in its cultural and political aspects. Our purpose is to elucidate the relevance of the colonial world for the development of Greek culture as a whole and to focus on phenomena that contributed to Greekness in its multiple local variants. Research on diasporas, culture contact, cultural hybridity, and networks in other historical contexts offers new conceptual paradigms to approach the cultural history of the Greeks overseas. In addition, the amount of material evidence available has increased in quantity and quality over the last few decades, thanks to the activity of archaeologists all around the Mediterranean, from Spain to the Black Sea.

Our hope to undermine the divide between "colonial" and "metropolitan Greeks" is admirably furthered by this volume from Irad Malkin. Originating in his Nellie Wallace lectures at Oxford (2005), the author draws on the latest concepts from network theory stemming from work in history, geography, sociology, physics, computer science, economics, and many other disciplines. In this thoroughly new approach, Malkin takes the notion of "connectivity" and an emphasis on the Mediterranean as a medium of communication rather than separation and extends it to both explain and describe Greek culture as a "small world." In network theory, this term encompasses a network of nodes that are interconnected without geographical distance or even time as a factor. Malkin concludes that network theory is useful when applied to Greek colonization—Greeks moving out—and the formation of Greek identity at the same time. These two apparently divergent phenomena are not contradictory scenarios at all, as his framework demonstrates.

We trust that this book will stimulate further debate and research on early Greek identity formation, comparative colonial studies, and a broad range of phenomena in Greek history and culture. We are proud to publish this truly original contribution in the Greeks Overseas series.

Carla Antonaccio
Nino Luraghi

Table of Contents

List of Illustrations

Acknowledgments

This book has its beginnings in the Nellie Wallace Lectures I gave at Oxford University in 2005. I am grateful to the Oxford Faculty of Classics, who elected me for these lectures. Special thanks go to the late and beloved Peter Derow, who hosted me at Wadham College; to Nicholas Purcell and Robert Parker, who made my stay a particularly welcome one, and to my friend Josephine Crawley Quinn, who hosted me for short periods at Worcester College and whose conversation and lucid advice are always most valuable. I am grateful to Robin Osborne, who invited me to Cambridge University and made my stay at Cambridge as a short-term fellow at King's College a happy and fruitful one. To the former director of the Centre Louis Gernet (now Centre ANHIMA [*Anthropologie et histoire des mondes antiques*]) in Paris, François Lissarrague, and to its current one, François de Polignac, I owe a warm, friendly debt for their consistent hospitality and thought-provoking conversations. I will always remember with affection and appreciation the late Pierre Vidal-Naquet, who was the first to introduce me to the Centre Louis Gernet and kept encouraging me over the years. I also wish to express my gratitude to Alan Shapiro and Matthew Roller, who, as chairs of the Department of Classics at Johns Hopkins University, have hosted me several times, and to my other colleagues there. I keep lamenting the passing away of Raymond Westbrook, a great scholar and friend. Very warm and special thanks go to Marcel Detienne, the first to bring me over to Paris to participate in a project on comparative foundations and who has remained a friend during the years that followed, both in Paris and in Baltimore. In recent years his interest in collective identities has proven provocative and important.

I wish to extend my warm thanks to Michal Molcho, my former student and research assistant, for her help and dedication throughout the work on this book. I owe a significant debt to the two anonymous readers of Oxford University Press for their helpful comments. Special thanks go to my friend Yoav Ben-Dov, a historian of physics (Ben-Dov 1995, 1997), who was the first to introduce me to the world of networks, pointed out some fascinating directions, and steered me off some tempting sandbanks.

With some additions and changes, chapter 4 in this book is based on my article "Herakles and Melqart: Greeks and Phoenicians in the Middle Ground" in *Cultural Borrowings and Ethnic Appropriations in Antiquity*, ed. Erich Gruen, 238–57, *Oriens et Occidens* 8 (Stuttgart: Steiner, 2005). I thank the publisher for the permission to include it in this book. I thank also my colleague and friend Sylvie Honigman for help with the transliteration of biblical Hebrew in this chapter.

The research has been made possible by a grant from the Israel Science Foundation (ISF). One year of research has been spent happily at the Institute for Advanced Studies, Jerusalem (IAS, www.as.huji.ac.il) with the Research Group on Urban Change, led by Gideon Avni and Ronnie Ellenblum. I wish to thank my colleagues and friends in the group for their comments and advice during the year. Finally, I wish to acknowledge my own Department of History at Tel Aviv University and my colleagues there. Placed in a small country in the eastern Mediterranean, within a few minutes walk from an ancient Philistine tell and just south of some Phoenician outposts, the department's international scope, intellectual vigor, and excellent students have provided a happy and thought-provoking home. Twenty-five years ago a group of historians founded the *Mediterranean Historical Review* at the (Graduate) School of History at Tel Aviv University, a biannual academic journal that publishes articles on issues of Mediterranean history that often transcend traditional periodization and categorization. I have learned much from my coeditor, Benjamin Arbel, from my colleagues on the editorial panel, and from the numerous articles and testimonia we have published. I am very encouraged to observe that the *Mediterranean Historical Review* is now part of a growing interest in Mediterranean studies.

List of Abbreviations

AION	*ArchStAnt* n.s. *Annali dell'Istituto Universitario Orientale di Napoli*, Dipartimento di studi del mondo classico e del Mediterraneo antico, sezione di archeologia e storia antica, nuova serie
AJA	*American Journal of Archaeology*
AR	*Archaeological Reports*. Published annually by the *Journal of Hellenic Studies*.
BASOR	*Bulletin of the American Schools of Oriental Research*
BCH	*Bulletin de Correspondance Hellénique*
BIFAO	*Bulletin de l'Institut français d'archéologie orientale*
BSR	*Papers of the British School at Rome*
BTCGI	*Bibliografia topografica della colonizzazione greca in Italia e nelle isole tirreniche*. Edited by G. Nenci and G. Vallet. Rome: Scuola Normale Superiore.
CPh	*Classical Philology*
CQ	*Classical Quarterly*
CRAI	*Comptes rendus des séances de l'Académie des inscriptions et belles-lettres*
DHA	*Dialogues d'Histoire Ancienne*
FGrHist	Jacoby, Felix (1923–1958). *Die Fragmente der griechischen Historiker*. Leiden: Brill.
FHG	Müller, Karl Otfried (1841–1872). *Fragmenta historicorum graecorum*. Paris: Ambrosio Firmin Didot.
GGM	Müller, Carl Friedrich Wilhelm (1855–1891). *Geographi graeci minores*. 3 vols. Paris: Ambrosio Firmin Didot.

IvO   Dittenberger, Wilhelm and Karl Purgold (1896). *Die Inschriften von Olympia*. Berlin: Asher.

JHA   *Journal for the History of Astronomy*

JHS   *Journal of Hellenic Studies*

LIMC   *Lexicon iconographicum mythologiae classicae* (1981–). Zurich: Artemis.

LSJ   Liddell, Henry George and Robert Scott (1996). A Greek-English lexicon with a revised supplement, 9th ed. rev. and augmented throughout by Henry Stuart Jones. Oxford: Clarendon.

MEFRA   *Mélanges de l'École française de Rome, Antiquité*

MHR   *Mediterranean Historical Review*

ML   Meiggs, Russell and David M. Lewis (1989). *A Selection of Greek Historical Inscriptions to the End of the Fifth Century B.C.* Rev. ed. Oxford: Clarendon.

OJA   *Oxford Journal of Archaeology*

PACT   *Revue du Groupe européen d'études pour les techniques physiques, chimiques, et mathématiques appliqués à l'archéologie*

PAPhS   *Proceedings of the American Philosophical Society*

PCPhS   *Proceedings of the Cambridge Philological Society*

PP   *La Parola del Passato*

RE   Pauly, August, Georg Wissowa et al., (eds.) (1894–1980). *Paulys Realencyclopädie der classischen Altertumswissenschaft*. Stuttgart: Metzler.

REA   *Revue des études anciennes*

REG   *Revue des études grecques*

RFIC   *Rivista di filologia e di istruzione classica*

RHR   *Revue de l'histoire des religions*

SCI   *Scripta Classica Israelica*

SEG   *Supplementum epigraphicum graecum* (1923–). Leiden: Sijthoff (vols. 1–27) and Amsterdam: Gieben (vols. 28–).

TAPhA   *Transactions and Proceedings of the American Philological Association*

ZPE   *Zeitschrift für Papyrologie und Epigraphik*

A Note on Transliteration

I try to be consistent in transliterating Greek words and names, prefer-
ring Greek forms (Hekataios rather than Hecataeus, Metapontion
rather than Metapontum). However, since so many Greek names have
become conventional in English (such as Corinth rather than Kor-
inthos, Cyrene rather than Kyrene) I have preferred them for clarity's
sake. Greek terms and quotations in the text are transliterated; Greek
may be found in the notes.

A Small Greek World

I

Introduction: Networks and History

Networks, the Archaic Mediterranean, and the Formation of Greek Civilization

Greek civilization came into being just when the Greeks were splitting apart. It took the form familiar to us during the Archaic period at the time Greeks were separating, migrating, and founding new communities in ever-widening horizons, reaching both the western Mediterranean and the eastern Black Sea (figure 1-1). On the coastal strips of these wide maritime horizons there were hundreds, mostly independent, Greek political communities with no contiguous territory and no single political center coordinating them. No pan-Mediterranean Greek empire had ever existed in the Archaic period (roughly from the eighth to the early fifth century BCE), and the numerous Greek communities functioned as a decentralized network. Imagine a circle of individuals, with each looking inward and facing each other, except that in this case we have a maritime circle, and the participants are *emporia* and city-states. In this maritime world they were interconnected mostly by the shared—though never owned—Mediterranean expanses. Greeks sometimes called the Mediterranean, together with the Black Sea, *he hemetera thalassa* ["our sea"] but only in a metaphorical sense. The equivalent Latin term, *mare nostrum*, conveys a diametrically opposed image of the maritime circle: The Mediterranean supposedly "belongs" to Rome, the center and capital of an empire. Instead of Greeks looking "inside," from their nodes on the shores

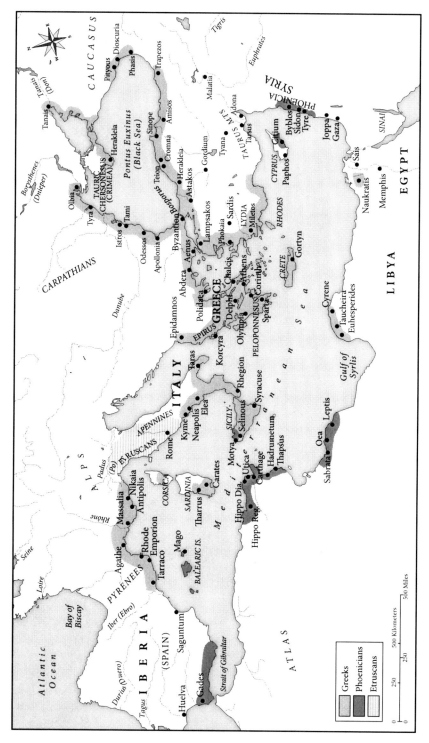

FIGURE I.I. Coastal areas of settlement in the Mediterranean: Greeks, Phoenicians, and Etruscans.

toward the shared sea, the Romans observed it from the center (Rome) outward, toward the coasts (figures 1-2 and 1-3).[1]

It was over the waters that Greeks migrated, founding new cities, creating regional identities, and transferring cults, myths, artistic conventions and artifacts, amphorae, and philosophies. Links, both planned and random, rapidly reduced the distance between the nodes of the network, turning the vast Mediterranean and the Black Sea into a "small world," a defining term in current network theory. These networks informed, sometimes created, and even came to express what we call Greek civilization.[2]

What we refer to conventionally as "Greek civilization" was formed during the Archaic period, between the second half of the eighth century BCE and the beginning of the fifth. This was the period of the formation of the city-state, the spread of the Homeric poems and the alphabet, and the emergence of Panhellenic cults, oracles, and monumental sanctuaries. It was also the time when literary, artistic, and architectural conventions spread among Greek communities, conventions that, for all their variability, are recognizably Greek. All this took place before the Classical period (fifth and fourth centuries) and a consolidation of a common, "confrontational" Greek identity in the face of the Persians in the east (beginning with Asia Minor) and the Phoenician-Carthaginians in the west (Sicily). The Archaic period was the time when Greeks, as Greeks, came to recognize specific commonalities among themselves, articulating them in terms of common narratives, ethnic genealogies, awareness of a common language, and access to Panhellenic cults, which were mostly reserved for Greeks alone.

The emergence of all of those commonalities was a process of convergence through divergence. By the end of the Archaic period, the greatest distance among Greek settlers was between modern Georgia in the eastern Black Sea and Spain in the western Mediterranean. The northernmost point was at the mouth of the River Don (at the northern Black Sea), and in the south, Cyrenaica (Libya) was Greek. What is noteworthy is that the more the Greeks dispersed, somehow the more "Greek" they became. This is an observable fact, but to date no one has sufficiently explained it. It would be natural to admire the Greeks for having achieved their civilization in spite of the consistently growing distance between their communities and the lack of contiguous territory. But why not reverse the approach? Greek civilization as we know it emerged, in my view, not in spite of distance but because of it. I will suggest that it was distance and network connectivity that created the virtual Greek center.

Unlike the Europeans in the New World, the Greeks who kept settling on the coasts did not have a notion of consolidated civilization from which they

---

1 Rubin (1986), pp. 14–26; Horden and Purcell (2000), pp. 10–12, 531.

2 For salient traits of what constitutes "civilization" and other similarly ambiguous concepts, see, for example, Braudel (1994), chapter 1.

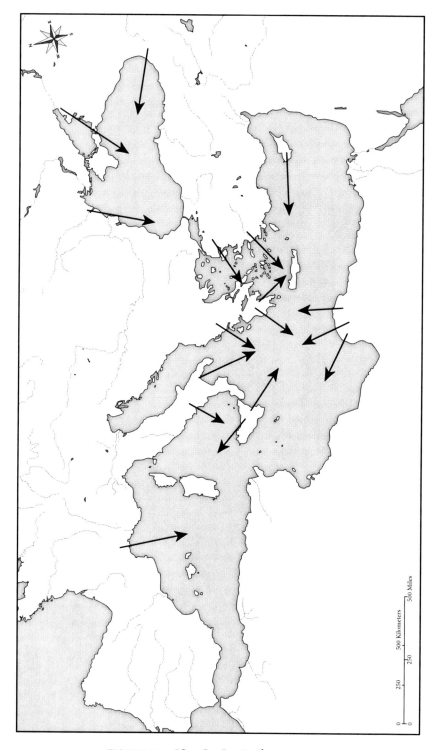

FIGURE I.2. "Our Sea," a Greek perspective.

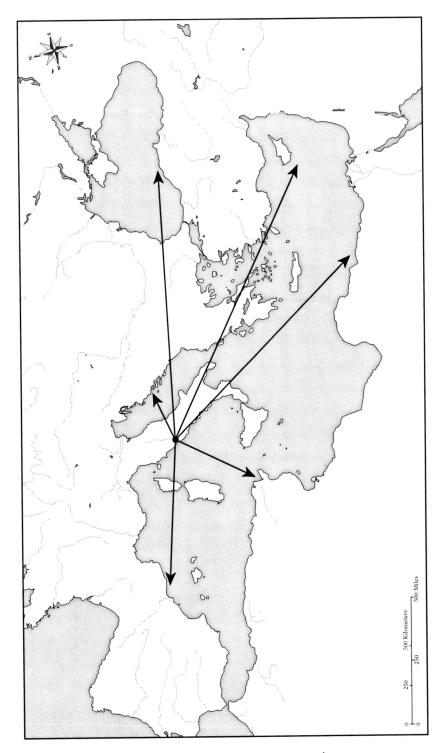

FIGURE I.3. "Our Sea," a Roman perspective.

Greece —not at a center looking out but peripheral.

departed and which they wished to export. Europeans observed the New World from a culture of the center, confident of their unquestionable superiority, and, most significantly, their monopoly over religious truth. In contrast, ancient Mediterranean religions were neither of the "revealed" type, nor were they monotheistic and exclusionary. Rather, the more syncretistic aspects of ancient Mediterranean religions facilitated the movement of religious notions along network lines. Religion sometimes served as a common matrix by mediating between Greeks, Phoenicians, Etruscans, and local populations. As far as we know, Greeks regarded "foreign" gods much as they did Greek ones, albeit with different names, rites, and representations. Religion was a universal *langue*; the local names of the deities the distinctive *parole*. Herakles (the Greek) *was* (the Phoenician) Melqart (chapter 4).

syncretism spread through networks

The notion of a superior center from which the world is viewed was almost certainly absent in the Archaic period. Greeks were familiar with the highly developed and more ancient cultures of the East, while their own position was peripheral. Their starting point was thus not a European center but a place between two worlds: the politically advanced Near East and the more fragmented Mediterranean and Black Sea areas.

With few exceptions, most of the more than one thousand Greek communities viewed their own origins in terms of migration and colonization. This observation applies equally to cities in "Older Greece," such as Corinth or Thebes, to the cities settled in Asia Minor during the Dark Ages (the "Ionian migrations"), and to the new "colonies" of the Archaic period, such as Syracuse. A common thread runs through the foundation stories of Greek cities, whether expressed in origin myths, quasi-historical accounts, or the better-evidenced historical narratives. A Greek *mentalité* is revealed, consisting of the notion that Greek history was young and on the move.

What is also clear is that separate, sovereign Greek communities had their discrete histories regardless of whether we assess them as true. Greek communities originated from different places, were founded at different times at distinct sites, and were led by different founders. Often they did not occupy adjoining territories. Neither in their historical narratives nor in terms of their lived experience was there a unity of time and space in the distinct narratives of the collective identities of Greek *poleis* (conventionally translated as "city-states"). The Greek starting points of "place" and "time" consisted of diffusion rather than concentration, occurring as a result of divergence rather than convergence.

divergence / convergence

With hindsight, the term "decentralized network" seems apt to describe the ancient Greek Mediterranean. As a descriptive term it is only slightly more useful than, say, the "Greek world." However, perhaps it is possible to ask whether the term "network" has an explanatory rather than just a representational value for the formation of the historical Greek network. Networks explain their own evolvement in terms of self-organization of complex systems,

network — how it evolved vs descriptive, representational

especially when applying new insights from network theory concerning the dynamics of network formation of small worlds, where connectivity and "distance" among nodes is measured by their degrees of separation rather than by physical distance (more on this later). We may question whether the dynamics that formed that decentralized Mediterranean network and its "flows" (contents) were also responsible for the general formation and the distinct attributes of Greek civilization. Having demonstrated that the Greek world was network oriented, can we move beyond the descriptive value of the term "network" and attribute to it a dynamic, creative role?

The question stems from contemporary concerns in more ways than one. For a historian to speak of networks as a heuristic concept requires a different way of observing, a new vocabulary, and a new definition of the object of observation. It is like asking a photographer to move to another position, to direct the camera elsewhere, and to replace its lens. It is difficult to avoid the term "network." Everyone is familiar with the "network news" of television. Most people are on the electrical grid or travel on a network of highways. The Internet introduced the wider public to the virtual World Wide Web, and an entire generation has been raised to think by means of lateral associations, opening "windows" on a computer screen, or reaching hypertexts with no necessary hierarchy of beginning and end. The globalized world is now familiar with networks that cross traditional boundary lines, and great corporations constitute their "hubs" with no necessary regard to the nation-state. Not too long ago it was impossible to travel from one major French city to another without first passing through France's capital, Paris. Indeed, the older French railway system represented the traditional, centralized, and hierarchical idea of a network.[3] (figure 1-5) Such a centralized network conforms to the image of the uniform and symbolically central nation-state. In contrast, the Internet and the World Wide Web have neither a "center" nor a hierarchy; although many persons access information through hubs, they do not have to. The World Wide Web does not stand in relation to its members in terms of "one to many" (cf. the Roman *mare nostrum*) but "many to many" (cf. the Greek *he hemetera thalassa*). The Internet lacks the hierarchical structure of the Cathedral and is more akin to the bazaar[4] and is therefore emblematic of the current view of decentralized networks. It is also a type of network remarkably similar to the structure of historical networks in the Archaic Mediterranean (figure 1-4).

Applying network concepts to historical civilizations seems to belong to our own Zeitgeist. "As a historical trend," says M. Castells, "dominant functions and processes are increasingly organized around networks. Networks constitute the new social morphology of our societies, and the diffusion of networking logic substantially modifies the operation and outcomes in processes

3 Dobbin (1994), pp. 111–13.
4 Raymond (2001).

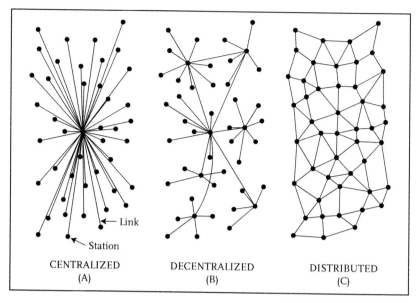

FIGURE I.4. Centralized, decentralized, and distributed networks. Paul Baran's suggested possibilities for the structure of the Internet (1964), with a preference for the less vulnerable distributed architecture. After Barabási (2003).

of production, experience, power and culture."[5] Castells's major interest lies in contemporary capitalism, studying globalization, state sovereignty, nongovernmental organizations (NGOs), and new social movements. Castells also points out a shift in mindset, probably linked to the postmodern sense of "shrinkage" and the blurring of conventional time-space categories.

Such "shrinkage" is well expressed in the work of Edward Soja, a groundbreaking thinker in the fields of spatial theory and cultural geography, following the pioneering work of Henri Lefebvre's *Production of Space*.[6] Soja's voice seems to best articulate the trend to reintroduce the concept of "space" into the humanities and the social sciences. He aptly quotes Michel Foucault's acute observation that illuminates both the anxiety and the options that networks have revealed:

> We are in an epoch of simultaneity; we are in an epoch of juxtaposition, the epoch of the near and the far, of the side-by-side, of the dispersed. We are at a moment, I believe, when our experience of the world is less that of a long life developing through time than that of a *network that connect points and intersects with its own skein.* (Soja 1989, 10; my emphasis)

5 Castells (1996), p. 469.
6 Lefebvre (1991); Soja (1989, 1996).

FIGURE 1.5. A centralized network: France's railway system ca. 1860 with Paris as a single major hub.

Foucault seems to express the postmodern lateral angst that has emerged following the loss of a sense of the linear progression of history, combined with the unprecedented contemporary experience of the shrinkage of geographical distances (e.g., via the Internet). Literature, too, seems to reflect the contemporary experience of the "spatiality of imagination." Soja refers to John Berger, a British painter, writer, art critic, and sociologist who has this to say about the novel, with a point pertinent to historians:

> It is scarcely any longer possible to tell a straight story sequentially unfolding in time. And this is because we are too aware of what is continually traversing the story line *laterally*. That is to say, instead of being aware of a point as an infinitely small part of a straight line, we are aware of it as an infinitely small part of an infinite number of lines, as the center of a star of lines. (John Berger, *The Look of Things* ([1974, 40])

Questioning the objectivity of geography

This approach, sometimes called the "spatial turn,"[7] has been revolutionary in overturning a common perception of geography as the "setting" for history and, specifically, of geographical space as a "container," existing objectively and independently of human activity:

> Space in modernity remained Cartesian and absolute, its language best described in Euclid's *Elements*. Space, like time, was treated as an objective phenomenon, existing independently of its contents. In this sense space was seen as a container that had effects on the objects existing within it, but was not itself affected by them.[8]

In this book, instead of viewing absolute space as a container, I am concerned with space that is relative and relational, a *historical* space that is both formed by connectivity among its proliferating nodes (here, "colonies") and simultaneously shaping their particular development, interconnections, and civilizational commonalities in the process. By the end of the Archaic period the result of such processes was an overarching Hellenic network where physical space and the space of the collective imagination converged.

The conventional claim that the subject of history is time, whereas that of geography is space, is now being seriously questioned. In some ways, we are returning to Strabo, who combined both.[9] Historians are being asked to reconsider their position: "The hoary traditions of space-blinkered historicism are being challenged with unprecedented explicitness by convergent calls for far-reaching spatialization of the critical imagination," says Soja, who continues to call for a "more flexible and balanced critical theory that re-entwines the making of history with the social production of space, with the construction and configuration of human geographies."[10]

Just as historians have been forever preoccupied with periodization, or time scales (contrast, e.g., a book titled *1789*, which focuses on a single year, with any long-term "history of the Middle Ages"), geographers have been concerned about scale. We have come to expect geographical studies in terms of "local," "regional," "national," and "global." Today, however:

> Both in theory and in practice, relative space more readily embraces the fact of *scalar continuity* and the constant blurring and interaction between scales that are always dependent on process and observation. "Local" spaces are as much a precipitate of "global"

---

7 On the "spatial turn" see Warf and Arias (2008); cf. Ethington (2007).

8 Cosgrove (2004), p. 58, goes on to say this: "Regarding space in this way corresponded well with the territorial imperatives of the nation-state as it had evolved within modern Europe, with the categorical administrative and organizational structures of state bureaucracies, industrial production, and social life in the modern city."

9 Clarke (1999) offers an excellent analysis of the time/space distinction.

10 Soja (1989), p. 11. Soja (p. 14) defines historicism "as an overdeveloped historical contextualization of social life and social theory that actively submerges and peripheralizes the geographical or spatial imagination."

processes. . . . Geographical "place" is today treated as an instantia-
tion of process rather than an ontological given. (my emphasis)[11]

The shift in perspective also applies to the shift of interest among some
historians, from reductionism, concentrating on the cellular, the institutional,
and the discrete political community—to relational models of fluidity and connectivity. Clearly, as Ian Morris shows, the effects of globalization on our perspectives are strongly felt in this shift.[12]

"Cellular history" has its corollary in geography in the study of "place" and
its nationalistic transformation into bounded *Landschaft*, comprehending the
"natural" territory of the *Volk* and its overlap with a given territory. Nineteenth-
century German geography was preoccupied with the relationships between
nation, state, and space (*Raum*).[13] Cosgrove traces this to Ptolemy's distinction
between a global earth geography and a geography of place (chorography), with
its peculiar features and history, as contrasted with the scalar continuity of geographical space.[14]

The modern, national issue of collective identity as bound up with a
national territory is something Greeks of the Archaic period did not have to
deal with—and not only because they lived in antiquity. Apriori, their space was
one of divergence. With no contiguous territory, with settlements sprinkled on
distant, disconnected shores, and with the "empty" sea as their center of connectivity, there was never a question of an overlap between a "Greek nation"
and its "land." Their mode of coastal existence lent itself rather to lateral connections (i.e., networks).

What also shapes our perspectives, at least in Western academia, is the
contemporary creation of the European Union, an overarching framework
that has been set up as a decentralized network. Europeans appear to be
structuring their European identity along distinctly Greek lines of affiliations. This is not meant to imply "the glory that was (Classical) Greece."[15]
Rather, what is striking is the structural similarity that combines, over enormous distances, an all-encompassing affinity with the preservation of the
discrete identities of the numerous political communities of the Archaic
Mediterranean. Ideologically, there is no center to the new Europe. It
constitutes a decentralized network, with Brussels as its "capital," Strasbourg the seat of the European Parliament,[16] Luxembourg that of its court,
and so on. Notionally, it is precisely the opposite of a centralized, hierarchical
empire.

---

11 Cosgrove (2004), p. 59.
12 Morris (2005).
13 The issue is of particular interest in Germany today. See Guenzel (2005). I thank my colleague Shulamit
Volkov for drawing my attention to this.
14 Cf. Clarke (2008).
15 The title of an often-reprinted book by J. C. Stobart—*The Glory That Was Greece*; see Stobart (1984).
16 http://europa.eu/abc/panorama/howorganised/index_en.htm#top.

global of particular structures

Historical uses of the network concept were prominent, particularly among "Mediterranean" historians. Curiously, the Mediterranean, both real and imagined, has a special role for this new Europe, especially after 1995, when the Euro-Mediterranean partnership was launched (the "Barcelona Declaration").[17] Bureaucrats and academics needed to begin thinking in terms of Mediterranean regionalism, oriented especially toward economic and educational networks. This particular vision of the Mediterranean meshes well with both its all-embracing aspects of metanational frameworks and the rise of particularized regionalism and "localism." The new Europe has witnessed a significant rise in the expression of regional identities, most probably because the nation-state is declining as the dominant focus of collective identity. "France" and "Spain" are making way for Brittany and Catalonia. The realignments along more specific regional networks are significant in that they stress affinities that not too long ago might have seemed a threat, if not outright treason, to one's national identity. Possible examples are Bavaria and Tyrol (Germany and Austria, respectively), French and Suisse Francophones, or the "Padanians" in Italy. Africa no longer "starts at the Pyrenees."[18] In fact, these mountains now unite more than they separate Catalonia and southern France, a situation not dissimilar to what existed in the Gulf of Lion in antiquity, between what are today Marseille and Ampurias. Such realignments stress affinities of dialect, environment, and lifestyle as perhaps more significant than their discrete identities as Austrians, Germans, French, or Italians.[19]

The combination of overarching, globalized structures, together with local identities and the circles of "lived experience," has given rise to a new term, "glocalization."[20] According to Roland Robertson, a reassessment of the "universalization of the particular and the particularization of the universal" leads to the blurring of the opposition between the forces of homogenization and heterogenization. In fact (through what he calls "interpenetration"), they actually complement each other.[21]

L'Europe des regions has become ubiquitous as a term in contemporary discussions of European identities, and network concepts have come to articulate identities that are both regional and European, or "local" and "global."[22] Ancient Greeks, living in more than one thousand independent states from the mouth of the Don (Tanais) to the Gulf of Lion, were well aware of both their commonalities and their individuality. Modern Europeans have much to learn from the ancient Greeks when it comes to glocalization.

17 http://www.delegy.ec.europa.eu/en/eu_and_country/4.pdf.
18 Ben Ami (1990).
19 Leclerc (2003); Keating (2004); Weatherill and Bernitz (2005).
20 Robertson (1992, 1995, 1997, 1998). For the evolution of the concept (apparently from Japanese business terminology) see Khondker (2004).
21 Robertson (1992, pp. 100–104; 1995).
22 The EU has set up a Committee for the Regions. See http://www.cor.europa.eu Bistolfi (1995); Bono (1999); Vasconcelos and Joffé (2000); Masala (2000); Brauch (2000).

Both the Europeanist and, to some extent, the Mediterraneanist discourses emphasize decentralization, bypassing sites of hierarchy (such as national capital cities) and are enthusiastic about networking.[23] As noted, the network approach of the twenty-first century deconstructs the meaning of "place" since the new technological, economical, and political connectivity often renders place insignificant. The more politically ideological Mediterranean discourse, best articulated in the early writings of Albert Camus,[24] bypasses the issue of national identities in favor of complimentary and non-exclusive identities, a middle ground of accommodation and mediation on a pluralistic level. Instead of bipolar, face-to-face conflicts, the European and the Mediterranean network approach dilutes the national foci while "enmeshing" societies that have been used to contact and conflict mainly through national modalities.

In sum, we can now see a convergence for a revitalized interest in networks as applied to collective identities with commonalities that take into account enormous distances, lived experience, and historical continuities; new prisms for historiographical research and historiosophical paradigms of structures and connectivity; a changing Zeitgeist of economy and cultural politics; a globalized-glocalized world, and a new framework of postmodern and postcolonial observation, as well as a contemporary Mediterranean agenda that is network oriented. It is a relevant approach, I think, to the Archaic Greek world.

The Network of Greece

"The shores of Greece are like hems stitched onto the lands of barbarian peoples," says Cicero,[25] and Plato famously compares Greeks to frogs living around a pond.[26] The pegs that fastened Cicero's hems to the shores that stretched from the eastern Black Sea to the western Mediterranean were hundreds of Greek communities. The sea (or Plato's pond) thus appears as the center of "Greece." It could be perceived as a *single sea* stretching "from the river Phasis to the Pillars of Herakles."[27] The land separates and the sea connects. When discussing the Mediterranean environment, Nicholas Purcell and Peregrine Horden stress the characteristic contrast between the "topographical fragmentation" of Mediterranean lands and the "connectivity provided by the sea itself." These are the "two key environmental ingredients" in Mediterranean history.[28]

23 Cf. Matvejevitch (1998); Bono (1999).
24 Ohana (2003); Foxlee (2006).
25 Cicero *de Rep.* 2.9.
26 Plato *Phaido* 109b.
27 Plato *Phaido* 109a–b.
28 Horden and Purcell (2000), p. 101.

Greek cities and their maritime connectivity may be interpreted in network terms. I discuss the network formation of the settlement dots along the coasts and the way in which networks may explain both the success and the dissemination of some major commonalities of Greek civilization and identity. Network theorists, both those who arrive at the subject by means of sociology and especially through physics,[29] claim that the principles of "small worlds" formation are universal, a point already acknowledged by several disciplines. Having observed the formation of actual networks among Greek cities and colonies, it may be fruitful to suggest an application of such principles and to allow the dynamics of the networks themselves an explanatory value.

"Network" in this book is not just a metaphor but a descriptive and heuristic term. It is another way of observing the Archaic Mediterranean. One may correctly anticipate that a clear distinction is drawn between networks that can be observed and described and networks in the sense that network theory attributes to the concept: that which happens to networks (especially the "small world" phenomenon) because they are networks. The question arises as to when a "network" is simply a network and when it is the "network" of network theory. The answer is that it is both. To the extent possible, I distinguish between networks and networks except that since the one often implies the other it is not always be easy to do so, and I therefore avoid the convenient but misleading capitalization of "Networks." My methodology consists of pointing out networks and processes of network formation while drawing the network implications to their most probable measure. In other words, the first goal of this book is to identify the phenomenon of network formation. Its second, and more suggestive one is an interpretation of its implications. Identifying networks and their overlaps involves much of the more familiar historical research and reconstruction, well known to historians of antiquity. Hopefully, as a result of this approach, some questions of Archaic history will be also seen in a new light.

The choice of subjects for analysis has proven difficult. For historians, precise applications of network analysis are possible today within limited and well-defined corpora of evidence, such as archives of letters,[30] prosopographical databases, catalogues of temple dedications, the personal networks of individual "connectors,"[31] transfer of knowledge and technology,[32] discrete textual corpora,[33] and so on. Discussion groups relating to network issues begin to appear and hopefully will widen the spectrum of issues to be discussed.[34] The more

---

29 L. C. Freeman (2004). Note the diagram on pp. 165–66, which shows how the two communities of physicists and social scientists rarely cite one another.
30 See the remarkable work of Ruffini (2008).
31 Cf. Hezser (1997); Collar (2007). See also Malkin, Constantakopoulou, and Panagopoulou (2009).
32 Http://www.tracingnetworks.org. For archaeological implications see Brughmans (2010).
33 For example, the Hestia Project on networks in Herodotus: http://www.open.ac.uk/Arts/hestia/.
34 See http://groups.google.com/group/the-networks-network?hl=en-GB.

specific and narrow the database, the more quantifiable would be the network, yet at the risk of losing the general civilizational implications.

Among the numerous aspects of network connectivity that come to the foreground it would be possible to select the spread of literary, artistic, and architectonic styles; the (almost too obvious and often-studied) role of Panhellenic sanctuaries; the human mobility of specialists; diffusion of dialects and scripts; provenance and destiny of temple dedications; amphorae stamps; and much more. However, in linking network dynamics and actual space, I prefer to present a few case studies that revolve around the creation of the permanent nodes that allowed for network connectivity, namely, Greek colonies. Our sources for the Archaic period are meager and varied, yet one certain datum is the sheer number and distribution of new Greek cities. These cities also provide examples for regional clusters of settlements, for middle-ground areas of mediation with non-Greek populations, for the emergence of Greek regional identities, and for the type of connectivity that allowed for the overarching formation (a kind of "self-organization" in network terms) of Greek civilization. The idea is not to essentialize the Mediterranean above history but to observe and analyze its patterns and networks. It is my hope that the articulation of the general approach, as well as the case studies presented here, will generate further application of network theory to some of the historical issues mentioned earlier, as well as to other aspects or periods of Hellenic history.

The first step may be a simple illustration: Imagine filling up the coastlines with dots (or "nodes," in network parlance), representing all Greek maritime cities. Imagine the connecting lines ("ties") among them, as well as some content moving along those lines ("flows"). What then comes to the foreground is a decentralized network. A closer look will reveal regional "clusters," such as Rhodes, with its emerging "island identity" and its three poleis (chapter 2); the Phokaians and Massalia (Marseille) in southern France (chapters 5 and 6) or Cyrene in Libya[35] (both with more centralized aspects); or Archaic Sicily, with its ritual expression of regional Greek ("Sikeliote") identity (chapter 3). Such clusters may overlap with trade and settlement clusters of other maritime civilizations, such as the Phoenicians and the Etruscans. Sometimes these resulted in pan-Mediterranean exchanges or religious syncretisms, such as Odysseus (Greek) and Utuzde (Etruscan),[36] or Herakles (Greek) and Melqart (Phoenician) (chapter 4), or the cult of Artemis "of Ephesos" in Iberia, France, and Italy (chapter 6). Settlement clusters were often connected via long-distance "ties," such as Massalia and its mother city, Phokaia (Foca in modern Turkey), or Taras (Taranto, in southern Italy) with Sparta.

If, for example, we have a map of the Mediterranean and mark all the "Greek dots" around 500 BCE, then superimpose on it a map with all the lines

---

35 Malkin (1994b), pp. 143–91.
36 Malkin (1998), pp. 156–209.

indicating known festivals and dedications in major sanctuaries, such as Olympia, Delphi, or the temple of Hera at Samos, the resulting lines would quickly multiply and overlap. On top of this we place a map that illustrates imaginary genealogies and mythical itineraries, such as those of the descendants of the "Cow Maiden" Io, or Herakles, or those of the Dorians and Aiolians, or those linking Athens with the Ionians as their mother city. On top of that we may superimpose a map that illustrates all real and imagined ties between colonies and mother cities. Yet another map may express artistic and architectural trends or material evidence for trade relations, such as wine or oil amphorae. The superimposed maps will reveal a dense, if somewhat messy, palimpsest of lines that connect "nodes" via "ties" and express different contents ("flows"). The flows appear mostly across open maritime spaces and, perhaps most important, they move along *multidirectional* network lines.

The ties overlap not just graphically but also historically. The Corinthians, for example, expected to develop conventional religious, commercial, and political ties with the cities they had founded. Such cities also tied themselves directly to other networks. When the people of Apollonia in the Adriatic (originally a Corinthian foundation) won a significant victory, they set up a victory dedication not at the mother city but at the Panhellenic sanctuary of Olympia.[37] An Apollonian, therefore, belonged to several networks, each somewhat overlapping with the other, yet each reaching different nodes: "Corinth" was his "mother city," Delphi had prophesied Apollonia's foundation, Apollo himself came to be considered the founder, and Olympia provided the link to the larger network of Hellenic belonging.

Each network involved a different circle of identity: the civic and political "citizen of Apollonia"; the identity of origins, the "Corinthian colonist"; the subethnic identification with the "Dorians," and the belonging to the "Greeks." Any Syracusan citizen was also a Corinthian colonist, a Dorian, a Sikeliote (a regional definition for Greeks living in Sicily), and a Greek (chapter 3). In more general terms, the circles of identity are the nonethnic identity of the polis; the region, subethnic grouping, and the Panhellenic, "Greek" identity. The flexibility to move among such circles, continuously expanding or contracting and sometimes operating on several planes at the same time, made Greeks experience networks of belonging differently from what is familiar to us, yet in a way that was recognizably common to diverse Greeks, thus providing them with a measure of "Hellenicity." They all knew (and mutually recognized) similar and multiregistered networks of belonging (figure 1-6).

Graphic illustrations of wide-ranging Mediterranean networks in the form of connective graphs usually prove to be unhelpful. Two-dimensional representations of connectivity mostly turn out to be messy "spaghetti monsters" with very long verbal explanations that are needed to accompany them. Missing are

37 Malkin (2001a), pp. 191–94.

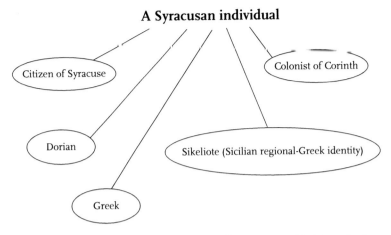

FIGURE I.6. Greek circles of identity: example of a Syracusan. No hierarchy is implied; circles of identity depend on context.

the networks' multidirectionality, multidimensionality, and multitemporality. We are in need of new modes of graphic representation that would avoid the more precise, yet messy, "lines connecting dots" and avoid the pitfalls of dazzling oversimplifications.[38] I have opted for the larger canvass of what seems to me highly probable at the risk of not presenting statistics and formulae that I am incapable of offering due to the state of our sources of knowledge.

It is not too difficult to describe Greek connectivity by using network terminology (all those nodes, ties, and flows overlapping). However, the goal here is to use network perspectives in order to see what otherwise might have escaped our attention. Network perspectives reveal much more about ancient mental maps of space and connectivity than modern atlases and historical maps of "ancient Greece" (see later on cognitive maps). When the subject becomes one of identity, of what it meant to be a Greek during the Archaic period, networks provide a framework in which various types of collective identities in the Greek world could form, coexist, and interact.[39]

A network approach provides a wide-angle vision of the ancient Mediterranean. It is very different from a "cellular" history of Corinth. Our final glance at the map will reveal Greek settlements and their territories, created between the end of the second millennium and the fourth century BCE, which were dotted along the coasts of mainland Greece, the Aegean, Asia Minor, the Propontis, the Black Sea, Italy, Sicily, France, Spain, and north Africa. Each political

38 Perhaps one venue to explore would be the visual program called Personal Brain (http://www.thebrain.com), where clicking on a particular node shifts the emphasis to that node while retaining its ties with the others, yet offering a different hierarchy each time. This would be impossible in book form, however. See also http://www.visualcomplexity.com.

39 On "Hellenicities" cf. Tuplin (2005).

community, whether a city-state or *ethnos* (a regional and ethnic political group-ing, although no *ethnê* were founded as colonies), had its own microregion, with varying relationships among components such as towns, sanctuaries, and neighbors, both Greeks and barbarians. Nonetheless, these political communi-ties, particularly the city-states, also form an overall network, itself subdivided, sometimes differently from the components that brought it about, according to kinship models and regional, religious, or ethnic affiliations.

A Theôria Network

For an illustrative, explicit example, let us examine the case of a ritual net-work that was both formative and expressive of its role of "Greek" conver-gence. Perhaps as early as the seventh century,[40] every four years sacred ambassadors set out from the Delphic Oracle to various corners of the ancient world where Greeks resided. They were called *theôroi* (those who see, observe; the origin of our "theory"), and their purpose was to announce the forthcoming Pythian festival and Panhellenic competitions.[41] Greeks from east and west came voluntarily, protected by a Panhellenic sacred truce. It was a world with no grand hotels, and the Delphic announcers were hosted by *theôrodokoi*, "*theôroi* hosts," a highly regarded position that often became hereditary. The *theôrodokoi* constituted a long-term network, expected to exist reciprocally among Greek cities. For their part, Greek poleis, city-states, sent their own "pilgrim" *theôroi* to the festival at Delphi to "observe" and partake in the rituals. Thus, a "theoretical" network comes to the foreground, the "center" of which was Delphi, a sanctuary in the wilder country of central Greece. Delphi was remote and had no political power. Although the sanctuary could be envisaged as the "navel (*omphalos*) of the earth," this was a religious-geographic metaphor with neither political nor ethnic connotations.

In the Greek world were other *theôriai*, related to other sanctuaries, some quintessentially Panhellenic (Olympia), some regional (Epidauros, Delos), and some merely ambitious. Sometimes *theôriai* were reciprocal, with *theôroi* attending each other's festival, thus joining together the smaller networks, or "clusters," of each festival in an even larger network. Itineraries were tradi-tional, "tying" together the cities and constituting both mental maps and phys-ical routes. The sum of all *theôriai* may be perceived as a "hypernetwork" that connected the entire Greek world. This observation seems valid especially for

---

40 Giovannini (1969), esp. pp. 51–71, with suggested theoric itineraries on p. 60. For early *theôriai* see Kowalzig (2007), p. 123 (especially for Eumelos in Paus. 4.4.1, 33.2), with D'Alessio (2009). However, precise attestations are hard to come by. See more in chapter 3.

41 For discussion and references of *theôria*, see chapter 3. See especially Rutherford (2007).

the four major Panhellenic festivals, arranged so as to follow each other in consecutive years (Olympia, Delphi, Isthmia, and Nemea).[42]

In practice, not everyone came every time, but what matters is that the network of *theôroi* signified an expectation common to all Greeks. Sometimes, as at Crete, it was enough that *theôroi* from only one or two cities would come, as long as that city had its own regional network that the *theôroi* "represented." Such *theôroi* would function as a shortcut, or a "link," with the meganetwork. When relating to all of the major sanctuaries together, as Greeks sometimes did, we have "a massive coordinated system, with major festivals staggered over a four-year period."[43]

Delphi and its *theôria*, which were self-aware and intentionally symbolic (unlike some of the networks discussed in this book), provide but one illustration for the way in which the Greek world was connected by multidirectional, noncentralized, and nonhierarchical networks. Greeks expressed, maintained, expanded, and kept revitalizing their networks throughout centuries of Greek history, while bringing to the foreground and shaping Hellenic identity in the process.

Networks in Place

The opposite of mental or symbolic networks, such as those of the Panhellenic sanctuaries, are those network patterns that were not self-aware, networks that were "in place" and developed because of geographical determinants and human practices from time immemorial. Mycenaean Greeks, for example, were active in southern Italy in the area of Taras (Taranto, in the "heel" of Italy), centuries before the Spartans sent their colony there around 706 BCE.[44] Phoenicians may have been around Huelva in Spain (to mention the farthest site) as early as the tenth century.[45] Such networks were a formative force. Some prehistorical networks of maritime travel and commerce, such as the famous tin or amber routes, had been in existence perhaps since the sixth millennium BCE. These were determined mostly by ancient Mediterranean geography, wind and current patterns, the locations of anchorages and ports, river mouths, and offshore islands. Fernand Braudel, the great Mediterranean historian, may have overemphasized the determinism of Mediterranean geography and certainly painted it in sweeping brushstrokes.[46] Yet he is basically correct: A ship will look for the expected wind and its planned-for stop at a known river mouth, moving from one port or anchorage to the next.

---

42 Cf. Valavanis (2004).
43 Rutherford (2007), p. 26.
44 Gale (1991); Cline (1994); Malkin (1994b), pp. 115–42.
45 Aubet (2008) for a reassessment of pre-eighth-century Phoenician colonization.
46 Braudel (1972).

It is no accident, for example, that Corinth was the mother city of both Corcyra (Corfu) in the Ionian Sea and Sicilian Syracuse (both founded around the same time)[47] since to reach Sicily from mainland Greece it was wise to make a maritime journey "up" before "descending," with the northeasterly winds (the entire Athenian navy repeated the pattern when sailing to besiege Syracuse in the late fifth century). Finally, maritime straits such as Messina, the Bosporus, or the Crimean Bosporus did not wait for modern strategists to evaluate their importance, and Greek colonies were settled, sometimes in pairs, to control them.[48]

Networks may be transformed, especially with the proliferation of permanent nodes and the intensification of flows. Dormant for long periods, trade networks underwent a period of intensive activation and qualitative change. It started during the first part of the eighth century, with "proto (or 'pre-') colonial" contacts.[49] The second half of the century witnessed an intensive founding of new cities that qualitatively changed the more ephemeral networks of trading stations (*emporia*).[50] "Towns are like electric transformers," says Braudel.[51] The eighth century started the process of transforming disparate maritime cultures into a Mediterranean civilization based on ties among mostly city-oriented nodes. Phoenicians, Greeks, and to some degree Etruscans were founding new settlements, thus signaling a social and political model diametrically opposed to what the far more affluent ancient Near East had to offer. Instead of a multiethnic empire, with a King of Kings at its head and "subjects" for a population, they created networks of numerous, independent, political communities made up of "citizens." This became a *longue-durée* contrast between the political cultures of the ancient Near East and the Mediterranean, expressed in the conflicts between Greeks and Persians and replicated in later periods, especially by the conflicts between the Mediterranean republics and the eastern empires of Byzantium and the Ottomans.[52]

The transition to intensive connectivity among cities and *emporia* may be illustrated by a Greek literary representation of a Phoenician example: The *Odyssey* describes a floating Phoenician *emporion*, a ship anchoring for one year, trading with the natives, yet making it impossible for the Phoenician traders to ever return because, just before leaving, they also abduct the prince Eumaios, who ends up as Odysseus's pig farmer in Ithaca.[53] Think, by contrast,

47 Malkin (1998), pp. 74–81.

48 Vallet (1958, 1996). Cf. Gentili and Pinzone (2002). See, for example, Thuc. 6. 48, illustrating the maritime significance of the Straits of Messina.

49 Graham (1990).

50 Purcell (2005), esp. at p. 120, claims the *emporia* were used to distribute wealth amassed in colonies, a view that basically sees them as part of an overall network.

51 Braudel (1981), vol. 1, p. 479. In general, Horden and Purcell somewhat diminish the role of cities, a point answered by Fentress and Fentress (2001), pp. 212–13.

52 For a wide-reaching emphasis on the role of the long and fragmented European seashores as the *longue-durée* cause for the "Rise of the West," see Cosandey (2007). Cf. Mollat du Jourdin (1993).

53 Homer *Odyssey* 15.403–84.

of Phoenician Motya, a tiny offshore island in western Sicily that served as a permanent base of commerce and contact also with Carthage, itself a major Phoenician foundation (from Tyre) dating back perhaps to ca. 800. The distinction between the temporary *emporion* and the permanent colony (the two forms of settlement existed side by side throughout the Archaic and Classical periods) illustrates that both Greeks and Phoenicians knew the difference between intentional foundations and temporary *emporia*. The latter could grow into permanent cities (e.g., Greek Emporion, modern Ampurias, in Spain, or Naukratis in Egypt) but were forever remembered as having gone through a transformation into a polis. Such stories of evolution were never told about city-states reputed to have been established as foundational colonies.

The general view among scholars about city foundations in the Archaic Mediterranean follows the basic outline provided by ancient sources (aside from their folkloristic and legendary motifs). They describe Archaic settlements as deliberate acts of "foundation": an identifiable mother city (*metropolis*) sending out a group of its own (*apoikia*, "colony"), led by a founder (*oikistês*), who goes to Delphi and is provided with a foundation oracle. He then sets out and usually conquers the settlement site (unless he is lucky enough to marry a local princess), establishes the rituals and institutions of the new society (*nomima*), plans and executes the territorial division, and distributes (probably by lot) plots of land (*klêroi*) to both settlers and Gods (sacred precincts, *temenê*). After his death the founder is buried in the *agora*, and the city accords him an annual hero's cult. We usually never hear of his descendants, and it seems clear that founders did not institute dynasties (with the notable exception of the kingdom at Cyrene). In sum, the term "foundation" may signify the entire period of the founder's mature life from arrival at the site to his death, as well as the hero cult founded in his honor, which provided the foundation with a closure. This, of course, is a general scheme, with many particular varieties relative to circumstance. However, an analysis of both ancient sources and archaeological evidence seems to confirm the general picture of the processes of foundation, perhaps with less emphasis on the a priori organization at the "mother city," which seems to have been consolidating as a political community in tandem with the early phases of colonization.[54]

The point is of importance for the formation of the Mediterranean nodes, especially since the foundational aspect of colonies may also explain the rapid pace of the overall network formation. However, some dissenting yet influential voices now view the scheme as anachronistic, although except for an a priori position that prefers history to be processual (cities come into being, evolve) rather than eventful (cities deliberately founded), what they express is more a scholarly mood than an argument, and I believe that they have failed to produce

---

54 Malkin (1994a). For a general review of the scholarly discourse on ancient foundations, see Malkin (2009).

any significant evidence for this.[55] However, even if merely "evolved," there is no doubt that by the end of the sixth century BCE, we find well-established networks of city-states active in reciprocal exchanges of trade, religion, language, art, literature, and philosophy. They usually followed similar options for social and political organization, a Greek way of doing things, and shared a common orientation toward Panhellenic sanctuaries. The result was a civilization that was undeniably Greek.

The study of Greek colonization has been enriched in recent years with more discoveries of mixed habitations. Archaeology has contributed to our understanding of settlement processes in the Archaic period by bringing to light a dimension of settlement of which the texts say little, that of the mixed communities and individual farmsteads. In Dobrudja (Black Sea), for example, a series of farmsteads has come to light, implying some *modus vivendi* with non-Greek, local populations. Places like Incoronata, San Salvatore, l'Amastuola,[56] Baou St. Marcel, Arles (chapter 5), and others are all different from each other, yet all seem not to have been Greek poleis, and all indicate some degree of mixed population. We need to be wary however, of the inclination to generalize from such sites an entirely new pattern for the history of Greek colonization. This is not a zero-sum game between those who accept the notion of "foundation," as is reported in the sources and seems to be strongly supported by the archaeology of sites such as Megara Hyblaia and many others, and by those who believe in a jumbled pattern of immigration that only gradually crystallized into homogenous poleis (but never quite explain why this should have happened). The two patterns are in no way mutually exclusive, and the example in chapter 5 of Massalia ("foundation") and related sites (mixed, as in Arles), demonstrate that both existed and quite possibly benefited each other as regional networks.

There is absolutely no need, therefore, to deny the "node" aspect of Greek cities around the coasts of the Mediterranean and the Black Sea merely because we have found another but by no means alternative form of settlement. Yet even for those who insist on denying foundational aspects of Greek colonization, the network approach suggested in this book may afford a way to explain why all of those sites (to use a neutral term), which they believed began as a settlement of a mixed bag of people, became Greek by means of a pan-Mediterranean co-optation. The difference between their approach and mine would then shrink significantly: According to the more accepted view, which I share, Greeks founded organized settlements with some a priori collective identity that rapidly crystallized into a polis form. The network attraction among such nodes significantly enhanced their common Hellenic characteristics across

55 See especially Osborne (1998); cf. Yntema (2000), for foundation stories as sixth-century inventions; replies: Malkin (2002b, 2003c).

56 Burgers and Crielaard (2007). Cf. Herring (2005), who seems to draw wide-reaching implications from a rather narrow corpus.

the sea and perhaps also helped to explain the overall similarity in their polis attributes. Those denying "foundation" may accept the explanation of the network process (for they must accept the very existence of a civilization that was markedly Greek by approximately 500 BCE), with the difference that they view the initial formation of its nodes differently.

Network Theory and Mediterranean History

Once in place, did these historical networks have dynamics that are characteristic of networks as such? Having been "electrified" by the foundation of numerous new city-states, did networks function according to "laws" that govern networks in general? In other words, might there be something common to rhizome plants, molecular biology, brain science, the Internet, crickets chirping in synchrony, and Greek civilization? The temptation to use "power laws" of network behavior as explanatory or even predictive must be resisted or at least seriously qualified. Albert-László Barabási rightly reminds us that uncovering sophisticated network laws has been made possible only with the World Wide Web because, in order to have any statistical significance, it is necessary to study millions of data.[57] Sadly, historians of antiquity do not possess so comprehensive a database, and the application of network concepts must follow the more basic terminology and observations of network theorists. In the future we may be able to improve on this.

So what may be done today? I believe that the first task is the identification and recognition of historical networks. The second is to understand the implications of network theory and the specific network characteristics of the Archaic Mediterranean, which we will observe: The Greek Wide Web was multidirectional, decentralized, nonhierarchical, boundless and proliferating, accessible, expansive, and interactive.[58] The third guiding principle is not to put too much significance into the discovery that "everything is connected" but to locate those problems that are better served by a network approach. The fourth is to examine the implications of the network approach for Archaic Greek history, particularly with a view to the formation of Greek identities and Greek civilization.

"The word 'network,'" says Darin Barney, "describes a structural condition whereby distinct points (often called 'nodes') are related to one another by connections (often called 'ties') that are typically multiple, intersecting, and often redundant." A node is a distinct point connected to at least one other node, yet often serving as the tie between them, whereas "flows are what pass between nodes along ties."[59]

node = point { also tie

57 Barabási (2003), p. 227.
58 For such attributes of networks, see Barney (2004), p. 26.
59 Barney (2004), p. 2.

In the past decade network theory has become popular in fields as far apart as business and biology.[60] In neurobiology and especially brain science, for example, there is a new emphasis on the entire network of the brain that sometimes compensates for damaged areas. A system of rapidly changing connections and "bypasses" appears to be at work. Immunologists are particularly eager to understand the spread of disease according to network principles. Barabási comments on the spread of early Christianity in network terms, and an interesting study of the Jewish Diaspora of the seventh century CE indicates that connections among rabbis, living in communities far apart from each other, should be understood in terms of network theory.[61] In fact, any interconnected Diaspora, especially one without a homeland, may constitute a network where distance works to enhance commonalities across physical distances.[62] Unlike the ancient Greek Diaspora, the Jewish Diaspora, with its narrative of exile, had a strong sense of origins and a homeland. In contrast, the Greeks experienced Diaspora in the reverse order: First they colonized from a variety of mother cities (also believed to have been originally founded as colonies) and only then created their virtual center.

In sociology, network theory (or "social network analysis") has been in use since the late 1960s, concentrating on networks formed by individuals but using terminology that is either borrowed from or applicable to other fields.[63] The pioneering experiments of Stanley Milgram (1967) indicated that the "average path length" among social networks of people is much shorter than might be expected. Milgram had letters sent by individuals to someone unknown to them (his stockbroker in Boston), with many of the letters reaching their destination within two weeks and usually by means of no more than six persons (hence, the popularized concept of "six degrees of separation").[64]

Mark Granovetter uses a network theory of the "strength of weak ties" that also explains Milgram's surprisingly small number of links:[65] Our acquaintances (weak ties) are less likely to be socially involved with one another than are

60 Barabási (2003), p. 228; Buchanan (2002).

61 Barabási (2003), pp. 3–5; Hezser (1997) (I thank Maren Niehoff for drawing my attention to this work). Cf. L. Michael White (1992); Collar (2007). For a review of works related especially to early Christianity, see Ruffini (2008), introduction. It is curious that Plato's characterization of the Greeks as frogs around a pond is echoed in Origen, *C. Cels.*4.23–25, on the Jews (a Diaspora) as frogs round a marsh. Philo understands the Jewish Diaspora in Greek terms, speaking of Jerusalem as if it were Athens: Jerusalem, he says, is a metropolis not of a single country but of many, sending out colonies to Egypt, Phoenicia, Syria, and so on. *Legatio ad Gaium* 281–82. Cf. *Contra Flaccum* 46.

62 Cf. Goitein (1967–1993).

63 Cf. Watts (2003), p. 100: "Starting the research with social networks . . . the phenomenon itself is not restricted to the complex world of social relations. It arises, in fact, in a huge variety of naturally evolved systems, from biology to economics. In part it is so general because it is so simple. But it is not as simple as a mere lattice with a few random links added to it. Rather, it is the necessary consequence of a compromise that nature has struck with itself—between the stern voice of order and its ever subversive, unruly sibling, randomness." Cf. Degenne and Forsé (2010).

64 Milgram (1967); Barabási (2003), pp. 27–30; Watts (2003).

65 Granovetter (1973).

our close friends (strong ties). Each acquaintance will also have a group of close friends, one of whom may be precisely the eye doctor you happen to need. The weak ties exist in a "low-density network" and become, therefore, a crucial link between the densely knit clumps (or "clusters" in some network parlance, i.e., at least three interlinked nodes[66]) of close friends. It also follows that social systems that lack weak ties will be fragmented and incoherent, new ideas will spread slowly, and scientific endeavors will be handicapped.[67] In other words, the "strength of weak ties" may explain how very large networks that extend over great distances (by analogy, as were the Greek cities in the Mediterranean and the Black Sea) can have an all-encompassing, strong, and dynamic connectivity even though most of the "nodes" (city-states and their neighbors) usually function as a microregion, with most of the links connected no farther than the adjacent nodes.

The principle was analyzed mathematically by Strogatz and Watts, who confirmed that a small number of either random or long-distance ties among "actors" or "nodes" are sufficient for connectivity over the entire network, turning it into a "small world."[68] This is a return, in a way, to the early work on graph theory by Paul Erdös. It is enough, said the famous mathematician, to join only a few of a network's potential links to connect to every node in the network. Moreover, the larger the network, the smaller that percentage needs to become.[69] The research by Duncan J. Watts and Stephen H. Strogatz indicates that the addition of a small number of random links drastically reduces the longest direct path between any two "vertices" in the network (figure 1-7).[70] What is most striking about the work of Watts and Strogatz is their claim that both the natural and artificial worlds (for example, the neural network of the worm *C. elegans* and modern power grids) exhibit small-world properties. This is a claim that network principles are universal, provided the networks are dynamic and are in a state of neither total order nor complete randomness.

This foreshortening of the "diameter" of a network could be applied to the interrelation between the phenomenon of city foundations in ever-growing distances and the Hellenic commonalities of this expanding maritime civilization. Both formalized links, such as the ritualized relationships between a mother city and its colony, or a *theôria*, and, more important, the more frequent and ubiquitous links in the form of human mobility and trade created weak links and cultural shortcuts, or shorter paths, for the flows of Greek content to pass through.

Think, for example, of the prototypical human connectors in the archaic world: the doctor, the blacksmith, the priest, the poet, the trader, the teacher

---

66 See Wasserman and Faust (1994), p. 291ff.
67 Granovetter (1983).
68 Watts and Strogatz (1998); Strogatz (2003).
69 Barabási (2003), pp. 25–26, 36.
70 Watts (1999).

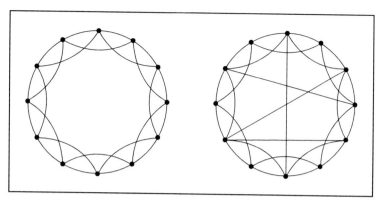

FIGURE 1.7. Random links and networks: the formation of a small world. Each node in the diagram on the left is connected to its four nearest neighbors. The addition of a few random links (right) drastically reduces the degrees of separation among all the nodes, increasing the connectivity of the entire system. After Barabási (2003).

(e.g., of the alphabet), the artist, the mercenary, the town planner (actually a specialist in territorial planning), a *geômetrês*, the constitution expert (e.g., Charondas), and the seer, *mantis* (e.g., the Iamidai), or even the mathematician (figure 1-8).[71] However, we rarely receive sufficient information about them, and studying them would necessitate a separate monograph. Some of these prototypical connectors are parodied in Aristophanes' *Birds*, which portrays them as *wandering* mercenaries trying to sell their expertise to the two Athenian founders of the birds' colony among the clouds.[72]

Aristophanes' founder deals harshly with "specialists" who arrive at the new foundation, expecting a handsome payment. A dealer in decrees wishes to sell him new laws. He is perhaps comparable to Charondas of Sicilian Katana, known precisely for providing states with "constitutions," or to Demonax of Mantineia, who was invited to reform Cyrene.[73] There is also a poet who arrives, claiming that he had already composed verses in honor of the colony, to the utter astonishment of the founder, Pisthetairos, who was just celebrating its foundation with a sacrifice and has only just named it, as is done with little babies (915–24). A professional land surveyor and town planner, appropriately named Meton, also wants to get in on the action. He wishes (verse 995) to "survey the plains of the air . . . and to parcel them into lots." He is also a town

71 Burkert (1983); Giangiulio (1996); Purcell (1990). Cf. Ampolo (1977); Netz (1997); D'Ercole (2005, 2007); D'Alessio (2009). Cf. Law and Hassard (1999) and Latour (2005) on actor network theory; Danowski (1990).

72 Aristophanes, *Birds* (esp. verses 905–1057), trans. O'Neill (1938).

73 Arist. *Pol.* 1247a22–25 says that Charondas became a *nomothetês* for his own citizens, as well as for others, both in Italy and in Sicily. For Demonax see p. 80.

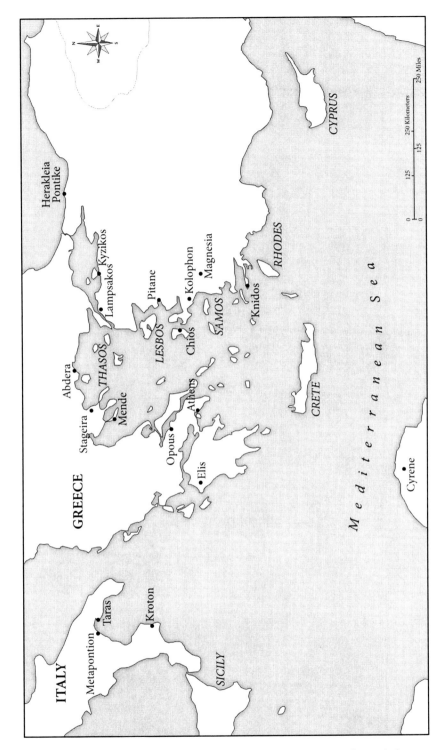

FIGURE I.8. Distribution of cities with resident mathematicians in the period before the founding of Alexandria (331 BCE). After Netz (1997).

planner: "With the straight ruler I set to work to inscribe [verse 1005] a square within this circle; in its center will be the market-place, into which all the straight streets will lead, converging to this center like a star, which, although only orbicular, sends forth its rays in a straight line from all sides." The *geômetrês* is indeed a figure known in the foundation decree of the Athenian colony to the site of Brea in the fifth century.[74] Of particular interest is the oraclemonger, who produces an oracle of Bakis, which exactly applies to Nephelokokkygia but seems to contradict the foundation oracle of Delphi, which was given directly to the founder: "This oracle in no sort of way resembles the one Apollo dictated to me," says Pisthetairos (960–92). Similarly, Antichares of Eleon provided the Spartan Dorieus with a charter oracle "of Laios," justifying his expedition to Eryx in western Sicily, apart from Dorieus's own consultation at the Delphic oracle[75] (chapter 4). Seers (*manteis*) accompanied founders for the purpose of divining and conducting rites and were probably instituting the general religious authority with which the oikist was invested by Delphi. For example, a family of professional seers, the Iamidai, was prominent in several places in the Greek world and seems to have practiced their trade in eighth-century Syracuse, of which they were "cofounders" with Archias.[76]

Sometimes we may notice prominent individual connectors, such as the seventh-century poet Archilochos, who is presented as having passed through various Mediterranean points. He came from Aegean Paros, spent time in Italian Siris, fought with Thracians, and settled in Thasos.[77] The Corinthian Demaratos has become almost proverbial in modern scholarship for being a connector, exemplifying individual mobility, fluctuating identities, modes of interaction, and cultural and political influence. He was a Herakleid, a Corinthian Bakchiad, of the same circle as Chersikrates and Archias, the Corinthian founders of Corcyra and Syracuse. Around the middle of the seventh century he immigrated to Etruscan Tarquinii, married, and eventually became the grandparent of a king of Rome (his integration is similar to the way the foreign Clodii, the later Claudii, are said to have integrated with the Roman nobility). He seems to have been an entrepreneur in more ways than one. He is said to have brought potters with him, thus creating local manufacturing of "Greek" pottery that eventually may have worked together with Gravisca, the Greek enclave-emporion at Tarquinii. His son (or grandson) is said to be the first "foreigner" to have made a dedication at Olympia. Demaratos was thus a true

74 *IG* I(3) 46 with Malkin (1984).

75 Hdt. 5.43.1.

76 Schol. Pind. *Ol.* 6 with Malkin (1987), ch. 2, esp. at pp. 93–97. Hornblower (2004), p. 185, sees this as a genuine historical tradition. Cf. Flower (2008), pp. 22–72. See Malkin (1987), ch. 2, and in general Flower (2008).

77 See more in chapter 2 at note 48. On poets as mercenaries: Kaplan (2002), pp. 234–35. On Archilochos and Paros: Gerber (1999b) *testimonia* 2, 6. On the battle with the Thracians: Gerber (1999b) *test.* 4. On Archilochos and Thasos: Gerber (1999b) *test.* 33, frg. 21. On Archilochos and Siris, compared with Thasos: Gerber (1999b), frg. 22. Cf. Clay (2004).

connector by linking Greek, Etruscan, and Roman elites, integrating into local society in Italy; providing a vehicle of trade and cultural transmission (pottery); and linking the "foreign" (but originally "Greek" in this case) with the meganetwork of Olympia.[78]

Network theory is really part of complexity theory, which seeks to understand emergent phenomena through the self-organization of large systems. Watts says that "one of the great mysteries of large distributed systems—from communities and organizations to the brain and ecosystems—is how globally coherent activity can emerge in the absence of centralized authority or control."[79] Watts lays particular stress on what is new in network theory, where the main advancements have been taking place since 1998. "It is this view of a network—as an integral part of a continuously evolving and self-constituting system—that is truly new about the science of networks."[80] The dynamics of self-organization seem to fit the Archaic Mediterranean world, where nobody planned, a priori, that which became the Greek network. For example, a colonist who ended up in Megara Hyblaia in Sicily was miserably trying out a few Sicilian sites until finally receiving an invitation from King Hyblon to settle in an unprotected plain (around 728 BCE). He would then have been busy building, tilling the land, participating in the new social order, and so on. It is unclear how aware he could have been that he was also participating in the creation of a Megarian network that eventually involved cities such as Chalkedon and Byzantion at the Bosporus and even Selinous (Selinunte), also in Sicily, founded from Megara Hyblaia a century later. With no colonial ideology to propagate these, the *nomima* (markers of social divisions, calendars, institutions, and cults) in all Megarian colonies were also similar (chapter 6). Moreover, he may not have been paying special attention to the fact that the foundation of Megara Hyblaia was also part of an overall process of exploration and city foundations in the Mediterranean by Phoenicians, Etruscans, and Greeks or that Delphi, as a result of Greek colonization, would consolidate its influence to create a *theôria* network for the expanded Greek world. "A series of small random events—that would go unnoticed under normal conditions—can, at the critical point, push the system into a universally organized state, giving it the appearance of having been directed there strategically," observes Watts, ". . . even when every element in the system is only paying attention to its immediate neighbor."[81]

The network dynamics, then, shapes the network. Chris Langton uses an example from the world of entomology to further illustrate the dynamics of self-organization and its implication for the formation of "society," in this case the formation of the "ant path" as equivalent to shaping a major characteristic of "ant society": An individual ant finds food and leaves odor trace marks to be

78 For discussion and sources, see Ampolo (1977).
79 Watts (2003), p. 64. Cf. Portugali (2000) for self-organization in the city.
80 Watts (2003), p. 29.
81 Watts (2003), p. 64.

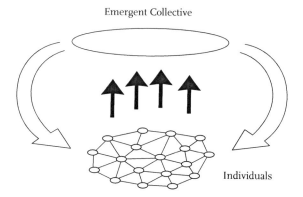

FIGURE 1.9. Chris Langton's ants. An interview with Christopher Langton with Yoav Ben-Dov. http://bendov.info/heb/sci/lang.htm.

identified by other ants that arrive there individually. While returning, they leave more traces for others to follow; a few paths form, but the path with the shortest route attracts more and more ants until finally a single, bidirectional ant path, with its characteristic attributes, is formed. Thus, while haphazardly forming their path, the ant society is being simultaneously shaped by it, a process that may be paralleled to a network being formed unintentionally, which, in turn, as a network with more rapid and efficient connectivity, shapes the "behavior" of the entire system (figure 1-9).[82]

We know that it was during the Archaic period that the Mediterranean basin came to have, for the first time ever, a "Mediterranean civilization." It comprised mostly the discrete political and commercial communities established along its coasts, mainly cities and *emporia* ("trading stations"). It is within this overall network of the maritime civilization of city-states that the more distinct civilizations of Greeks, Etruscans, and Phoenicians emerged, and I will describe some of the characteristics and modalities of this process. For Greeks, foremost among these characteristics is the lack of any "center" that emanates outward or provides direction. Some cities, such as Corinth, tried to exert stronger control over cities of Corinthian origin, with varying successes and conflicts. Others do not seem to have tried at all.[83] Whereas in Phoenician colonization the role of Tyre as a mother city was paramount, at least symbolically, the Greek mother cities were numerous, and often colonies also became mother cities. It was a wide-ranging process with no central direction. Yet the result is undeniably a Greek Wide Web. "What if there are many "centers" that are not necessarily coordinated or even on the same side? What if

82 Christopher G. Langton: interview with Dr. Yoav Ben-Dov, http://www.bendov.info/heb/sci/lang.htm.
83 Graham (1983), pp. 118–53.

important innovations occur not in a core of a network but in its peripheries, where the chief information brokers are too busy to watch? *[T]he center*," concludes Watts, "*emerges only as a consequence of the event itself*" (original italics).[84]

Greek cities and their comparatively small territories normally formed clusters of varying degrees of settlement nucleation, comprising both urban and country sites. Whereas Greek cities were adjacent to non-Greek populations (almost everywhere, aside from what is today the Greek mainland and some Aegean islands, and even there the situation is far from simple), the clusters also included the circles of exchange with neighbors, both Greek and non-Greek. Greeks in Asia Minor were no different in this respect from Greeks in the western Mediterranean. With some Greek islands, such as Rhodes and Sicily (chapters 2, 3), clusters were also translated into regional identities, and perhaps similar processes, with the region defining collective identity, took place in Greek *ethnê*, such as Phokis.[85] Cities such as Massalia or Cyrene established regional subcolonies and *emporia*, thereby adding to the diversity and complexity of clusters.

The term "cluster" may seem forced, but it successfully expresses the situation where most exchanges would take place on a local plane, yet with some links connecting clusters (and potentially all that is within them) with other clusters. This would seem self-evident when the process is intentional, as when representatives of one or two Cretan cities travel as *theôroi*, "representing" other Cretan cities. But what if the links are few and random? The application of random links, as revealed by Watts and Strogatz, creates shortcuts that drastically contract the path lengths between distant nodes. Only a few random links can generate a large effect. And they were "random": It is enough to observe cargoes of ships from this period to see how Greek, Phoenician, and Etruscan items were carried by everyone with mixed cargoes. Braudel's notions of "exchange" were, of course, innocent of the dynamism involved in the shortcuts and the shorter path length forming the networks, and as a result his networks (*réseaux*) appear simplistic. In network terminology the result of the random links and consequent shortcuts is a "small-world" phenomenon, which is precisely what was happening to the Mediterranean in the Archaic period. "Roughly speaking," says Watts, "this is how the small-world phenomenon works. In a large network, every random link is likely to connect individuals [or polities, in our case] who were previously widely separated. And in so doing, not only are they brought together, but also large chunks of the rest of the network are made much closer." The emergence of the Greek network, which crystallized commonalities of Greek civilization in the process, corresponds to "global emergence from local interactions."[86]

---

84 Watts (2003), p. 54.
85 McInerney (1999); Morgan (2003).
86 Watts (2003), pp. 89, 100.

In historical terms, we observe the contrast between clusters of proximate settlements, such as those in southern France, under the direct influence of Massalia (Marseilles), and Massalia's weak ties with the Etruscans, Rome, its own mother city, Phokaia (in Asia Minor), the various *emporia* in the western Mediterranean (Greek, Phoenician, Etruscan), and with the Panhellenic sanctuary of the Delphic oracle (chapter 5). Another example is the island of Rhodes. It became a single political entity only at the end of the fifth century, but the regional island identity of the "Rhodians" was formed much earlier. It is not enough to observe what was happening at Rhodes; we must also understand what Rhodians were doing in Egypt, Phoenicia, the Aegean, and especially Sicily. Rhodian ties with the entire Mediterranean were also responsible for a backward ripple effect and a Rhodian convergence at home (chapter 2).

It is possible to think that propinquity (sharing a neighborhood or territory) and frequency of contact stand in direct proportion to their significance in constituting people's identity. Counterintuitively, perhaps, the reverse seems to be true. Greek networks emphasized Hellenic identity not in spite of distance but often because of it. Jeremy Boissevain, an early social theoretician of networks,[87] says that although he sees his milkman every day, far more frequently than he sees his own brother, who has been living abroad for a few years, a far larger variety of contacts, both practical and emotional, exists with the faraway brother. The relations belong mostly to the expectations of potential family contacts—whether directly, calling him on the phone, or through a network of friends and relatives. The observation may serve a cautionary note for the implications of material evidence when assessing links. An archaeologist might become overenthusiastic about the concrete evidence of broken milk bottles, which implies an intense relationship with the milkman, while missing the richer relationship with the faraway brother—or even his very existence.

This is perhaps something to remember when considering, for example, cases of relationships between mother cities and colonies that crisscross the Mediterranean, with intermittent contacts among the colonies that sometimes bypass the mother city altogether. Such decentralized networks may not be actualized on a basis observable to us (frequency or intensity), but that does not mean they did not exist or at least were expected to function in a meaningful way. Factors of space and time can determine when an apparently dormant network is suddenly activated. Historical networks rely not just on the actual volume of traffic but also on horizons of expectations that persist through time. As such they form a mental framework that could have a significant historical role in certain occasions. For example, Sparta kept sending her generals to the "heel" of Italy to the aid of her colony Taras. This was centuries after Taras's

---

87 Boissevain (1974); cf. Boissevain and Mitchell (1973). Boissevain's contribution also relates to the role of "contact strength" within a network rather than to its systemic, or structural, position.

foundation (ca. 706), with no evidence for similar, direct contacts in the intervening periods. A cynic might say that both cities exploited the notion of Sparta as mother city to their ad hoc advantage. This comes as no surprise. "Uses of the past" have always been common for politicians and generals.[88] However, this was no ad hoc innovation, and Taras's need apparently struck several widely responsive chords. Taras and Sparta relied on a mental infrastructure, an imagined network of Sparta as a mother city and Taras as her colony (yet based on the fact that Taras was indeed its colony), which provided the expected response both at Sparta and at Taras. The same may be said about Dorian Sparta helping its own, perhaps mythical, mother city, Doris, twice (in the fifth century) sending armies to its aid with little evident advantage to itself.[89] Similarly, although Corinth and Corcyra, its colony, were often at odds from the seventh century on, culminating in their rivalry, which ignited the Peloponnesian War, we also find them as joint arbitrators giving Kamarina to Hippokrates over Syracuse (another Corinthian colony).[90]

To personalize the issue, we may look at what happened to some Persians in southern Italy. They were chasing Demokedes of Kroton, a famous doctor bound to involuntary service at the Persian court. Demokedes convinced the King of Kings to send him as a scout to Italy, to prepare the conquest of this "further part of Hellas" (*to prosôterô tês Hellados*)[91] by the Persian Empire. Once in Italy he jumped ship and escaped his Persian pursuers, who were in turn shipwrecked and captured in Taras. The Persians were finally released thanks to a supportive network: a Tarentine exile, Gillos, interceded on behalf of the captives. He also had his own agenda with Taras, his hometown. Gillos sailed to Italy with an escort of men of Knidos "for he supposed that thus the Tarentines would be the more ready to receive him back, because the men of Knidos were their friends."[92] Earlier still (around 520), the Knidians rescued prisoners from Cyrene whom Arkesilas III, King of Cyrene, had sent to be executed on the island of Cyprus. The Knidians saved them and brought them to Thera (modern Santorini). What underlies all these episodes is a connection that must have been obvious to Greeks at the time. All four, Cyrene (Libya), Thera (the Aegean), the Peninsula of Knidos (by Asia Minor), and Taras (southern Italy) were "family." Sparta was regarded as the mother city of Knidos, Thera, and Taras, and may have sent a cofounder (Chionis) when Thera, its own "daughter," founded Cyrene. That is why people as far apart as Knidians and Tarentines were "friends" (*philoi*). In all these episodes the metropolis Sparta is absent, nothing passes through it (unlike

---

88 Urso (1998). Cf. Revel and Levi (2002).
89 Thuc. 3.92 with Malkin (1994b), pp. 221–27. On "imagined communities" see the seminal work of Anderson (1991).
90 Hdt. 7.154.3; cf. Plut. *Timoleon* 8.4.
91 Hdt. 3.137.
92 Hdt. 3.138.1.

Paris and the old French railway) but its existence in the network is implicit (figure 1-10).[93]

Much effort is being invested in network theory to draw descriptive and evaluative graphs that illustrate the difference between the ways nodes are connected. For example, a node may be locally central. Examples of such nodes are apparent when we examine the "gateway communities" around Massalia. A node can be relatively central, compared to its position in relation to the others, such as the Greek enclave community at the *emporion* of Gravisca, in Etruria, serving both the long-distance Phokaian routes, as well as regional connectivity. Finally, it is "globally" central when it exists at short distances (not necessarily physical distance) from many other points. In contrast, peripheral points are those with the lowest degree of centrality (or the fewest number of links). With the meager data at our disposal, we can apply such differentiations only with extreme caution.

Certain observations of network theory in mathematics and physics may be useful. A "phase transition,"[94] such as the freezing of water, may happen between disconnected and connected networks when a network reaches a point when nodes appear in clusters with only a few links connecting them. The addition of a relatively small number of links can result in isolated groups suddenly coalescing into a giant cluster (or a "giant component"). The giant cluster engenders multidirectional ripple effects. Whatever happens at one point may have an effect on any other point in the network.

A cultural negotiation among the newly founded city-states probably accompanied their foundation and was related to the novelty of distant city foundations. Similar patterns of settlements (with public, sacred, and private spaces; similar pantheons; patterns of land allocations) can be traced on the ground from the Ukraine to Spain. Similar patterns of societies appear as if they were almost replicated. Regional architectonic styles flourished, and burial customs followed less those of the mother cities and more those of neighbors, as in Sicily.[95] For the new settlers, the founding of a new society implied the need to imagine and articulate what their social order should be. From their similar responses, we can observe a common set of Greek concerns: the social divisions and magistracies of the new society, the sacred calendar involving communal sacrifices, the hierarchy and makeup of the city's pantheon, distinguishing and choosing private, public, and sacred spaces. It is no accident perhaps that the first reputed Greek lawmakers, Zaleukos of Lokroi (Italy) and Charondas of Katana (Sicily), came not from the older, mainland Greece but the West.[96] Contacts among the expanding network of settlements were multidirectional, and Greeks were copying each other, perhaps through the agency

---

93 Hdt. 3.181.1 with Malkin (1994b), pp. 81, 110.
94 Barabási (2003), pp. 73–78; Collar (2007).
95 Shepherd (1995, 2005); Mertens (1990).
96 Aristotle *Politics* 1274a–b; Gagarin (1986), p. 52.

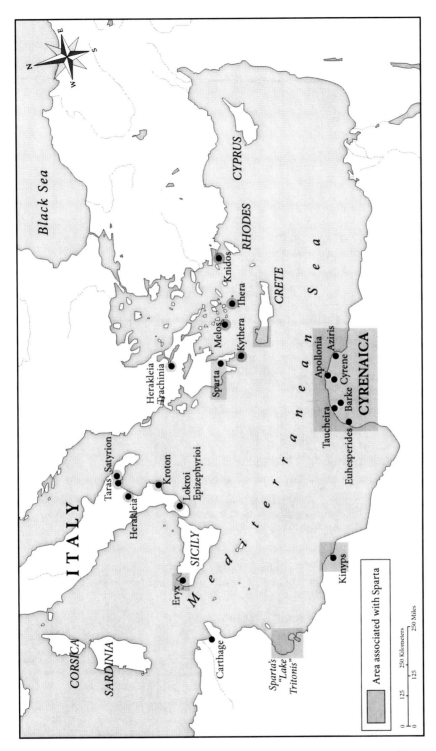

FIGURE 1.10. The "Spartan Mediterranean" in the Archaic and Classical period.
After Malkin (1994b).

of specialists such as those parodied by Aristophanes. The colonial experience made commonalities come to the foreground, rendering them "Greek" in the making. The best evidence for this is the well-known, special investment of the western Greek colonies in the Panhellenic sanctuaries, both in terms of dedications and their participation in the Panhellenic festivals.[97]

In periods when horizons suddenly open, when vast spaces shrink because of better communication, and when connectivity moves to a more efficient and richer level, identities seem to acquire new perspectives and undergo quick realignments. The newly founded Greek colonies, looking toward each other across the waters, were undergoing similar, almost simultaneous experiences, yet at great distances from one another. The turning of the Mediterranean from a sea of connectivity among unstable nodes, such as temporary *emporia*, to a sea of colonization (whether Greek or Phoenician) was an "emergent process," in which commonalities apparently consolidated into identity. Some of the major work of Watts and Strogatz has been concerned with synchronicity (for example, why do crickets seem to chirp in a chorus?), the nature of which can be explained by "small worlds" and networks.[98] For a historian the interesting implication would be that simultaneous or contemporary perceptions and actions, within social groups or among them, can be explained with regard to the existence of networks, especially when those reach a "tipping point," a kind of critical mass that serves as a catalyst for mass change.[99]

An emergent process is a salient aspect in network theory of "information cascades," the social scientist's version of the physicist's "phase transition." To quote Duncan Watts, "What all information cascades have in common is that once one commences, it becomes self-perpetuating; that is, it picks up new adherents largely on the strength of having attracted previous ones. An initial shock can propagate throughout a very large system, even when the shock itself is small."[100] Historical networks of the decentralized type, as were the Greek networks of the Archaic Mediterranean, share the physicist's decentralized, "emergent process," where no single molecule of water makes the decision to freeze up the entire pond. The emergent process transformed discrete networks, such as those of settlement, trade, pilgrimage, migrations, and individual mobility into an overarching framework of reciprocally recognizable traits that may be recognized as a civilization.

Yet networks rarely remain static. The idealism of the early days of the World Wide Web, which envisioned an egalitarian, "many-to-many" type of network,[101] has been set aside in favor of taking paths through hubs, portals, or

---

97 See articles in Mastrocinque (1993b).

98 Strogatz (2003).

99 Cf. Gladwell (2000), who says that the transition between *isolation* and *connectedness* is an important threshold for the flow of information, disease, money, innovations, and so on.

100 Watts (2003), p. 206.

101 Raymond (2001).

search engines such as Google. In fact, a kind of pessimism is embedded in Albert-Lásló Barabási's book *Linked* and the discovery (in 1999) of scale-free networks. "The architecture of the World Wide Web is dominated by a few very highly connected nodes, or *hubs* (original italics)."[102] Barabási pays special attention to "connectors," "nodes with an enormously large number of links which are present in very diverse complex systems, ranging from the economy to the cell. They are a fundamental property of most networks (biology, computer science, ecology). Their discovery has turned everything we know about networks on its head."[103]

When I began thinking about the subject, my automatic association with the word "network" was a grid, with the mental image of a fishing net that, like Cicero's toga, is strung over the entire Mediterranean basin. Lasló Barabási draws on the image of a similar grid, the American road system, with lines crisscrossing each other at right angles and with each crossroad having only four links. In contrast, says Barabási, consider a map of various American airlines, where the connections usually converge in hubs, such as the Chicago O'Hare airport. There is no single center—there would be no point—but rather numerous airlines and several hubs. Like the road system, it is a traffic network but with fewer points of convergence yet with more concentrated cross-links. Barabási concentrates on hub networks as being "scale free": The pattern of links is not distributed according to any particular scale (such as a bell curve); some nodes have few links, and some have many.[104]

The concepts of hubs and networks should prove useful when analyzing the nature of the Greek presence in the Mediterranean because they allow us to combine many-to-many types of networks with the more distinct hubs and subnetworks of mother cities and colonies, religious and pilgrimage networks, regional networks and regional identities, networks of commercial exchange and redistribution, or *emporia* as regional networks at the "middle-ground" frontiers (see below on "middle ground"). The eventual concentration of networks through hubs—nodes with numerous links— may contribute to our understanding of the growth of networks through "preferential attachment": "[R]eal networks," says Barabási, "are governed by two laws: *growth* and *preferential attachment*. Each network starts from a small nucleus and expands with the addition of new nodes. Then these new nodes, when deciding where to link, prefer the nodes that have more links."[105] Such dynamics illustrate, if not actually explain, the quick, independent growth of colonial areas both in regional, middle-ground terms and in relation to major connectors such as Corcyra or Massalia, independently of any mother city.

[hub= node with numerous links]

102 Barabási (2003), p. 56.
103 Barabási (2003), p. 56.
104 Barabási (2003), p. 65.
105 Barabási (2003), p. 86.

There is one major difference between Barabási's scale-free networks and historical (or sociological) networks: Unlike mathematical computations and the seemingly endless World Wide Web, historical networks are limited and contingent. They must have a cutoff point somewhere.[106] In the Archaic Mediterranean the cutoff points correspond to where Plato's frogs sit down to croak: These are the coasts and the narrow hinterlands of Greek cities, where the coastal *chorai* become regional middle grounds. Unlike the networks of the mathematicians and physicists "to whom the idea that a network node possessing an identity sounds vaguely ridiculous,"[107] real nodes have a "social identity" and contingent reasons for preferential attachments.

However, Barabási's discoveries may explain the modalities of historical transition from the more mixed, many-to-many, decentralized networks of the early Archaic Mediterranean to the more homogenized ones of the late Archaic period (ca. mid-sixth century), where many actors or nodes had fewer links, and few nodes acquired a growing number of links. We may observe one major historical change of what may be termed "network homogenization." The early Archaic Mediterranean started out as a free-for-all, many-to-many type of network, where Greeks and non-Greeks were trading, creating *emporia* and permanent colonies.[108] In the early sixth century more Etruscans, for example, seem to have frequented the area of Massalia than Greeks. Earlier still, as David Ridgway notes, we find at "Euboian" Pithekoussai (in the Bay of Naples) evidence of Corinthian artisans, North Syrian seal scarabs, and inscriptions testifying to the presence of Phoenicians (or other Semitic-speaking people). Conversely, Euboians may have been "partners" in early Phoenician Carthage, and we find Euboian material at Sant'Imbenia, a native Nuragic settlement in Sardinia, an area heavily influenced by Phoenician material culture.[109]

By around 500 BCE, the many-to-many aspect of ancient Mediterranean networks had transformed somewhat into one more familiar to the modernistic perspective of "zones of influence." By 540 the Carthaginians and Etruscans dislodged the Phokaians from Corsica, and by the end of the century Greek Sicily had been more firmly divided along Greek and Phoenician lines, some Greek *emporia* had been lost in north Africa, and most of the southern Mediterranean (except Cyrene and Egypt), together with significant parts of Iberia, had become "Phoenician." The Etruscans were still influential in Liguria, the Adriatic, and central Italy. Maritime straits were firmly in either Greek or Phoenician hands (never both), and around 509 BCE Rome signed a treaty with Carthage dividing up maritime sailing routes (p. 123). Thus, we see a movement toward the creation of more homogenized areas of maritime traffic and settlement. These are

106 Watts (2003), p. 111; For the limitation of power laws in social networks, see Schengg (2006).
107 Watts (2003), p. 116.
108 Cf. Gras (1995a).
109 Ridgway (2007); Docter and Niemeyer (1994); cf. Peserico (1996); Rolle, Schmidt, and Docter (1998). Cf. Nijboer (2008).

not, of course, the zonal divisions of modern powers, but the effects are not dissimilar. In a wider perspective this took place when a general consolidation of what we call Greek "civilization" took place, a result of the increased volume of the network and of the decreased variety of the agents of exchange.

The network prism allows us to bring together two opposing attitudes or positions, best represented in the debate between the modernist and the primitivist perspectives on ancient economy and politics.[110] The modernist approach treats the ancient Mediterranean in modern strategic terms; the primitivist sees anachronism in terms such as "maritime routes," "strategic points," and "areas of influence."[111] The network approach may resolve the contradiction. The change in networks from disparate, many-to-many types to more centralized hubs and ethnic divisions of the late sixth century is equivalent to a change from a primitivist situation to a modernist one. Thus, the latter approach would not be anachronistic for these later networks, whereas the former approach is better suited to the earlier periods. Moreover, depending on the degree of network homogenization, aspects of both overlapped during the entire Archaic period.

By the sixth century, Greeks, Phoenicians, and Etruscans were collectively identifiable entities with geographically specific areas of presence or influence. Greeks now fought not just the city of "Caere" but "Etruscans." More distinctively, the lines between Greeks and Phoenicians were clearly drawn in the battle of Himera in 480, when Phoenician Carthage invaded Greek Sicily in tandem some would say, with the Phoenician ships fighting for the Persians when they invaded Greece that same year.[112] In short, a centralization process, the concentration on major hubs that control or direct the links among the clusters of networks (e.g., at Massalia) is a feature common both to the ancient Greek Wide Web and to the contemporary World Wide Web.

Networks in Modern Historiography

The network concept seems to be filtering in everywhere, changing sets of values, and breaking up assumed hierarchies of centers and peripheries. It is characteristic of both postmodern and postcolonial thinking; it presents a new vision of geography and human space. Most significantly, network thinking has transformed the botanical metaphor, so influential in the nineteenth and twentieth centuries, of the tree: "Roots," "stem," and "branches" were used

110 Finley (1999 [1973]). Essentially, the modernist position sees "laws" in economics that are universally applicable (such as supply and demand) and the difference in economic activity in premodern times basically as a difference in scale and efficiency. The primitivist approach attaches importance to different social values linked to economic activity, especially in premonetary systems, where values are imprecise and the economic transactions are "embedded" in the social matrix; hence, economic behavior is more context specific.

111 Horden and Purcell (2000), pp. 123–52.

112 Hdt. 7.166. Cf. ML 27; Pindar Pyth. 1, 27; Diod. Sic. 11.24.

to denote genealogies of kinship, races, languages, and entire civilizations. In current philosophical discourse, Felix Guattari and Gilles Deleuze criticize such "arborism," as they call it, in their book *A Thousand Plateaus*, in which they argue for a network model. Their figurative term is that of the *rhizome* plant stem, an "endless" interconnected root system with individual leafy shoots that appear over the surface. It "assumes very diverse forms, from ramified surface extension in all directions to concretion into bulbs and tubers." "Any point of a *rhizome* can be connected to anything other, and must be. This is very different from the tree or root, which plots a point, fixes an order."[113]

Historical discourse has been long dominated by "arborism," with its implied spatial hierarchies of centers, peripheries, and temporal hierarchies of "origins." While both spatial and temporal hierarchies are important, they are neither exclusive nor universally applicable. A "center vs. periphery" tool of analysis may be applied with more profit to perhaps the Persian Empire than to a Greek civilization that comprised *ethnê* and hundreds of poleis, spread all the way from modern Georgia in the eastern Black Sea to Spain in the western Mediterranean.

A concept of network (*réseau*) is not new to historians. It is central to Mediterranean studies, where the network concept has been operating with relative ease and a sense of validity long before the emergence of the postmodern mindset. Over the past twenty-five years, as cofounder and coeditor of the *Mediterranean Historical Review*, I have followed this concept as it emerged over different historical periods.[114] Shlomo Dov Goitein's *Mediterranean Society*, a study of Medieval Jewish and Muslim society based on the Geniza archive in Fustat (old Cairo), emphasizes cross-Mediterranean networks, involving aspects such as commerce, loans, information, and marriage contracts.[115] Neither Shlomo Dov Goitein nor Fernand Braudel has read each other's work, to their expressed, mutual regret.[116] Braudel's networks are more sophisticated in having introduced a multilayered temporality into the discourse. His famous category of history "in the long term" (*la longue durée*) directed the historian's gaze to noticing *structures* and networks (*réseaux*) that persist throughout conventional divisions of time and place. Historians often have difficulty in defining "periods," weighing "process against event," and deciding between change and continuity. Since antiquity, the pendulum of historical thought has been moving between Parmenides' fixity and Herakleitos's fluidity. The current debate as to whether Greek colonies were founded or simply evolved is but one example of this issue.

113 Deleuze and Guattari (1987), pp. 6–7.
114 Founded in 1986 at the School of History, Tel Aviv University, under the direction of Shlomo Ben Ami. Published by Taylor and Francis (Routledge); http://www.tandf.co.uk/journals/titles/09518967.asp. Cf. Alcock (2005).
115 Goitein (1967–1993).
116 Kraemer (1990).

Herakleitos in particular makes life difficult for the historian: If all is in flux, including the historian's own vision, how is it possible to objectify or isolate any phenomenon? One may not enter the same river, not even once. However, if historical phenomena can be viewed as studies in temporal scales that are different from those of the observer, that would provide a way out of the dilemma posed by Herakleitos, for whom the time of the river and the time of the one entering it are the same. Although Braudel did not articulate a systematic historiosophy, his *longue durée* indicated a way out of the Parmenides-Herakleitos difficulty. History was given several time dimensions with certain "structures" persisting, at different rates, throughout time. There are, he claimed, different rates of change and continuity in relation to various factors or forces. Compared with the agitated history of headline news, some structures display a rate of change that is almost "geological," compared with the short life span of human agents and the events in which they are involved. Structures can thus become an "object" of inquiry whose "time" and "space" are measured differently from those of the observer. Moreover, as structures, they are not necessarily dependent on any religious, national, or political color. In fact, they often persist as structures through their transformations. In his further work this concept also underlies Braudel's notion of *civilizations*. For example, Braudel finds a geographical overlap and a pattern of civilizational continuity between the ancient Latin civilization (Rome and the western Mediterranean), the Greek (Greece, Anatolia, and the Near East), and the Phoenician (also the Near East and especially north Africa), overlapping with the blocks of the Latin and Byzantine churches, and Islamic areas of domination and influence.[117]

Braudel's *La Méditerranée* stresses the notions of "exchange" and *réseaux*, networks. "The Mediterranean is exchange," he often says.[118] No port is without its counterpart elsewhere in the Mediterranean, and their connecting lines are substantive. This approach has its background in the work of the geographer Theobald Fischer, who, following in the footsteps of Karl Ritter, perhaps the first geographer to define the Mediterranean as a region, emphasized the connection between "opposite shores" as the key to understanding the history and the economic development of a region. For example, he writes that the western shores of the Iberian Peninsula and Britain were marginal until the wealth of the "coast across from them"—America—was revealed. Then, at once, their status changed, their wealth grew, and they became a connecting link between Europe and America.[119]

The implication that emerges is that instead of overemphasizing the individual history of this city or that, it is also necessary to examine what takes place

117 Braudel (1994).
118 "Exchange": a phrase often repeated in various forms in Braudel (1972), for example, vol. 2, p. 761. Cf. Gras (1995b).
119 Fischer (1882). See also Fischer (1877). Cf. Schott (1977); Burr (1932). Ben Artzi (2004); Portugali (2004); Nordman (1998); Brun (2007), pp. 47–55, also for a different approach to Ritter.

on their interconnecting lines and to observe intensity, volume, and types of exchange.[120] If the network persists for several centuries in spite of great events such as wars or revolutions, it is observable through the prism of the *longue durée*, the slower tempo of history that allows for patterns of continuity to endure through change.

Braudel was heavily indebted to Claude Lévi-Strauss and in general to structuralism. One major criticism of the structuralist approach has been that structures tend to be viewed synoptically and synchronically, whereas history is diachronic since it is also about change and continuity, time and transformation. Each element of Lévi-Strauss's structures may contain its own history and could (and would) develop at a rate different from that of others, thus rendering the structures unstable and diminishing the validity of general statements about them.[121] Here again, the variety of Braudel's temporal categories could offer a more acceptable explanation for historians.

The real weakness lies elsewhere: Braudel tends to treat networks as the embodiment of those forces that created them. The Mediterranean for him is too much an *espace* in the sense of "environmental container," as discussed earlier (p.12). He misses out on the dynamics of network formation in terms of an emergent process and the dynamics on the network lines, which are responsible for historical processes such as homogenization (aside from the obvious, that *réseaux* serve as an exchange mechanism). He is not at fault, of course, since network theory has advanced by leaps and bounds since the publication of *The Mediterranean*. Similarly, Horden and Purcell's more recent *Corrupting Sea*, while laudably analyzing and stressing connectivity, pays little attention to the formative dynamics of the networks that allow for that connectivity. Again, although *Corrupting Sea* was published in 2000, it was only about that time that significant breakthroughs in network theories occurred. "Dynamics refer to the evolving structure of the network itself, the making and breaking of network ties."[122] For Braudel the networks are basically a representation and a result of exchanges and influences that run along its ties. In contrast, current network theory stresses the role of the network itself, its dynamics of evolvement, in forming the result.[123]

One of the fascinating achievements of *The Corrupting Sea*[124] is the emphasis on Mediterranean microregions. Many of the Braudelian patterns appear in each of these regions, although Braudel presumed them to be applicable only to the Mediterranean as a whole. For example, Braudel's "mountains," where

---

120 Cf. Harris (2005a), p. 24.
121 Finley (1975), pp. 109–11.
122 Watts (2003), p. 54.
123 Cf. Watts (2003), p. 50: "Instead of thinking of networks as entities that evolve under the influence of social forces, network analysts have tended to treat them effectively as the frozen embodiment of those forces. And instead of regarding networks as merely the conduits through which influence propagates according to its own rules, the networks themselves were taken as the direct representation of influence."
124 With Harris (2005b).

people are less prone to be subjects of central authority, emerge when observing the Lebanon together with the Biqa valley, as containing a whole spectrum of characteristics (e.g., climatic, economic, social) that, according to Braudel, could be depicted only with very wide brushstrokes. The Mediterranean, therefore, still appears as it does in the Braudelian model ("The Mediterranean is exchange," or "the whole Mediterranean consists in movement in space") but more as a network connecting the microregions or micronetworks, with the added recognition that the pattern itself is replicated within each microregion (or, conversely, what happens in each is replicated in the entire Mediterranean). In other words, micronetworks are structurally similar to the meganetwork within which they exist or with which they coalesce.

Finding the correct vocabulary is not easy. The term "connectivity," which appears throughout the *Corrupting Sea*, seems to have been appropriated from communication theory. I believe that the microregions are equivalent to "fractals," a concept borrowed from fractal physics and chaos theory.[125] It is curious that a prominent example used by the mathematician Mandelbrot, who developed fractal theory, was maritime, fitting the Mediterranean context of this book. He observed that sections of coastlines replicated the patterns and contours of much larger sections. Fractals are everywhere. A section of a snowflake replicates the entire snowflake, that of a tree leaf the entire leaf, in fact—the entire tree, and so on. In a sense, each microregion in Horden and Purcell's *Mediterranean* is also a "fractal" of Mediterranean networks.[126]

In sum, instead of looking at nodes as solid points, we may now, with greater sophistication, approach the issue of microregions, serving as regional network clusters. In historical terms (rather than environmental terms) this involves observation of areas such as Sicily (chapters 3, 4) or southern France and Spain (chapters 5, 6), the regions that constituted a middle ground of settlement and cultural transfers.

Middle Grounds

The term "middle ground" may be applied in particular with regard to regional (or microregional) networks, forming local, intensive clusters with a few significant links to long-distance Mediterranean networks. Aside from the middle ground in western Sicily, where the heroes Herakles and Melqart mediated between Greeks and Phoenicians and later served to justify their antagonism (chapter 4), we will also observe middle ground networks in southern France and eastern Spain. They were particularly important around the settlement, trade, and even religious activity of the Phokaian Greeks (chapters 5, 6).

125 Mandelbrot (1967, 2004); Peitgen, Jürgens, and Saupe (2004); cf. Cosandey (2007), pp. 563–69.
126 Mandelbrot (1983); cf. Mandelbrot (1967).

As a heuristic historical term, middle ground was coined by the historian Richard White in his study of Native Americans and whites in the Great Lakes region of North America (1650–1815).[127] "Middle ground" refers to what emerges from the encounters between colonists and "native populations." White is interested in how various "sides" (e.g., whites, Fox, Hurons, Iroquois) reached an "accommodation" and constructed a common and mutually comprehensible world beyond a mere "contact zone."[128] The context of these encounters was not the sweeping territorial conquests and the destruction of Indian peoples of later periods but that of significantly long periods when no single, dictating authority existed in most of the areas concerned. Too often we think of colonization activities in terms of the conquests that they became in later generations. However, it is the *inability* to dictate, that is, the lack of a hegemonic power controlling vast territories, which lies at the heart of the colonial experience. There are many parallels to this in antiquity, and similar processes (without the application of the middle-ground terminology) have been identified by Robert Bartlett with regard to the colonization of Europe during the Middle Ages, by Solange Alberro for Mexico, by Thomas Kelley for Dahomey, and by Norman Etherington for South Africa.[129]

The middle ground is characterized as a field with some balance of power in which each side plays a role dictated by what it perceives to be the other's perception of it, resulting from mutual misrepresentation of values and practices. The cult of Artemis of Ephesos may have functioned along such lines in the western Mediterranean (chapter 6). In time this role playing, the result of "creative misunderstandings," a kind of imprecise double mirror reflection, creates a "third" civilization that is neither purely native nor entirely colonial imported. White observes that when people apply their conventions and cultural expectations to new situations, their performance generates a change in culture and eventually results in a shift in the conventions of both colonizers and colonized. Due to its insistence on historical contextualization and the careful study of social practices and representations, the middle-ground approach is an effective mode of interpretation. Perhaps because of the influence of postcolonial studies, other concepts have overshadowed the middle ground, even though, to my mind, they are somewhat

---

127 Richard White (1991, 2006). Issue 63(1) of the *William and Mary Quarterly* is dedicated to White's middle ground. I wish to thank Carla Antonaccio for drawing my attention to this publication. The term "middle ground" has influenced my previous work on Odysseus in Italy as a mediating hero. Malkin (1998, 2002a).

128 For "contact zone" see Pratt (1992). White (2006, p. 9) summarized his approach as follows:

First, I was trying to describe a process that arose from the "willingness of those who . . . [sought] to justify their own actions in terms of what they perceived to be their partner's cultural premises . . ." [quoting from White (1991, pp. 52–53] I was fairly specific about the elements that were necessary for the construction of such a space: a rough balance of power, mutual need or a desire for what the other possesses, and an inability by either side to commandeer enough force to compel the other to change . . . but the critical element is mediation.

129 Alberro (1992); Bartlett (1993); Etherington (2001).

less satisfactory.[130] The better known are "creolization,"[131] "hybridity,"[132] and "contact zones."[133]

While providing a perspective for the phenomenon of "mutualities and negotiations across the colonial divide,"[134] these terms are often too broad and too detached from historical processes, causes, and conscious agendas. "Contact," in particular, is unsatisfactory. Like "connection," it is always true in some sense, yet precisely because of this it signifies little unless heavily qualified. The term "hybridity" has too many biological connotations and, again, is obscure and as such means little. "Creolization," as a linguistic metaphor,[135] is perhaps the closest term for describing cultural negotiation and mediation involving a clearly defined cultural change (an aspect missing from both "hybridity" and "contact"). "Middle ground," despite its advantages, is also rather vague, and, without White's entire book describing its function, the term would have been of little use to historians.

The concept of the middle ground is particularly appealing in the Archaic Mediterranean, where there was nothing in the order of the Roman Empire's *mare nostrum* of later times. The middle-ground approach also allows us to see the issue of "Greek vs. native" in terms of networks of exchange. Moreover, it permits us to eliminate the highly misguided term, current in studies of ancient Greek colonization, of "native populations."[136] Simply put, most were not native, at least not to the specific regions of Greek settlement. Many of the settlements around the territorial countryside of Massalia, for example, were founded later on and in response to Greek settlement. Emporion in Spain was uneasy with its neighbors, the Indiketans, yet the Greeks lived together with them in a single city subdivided by a wall, and together the Greeks and the Indiketans were allies against other Iberians of the hinterland (see pp.167–68). Greek colonization prompted immigration toward the coast from the hinterland, which resulted in newly established gateway communities that often contained a mixed population (chapter 5). At times the reverse might have been the case: Greeks' paying attention to coastal areas because of hinterland migration toward them.[137] In either case, however, the term "native" loses its salience. There are historical parallels for this phenomenon, characteristic of the role of coastal areas and the encounter between maritime arrival and hinterland migration to the coasts. Middle grounds, in this book, characterize regional clusters of net-

---

130 Malkin (2004).
131 Fabre (2002).
132 See the perceptive series of discussions by van Dommelen (1997); van Dommelen (2006a); van Dommelen (2006b, 2005).
133 Pratt (1992).
134 Moore-Gilbert (1997), p. 116.
135 Fabre (2002).
136 Descœudres (1990).
137 A major, original point raised by Sara Owen (forthcoming) with regard to the Thraceward region.

what were the political identities in these middle grounds?

works where Greeks founded colonies or lived in *emporia* and mixed settlements. Sometimes, again as at Massalia, Greeks were not the only ones to arrive on the coast by sea. There were many Etruscans as well whose presence enriched the middle ground with yet another dimension. Such middle-ground networks constituted the cutoff areas of the greater Mediterranean networks. They contributed to and shared in pan-Mediterranean connectivity through the major Greek hubs.

From Ship to Shore: The Maritime Perspective

A Mediterraneanist historian may adopt the maritime perspective of the ancient Greeks, Phoenicians, and Etruscans. These major trading and colonizing peoples usually preferred to settle on offshore islands and promontories, sites easily defensible and accessible from the sea, yet at the same time perhaps regarded as marginal from an inland perspective. For those maritime civilizations the sea was their "hinterland," and all those islands, promontories, and river mouths spoke to each other across the waters of the Mediterranean.

shore – own space

With the emergence of maritime civilizations in the Mediterranean and Black seas, and with a ship-to-shore orientation, large sections of the coasts, with their maritime orientation, functioned effectively as "islands."[138] A maritime perspective finds expression in Greece in geographical names and terms: Epirus (*Epeiros*), the significantly large landmass of northwestern Greece, means the "land opposite," or "mainland." The term was undoubtedly derived from a maritime frame of reference (perhaps that of Ithaca and some other Ionian Sea islands).[139] Similarly, as Horden and Purcell note, the colonial term *peraia*, the territory on the mainland opposite, belonging, for example, to islands such as Samos or Thasos, implies the same perspective.[140] Glen Bowersock correctly observes that ancient Greek and Latin geographers and travelers used expressions such as *hyper, anó, ultra, superior*, and their opposites to indicate places and territories from that of a ship-to-shore context. "Upper Libya," for example, the territory of the Pentapolis of Cyrenaica, lies to the west and north of "lower Libya." "It was thus remote from the Nile Delta, which must therefore have been considered the maritime point of reference."[141]

Greg Dening, in his suggestive book *Islands and Beaches*,[142] elaborates on the theme of the shore as a middle ground of commerce and settlement, both for people arriving from ship to shore and for those coming from the hinterland to the beaches. Odysseus had already observed that the island across from

138 See the perceptive study of Shaw (2004).
139 Malkin (1998), p. 135; Malkin (2001a), pp. 188–91; cf. Morgan (1988).
140 Horden and Purcell (2000), p. 133.
141 Bowersock (2005), pp. 174–75, with Prontera (1996a).
142 Dening (1980).

the terrible Cyclopes was "good-to-settle," not least because the Cyclopes possessed no ships.[143] The observation may serve as a blueprint for Greek perspectives of settlement, consistently maritime since the Dark Ages (settlements in the Aegean and Asia Minor) and the Archaic period (city foundations in the Mediterranean and Black seas). One advantage of the network approach immediately comes to the foreground: The ship-to-shore perspective is consistent throughout periods that historians like to maintain as distinct, precisely the Dark Ages (ca. 1200–750 BCE) and the early Archaic period (ca. eighth–sixth centuries BCE). Odysseus's observation may belong to either one, thus providing a *longue durée* to the history of Greek settlement and city foundations.

Greeks have been accumulating the experience of applying the same patterns of choice of sites, advancing relatively little inland, and also serving short-distance coastal navigation and *cabotage* trading (long-distance trading done via short hops and changing agents),[144] while keeping in touch by means of lines of long-distance sailing (lines that were growing longer due to further settlement). This Mediterranean movement in space, following a consistent pattern of experiencing sea and land from ship to shore, not only created a "Greek" network but also informed the pattern for further settlement.

Maritime connectivity obviously depended on the technology of ship-building and ship-related matters. Long-distance shipping represented a technology alien to the great Near Eastern empires, and the frustrated ambitions of the Persian king to rule the sea provides a good illustration of what he failed to achieve.

"Technology in general embodies and enforces a particular way of being in the world, a particular conception of human relations."[145] Can we speak of ancient ships as providing this type of technology of communication? It appears so. No one in antiquity had a monopoly over shipbuilding, just as no one had a monopoly over maritime routes. Ships, relatively free to move across maritime spaces (in contrast to controllable routes over land and river) could skirt around controlling hubs. The result in the Archaic Mediterranean was the creation of numerous, independent political communities. It is no accident, perhaps, that the few maritime civilizations in the Archaic Mediterranean, namely the Etruscans, the Phoenicians, and the Greeks, all developed city-state cultures and that all expanded by means of maritime colonization, some more significantly than others.[146] Moreover, both Greeks and Phoenicians (we know too little of the Etruscans) retained a sense of wider connectedness (e.g., through Delphi for the Greeks or the annual religious expeditions to Tyre and the god Melqart by Phoenicians) (see chapter 4).

---

143 Homer, *Odyssey* 9.115–30.
144 Horden and Purcell (2000), p. 144.
145 Barney (2004), p. 38.
146 Note the interesting ideas advanced by David Cosandey (2007 [1997]) about the role of the sea and what he terms *articulations thalassographiques* for the spread of scientific knowledge and the rise of the West.

move populations [handwritten marginal note]

Ships are usually designed for warfare or trade, but they can effectively move about entire populations, thus retaining an ad hoc option for which they were not originally designed. On the eve of the battle of Salamis (480 BCE), fearing that their allies would abandon them, the Athenians under Themistokles threatened to remove their entire population by sea to Siris in Italy because it was theirs "from long ago."[147] The threat was effective. What matters here is the appearance of a decentralized network that, while retaining *hoi Athenaioi* as a viable political entity, was in place to relocate the Athenians, compensating for the loss of the town of Athens. The Themistokles episode is particularly significant as, when Themistokles made his threat, Italian Siris had long been in ruins. It was "Athenian" only by a second-order implication: Athens was supposedly the mother city of Kolophon (in Asia Minor), and it was Kolophon who had once founded Siris.[148] This episode clearly illustrates the overlap between actual networks (Kolophon apparently did have a role in founding Siris) and mental and symbolic ones: Athens presented itself as the mother city of all Ionian Greeks (Kolophon was Ionian), something that contemporary, non-Athenian Greeks, seem to have accepted. Note the three points on the map: Athens in the Greek mainland; Kolophon in the east, in Asia Minor; Siris in the west, in Italy—all illustrating how the entire Mediterranean was imagined in terms of a potential network of settlement.

More concretely, in 545 BCE the Phokaians packed their women, children, men, and gods on board their ships and abandoned Asia Minor rather than submit to the Persians.[149] They were not sailing into the unknown. Although they had lost their city, they could still rely on their decentralized network, whose other nodes had remained untouched by the Near Eastern empire. They first headed to Corsica, where twenty years earlier they had founded a colony at Alalia. Some probably continued on to Massalia, their foundation in southern France of ca. 600, and some possibly journeyed even farther west to Iberian Emporion, also a Phokaian (or Massaliot) foundation. Abandoning Alalia five years later (following their costly naval victory over the Etruscans and Carthaginians) and with the friendly cooperation of Rhegion in southern Italy, they took over Elea (Velia) and turned it into a new polis, later famous for its philosophers (notably Zeno) and as a place of refuge for fugitive poets such as Xenophanes.

Cognitive Maps and the Effects of Distance

To apply a network approach to the Archaic Mediterranean it is necessary to revise the conventional cognitive map of ancient Greece. The historical maps we are accustomed to usually imply a center-periphery vision of the Archaic

147 Hdt. 8.62. Cf. Raviola (1986).
148 Cf. Malkin (1998), pp. 226–31.
149 Hdt. 1.164 with chapter 5.

Mediterranean. Teachers of the Classics are all too familiar with wall maps that, although labeled "ancient Greece," often illustrate merely the Aegean circle. The Routledge teaching map,[150] for example, excludes even Crete. Such representations imply a distinction between a primary center (Greece), where the main action of Greek history took place, and what is beyond the scope the map, which is by implication secondary, or "backwaters," such as the Greek colonies.

However, ancient Greece was not in Greece, which is a modern national country that was first proclaimed in 1821 and is now a member of the European Union. Ioannis Kolettis echoed ancient sentiments when he claimed, in 1844, that "a Greek is not only a man who lives within this kingdom but also one who lives . . . in any land associated with Greek history or the Greek people."[151] "Greece," in other words, is where Greeks came to be. There was no country called Hellas in antiquity and, apart from several inconsistent geographical statements about "Hellas" that would seem dissonant to a modern Greek (Epirus, for example, is sometimes excluded in ancient sources), Hellas functioned more as an abstract term that covered the wide, fragmented Greek horizons of the islands and coasts of the Black Sea and the Mediterranean.[152]

After the Dark Ages, when Greeks established settlements far beyond the Aegean circle, the name "Greece" accompanied them. We saw how the Persian ship carrying Demokedes to Italy tried to reach "the further part of Hellas."[153] The founders of new city-states during the Archaic period were usually citizens of their new, independent communities. Except for the Athenian *klerouchoi* ("Athenians abroad"), the status of most Greek colonists was the opposite of, for example, the French citizens *outremer* of modern colonialism. As Jean Bérard noted in 1960,[154] this independence was a salient feature of the Greek "colonies" and thus renders the term "colonization" anachronistic. Curiously, in spite of much reawakened criticism of the term "colonization,"[155] no one has come up with a successful replacement. What is more confusing, especially for those who are used to seeking ancient realities in philology, is that ancient Greek terms tend to be historically paradoxical. Greeks spoke of a "mother city," *metropolis*, and its home offshoot, the *apoikia*, terminology that could be understood as signifying political hierarchy, something that most Greeks rejected. Paradoxically, it is the ancient terminology that appears anachronistically modern.

However, colonies (I continue to use the conventional term) were neither secondary nor "backwaters," and some were not even "overseas," as the general

---

150 Stoneman and Wallace (1989). Crete has been added in the 2010 edition: http://www.routledge.com/books/details/9780203838846/

151 Quoted by Clogg (2002), p. 47.

152 Jonathan Hall (2002), pp. 125–29.; Malkin (2001a), pp. 198–200.

153 Hdt. 3.137.

154 Bérard (1960).

155 See, for example, Hurst and Owen (2005).

accounts of Greek colonization erroneously continued to label the phenomenon.[156] At least fifty percent of all Greek *poleis*—whether "colonies" or not, whether inside the arbitrary Aegean circle or outside it—were established only after the mid-eighth century, to which the beginning of city-state colonization is usually dated.[157] City-states such as Syracuse, Cyrene, or Herakleia on the Black Sea ruled enormous territories, participated fully in the Panhellenic games, were affluent, and enjoyed a vigorous intellectual life. In 480 a Sicilian Greek facing the Carthaginian invasion must have felt no less at the center of things "Greek" than his counterpart in Athens, who, in the same year, was facing the Persians. "Centers" and "margins" are points of reference resulting either from our slanted sources (mostly Athenian) or from the historical constructs that determine our perspective.

In both the Archaic and the Classical period, Greeks also continued to colonize in the center of the "ancient Greece" of the teaching maps, not just "overseas." There were, for example, new colonies in the Aegean (e.g., at Amorgos, Thasos, Lemnos, and Skyros), as well as in what is today modern, mainland Greece (e.g., at Amphipolis and Herakleia Trachinia) and in the Ionian islands and Epirus. Sometimes they confronted non-Greeks ("barbarians") in areas that to modern eyes might seem entirely Greek. In other words, only a map pinpointing where Greeks had their settlements, encompassing the wide horizons of the coasts of the Mediterranean and the Black seas, can justifiably contain "ancient Greece."

In addition, the revision of the arbitrary map frames within which it is customary to work provides a wide-angle lens for viewing the interlinked processes of settlement and identity formation that took place at a distance. For example, the three Rhodian poleis (Lindos, Kameiros, Ialyssos) were undergoing converging processes in terms of Rhodian identity that were interlinked with Rhodian actions overseas, especially in Sicily and Egypt (chapter 2). Processes of social and political cohesion, forming the home community as a city-state, were contemporary with and often dependent on sending out sections of the population to colonize elsewhere.[158] Thus, the distinction between "home" and "overseas" becomes blurred from yet another angle. Think, for example, of the so-called internal colonization of the territories of Corinth or Eretria, both great *metropoleis* that coalesced as *poleis* and urban centers at the same time as (or even later than) the city-states that their colonists founded in Italy and Sicily.

It is no accident that Spartans were concurrently busy conquering and founding dependent settlements in the Peloponnesus, a short distance from Sparta, while Spartan "bastards" founded Taras in southern Italy (ca. 706) right after the First Messenian War, or that Spartans were directly involved in *emporia*

---

156 Boardman (1999); Tsetskhladze (2006b).

157 For a review of Greek cities and their polis status, see Hansen and Nielsen (2004). For a list of cities classified as "colonies," see Tsetskhladze (2006a), pp. lxvii–lxxiii.

158 Malkin (1994a).

in north Africa. This was also a time when a new division of plots and citizen status as *homoios* (someone who is "equal," being "like" another) apparently took place.[159] The variety of settlement activity abroad and the processes of social and political homogenization at home (now finally free of the "bastards") is interconnected within a Mediterranean web of social, political, and religious processes relevant to both communities and individuals.

Cognitive maps sometimes determine our historical hierarchies since they might imply a differentiation between center and periphery, an implication that can be misguided. Their revision allows us to better observe concurrent processes. Founding a colony, an *ap-oikia* away from home, could save the home, *oikos*, and turn it into a *polis*. It was probably later on that the term *metropolis* emerged as it has no semantic touch point with the Greek word *apoikia* (Greek has no "daughter colonies").[160] Colonization could be equivalent to the foundation of the mother city.[161] Here, the wide angle of observation is particularly important, as it needs not just to encompass in its vision the political community of the island of Paros (a *metropolis*) or Thasos (its colony) but also to understand what went on at both because they belonged to the same network (chapter 2). In fact, the island of Paros provides an intriguing example that combines a regional network forming an island identity, together with colonization across the waters. The Parian hill site of Koukounaries was abandoned at the same time as the new settlement of two new towns at the Bay of Naussa in Paros itself. Approximately contemporary with these was the overseas foundation, by "Paros," in Thasos (p. 77). All of these foundations belonged more or less to a single generation, and it is easy to envision sons from the same families participating in all of these settlement projects. Thus, polis formation, "inner colonization," and overseas settlement all form part of a single process. Rather than in isolation, the issue is best approached in network terms.

The Colonial Experience and the Greek Convergence

The networks of Greek colonization encouraged the formation of more generalized Hellenic categories for its participants. Instead of merely "Therans," for example, we find "all the Greeks" explicitly mentioned as potential colonists at Cyrene. This is perhaps also because colonial practices became Greek in the making, in tandem with the rise of Delphi. Combined with the extended and increasingly varied geographical horizons, commonalities of experience and the resulting commonalities of practice probably taught Greeks that the overall

---

159 Malkin (1994b), pp. 67–113.
160 For the terminology of ancient Greek colonization, see Casevitz (1985).
161 Malkin (1994a).

differences and variety among themselves were comparatively far less significant than the differences between the Maryandinoi in the Black Sea, the Etruscans in Italy, the Iberians in Spain, or the Libyans in north Africa. These groups of people, among whom Greeks were founding their new cities, were all distant from one another, a situation unprecedented in previous Greek history. The "perceptual continuum" of the sea (of which Horden and Purcell speak), those fragmented lands vs. the unified sea, found its historical counterpart in fragmented barbarian lands and a common Greek civilization that was stitching its hems to their terrain.

Greeks continued to found settlements farther away from each other. The Phoenicians of Tyre were following a similar pattern, particularly in north Africa and Spain, and ritually compensating for the growing distance from their mother city. They were still practicing the annual ritual pilgrimage to participate in the cult of Melqart in Tyre when Alexander the Great besieged the city. The questions as to how much of "Phoenician identity" was determined by the growing distances and their ritual "compensation" over the sea is an interesting one.

Awareness of affinity or even "sameness" occurs not when people, such as the Homeric heroes, are close to each other (in fact, that is when they pay particular attention to their differences) but when they are far apart (and that is when they condense their vision to some salient and common characteristics of identity). A new kind of "Greek" convergence around the ancient Mediterranean came about because of the great number of settlements, the relatively short time in which they were established, and their wide-ranging geographical horizons. It is the distance that creates the virtual center. The longer one stretches the connecting cables, the thicker they become. The farther the shores of these maritime settlements, the closer Greeks felt toward one another, as the ritual investment in Panhellenic sanctuaries expressly indicates. In other words, colonization was responsible, to a significant measure, for the rise of Hellenism. In spite of the fragmented state of our sources, archaic networks of colonization provide us with some rare examples of the explicit enlargement of categories of Hellenic identities. Let us observe the modalities of this process and point out the relevant cases.

Greek colonization rapidly expanded categories of belonging because early settlements came to include immigrants who would join the original nucleus of settlers. Otherwise it would be difficult to explain the relatively enormous number of colonies founded by mother cities such as Miletos or Chalkis, both unlikely to have had sufficient population resources for all of them. Early colonization involved significant processes of Hellenic convergence because of the nature of the colonizing projects themselves. I believe that these were often conducted as the project of a core group of settlers who set out from a specific community and were led by a known oikistês. Many would join, either at the time of foundation or, more commonly, in later generations or in secondary foundations, and were assimilated to the nucleus by means of the formal social, ritual, and political modalities established at the start.

As explained in detail in chapter 6, the filter through which settlers integrated and became "Corinthians" or "Milesians" was that of *nomima*. These were the "diacritical markers" of a community and involved social divisions such as the name and number of "tribes," sacred calendars, and types and terminology of institutions and magistracies. *Nomima* were mostly "assigned" (*etéthe*) and implemented as entire sets for the community by the oikist.[162] They basically constituted the social and religious order of the new community and served as an efficient mechanism for assimilating disparate groups of other immigrants, who, as at Cyrene, could outnumber the original colonists. Greeks cared about *nomima* and employed them, for example, to identify a colony as "Chalkidian." *Nomima* served to assimilate all individual migrants into the new social order so that after one generation all would become "Chalkidians" or "Phokaians." Moreover, sometimes "Chalkidians" (especially in Sicily) or "Phokaians" (in the western Mediterranean) eventually came close to what "Graikoi" signified in Italy or "Ionians" in the east: a generalized ethnic or subethnic category. From a historical perspective, it is noteworthy that the comprehensive ethnic names given by "foreigners" to Greeks, namely, *Graeci* in Latin, *Yavanim* in Hebrew, *Wynn* in Egyptian—emerged due to processes of settlement and colonization.

The Greek cities, especially in the western Mediterranean, were often connected with the oracle of Delphi, who not only had provided them with a foundation prophecy but also functioned as an ongoing mediator between Apollo, the sending communities, the settlers, and further migrants.[163] Delphi, emerging as a major Hellenic hub in tandem with the spread of Greek colonization (eighth–seventh centuries), was also in a position to place specific colonization projects within Panhellenic contexts. Approximately three generations after Cyrene was founded (traditional date: 631 BCE), Delphi provided it with a second colonization oracle in order to encourage further immigration. This time it was addressed neither to an *oikistês* nor to a specific mother city but to "*all the Greeks (Hellenas pantas)* to sail across the sea and live together with the people of Cyrene in Libya for the Cyrenaeans invited them, promising a distribution of land."[164] So many came from all over that eventually a redistribution and renaming of tribes was implemented by an external arbitrator that Delphi was asked to send to Cyrene to help settle its internal affairs: (1) Therans (the original settlers) and *perioikoi* ("dwellers around," probably local populations or mixed Greek-Libyan groups, but the meaning is not clear); (2) Peloponnesians

---

162 This is the word used by Thucydides in the beginning of the sixth book when describing the foundation of colonies in Sicily, clearly seeing *nomima* in terms of a comprehensive choice and implementation. See chapter 6.

163 For an assessment of Delphi's role in Greek colonization, see Malkin (1987), pp. 17–91.

164 Hdt. 4.159.2 with Chamoux (1953), pp. 72, 124–25, 134. Cf. Giangiulio (2009).

and Cretans; (3) islanders.[165] Thera was an exceptional "mother city," and in the new tribal division the original nucleus dwindled to about one-sixth of Cyrene's citizens even though its Theran rituals (e.g., the *karneia*) and the Theran founder cult remained consistent during later centuries as a focus of collective identity.

This is a rare glimpse of how colonization provided opportunities for Greeks to "mix" and to refer to their overarching, Panhellenic identity in terms of "all the Greeks," a phrase apparently quoted from Apollo's prophecy. This foreshadows Hellenistic colonization, where people would settle as "Greeks" (no longer as "Corinthians" or "Chalkidians"). The Cyrene episode in particular illustrates the dynamism of colonial networks and stretches the notion of inclusiveness, which was based on generalized Hellenic identity. This was not an isolated phenomenon.

As noted, there was much individual human mobility around the Archaic Mediterranean, including that of traders, artists, seers, arbitrators, professional "lawmakers," soldiers, and individual migrants.[166] In a colonization context, the earliest explicit example of Greeks of varied origins converging on a new colony is found in the poetry of Archilochos of Paros (ca. mid-seventh century). He speaks of himself at Thasos, Paros's colony, yet complains bitterly that "the misery of all the Greeks (*panhellenes*)" is converging on the island.[167] He was clearly not referring to his fellow Parians. The context of colonization, then, encouraged a man from Paros to articulate the identity of non-Parian migrants, arriving through networks unknown to us, to join in the new foundation in relation to the wider concept of "*Hellenes*."

The colonial context that expresses the extension of collective identities is also found in detailed accounts. Note that Thucydides says that the original colonists of Epidamnos, a colony of Corcyra (late seventh century), also included Corinthians and "other Dorians"; before the Peloponnesian War Corinth called on "whoever wishes" to join in its recolonization "on fair and equal terms." Also note how he describes the foundation of Zankle (later Messana) in Sicily: First it was "pirates" who settled it: "Zankle was originally colonized by pirates who came from Kyme, the Chalkidic city in Opikia." Thus, it started as a type of secondary foundation from another colony. However, it quickly became formalized: The original settlers "were followed later by a large body of colonists from Chalkis *and the rest of Euboia who shared in the allotment of the land* [note the similarity in expression with Cyrene, given earlier]. *The oikists were Perieres of Kyme and Krataimenes of Chalkis.*" On the one hand, the formal aspects of two founders, one from Chalkis, the mother city of Kyme, the second from Kyme itself, are clearly "Chalkidian." On the other, we hear of other settlers "from the

165 Hdt. 4.161.
166 Giangiulio (1996); Purcell (1990). Cf. Ampolo (1977); D'Ercole (2005).
167 Frg. 102 in Gerber (1999a), p. 142: Πανελλήνων ὀϊζὺς ἐς Θάσον συνέδραμεν.

rest of Euboia." We now see both aspects: Colonization was correctly perceived as oriented to identifiable mother cities and human founders, serving as the focus of collective identity. Yet, in reality, many others joined in. Perhaps it is not by chance that the small subcolony of (Chalkidian) Leontinoi in Sicily was given a much more encompassing name, "Euboia," after the entire home island, whence we may assume that others came, joining the "Chalkidians" at Leontinoi.[168] Examples abound across the chronological spectrum: There were Megarians, for example, who joined the Corinthian founder, Archias, at Syracuse (733 BCE);[169] we hear of Samians *and other Ionians* colonizing Sicily (first at Kale Akte, then taking over Zankle), and so on.[170] In sum, whether as "Ionians" (cf. chapter 6) or as "all Greeks," it is within the context of colonization that the colonists would refer to themselves in terms that transcended a specific polity.

If we shift our gaze from the colonists to the lands of settlement, we note the same all-encompassing expressions of identities that transcended the individual city. The altar of Apollo Archêgetês in Sicily (chapter 3) came to signify the opening up of a new land for *Greek* settlement. In chapter 6 I point out a parallel development in Massalia, where the Phokaian colonists established a cult to Apollo Delphinios, to be common to all Ionian Greeks. Like Naxos, Massalia was the first Greek city in a new country where no other Greek had settled before. Although this is a case of a single mother city (Phokaia) in contrast to the numerous mother cities active in Sicily, I argue that at the time this was taking place, with the fall of the Assyrians, the pressure of the Lydians, and eventually the rise of the Persians, many other Ionians might have been expected to rush to the west. I claim that, precisely because of the great distances, settlers of Massalia felt a need to assert, in a "new" land with no Greek poleis preceding them, a collective identity that transcended the limited connection with their mother city, Phokaia, to belong to a wider "Greek" network.

The implication that in the early periods of colonization somehow Greek settlers had some concept of shared identity articulated in lands with no previous Hellenic settlement in them—in fact, that certain aspects of "Hellenicity" emerged because of colonization—may seem far reaching. However, the ritual consistency seems to indicate this. Something analogous seems to have happened in Cyrenaica. There, with only one mother city (Thera) and only one major colony (Cyrene) serving as a subsequent mother city to other cities in Libya, prominence of cult was accorded to Apollo Karneios, a Dorian (and prominently Theran) God of migration, as well as to the regional, or "local" (Zeus) Ammon, with some Panhellenic connotations. Libya in its entirety was perceived as Zeus Ammon's "precinct" (*temenos*), and from Libya his cult and

168 See Hodos (2006), p. 91; Frasca (1997).
169 References in Malkin (1987), pp. 93–97, 210.
170 Thuc. 1.24, 26, 1.27.1 (Epidamnos), 6.4.5 (Zankle).

the fame of his oracle spilled over into Greece, a kind of "back-ripple" effect along the network lines.[171] By the late fourth century, it was not in any major temple on the Greek mainland but at the oracle of Zeus Ammon in Siwa that Alexander the Great chose to be recognized as the son of Zeus and, by implication, as a Panhellenic leader. We may also consider the regional-maritime cult of Achilles Pontarches for Black Sea colonies.[172] This was a Platonic "frog" cult of a hero-god whose presence was felt across the sea and in the narrow coastal strips of the Greek colonies. Its presence over the water and at points of terrestrial contact may be analogous to the curious Mediterranean dialect known as *lingua franca* (not to be confused with the generic meaning of the word), spoken mostly by sailors on board ships and in ports.[173] In other words, networks of cults expressed the "tying in" of the coasts with the sea as a virtual center. They also illustrated the double-ripple effect of Greek networks: Wider frameworks of identity were formed across the sea due to the dynamism of connectivity that followed the network links, reinvigorating the network as a whole and giving it a new meaning in the process.

Overseas settlement, then, extended network lines and made identities more inclusive and all-encompassing. As we will see in chapter 6, this is not merely a matter of the historian's hindsight but is integral to a Greek view of the world, at least as it was expressed in the sixth century BCE. The Ionians again provide interesting examples. In their collective *imaginaire* the Ionians viewed themselves as having once colonized in Asia Minor, where they split into discrete political communities. From around 600, some were redirecting their gaze westward. The Kolophonians settled Siris; Ionian cities toyed with the idea of founding a new Ionian state at Teos (Thales' idea) or migrating and doing the same in Sardinia (suggestion of Bias of Priene) or immigrating under stress to Sicily and settling *together* at Kale Akte or, just after the Persian Wars, immigrating en masse to some unspecified place. These pan-Ionian projects indicate how, on the contemporary horizon of Greek expectations, colonization and new foundations could conceivably result in the political and ethnic homogenization of "the Ionians."[174] A less voluntary characteristic of mixture appears later, in the fifth century, when some Sicilian tyrants were

171 On the cults of Apollo Karneios and Zeus Ammon see Malkin (1994b), pp. 143–68.

172 *RE* s.v. Pontarches (Diehl); *New Pauly* (English), s.v. Achilles (Ley): "According to later sources . . . under the name of *pontarchoes* he was venerated on a par with Poseidon among the inhabitants of the Pontus Euxinus coast, as protector of sea voyages and seafarer" (p. 91). Also Graf (1985), pp. 351–53; Hooker (1988) argues against Hommel (1980), who suggests that Achilles was worshipped both as a hero and as a god. Hooker focuses his criticism on differentiating between the Homeric tradition, in which Achilles died, and later traditions and sources that offered alternative stories in which he is resurrected. See Quintus Smyrnaeus: "to Thetis, of Achilles: '. . . and I will give to him a holy island for my gift: It lies within the Euxine Sea: there evermore a God thy son shall be. The tribes that dwell around shall as mine own self honour him with incense and with steam of sacrifice.'" Quintus Smyrnaeus 3.775–90, trans. A. S. Way (1913). Also Pindar, *Nemean Ode* 4.49–50. On the cult of Achilles in the Black Sea, see also Belin de Ballu (1972), pp. 77–82; Hedreen (1991); Buskikh (2005).

173 Kahane, Kahane, and Tietze (1958).

174 The case is different from other relocations en masse as a single polis, as Themistokles famously threatened to do before the battle of Salamis; Hdt. 7.143.

forcefully relocating and blending entire populations (chapter 3). In authentic
Greek terms, it seems that what erases differences and consolidates identities
is not permanence but rather movement and distance.

A "Hellenic" convergence in a colonial context, explicitly articulated as
such, took place at Naukratis, in Egypt. Under the direction and protection of
Amasis, the *emporion* of Naukratis was reorganized: Nine Greek poleis (four
Ionian, four Dorian, and one Aiolian), established and ran the "Hellenic temple," the Hellênion, where inscriptions to the "gods of the Greeks" have been
found (chapter 2). It is noteworthy that Hellenicity acquired an express articulation not in any "Greek place" but in Egypt, where Greeks converged from all
over. Aside from being a self-referential identity, as the inscriptions seem to
indicate, Hellenic Naukratis also depended on Egyptian perspectives and practices that condensed the identity of foreigners (beginning with mercenaries)
into larger ethnic categories. Something similar happened to the Karians that
were serving in Egypt and to the Phoenicians: A discrete group of the latter, for
example, although known to be "Tyrians," was also regarded as "Phoenicians,"
a much wider ethnic category (chapter 2). Naukratis also indicates the "fractal"
nature of Hellenic convergences overseas: Three Rhodian poleis, Lindos,
Ialyssos, and Kameiros, were officially "represented" at Naukratis together as
"Rhodians." Since the state of Rhodes (or "the Rhodians" in Greek) was united
only about a century and a half later, the fact that three Rhodian *poleis* made an
official decision to define themselves as "Rhodians" is remarkable. It happened
early on, not at "home" but overseas. The ad hoc reason may have been profit:
Three poleis received their share as one of the four "Dorian" cities. In contrast,
although Lesbos, too, had a small "Lesbian" sanctuary on Lesbos, no other Lesbian polis aside from Mytilene had a share in the Hellênion. Naukratis, then,
illustrates from another perspective how distance affects Hellenic convergences. Because of the alien and dependent circumstances, three Rhodian
poleis converged into one. Greeks needed to officially organize themselves
according to their subethnic categories of "Dorians, Aiolians, and Ionians,"
something they would hardly have done in other contexts, and all of them now
officially employed the term "Hellenes."

As this book is concerned more with Greek civilization and identity and
less with ethnicity as such,[175] I refer to "Hellenic" terminology in relation to
its place within network contexts. Again, the sanctuary of Apollo at Delphi
may be relevant for the term "Hellenes" and to the network mode of its formation. The Delphic (Anthela) amphiktiony (a ritual network or grouping of
political communities, mostly *ethnê*, supervising the Delphic sanctuary, centered on Thermopylai and with a strong Thassalian influence)[176] undoubtedly
played a significant role in the original spread of the term "Hellenism." All who

---

175 Jonathan Hall (1997, 2002); Malkin (2001b and the other papers in the volume; 2003a).
176 Tausend (1992); Sánchez (2001); Bowden (2003).

joined in the Delphic network probably became Hellenes, a term originally associated with only a section of the amphiktiony.[177]

In Homer's *Iliad*, the term "Hellas" denotes the area of the kingdom of Hellen and later that of Achilles in Achaia Phthiotis, in western Thessaly.[178] Herodotus and Thucydides, for example, witnessed the spread of the term mostly as a matter of acculturation. Greeks could accept the idea that one could *become* a Greek. Margalit Finkelberg aptly quotes Plato's Menexenos, which apparently reacts against this notion:[179]

> We [the Athenians] are pure Hellenes, who have not mixed with barbarians (*amigeîs barbáron*). For we are not like the descendants of Pelops or Kadmos, Aigyptos or Danaos, nor many others who, being barbarians by nature (*phúsis*) and Hellenes by convention (*nomos*), dwell among us (*sunoikoûsin hemîn*)—we reside here as genuine Hellenes, not as half-barbarians (*meixobárbaroi*).[180]

In contrast, Herodotus, who believed that Hellenicity was a matter of diffusion, was only too happy to inform the Athenians that their pride in being autochthonous was double edged. If Hellenicity was a matter of *becoming*, that meant they could not possibly have originally been Hellenes but rather Pelasgians.[181]

The point here is not to decide between Herodotus and Plato on the issue of "pure" Athenians but to refer to the ancient debate precisely to demonstrate that such a debate was taking place and that Greeks were perfectly happy with the idea that some Greeks (albeit usually Greeks other than the speaker) were simply acculturated into becoming Greeks. Hellenism was perceived by the Greeks as something that could spread from some *point* (for example, "Hellas" in Achaia Phthiotis) outward. Many modern scholars follow the same line of reasoning, and the case for the Delphic Amphiktiony as a mechanism for this spread seems convincing. A further implication might be that such *Hellenes*, when sailing overseas under the auspices of the Delphic oracle, may have been responsible for the spread of the term in the Mediterranean at large, with Greeks referring to themselves as Hellenes across the Mediterranean but no longer only in reference to Delphi. However, being *called* by comprehensive names (Hellenes, Ionians, Phokaians—(chapter 6) and forming and sharing Hellenic commonalities is not the same. All of this may warrant further study beyond the scope of this book.

The issue is not a simple one since, as noted, in the west Greeks came to be known by non-Greeks not as Hellenes but as Graikoi (Latin *Graeci*, hence

---

177 Fowler (1998), p. 11; Jonathan Hall (2002), pp. 134–54 with references to the previous discussion.
178 Cf. Thuc. 1.3 with Hall (2002), pp. 125–34.
179 Finkelberg (2005), p. 37.
180 Plato *Mx.* 245d.
181 Thomas (2001).

our "Greeks"). The process could not have been simply one of spreading one's own identity outward in concentric circles. Aristotle places "ancient Hellas" (*he Hellas he archaia*) not in Thessaly but around Dodona: "It was there that the Selloi [Zeus's priests at Dodona] and those who were then called Graikoi and now Hellenes used to live."[182] Elsewhere I have suggested that the *Graikoi* around the oracle of Dodona, who claimed they were the most ancient of Greeks, were somehow responsible for the transfer of the term through the nearby Straits of Otranto to Italy.[183]

Common action may seem to constitute an experience formative of collective identity. Hellas never did anything in common before the Trojan War, says Thucydides.[184] Following the Trojan War, the Age of Heroes died out, and the war was perceived as the first and only Panhellenic project before the Persian Wars. The common action of the Greeks (called mostly "Achaians" by Homer) was to converge on a single spot, Troy. In contrast, the returns of the heroes, such as Diomedes, Agamemnon, and Odysseus, signified the great *kinêsis* (movement, turbulence) with heroes spreading apart, as well as bringing about revolutions and movement of entire populations. Troy provided an imagined unity or at least an imagined concerted action, which Greeks in later periods, like the Spartan Agesialos or Alexander the Great, attempted to replicate when warring against the new Troy, the Persian Empire. In contrast, the heroes of the *nostoi* (returns) provided an explanation for the fragmentation of the entire Greek world.[185]

In contrast to this quasi-historical *imaginaire*, the historical Greek networks during the Archaic period indicate the reverse: Greeks set out not to converge on a "Troy" but to diverge by spreading far and wide. Their common action was dispersal to new foundations, followed by more dispersal and more foundations. They were not like the heroes of the returns: Those wandered either because they wished to return home or, finding their home had turned against them, went into exile. In contrast, Archaic Greeks were on the move as entire communities or as migrants joining new foundations. They dispersed without becoming atomized. In short, it was not concerted action but divergence through colonial networks that created some of the important commonalities of the civilization we know today as Greek. The spatial distance and the network dynamics formed its virtual center.

Jonathan Hall (1997, 2002) emphasizes images of blood kinship as the salient definition of "Hellenicity" during the Archaic period. He is clearly correct in claiming that genealogical *stemmata* provided outlines of kinship and that Greeks loved to experiment with genealogies. Moreover, genealogies may also fit network models. I have some doubts as to their salience, especially

---

182 Arist. *Mete.* 352a33–34.
183 Malkin (2001a), pp. 198–200.
184 Thuc.1.3.1.
185 Malkin (1998), p. 3.

because as a genre or subgenre genealogy had its own "textual" life. It is possible that the genealogical poets were mainly speaking to each other, in contrast to the general mindset that relied more on common historical experiences than on kinship. Such experiences spoke of migration and colonization, namely an experience of drawing lines across lands and waters. The seventh-century poets Mimnermos and Tyrtaios, for example, seemed to define their collective identities as Spartans or Kolophonians in terms not of genealogy but of the *ktisis*, the foundation story of their respective cities.[186] By analogy, the Hebrew God is both the "God of Abraham, Isaac, and Jacob" (genealogy) but more prominently "the Lord God who took you out of the Land of Egypt" (a *ktisis*, a common historical and foundational experience). Whereas the Hebrew genealogies found no ritual expression, the Exodus from Egypt came to be celebrated at Passover, one of the three most important Jewish holidays.

While the Hellenes of the Delphic amphiktiony and the Hellenic genealogies surely had a role to play, there is no reason to discuss their role in the formation of Greek identity by downplaying the role of colonization. Collective identity is not a zero-sum game. Others have made the point that colonization, especially because of the contrast with non-Greeks, was a fundamental historical experience that shaped the Greeks' view of themselves as Greeks. The idea has been around for quite a while. Jonathan Hall aptly quotes John Bury, who wrote in 1895 that "No cause . . . more powerfully promoted the growth of a feeling of unity among the Greeks—the consciousness of their common race and common language—than the institution of colonization which brought them into contact with many various kinds of non-Greek peoples."[187] Similarly, Gustave Glotz argued that "colonization made more clearly perceptible to the children of Hellen those mysterious bonds—race, language and religion— which had unconsciously united them. Living on the far-off margins in contact with populations that neither spoke nor thought like them, they more proudly sensed themselves as Greek."[188] In contrast, Hall claims that "To trace and understand the construction of a specifically Hellenic identity, it is not to the *margins* that we must direct our sight but to the *heart* of the Greek mainland itself" (my emphasis).[189]

The alternative network approach emphasizes not only the encounter with non-Greeks (Greeks looking *outward*, toward the terrestrial hinterlands and being observed from there) but also the resulting commonalities (Greeks looking *inward*, at each other across the waters). A network perspective does not take it as self-evident that "Firstly, cultural self-reflexivity is typically triggered

186 Mimnermos: frg. 9 in West (1993) and frg. 3 in Gentili and Prato (1988); Tyrtaios: frg. 1a in Prato (1968) and frg. 2 in Gerber (1999a). See in more detail chapter 3, pp. 99–100.

187 Hall (2002), p. 90, with reference to Bury (1895), p. 236. (Note that when Bury was writing, the meaning of "race" in English could function as our "nation.")

188 Glotz (1948), p. 216.

189 Hall (2002), p. 124.

by an awareness of difference, not similarity." More important, in direct contradiction to Hall's position, a network approach sets aside concepts such as center vs. periphery or margins vs. "the heart of the Greek mainland itself."[190] These imply temporal and spatial hierarchies that, rather than being self-evident, are themselves in need of justification.

I believe that colonization informed and strengthened the nascent idea of Greekness primarily because the initial colonial experience was similar and common, and its initial problems and solutions were quickly copied among colonies that had different origins and were at great distances from each another. A list of such common problems may include the role of Delphi (foundation prophecies and ongoing relationships); the negotiation with various "Others" and the unwilling or suspicious acceptance by local populations; the authoritarian role of the founder (oikistês) and leader of the settlement expedition; the adaptation of a social order and a code of nomima, usually from the mother city; the age average (most new settlers were young and more open to experimentation); similar social orders that included, with one known exception (Cyrene), the rapid disappearance of all oikist families (that is, no dynasties); the ongoing tensions of identity with, independence of, and dependence on the sending community; the assimilative social forces of nuclei of organized settlers for disparate groups of colonists; the similar needs to organize the physical space of the new territories according to very similar criteria and functions that are apparent from the Crimea to France; a common visual language, often expressed in similar motifs in art and architecture; and the special investment in the great Panhellenic sanctuaries and participation in the Panhellenic games.

The settlers of the new city-states met an enormous variety of populations. Images of the new places and especially their marked differences from what now came to be understood as "familiar," or "Greek," as well as the commonalities of colonial experiences, must have been spoken of along sea lanes and in ports, in the same way that overseas adventures were the stuff of the epic poetry of Homer.[191] Combined with the phenomenon of the mobility of individuals and small groups, as well as the changing roles of traders, mercenaries, warriors, and settlers, information was moving along the newly expanded network lines across the Mediterranean and the Black Sea. Perhaps a principle of "peer polity interaction" (everybody tries to keep up with the Joneses) was at work and existed among entire communities along network lines.[192]

---

190 Hall (2004), p. 124; Hall (2002, chapter 4) presents a detailed and highly sophisticated discussion of issues such as acculturation and encounters, stressing their variability, and rightly argues against applying simplistic Greek/barbarian divisions. Yet his terminology retains the notions of "margins" and "heart," and the "direction" for the spread of Hellenic identity resembles the concentric circles that result from throwing a stone into a pond. I consider the back-ripple effect to be equally important.

191 Cf. Andreau and Virlouvet (2002).

192 Renfrew and Cherry (1986); cf. Herring (1991); Ma (2003).

In the words of John Ma, who brilliantly applies this to the Hellenistic period, "The concept [of peer polity interaction] promotes the study of equipollent, interconnected communities, which must be considered *qua* network rather than by trying to differentiate between core and periphery." The approach of peer polity interaction stresses competitive emulation among city-oriented elites: "structurally homologous, autonomous states of the same size, linked by networks of concrete and symbolic interaction, where changes occur across the board rather than in top-down diffusionist waves."[193] In this respect it clearly foreshadows certain characteristics of the application of network theory to historical studies.

What matters within our historical context is that the growing distance of the settlement horizons in the Archaic period, together with the crystallization of practice, connectivity, and the eventual need to refer to a framework of a wide-reaching, "imagined community,"[194] probably had an impact on the way the people we refer to as Greeks came to view themselves. Widely distributed commonalities come to the foreground. "Distance gives the objectivity that time will eventually provide even to compatriots," says Edmund White in *The Flâneur*.[195] Geographical distance fulfills a similar function to a temporal one: We forget many differences in order to affirm some sameness. Common forgetfulness, not common memories, says Ernst Renan, is what unites the nation. (What French person would like to remember the massacre of the Protestants on St. Bartholomew's Day?)[196] Modern Greeks make deliberate choices of what to see in the past so that they may forge a neoclassical, national, modern identity.[197] For ancient Greeks, distance functioned as a mental filter. It is not Edmund White's "objectivity" that I seek but the sense of it—a realization that things are common, shared, and similar and that so many elements of sameness constitute an identity. Through network dynamics, Hellenization became shared across vast expanses. It followed geographical expansion down to the Hellenistic period and Hellenistic colonization, which reached all the way to Afghanistan, and the emergence of a new common dialect, *koinê*, the first ever, truly Panhellenic language.

---

193 Ma (2003), pp. 15, 23.
194 Anderson (1991).
195 White (2001), p. 28.
196 Renan (1882).
197 See, for example, Liakos (2001) with Just (1989).

2

Island Networking and Hellenic Convergence: From Rhodes to Naukratis

The rise of networks in the Archaic Mediterranean had a significant impact on the emergence of newly defined, regional identities. In contrast to affiliation by means of fictitious bloodlines or through the civic organization of this or that polis, regional identities signified a convergence that bypassed these traditional lines. What is remarkable, too, is the interlinked character of the rise of regionalism (itself a subject for network analysis) with the overall emergence of generalized Hellenic articulations. In this chapter and the next I focus on two large Mediterranean islands, Rhodes and Sicily, to see how the network prism is beneficial to observing these phenomena.

The issue of regional identities and their connectedness with overarching identities is as ancient as it is contemporary. As noted, the rise of the European Union was accompanied by the shrinking role of the nation-state and the growth of regional identities that often transcended national boundaries (*l'Europe des régions*). Our changing perceptions of regionalism, especially nonhierarchical, network-oriented regionalism, facilitate the application of this concept to antiquity and the ability to search for the kind of cultural, religious, and functional identities that existed among an individual polis, its regional identity, and the overarching Hellenic civilization. I intend especially to illustrate and analyze, in network terms, the multidirectional influences both on the rise of regionalism, such as Rhodian or Sicilian identity, and of Hellenism, with colonization and emporic activity as the mediator between these two phenomena.

Rhodian Identity at Rhodes and Overseas: Myth and Cult

The island of Rhodes lies off the southwestern corner of Asia Minor, some-what resembling a bit of the landmass that has been pinched off and placed in the sea. It was sufficiently far from the mainland (18 km) to keep it safe, yet sufficiently close to enable it to conquer some of the land across the mainland facing the island (*peraia*) in various historical periods. The island is about 80 km long and 38 km wide, with a total area of approximately 1,400 square km and a coastline of about 220 km. The modern city of Rhodes overlaps the site of the city that was founded at the end of the fifth century (408 BCE). This was a result of the political unification of the island (*synoikismos*), when its three independent states (Lindos, Kameiros, and Ialysos) relinquished their sover-eignty.[1] During the Hellenistic era Rhodes became a miniempire, and some aspects of its maritime code still exist today. The long-term perspective high-lights the advantages of its maritime position, as expressed in antiquity and the Middle Ages (the Knights Hospitaller, 1309–1522), but always present is its significant role in relation to the mainland and to maritime trade routes (figures 2-1 and 2-2).

Rhodes as a single unit first emerges in the Greek *imaginaire* as a physical entity. A "land myth" explains its emergence: The island was made to rise out of the sea[2] because the god Helios missed out on the divine lottery and needed a land to worship him. In a physical and cultic sense, the god Helios came to be considered the *archêgos* (primordial founder) of Rhodes.[3] Upon that island we then find various mythological inhabitants, such as the Telchines.[4] In a transi-tion from the idea of "land" to that of the foundation of a political community, we hear of the grandsons of Helios, the eponymous founders of Rhodian cities: Ialysos, Kameiros, and Lindos. "They (Kameiros, Ialysos, and Lindos) divided their inherited land into three parts and separately held their allotment of cit-ies, places that still bear their names."[5]

It is interesting that the earliest source to mention Rhodes represents it as a complete entity, an entire human community divided according to city "divi-sions," and does so in an overseas context: Homer says that Tlepolemos, a son of Herakles, led nine ships to Troy carrying Rhodians "who lived in Rhodes in three divisions, in Lindos and Ialysos and Kameiros, white with chalk." Homer also provides a *ktisis* (foundation story) that explains Tlepolemos's

---

1 Diod. *Sic.* 13.75.1 with Moggi (1976), pp. 213–26; Gabrielsen (2000). For a review of Rhodian poleis see "Rhodos" in Hansen and Nielsen (2004), pp. 192–210.

2 Pind. *Ol.* 7. 54–63. Cf. Malkin (1996a, 1996b).

3 Diod. *Sic.* 5.56.4. For Helios and his sons as mythological progenitors and founders see Kowalzig (2007), pp. 239–57.

4 Blakely (1998, 2006).

5 Pind. *Ol.* 7.74–76, trans. William H. Race in Race (1997a).

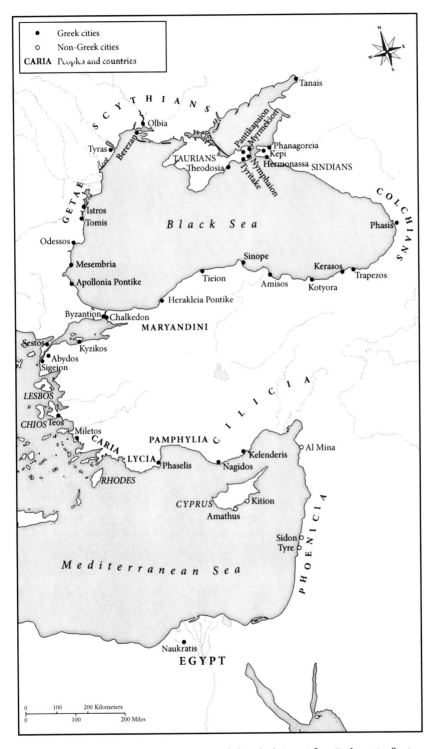

FIGURE 2.1. The Eastern Mediterranean and the Black Sea. After Graham (1982a).

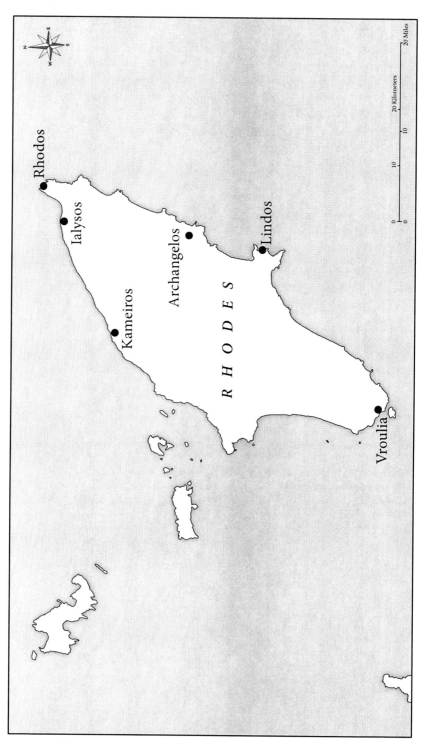

FIGURE 2.2. The island of Rhodes. After Gabrielsen (1999).

status: Tlepolemos fled from Argos, where he had grown up, having killed his uncle. "So he immediately built ships, and when he had collected a host of people, went forth in flight over the sea, because the other sons and grandsons of mighty Herakles threatened him." After many wanderings Tlepolemos finally reached the island of Rhodes, where "his people settled in three divisions by tribes" and enjoyed the favor of Zeus.[6] Pindar speaks of Tlepolemos as *chthonos oikistêr*,[7] "the founder of the land." This refers to all of Rhodes rather than to one of its particular cities, Kameiros, Ialysos, and Lindos.[8] Aside from poetical references, Tlepolemos existed as a cultic reality: He enjoyed a pan-Rhodian cult, consisting of sacrifices, processions, and games.[9]

This is a very peculiar Dorian-Herakleid myth. It is similar to the Peloponnesian myths of the return of the Herakleidai but with a twist:[10] Tlepolemos flees other Herakleidai[11] and has no "right of return" to Rhodes, in contrast to the Spartan Herakleidai, who claimed they were "returning" to claim their inheritance in the Peloponnesus. However, his myth is commonly "Dorian" in relation to the concepts of "foundation," in terms of conquest and discontinuity: Just as Sparta had been in existence before its Dorian conquest, so, too, were Lindos, Kameiros, and Ialysos, originally founded not by Herakleidai but by the descendants of Helios.[12]

Therefore, although we have three distinct *poleis* on the island, they form a single unit in the *Iliad* when sailing overseas to fight at Troy, an occasion that prompts Homer to provide us with the *ktisis* that at once distinguishes the three cities yet provides them with a common Dorian-Herakleid foundation. It is only from a distance, in an *overseas* context, that Rhodian identity is condensed. The Tlepolemeia, the pan-Rhodian festival, provides us with its cultic expression as a living reality for Rhodians in historical periods.[13]

There is little doubt that the three Rhodian cities were poleis. Pindar calls Rhodes a *tripolis nason*, "a three-poleis island," and Herodotus informs us that of the five Dorian poleis that made up the Dorian *Pentapolis*, three were Rhodian.[14] Gary Reger and Christy Constantakopoulou have studied some

---

6 Homer *Il.* 2.653–67, trans. Lattimore (1961).

7 Pind. *Ol.* 7.30.

8 Cf. Pind. *Ol.* 7. 13–19.

9 Pind. *Ol.* 7. 79–80.

10 Similar also to the myth of other Heliadai (descendants of Helios), four of whom had to escape Rhodes after they murdered their brother Tenages. See Diod. *Sic.* 5.57.2 with Craik (1980), pp. 155–57.

11 See Craik (1980), pp. 165–67.

12 Prinz (1979), pp. 78–97, gives a good summary of sources; cf. Craik (1980), pp. 153–67, who thoroughly discusses Rhodes's foundation myth; cf. Dougherty (1993), pp. 189–94.

13 On the Tlepolemeia as a pan-Rhodian festival, see Arnold (1936), pp. 432–33; Bresson (1986), p. 414, for a discussion of the place of Tlepolemos in Rhodes. Kowalzig (2007), p. 225, believes that Pindar's *Ol.* 7 was performed at the Tlepolemeia.

14 Pind. *Ol.* 7.18; Hdt. 1.144. Cf. Gabrielsen (2000), p. 181. What is more striking is that Rhodians expressed a common identity in spite of that division. Homer regards all Rhodians as *Rhodioi* (Hom. *Il.* 2.653–56). See also Hekataios *FGrHist.* 1 F 246, Korydalla (in Likya) as *polis Rhodiôn*, but the expression may be a paraphrase by Stephanus of Byzantium, who quotes Hekataios.

fascinating expressions of "island identities" in the Greek world, and Rhodes seems to be a prominent case in point.[15] In external Hellenic contexts, a Rhodian, expressly and even proudly, may have wished to appear as a "Rhodios" rather than coming from a particular polis in Rhodes. This is especially noteworthy in the Panhellenic, Olympic context: Dorieus, a Diagorid from the polis of Ialysos, dedicated a statue at Olympia and proclaimed himself "Rhodios";[16] thus, too, apparently his brother, Damagetos,[17] and Diagoras himself.[18] Note that Thucydides also refers to Dorieus, a victor at Olympia in 428 as "Rhodios."[19] This is particularly important as a proclamation of his Rhodian identity to the Greek world and should serve to qualify the notion (advanced by Leslie Kurke) that Olympic victories were directed at the polis in its more conventional sense.[20] Moreover, this time from a Rhodian perspective, the *Seventh Olympian Ode*, which celebrates Diagoras, was apparently dedicated at the temple of Athena at Lindos even though Diagoras himself was from Ialysos.[21]

In military contexts outside of Rhodes itself, as, for example at Athens, we find mention of two "Rhodian" pentekonters (fifty oared ships) and seven hundred "Rhodian" slingers.[22] Similarly, notes Christy Constantakopoulou, Thucydides' list of allies includes "Lemnians," "Keians," and "Rhodians."[23] Conversely, during the revolt of 412, a few years before the *synoikismos*, all of the Rhodians seem to have fought against Athens.[24] How did this Rhodian convergence come about? Natural circumstances, with Rhodes being an island, probably helped, but as there are many islands where such developments did not occur, we need to look for a wider Mediterranean context whereby the dynamics of networks consolidated a Rhodian identity in relation to itself and to Hellenic identity at large.

15   Reger (1997), Constantakopoulou (2005). Cf. Knoepfler (1974, 1976).

16   Paus. 6.7.1 describes these as "the statues of the Rhodian athletes." On the statues and their inscriptions, see Frazer (1898), note 7.1, on Paus. 6.7.1. The Dorieus inscription is usually attributed to Dorieus, though it has been argued that it is not certain whether the athlete to whose name the inscription refers was Dorieus of Rhodes or Theagenes from Thasos. See *IvO* no. 153.

17   *IvO* no. 152.

18   *IvO* no. 151.

19   Thuc. 3.8.2. Cf. Hornblower (2004), pp. 131–45.

20   Kurke (1991).

21   The Scholia to Pindar's seventh *Olympian Ode* suggests that Gorgon, the historian of Rhodes, spoke of a copy of the ode written in gold letters, which was set up at the temple of Athena at Lindos. See Gorgon, *FGrHist* 515, frg. 18. Also *FHG*, vol. 4, 410, frg. 3 = Sch. Pind. *Ol.*7 in Drachmann (1903), p. 195, lines 13–14. Momigliano (1975), p. 514, emphasizes the pan-Rhodian aspect; the point has been made long ago. See Graux (1881), who suggests that the ode may have been written in golden ink on parchment. Cf. Arnold (1936), p. 433; Morelli (1959), p. 81; Parker (1998), pp. 15–16.

22   Thuc. 6.43.

23   Thuc. 7.57.2, 7.57.4, 7.57.6, respectively; see Constantakopoulou (2005), p. 8.

24   Thuc. 8.44.2.

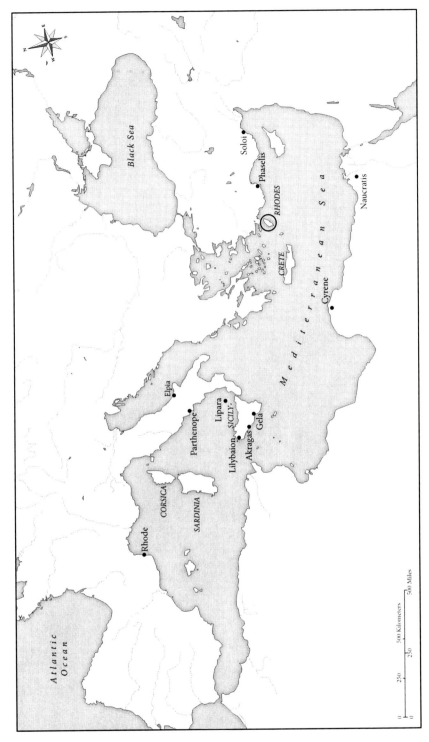

FIGURE 2.3. Colonies associated with Rhodes.

Rhodian Colonization: The Seventh Century

In the early seventh century we find the "Rhodians of the Sea"[25] colonizing in the east, in southern Asia Minor at Phaselis, and in Sicily (figure 2-3). Rhodian wares reached far and wide, for example to Histria in the Black Sea.[26] Some have suggested Rhodian involvement in a temple to Helios, a prominent Rhodian deity, at Tell Sukas in north Syria (see Hodos 2006, pp. 55–58; alternatively, this may have been a Phoenician temple dedicated to Rashaph). Another possible Rhodian involvement in colonization was the founding of Soloi in Lycia, but the tradition may be based on guesswork.[27] Anecdotal traditions speak of the founder of Phaselis as Lakios, a brother of Antiphemos, the Lindian founder of Gela in Sicily,[28] and the *Lindian Chronicle* (xxiv) proudly tells of Lakios's dedication to Athena Lindia.[29] By the early sixth century, Phaselis, as a Dorian city, was a member of the Hellênion in Naukratis.[30] According to Egyptian harbor accounts from probably the first half of the fifth century, discovered in the Aramean Akhikar palimpsest, Phaselis achieved particular commercial prominence in Egypt: Thirty-six ships from Phaselis are mentioned, no Greek ships are listed, and only six Phoenician ones are cited.[31] The lack of other Greek ships may easily be explained by the conditions following the Ionian revolt (Egypt was then under Persian rule).[32] The harbor accounts reveal how the commerce and presence of Greeks must have affected the Egyptian economy by drawing it outward to the Mediterranean. It appears that the royal Egyptian treasury received its taxes in Greek coin, signifying the potential growth of commerce, which is expressed in the recorded imports of metals, worked wood (boards, planks, etc.), wine, and perfumed oil (wool).[33] We have no information about the ongoing relations between Rhodes and its colony Phaselis, yet the participation of both Rhodes and Phaselis in the Hellênion in Egyptian Naukratis points to some cooperation in the same commercial network. One wonders how many of the thirty-six ships that were officially registered under a "Phaselis flag" were actually from that city.

25 Pind. *Ol.* 7 13–14.

26 Krebs (1997), p. 52.

27 According to Strabo (14. 5.8 C.671), the founding of Soloi in Lycia was conducted by "Achaians and Rhodians from Lindos." For Korydalla see Hekataios *FGrHist* 1 F 246. Cf. Ps. Scymn. 75; Arrian *Anab.* 1.26.4; Polyb. 21.24.

28 Aristainetos *FGrHist* 771 F 1; cf. Philostephanos *FHG*, vol. 3, p. 28; Heropythos *FGrHist* 448 F 1. See Malkin (1987), pp. 196–97.

29 Higbie (2003), p. 104.

30 Hdt. 2.178.2; Bresson (2000c, pp. 41–42; 2000b, p. 68), with updated bibliography.

31 Porten and Yardeni (1993). Commentary: Briant and Descat (1998), pp. 60–62, for a possible later chronology. Cf. Tammuz (2005).

32 Bresson (2000b), pp. 68–73.

33 Briant and Descat (1998), pp. 69–73, 77–78.

Turning west to Sicily, we find Lindians "solidifying" as Rhodians, as well as "Cretans," who are submerged in a new identity overseas. In 688, says Thucydides, "Antiphemos of Rhodes and Entimos of Crete led colonists and founded a joint colony at Gela . . . and the name for the city came from the river Gelas, while the land which is now the acropolis and which was the first to be fortified is called Lindioi; their *nomima* were established as Dorian."[34] The name "Lindioi" points to the fact that Antiphemos, "from Rhodes," actually sailed from Lindos. In fact, Herodotus, without mentioning Entimos and the Cretans, explicitly says that "Gela was colonized by the Lindians of Rhodes and Antiphemos."[35] A fifth-century dedication inscribed on a cup (*kylix*) from Gela testifies to a cult to "Antiphamos" (*Mnasithales anetheke Antiphamôi*),[36] thus appropriating the name of the founder from the domination of literary tradition and firmly anchoring it in a social and ritual reality. And Antiphemos is mentioned alone. His name is also mentioned, again sidestepping the Cretan cofounder, Entimos, by Pausanias, who says that Antiphemos returned victorious from the Sicilian town of Omphake and brought back a statue made by Daidalos. The statue probably alludes to the myth of Daidalos, who had sought refuge from King Minos at the court of King Kokalos in Sicily. The symbolic relic, with its Cretan resonance (Minos), yet in the hands of a Rhodian founder, probably implied some claim to mythic legitimation.[37] We see, then, that at Sicilian Gela, Antiphemos and the Rhodians overshadowed Entimos and the Cretans in the historical tradition, in oracular folklore, and in cult.[38]

However, while overshadowing the Cretans, the generalized identity of Rhodians as expressed in Sicily also diluted the more specific "Lindians." The apparent intention to make Gela a New Lindos, Lindioi, failed, and the *nomima* that were established were not Lindian but generally "Dorian," probably to also accommodate the Cretans. Thucydides recognized *nomima* as a defining attribute of a Greek city and was very specific about *nomima*: In his introduction to the sixth book he is careful to mention them and usually cites them according to *poleis* (see chapter 6). In other words, he is aware of the distinction and uses "Dorian" intentionally. It seems, therefore, that in establishing the

---

34 Thuc. 6.4.3 For more on *nomima* see pp. 189–197.

35 Hdt. 7.153.1. Cf. Call. *Aet.* Fr. 43, 47, with Malkin (1987), pp. 52–53. For Rhodians and Cretans see also Diod. *Sic.* 8.23; Artemon 569 *FGrHist* 1; *Et. Mag.* 225.1. See Hornblower (2008), p. 290.

36 Ciaceri (1911), p. 311. For the inscription see Guarducci (1967), vol. 1, pp. 254–55, with bibliography. Dubois (1989), vol. 1, no. 135, pp. 159–60. Also, Orsi (1900) and "L'Heroon di Antifemo" in Orsi (1900), pp. 558–60, for the first publications.

37 Paus. 8.46.2; 9.40.1. On the myth of Daidalos in Sicily see Hdt. 7.170; Diod. *Sic.* 4.77–79; Apollodoros *ApE* 1.14–15; Zenobios 1.92; Schol. Nem. 4.95. Sophokles' lost play, "Kamikioi" [The Men of Kamikos], is thought to have recounted the myth; surviving fragments (Soph. fr.324R) speak of the shell brought over by Minos in his search for Daidalos. See Dunbabin (1948b); Lloyd-Jones (1996), pp. 178–81; and for a more general discussion of the myth, Gantz (1993), pp. 273–75; "Chez le roi en Sicile" in Frontisi-Ducroux (1975), pp. 171–90.

38 Malkin (1987), pp. 52–4, 194, 259–60. Hornblower (2008), p. 290, notes the recurrence of the name Entimos in Hellenistic Rhodes and even Telos.

social, political, and religious order of their new colonial city, an interest emerged in finding common ground articulated in terms of more generalized groupings: Lindians become Rhodians while Rhodians and Cretans have "Dorian" *nomima*. The Mediterranean colonial network, involving three of its largest islands—Rhodes, Crete, and Sicily—thus encouraged not only a generalized Greek identity but also provided new salience to its subethnic components. To be a "Dorian" became a formal status in a foreign land.

The importance of the distinction between city-specific *nomima* and the more generalized ethnic ones becomes clear when Gela itself became a mother city in Sicily and founded Akragas. Thucydides, now careful about *nomima*, says that its *nomima* were specifically "those of Gela," not "Dorian." The mother city, not the generalized, shared ethnos, becomes definitive. This also implies that circles of identity could either expand (Lindians-Rhodians-Dorians) or become city specific (Geloan *nomima*), depending on circumstance and distance. On the one hand, it seems that the shorter the distance between a mother city and its colony, the more specific was its identity. For example, Akrai and Kasmenai, two nearby, possibly military establishments of Syracuse, were not considered independent poleis. On the other hand, when Hieron of Syracuse "founded" Aitna (having destroyed Katane), he was celebrated by Pindar for implementing "Dorian laws,"[39] perhaps because of the mixed nature of his new establishment.

Additionally, we can identify a Sicilian interest in later periods that also prompted this emphasis on the generalized Rhodian identity. Herodotus[40] says that Deinomenes, the ancestor of Gelon, joined the founders, coming not from Rhodes but from the island of Telos, which lies opposite Triopion; "when Gela was colonized by the Lindians of Rhodes and Antiphemos, he was not left behind" while the *Lindian Chronicle* (xxxviii) provides the exaggeration that "Deinomenes [here a 'Lindian'] colonized Gela together with Antiphamos." It seems, therefore, that, from a "Sicilian" angle, looking back at the origins of Gela, a generalized, regional Rhodian perception suited the non-Lindian Deinomenidai more than the politically specific "Lindian" to which they did not belong. Again, the colonial situation encourages a wider identity formation.

Deinomenes of Telos, joining the founders of Gela, also illustrates how the network dynamics of colonial projects combined the elite and the political community in the Archaic period, while subsuming all of the participants in a more generalized identity. The lateral social network of aristocrats, which transcended local polities (here, Antiphemos, Entimos, Deinomenes), seems to have pulled together settlers from more disparate regions while consolidating a single identity in the process, reflecting both the "home" (predominantly

---

39 Pind. *Pyth.* 1.64–65.
40 Hdt. 7.153.1. Cf. Hornblower (2008), p. 289 *infra*.

Lindos in Rhodes) and the new, "mixed" colony, which was named Gela after the local river, but emphatically not "Lindioi," after Lindos. Similarly, the "Cretan" immigrants, who were themselves apparently a mixed lot, probably also encouraged a more generalized notion of regional-island origins rather than city-specific ones, thereby avoiding group hierarchies that might have been based on specific localities in Crete.

Aristocrats would sometimes use their lateral social networks to join other aristocrats, who were serving as oikists on behalf of their community. This is a prominent aspect of the social compromises of the Archaic period, when aristocrats had to find their place within the context of the rise of the political community. For example, Sparta was the mother city of a colony that left for Sicily under the leadership of Dorieus when Dorieus set out at the head of an official expedition to Sicily, and Philippos of Italian Kroton joined him with his private ship and followers.[41] A parallel (later) case would be Dorieus the Rhodian, an exiled Diagorid who, when revolting against Athens, had ten ships of his own.[42]

In sum, Gela, perhaps in spite of the intention to make it just "Lindian," became a "Rhodian" project, to be remembered as such for generations to come, paralleling and reflecting on the process of Rhodes's own convergence. These two nodes—Rhodes and Sicily—shaped each other through the dynamism of network attraction over long geographical distances. The vision from colonial Sicily in the western Mediterranean encouraged an all-encompassing vision of Rhodes, and "Rhodian identity" can be seen to some extent as the result of Rhodians' participating in overseas colonization. For their part, Lindian colonists at Gela, for local Geloan reasons, apparently also preferred their identity to be articulated as having the more generalized "Rhodian" origin, another illustration of how local behavior influences "global" patterns in a mode of self-organization throughout the Mediterranean. There must have been a significant amount of travel between Rhodes and Sicily, of which we know little. This might explain how Rhodian/Sicilian identity was revitalized a century later at Gela's colony Akragas, with new colonizing waves that involved Rhodians arriving this time via Gela. Polybius even states that Akragas was a "Rhodian" colony, disregarding Gela altogether.[43] In network terms a double-ripple effect is newly evident: Something happens again to Rhodes because Kameirians, Ialysians, and Lindians travel overseas, where their distinct polis origins become less relevant, thus reflecting a condensing or contracting view of "Rhodians." This was not by design, yet the self-organizational aspects of this networking identity are apparent. Paradoxically, one might say that Rhodian

41 Hdt. 5. 43 with Malkin (1994), pp. 203–18. The official aspect is revealed by Herodotus's expression ("from the tribes"). Had Philippos not died in the field, he may have been remembered differently.

42 Thuc. 3.8.1; 8.35.1 Xen. *Hell.* 1.5.19; Paus. 6.7.1, 4–7 = Andronion *FGrHist* 324 F 46.

43 Polyb. 9.27.7–8. See also Schol. Pind. F119, where Theron's ancestors came to Akragas directly from Rhodes.

identity was not locally Rhodian as such but was predicated on Rhodian Mediterranean networks with their own, sometimes independent, dynamics.

The Decade of Expanding Networks: 580–570

The early sixth century, particularly the decade between 580 and 570, may be seen as crucially important for the development of both regional and Panhellenic identities within Mediterranean networks. Within a short period, we find significant changes at Rhodes itself that are directly linked to the contemporary, wide-ranging Rhodian immigration and colonization overseas. For approximately fifty years the site of Vroulia, a port in southern Rhodes, was active, probably as the Rhodian port conducted commerce with the East (Phoenicians) and Egypt.[44] It is important to understand the peculiarities of the site, particularly its abandonment, in the context of its overseas orientation and function. While Vroulia sits at the end of the route from Lindos to the south of Rhodes, there is nothing to make it specifically Lindian. It could easily have served others on the island as a port. In fact, the short history of Vroulia exemplifies the multidirectional ripples of the new Mediterranean networks: With a stronger push overseas a more "pan-Rhodian" settlement, sufficiently small not to pose a threat to the other polities, was probably settled with the consent of all concerned. It was, so to speak, a "colony" of an emporic type, serving Rhodes itself and binding it more closely as "Rhodes" in the process. Conforming to the Braudelian notion that one port enhances another by its dynamics of communication, Vroulia could develop with its direct overseas contacts. However, Vroulia was abandoned precisely during the early sixth century, when Rhodians were immigrating in large numbers toward ever-widening horizons. The new scale and the more distant lines of the network probably made Vroulia's mediating function obsolete. Fractal imagery comes to mind: Instead of Rhodian cities working in relation to Vroulia, we now have Rhodes in its entirety working in relation to the Mediterranean at large.

It seems that the following inferences may be drawn: (a) Vroulia seems to have been on a practical level a pan-Rhodian "foundation" as a port oriented toward the south; (b) overseas contacts prompted this development, reflecting on Rhodes to create its "local" city foundation; and (c) the widening of the

---

44 Kinch (1914); Morris (1992), pp. 174–99. For possible Phoenicians (artisans) in Rhodes, see Coldstream (1969); Markoe (1996), p. 54, on maritime routes of transmission of ceramics, stone objects, faience: Levant-Cyprus-Rhodes-Cyclades-Aegina with Rhodes as a probable redistribution center. Rhodes was a center for the manufacture of Greek faience in the early Archaic period. For Egyptian and Egyptianizing small finds, including scarabs that were found in Athena's temples on the island, see Lloyd (1975b), vol. 3, p. 239, and Kowalzig (2007), p. 232 for more references. That the sailing route between Rhodes and Egypt was accessible also in winter was something worthy of comment: Dem. 56.30.

scales of overseas activity enhanced the pan-Rhodian aspect and finally made Vroulia irrelevant. One suspects that Vroulia's enterprising inhabitants simply left it for new opportunities offered farther away.

I believe this is not an isolated phenomenon. What was happening within each island ought to be correlated with the islanders' involvement overseas. Take Paros, for example. Koukounaries, a hilltop site overlooking Naoussa Bay, was abandoned around 700 BCE. Apparently, as a result of the abandonment, a new temple to Athena was dedicated there, with evidence of cult continuity at the abandoned site until the Classical period.[45] Incidentally, this is an effective reminder that new cult activity is not the same as settlement activity; in fact, in this case the establishment of the cult signifies abandonment. About the same time two new foundations in the Bay of Naoussa appear directly on the coast, apparently with better agricultural hinterland and improved access to the sea.[46] How are we to refer to these new settlements? They were not meant to be new *poleis*, but they do not seem to be regulated by any central authority. It is not clear how Paros became the polis we know from later periods. I therefore hesitate to use the term "internal colonization"[47] as the word "internal" signifies a bounded Parian territory.

Around the same time (ca. 680) Parians were also settling overseas at Thasos and fighting Thracians on the opposite coasts. Perhaps some of the people involved came from the same families. One can imagine a family from Koukounaries moving to a seafront location in the Bay of Naoussa while one of its sons, perhaps of Archilochos's age, joined Archilochos's father, Telesikles, who was the founder of Thasos.[48]

The eighth and seventh centuries witnessed all kinds of human mobility, migration, and especially settlement activities that are classified differently by scholars. This is another illustration of how the term "colonization" can be misleading, especially because of its modern connotations.[49] There is a danger that, because of the emphasis on *overseas* activities, one might overlook other categories of settlement and mobility that in fact belong to the same network.

The "internal" settlement activity in Rhodes and Paros brings us back to the effects of distance. Close-range settlements were either founded as dependencies or tended to become dependent, thus forming clusters of smaller-scale

---

45 Schilardi (1983), pp. 178–79. For more on Koukounaries, see Reger (1997), p. 460; Schilardi (1988, 1996).

46 Reger (1997), pp. 460 and 462, where he considers the move nearer the sea in terms of agricultural advantages, underemphasizing the seaward orientation. For Oikonomos and Koukounaries see Berranger (1992), pp. 121–22, and Schilardi (1975). Also on Oikonomos, Schilardi (1973). See also Reger (2004), no. 509 (Paros), for a discussion of the various Parian settlements.

47 Snodgrass (1980), p. 34; Morris (1987), p. 205. Cf. note 56.

48 Graham (1978); for the publications of the École Française d'Athènes on Thasos see *Études thasiennes* (1944–). For issues concerning a historical Archilochos and the limits of the evidence see Owen (2003); cf. Clay (2004); Tandy (2004); Rougier-Blanc (2008); D'Ercole (2010), pp. 71–77.

49 See, for example, Hurst and Owen (2005).

networks of a more hierarchical type. Sicilian Syracuse, for instance, was independent of its mother city, Corinth, but Kasmenai and Akrai (Syracuse's short-distance colonies in Sicily) were dependent on Syracuse.[50] In "Old Greece" Argos expanded by obliterating nearby cities (such as Asine) and taking possession of their territory. Sparta, after winning the First Messenian War, colonized (ca. 700) the fugitives of Asine and founded New Asine on the southeastern Rhion peninsula to serve its own interests in relation to Messenia.[51] Mothone, the corollary of New Asine in the southwestern region (on the Pylos side) of the same peninsula, was settled by Sparta ca. 600 by refugees from Nauplia, also fleeing the Argives.[52] In 431 Sparta settled the Aeginetans, who were driven out by Athens in Thyreatis, at the frontier between Argos and Lakonia. These three cases (Asine, Mothone, Thyreatis), from the end of the eighth century to the fifth, indicate a consistent colonial use (of non-Lakedaimonian populations) to serve Sparta's regional interests.

In addition, during the eighth century Sparta was busy with both short-distance colonization and conquering lands in the Peloponnese, while also sending groups of settlers overseas—to Taras (706).[53] Earlier settlers might have left Lakedaimon for Thera[54] and Melos.[55] Sparta thus exemplifies settlement and foundational activity in a combination of features that are at once singularly Spartan and generally Greek, a combination that is itself a salient feature of the Archaic Greek world. Conquest, expansion, and annexation, individual migrations such as that of Hesiod's father, who left Aiolian Kyme to settle in Boiotian Askra,[56] mercenary service overseas, short-distance settlements, colonization in the Aegean and Italy—all were taking place concurrently.[57]

Athens is reputed to have sent only a few colonies overseas,[58] yet Attica was "internally settled" and its countryside "filled" during the eighth and seventh

50   Hansen includes Kasmenai and Akrai in his discussion of dependent poleis in Hansen (1997b), p. 36. See also Fischer-Hansen, Nielsen, and Ampolo (2004b), no. 29 (Kasmenai), no. 10 (Akrai), and no. 8 (Heloron). The polis status of the three is uncertain, and it is suggested that they were perhaps founded as fortresses.

51   Paus. 2.36.4; 3.7.4, 4.14.3, 4.34.9; Hdt. 8.73.2, Theopomp. *FGrHist* 115 frg. 383 = *FHG*, vol. 1, 311, frg. 191 (= Strabo 8.6.11 C373). Paus. 4.8.3. cf. 4.24. See Styrenius (1998), p. 54. Cf. Frödin, Persson, and Westholm (1938), p. 437, for the date of the destruction of Argive Asine, around 700 BC. Cf. Courbin (1966), p. 565, note 6, and Kelly (1967); Harrison and Spencer (1998), p. 154. On the new Messenian Asine see Shipley (2004), no. 313 (Asine). A Spartan garrison still existed in Messenian Asine in 369 or 368 (Xen. *Hell.* 7.1.25), and Asine was within the territory of Sparta until 338. On the status of Messenian Asine as a polis see Shipley (1997), p. 209. On Messenia see Luraghi (2008).

52   Paus. 4.24.4, 4.35.2; 4.27.8; cf. Theopomp. *FGrHist* 115 frg 383 = *FHG*, vol. 1, 311, frg. 191, in Strabo 8.6.11 C373.

53   See Fischer-Hansen, Nielsen, and Ampolo (2004a), no. 71 (Taras) for ample bibliography; also Graham (1982a), pp. 111–13; Malkin (1994b), pp. 115–42; Nafissi (1999).

54   Reger (2004), no. 527 (Thera); Malkin (1994b), pp. 89–111.

55   Reger (2004), no. 505 (Melos); Malkin (1994b), pp. 74–77.

56   Hesiod, *Works and Days* 630–40. Verses 639–40 are also quoted in the first paragraph of "The Contest of Homer and Hesiod"; see Evelyn-White (1936), pp. 566–67.

57   On Spartan mercenaries, see Trundle (2004), pp. 106–107, 122–24, 156–57.

58   Whitehead (1986), p. 8. Cf. Coldstream (2003), pp. 134–35. However, according to Hansen (2004), pp. 636–37, "That Athens did not take part in the Archaic colonisation is a widespread but seriously misleading belief." He names more than 40 (42) places settled by Athens.

centuries.[59] Corinth, a major mother city ruled by an aristocratic-family oligarchy of the Bakhiads, which sent colonies abroad (Syracuse, Corcyra) led by other Bakhiads, was itself not "urbanized" before the seventh century. Charles Williams speaks of small settlement points around water resources that intensified their interconnections through a network that eventually became "Corinth." This was taking place while some Corinthians were sailing with Chersikrates to Corcyra and with Archias to Syracuse, there to found an archaeologically attested "planned" city, far more advanced than the Corinthian home.[60] In short, like Rhodes, to a significant extent Corinth consolidated while trading and colonizing overseas.

Note how contemporary mobility and settlement affected Rhodes: During the axial decade of the early sixth century we find new waves of Rhodians immigrating to their own colony of Gela, participating in the foundation of Gela's colony, Akragas, probably settling in the Adriatic (Elpia, north of Mt. Gargano),[61] joining in the failed attempt of Pentathlos of Knidos to conquer Lilybaion in western Sicily (chapter 4), immigrating to Cyrene, and—perhaps most important of all—joining in the first explicitly Panhellenic temple, the Hellênion in Naukratis (later). Archaeological evidence seems to point to a new influx of Rhodians at Gela about 580,[62] precisely when Gela established Akragas with two founders, Aristonoös and Pystilos.[63] This duality could point to the Rhodians and Cretans of Gela, although it seems more likely that a Rhodian oikist was ceremonially invited from the mother city according to the ancient custom that Thucydides specifies à propos Selinous.[64] There are some other Rhodian indications: Theron's ancestors are said to have come directly from Rhodes,[65] and Polybius, who considers Akragas Rhodian, also claims that the cult of Zeus Atabyrios came from Rhodes.[66] Dunbabin[67] observes that Zeus Atabyrios was worshipped specifically at Kameiros. The Lindian Chronicle (xxvii, xxx) also mentions two dedications to Athena Lindia, one by Phalaris, the other by "Akragantines."[68]

59 Whitehead (1986), pp. 5–10, argues that the "colonization" of the Athenian chôra continued, though at a slower pace, throughout the seventh and sixth centuries. For a detailed discussion of Attika and its poleis, see Hansen (2004), pp. 624–26.

60 See "Corinth: The Settlement" in Salmon (1984), pp. 75–80; Williams (1995). For Syracuse see Domínguez (2006), pp. 269–75.

61 Cabanes (2008), p. 173, with Strabo 14.2.10; Steph. Byz. s.v. Elpia; van Compernolle (1985); cf. Salpia in Vitruvius 1.4.12. For possible Rhodian participation at Sybaris, implied by the pottery, see Morgan and Hall (1996), p. 202 and note 208.

62 Dunbabin (1948a), pp. 228–31; Domínguez (2006), pp. 279–80.

63 Thuc. 6.4.4.

64 Thuc. 6.4.2.

65 See scholia to Pindar Ol. II 15, 16, 29, probably based on Timaios FHG 214, F90. Cf. FGrHist frg. 556 92, 93b.

66 Polyb. 9.27.7–8 with Walbank (1999), vol. 2, pp. 159–60.

67 Dunbabin (1948a), p. 311.

68 See Higbie (2003) for translation and commentary.

Around 580 we also find the ambitious Pentathlos of Knidos trying to conquer Lilybaion in western Sicily, probably using his reputed descent from Herakles as a justification, similarly to what the Spartan Dorieus later attempted (ca. 509), more explicitly and equally unsuccessfully. Rhodians also participated in Pentathlos's expedition and, following the Sicilian failure, apparently went on to settle Lipara.[69]

The years around 570 were therefore pivotal for Rhodian Mediterranean networks. Rhodians were using preexisting network lines: Previous colonization at Gela and Herakleid legitimation stories applied to the last area in Sicily free from Greek settlers (see chapter 4). By using the network lines they were enhancing their volume and multiplying their number, following the basic network dynamics of the growth of multidirectional links and flows.

Rhodians were also "enmeshing" their network within Panhellenic projects, such as the second colonial immigration to Cyrene. Battos II, king of Cyrene, asked the Delphic oracle to encourage further migration. Delphi responded with a Panhellenic prophecy addressed not to an oikist or to a mother city but to "all Greeks (*Hellenas pantas*)" . . . "to cross the sea and dwell in Libya with the Cyrenaeans."[70] The episode illustrates the dynamism of colonial networks, which stretched the notion of inclusiveness to a generalized Hellenic identity. Rhodians apparently participated in significant numbers, and among them may have been the family of Pankis and his sons, who are mentioned by the *Lindian Chronicle* (xvii), with the usual exaggeration (the Rhodian becomes a cofounder of Cyrene) in the dedication of Athena's temple at Lindos: "Those of the Lindians who with the children of Pankis founded a colony on Cyrene with Battos to Athena and to Herakles a tenth of the booty which they took from . . . ," as Xenagoras states in the first book of his *Annalistic Account.*[71]

When the tribal reform that was planned by Delphi's arbitrator, Demonax of Mantineia, was implemented in Cyrene, redistributing its citizens into three "tribes," these Rhodian settlers were probably included in the tribe of the "islanders," a category that creates a converging image for the entire Aegean (except the Cretans, who were grouped with the Peloponnesians in the second tribe).[72] Christy Constantakopoulou, following Arnaldo Momigliano, discusses an inscription from the Lindian temple, dating from the fourth century, which mentions much earlier relations between a family from Cyrene

---

69 Diod. *Sic.* 5.9, probably following Timaios *FGrHist* 566 F 164.9; cf. Paus. 10.11.3, which is based on the excellent authority of Antiochos (*FGrHist* 555 F 1) but gives a very abbreviated account. More in Malkin (1994b), pp. 80–81, 211–14, 217–18.

70 Hdt. 4.159 (LCL) with Chamoux (1953), pp. 72, 124–25, 134. See pp. 55–56.

71 Translation: Higbie (2003), pp. 28–31. For Rhodian pottery at Cyrene see Boardman and Hayes (1966), pp. 16–20, 41–57.

72 Hdt. 4.161.

and Kameiros.[73] I believe this provides an excellent illustration of how the lines of the network could alternate back and forth: The family may have belonged to descendants of "Rhodian" colonists from Kameiros who came to Cyrene ca. 570. It points to a triangular network of Kameiros, Cyrene, and Lindos, with Kameiros and Lindos functioning together as "Rhodes." From the north African perspective of Cyrene, what apparently mattered most was the common origin in Rhodes as a whole.

In sum, overseas experiences and colonizing activities condensed the discrete political identities on the island into "Rhodian" ones, beginning with the image of the foundation of all the Rhodian poleis from overseas by Tlepolemos, the pan-Rhodian festival of the Tlepolemeia, through Homer's Rhodian contingents sailing to Troy and historical Rhodian colonization activity in Phaselis, Gela, Akragas, Elpia, Lilybaion, Lipara, and Cyrene. Moreover, the outsiders' vision, whether the condensing perception by other Greeks of "Rhodians" or by non-Greek traders and manufacturers (probably Phoenicians), also unified the self-referential view of the inhabitants of the island. Some aspects of these processes, especially the "back-ripple effects" (noted earlier with regard to network dynamics), may not have been evident to contemporaries. However, we find a self-referential Rhodian identity explicitly articulated precisely in network contexts (colonization, Panhellenic games).

Perhaps the most elaborate of these contexts, involving all circles of identity—the polis, the region, the subethnic, and the Hellenic—was a peculiar colonial experience overseas that at once condensed the identities of the Rhodian *poleis* to a regional identity and, at the same time, contextualized them as Hellenic. It was also roughly contemporary with the varied enterprises of the 570s. It took place in Egypt, at the *emporion* of Naukratis, where Greeks from different backgrounds were residing and trading and where all of Rhodes was represented as a polis more than a century and a half before its formal *synoikismos*.

Rhodes and Naukratis

Greeks had been arriving in Egypt since the seventh century BCE as mercenaries, traders, and individual settlers.[74] The first Rhodians we hear of by name are Anaxanor and Telephos, both from Ialysos. They belonged to a unit of soldiers who inscribed their names on the left leg of the colossal statue of Ramses II, some four hundred kilometers (two hundred and fifty miles) from the sea, near

    73 Segre and Pugliese Caratelli (1952), no. 105. See Momigliano (1975), pp. 511–14, and Constantakopoulou (2005), p. 16.
    74 Austin (1970); Boardman (1999), pp. 111–41; Braun (1982); Kaplan (2003).

the second cataract at Abu Simbel.[75] Their commander was probably a second-generation Greek bearing an Egyptian name, Psammetichos, son of Theokles. They all belonged to a unit of *alloglossoi*, "speakers of a foreign language,"[76] obviously implying an Egyptian point of view of Greeks as foreigners, perhaps together with other foreigners, especially Karians. The time was about twenty years before the foundation of the Hellênion at Naukratis. Anaxanor and Telephos may have thought of themselves as Ialysians, yet at the same time they recognized the external, Egyptian view of themselves as belonging to a wider category of the *alloglossoi*, foreigners. It is this comprehensive and condensing point of view that proved important in the charter of Amasis for Naukratis.

Naukratis in Egypt is the only "colonial" settlement in the Archaic period that points to an explicit concept of Hellenism. We find oppositional ethnicity there in terms of contrast with Egyptians and especially the condensing view by Egyptians of Greeks, but there is also an accommodated articulation of Greek identity among Greeks of varying origins and probably a generalized, self-referential Greek identity in relation to Egyptians as well.

When describing the charter of Naukratis by Amasis, Herodotus lists the following cities as members of the Hellênion, the "Greek" temple:

> [T]he best known and most visited *temenos* (sacred precinct, sanctuary) is that which is called Hellênion, founded jointly by the Ionian cities of Chios, Teos, Phokaia, and Klazomenai; the Dorian poleis of Rhodes, Knidos, Halikarnassos, and Phaselis; and of the Aiolians Mytilene alone.[77]

The list indicates that the colonial-*emporion* situation condensed Rhodian *poleis* into a single quasi-polis entity in Egypt. The Rhodian situation at Naukratis is the reverse of what Rhodians chose to do at the Dorian Pentapolis, where the political distinctiveness of each Rhodian polis was emphasized, thus giving Rhodians a majority.[78] In contrast, at Naukratis Herodotus represented "Rhodes" as one of the four Dorians "*poleis*" that shared in the Hellênion. But there had been no single polis known as "Rhodes" before the end of the fifth century.[79] In this respect Rhodes stands in marked contrast to Lesbos, whose island identity was also functional: all Lesbians shared in a common sanctuary at Mesa, but only Mytilene represented any Lesbians at the Hellênion. In contrast to Lesbos it appears that Lindos, Kameiros, and Ialysos all joined in the Hellênion as a single entity of "Rhodians." Alain Bresson provides a thorough

---

75 Meiggs and Lewis (1989), no. 7; Sauneron and Yoyotte (1952); Bernard and Masson (1957), pp. 1–20. On the Greek mercenaries in Egypt, see Lloyd (1975a), pp. 14–23; cf. Boardman (1999), pp. 115–17.

76 Lloyd (1975a), pp. 21–22.

77 Hdt. 2.178.2, translation adapted from Godley (1926), LCL.

78 Hdt. 1.144.

79 I would hesitate to see in this testimony to a *formal* pan-Rhodian organization. See Gabrielsen (2000), p. 184.

discussion of how and why this was possible. Perhaps the most obvious Rhodian interest was that this was an excellent deal, three for the price of one, an obvious advantage if the number of "Dorian states" in the Hellênion had been initially limited to four in order to achieve an equilibrium with the four Ionian cities.[80]

Nonetheless, commercial interests and cynical explanations, while valid, would be insufficient here. We are missing the Egyptian regard in relation to Rhodes, although there are some indications for such Egyptian perspectives. Special relations seem to have existed between "Rhodes" and Egypt, and it is likely that Rhodes, as a whole, enjoyed a favored attitude from Amasis, who also visited Rhodes and made costly dedications there to Athena. It was said he was following in the footsteps of Danaos and his daughters (who had set out from Egypt), the heroic founders of the temple at Lindos, thus making it, in Greek terms, a kind of an "Egyptian-Rhodian" mythological itinerary.[81] Other links between Rhodes and Egypt are implied by the large quantity of "Rhodian pottery" at Naukratis (although it could have been mediated by others),[82] by inscriptions from the Hellênion that appear specifically Rhodian,[83] and by a Lindian proxeny decree (proxenos: a kind of honorary consul; see later) that speaks of placing a copy in the Hellênion.[84] Furthermore, there are marked similarities between the scarabs found in Rhodes and those in Naukratis.[85] Finally, prior to the synoikismos of Rhodes, we find Ialysian, Kameirian, and Lindian coins in Egyptian temples and two Rhodian coins in Naukratis of the fourth century BC.[86] Although coins are problematic as evidence in terms of independent circulation, they are important for denoting pan-Rhodian tendencies. With the same horse protome shared among all three Rhodian cities, sometimes it is only the legend that distinguishes among them.[87] Rhodians,

---

80 Cf. Bresson (2000c), p. 40; (2005). Similarly, perhaps Herodotus (1.144.3) lists "Kos" as a member of the Dorian Pentapolis, although Kos-Astypalaia and Kos-Meropis seem to have been discrete poleis. The exact state of Kos at the time is, however, uncertain. See Sherwin-White (1978), pp. 46–47, with Constantakopoulou (2005), pp. 8, 13.

81 Hdt. 2.182 with 3.47; Cf. Call. Fr 100 Pf.; Diod. Sic. 5.58.1; 14.2.11; Apollod. 2.1.4; Diog. Laert. 1.89.

82 Bresson (2000c), p. 26.

83 Hogarth, Lorimer, and Edgar (1905), pp. 116–17.

84 Syll.3 110; see note 95.

85 Lloyd (1975b), pp. 226, on Hdt. 2.178. Jacopi (1932–41), p. 16. Petrie (1886), pp. 36–38.

86 See Dressler (1900), nos. 38, 39, for the coins from Kameiros and Ialysos found in Sakha in Egypt. For the Ialysian coin found at the site of Damanhur and the Kameirian coin from Zagazig (Bubastis), see Dressler (1900), no. 114, taf. II.114 and no. 243, taf. V 243, respectively. Cf. Gabrielsen (2000), p. 188. For coins from all three poleis found at Asyut, see Price and Waggoner (1975), pp. 94–96. For the two fourth-century Rhodian coins found in Naukratis, see Head (1886), p. 11.

87 Bresson (2000c), p. 26 with notes. See Head (1897), p. ci, on the similarity between the coins of the three poleis: "The peculiar form of the incuse reverses of the coins of Camirus (pl. xxxiv, 7–10, 12, 13) and Lindus (pl. xxxv, 7, 8, 9), consisting of a square divided into two oblong parts by a broad band . . . is original, and hardly ever met with outside Rhodes, except at Posidium in the neighbouring island of Carpathos (pl. xxix, 14)." For the distinctiveness of the coins of Ialysos (pl. xxxv, 1–6), see Head (1897), pp. c–cii, 223–39. See also Head (1911), pp. 635–37. Were they made on a Phoenician standard, as Berthold (1984, p. 48) deduces? If so, Rhodian networks would then acquire more "Mediterranean" salience.

long before the advent of the Euro coin, learned how to appear as if they shared a common identity while retaining a distinct one for each of their poleis.

Elsewhere in Egypt, probably before Naukratis's new charter, independent *emporia* may have been more common. Hekataios mentions Nile islands with names of Greek *poleis* and islands: "Ephesos, Chios, Lesbos, Cyprus, and Samos."[88] It is possible that such names were merely Greek geographical markers for the purpose of navigation,[89] although Ephesos was not an island, and the explanation would need to be supported by other parallel examples. I am more inclined to view them as *emporia* of sorts,[90] probably also functioning as service stations for ships that may have temporarily hosted mercenaries.[91] Their existence seems to reflect a situation that existed prior to the charter of Amasis, concentrating the commercial activities of Greeks, since we never hear of them again.[92]

Their particular historical function is not relevant to the discussion at hand, apart from what the Nile islands can tell us about the widening of the circles of identity due to distance and network contexts. Naukratis offers an interesting variability of expressions in these contexts, all reflecting the need to explicitly confront them. Poleis and the island-poleis Chios and Samos expressed their polis identity institutionally and let it be subsumed under "Naukratis" (Samos independently, Chios as part of the Hellênion). Lesbos and Mytilene took a different approach: As noted, Mytilene, together with the other "Lesbians," participated in the founding of the pan-Lesbian sanctuary at Mesa, thereby also stressing their "pan-Aiolianism." In the words of Alkaios: "The *Lesbians* founded this precinct . . . for all to share . . . and you, the glorious *Aiolian* Goddess . . ."[93] However, "Lesbos," also one of the Nile islands, and "the Aiolians" ("of the Aiolians Mytilene alone," says Herodotus) were represented in the Hellênion only by Mytilene (there were at least another five poleis in

---

88 Hekataios *FGrHist* 1 F 310 with Braun (1982), p. 47.

89 Cf. Austin (2004), p. 1237. The cases of Egyptian Abydos (cf. Hellespontine Abydos) and Thebes (cf. Greek Thebai) would be irrelevant as they are city names and not generalized geographical appellations.

90 Lloyd (1975a), p. 29; Braun (1982), p. 47; Shipley (1987), p. 86.

91 Cyprus may have been a source of mercenaries: Carpez-Csornay (2006), p. 215n7, sees the Cypriots as mercenaries. For Cypriote pottery at Naukratis, see Boardman (1999), p. 139, and pp. 25–26 for Cypriote statuettes. For a thorough discussion of Cypriote-like finds and the Cypriote presence at Naukratis, see Möller (2000), pp. 154–63, who argues for "the absence of conclusive evidence confirming a Cypriot presence in Naukratis" and for more limited "lively connections between the Greeks and the Cypriots" (p. 162). She considers the arguments in Davis (1979, 1980) in favor of such presence as doubtful and the evidence for it as unsatisfactory.

92 Fantalkin (2008) lowers the chronology for Naukratis and reverses the meaning of the reforms of Amasis: an opening up of Egypt for commerce instead of a concentrated monopoly. Fantalkin rejects the Nile-island *emporia*, at least as reflecting the origins of the merchants, yet is willing to accept the idea as possible if reflecting the situation *after* the charter of Amasis.

93 For Alkaios's mention of the sanctuary, see *P.Oxy.* 2165 frg. 1 col. i; see Lobel, Roberts, and Wegener (1941), pp. 30–31, 35; cf. Lobel and Page (1955) frg. 129 G1, 1–3; Campbell (1990), pp. 296–97, frg. 129, 1–3. See Reger (1997), p. 477 with note 159. The temple was excavated by Koldewey and published in his survey of Lesbos. See Koldewey (1890), pp. 47–61; also Plommer (1981). On the role and significance of the Mesa sanctuary cf. Robert (1960), especially pp. 302–15; Labarre (1994, 1996), pp. 42–50; Parker (1998), p. 15; Bresson (2000a). For further bibliography on Mesa see Spencer (1995), pp. 22–23, no. 103.

Lesbos: Methymna, Pyrrha, Antissa, Eresos, and Arisbe, the latter subjugated by Mytilene).[94] The contrast illustrates the tension between singular and "pan-" identities: A Mytilenaian was happy to be a "Lesbian" and an "Aiolian" in a common Lesbian sanctuary and probably did not mind accepting the name of "Lesbos" as one of the Nile islands. At Naukratis, however, the Mytilenaians insisted on their polis identity, while subsuming it under the Hellenic identity of the Hellênion. This was the reverse strategy of the Rhodians. In short, both Rhodes and Lesbos, two major islands, illustrate the tensions involved in the formation and renegotiations of their respective collective identities within the circles of the region, the polis, the subethnic, and the Hellenic. Those tensions evolved within the network context of the islanders' involvement in both regional networks (e.g., the Temple of Athena Lindia for Rhodes, the sanctuary at Mesa for Lesbos) and overseas projects, as at Naukratis.

While discerning the larger patterns, it is important to note examples of the actual participants. The paucity of the sources often prevents us from doing so, but there are two proxeny inscriptions from Rhodes that may enable us to do just that. Their significance has been well illuminated by Alain Bresson, and I would like to add some commentary to his penetrating observations. The first decree,[95] found in Egypt and dating to about 440–420, orders as follows:

> To inscribe Damoxenos, son of Hermon, a resident of Egypt (en aigyptoi oikeonta), as a proxenos and benefactor of the Lindians in the sanctuary of Athanaia, and that he will be exempt from taxes, he and his descendants, . . . that Polykles, son of Halipolis, will have it inscribed also in Egypt, in the Hellênion.[96]

The decree speaks specifically of "Lindians," yet the copy of the inscription is to be placed in the Hellênion at Naukratis, where "Lindos" was subsumed in the generalized category of "Rhodes." Damoxenos could be a proxenos (an honorary position that originates in practices of hospitality and is usually conferred on a citizen who hosts foreign officials and looks after the interests of another state) only of Lindos, not of Ialysos or Kameiros. He was not a prostatês, a Hellênion official, as that would have been a pan-Rhodian appointment, but a traditional proxenos. It is curious to witness the inner functioning of the Hellênion, where apparently each Rhodian city could use the Rhodian category of identity for its own, more narrowly defined, polis function. Aside from the prostatai the timouchoi were the magistrates responsible for the actual temple,[97] a reminder that the Hellênion employed various types of common administration. As it is

94 Hdt. 1.151.

95 Blinkenberg (1941) as an appendix to no. 16; Syll.3 110, note 4; SEG 32 1982, no. 1586; Bresson (2000c), pp. 27–31.

96 In my translation I follow Bresson's interpretation in Bresson (2000c), pp. 27–31. For the (uncertain) political and institutional implications, see Gabrielsen (2000), pp. 184–85.

97 Austin (1970), pp. 30–31 and p. 31n1. See Pébarthe (2005).

difficult to imagine a lack of interest by the cooperating cities in the choice of the *timouchoi*, it becomes evident that the "nine poleis" managing the Hellênion were repeatedly busy with at least two sets of appointments, thus maintaining a Mediterranean network of contacts that must have transcended Naukratis itself. Polykles, son of Halipolis, who was to set up the copy in the Hellênion, could have been a "Rhodian" *prostatês* or *timouchos*. Alternatively, and perhaps more likely, he may have been a merchant going to Naukratis since the decree was after all specifically a Lindian one.

For oaths and interstate agreements, it was a common enough practice to place two copies of an inscription in two separate temples. They would usually be placed in particular polis temples or in interstate, Panhellenic ones, such as Delphi and Olympia. However, to do so at Naukratis was to combine both since there was no other temple but the Hellênion that could serve a proxeny function for a Lindian. Yet it was also perceived as Panhellenic, especially when we remember that the Hellênion was probably managed somewhat like an amphiktyony (an association of states that manages and maintains a temple cult).[98] Three multidirectional networks, expressed as circles of identity, intertwined: Lindos into Rhodes, Rhodes into the Hellênion, and vice versa: Damoxenos was recognized at Naukratis as the *proxenos* of Lindos through the Hellênion, working from the outer into the inner circle, from the Hellênion, through Rhodes, to Lindos.

The second decree (*Syll.*[3] 110) from the acropolis at Lindos on Rhodes dates probably to the years around 411–408:[99] "Deinias, son of Pytheas, an Egyptian[100] from Naukratis, a *hermeneus* (interpreter) . . . will be a *proxenos* of all the Rhodians, he and his descendants, and that he shall have the right to enter and exit the port, he and his descendants."

This time it is expressly a decree of all the Rhodians. The inscription is to be placed in the temple of Athena of Lindos, but the *proxenos* is to be of all Rhodians. As noted, long before the *synoikismos* of Rhodes, the sanctuary of Athena Lindia had a pan-Rhodian function for the three Rhodian poleis. As also noted, the fourth-century inscription from the Lindian temple that mentions early relations between a family from Cyrene and Kameiros points to Athena's temple at Lindos as serving a family from Kameiros.[101]

The emphasis in the proxeny decree on the recipient, a translator, highlights the difference from the first decree. He may have belonged to the descendants of the Egyptian age group that Psammetichos I adjoined to the

98 Bresson (2000c), p. 47; Bowden (1996), p. 33.

99 Blinkenberg (1941), no. 16; *Syll.*3, 110; Kinch (1905), pp. 34–48. Also Bresson (1991), pp. 37–42; Bresson (2000c), pp. 28–36. See, however, Gabrielsen (2000), pp. 179–80, who considers an early fourth-century date acceptable.

100 Or Aeginetan? See "The Aeginetan Proxenos of Rhodes at Naukratis" in Figueira (1988), pp. 543–51.

101 See notes 25 and 77. See p. 80.

Greek mercenaries in order to learn Greek and serve as interpreters,[102] or perhaps he was simply a knowledgeable bilingual person, possibly, but not self-evidently, an Egyptian. He is not an official "resident" like other Naukratitai, but a local. His name (in Greek) is accompanied by the ethnic "Aigyptios" (if the likely reconstruction is accepted). Moreover, his profession, "interpreter," probably indicates an active mediation. He was probably a local handler, possibly political (dealing with Egyptians), and quite certainly commercial since he is to have port rights.[103] It seems as if each participant polis in the Hellênion could grant such privileges, perhaps from a standard quota. Again, we have three networks: first, Lindos and Rhodes; second, in relation to the other Greeks, the *proxenos* acted as if representing all Rhodians; third, in relation to the Egyptians, obtaining his "Greek privilege," he was a Hellenic representative.

Naukratis and Panhellenism

It is time to turn to the position of Naukratis in the overarching network of Hellenic identity. Naukratis is the only "colonial" settlement in the Archaic period that points to an explicit concept of Hellenism through the Hellênion, although in Egypt it was not an isolated case (discussed later). It reveals an Egyptian view of Greeks as foreigners, an accommodated articulation of Greek identity among Greeks of varying origins, and a generalized, self-referential Greek identity in relation to Egyptians.

The notion that the encounter of Greeks with non-Greeks in wide-reaching geographical horizons from the Black Sea to France was crucial to the formation of Panhellenic identity is not new (see p. 62). In general, the Greek/barbarian antithesis ought not to be viewed as the primary factor in determining Greek identity, especially in the Archaic period.[104] The picture is far more complex and concerns, aside from the "antithetical" barbarians, the "positive content" of the network of commonalties and similarities as expressed both among colonies, in relation to mother cities, and with regard to the Panhellenic centers such as Delphi and Olympia. The foundation of Naukratis embodies the problematic aspect of this network, the mutual regard of non-Greeks and Greeks, and the articulation of a Panhellenic identity around a local religious focus.

---

102 Hdt. 2.154. Cf. 2.164; Bresson (2000c), p. 36.

103 This is a strong argument as to why he could not have been an Aeginetan (see note 100), for whom this would have been superfluous since Aegina had its own presence in Naukratis.

104 Malkin (1998), p. 19.

Here is how Herodotus describes the settlement at Naukratis:

> Amasis, becoming/being a Philhellene, granted some Greeks certain
> rights, and in particular he gave those who came to Egypt the polis
> Naukratis to dwell in. And, what is more, to those among them who
> were going to sea and did not want to live there permanently he gave
> lands to erect altars (*bomous*) and sacred precincts (*temenea*) for the
> gods. Of these latter the largest which is also the best known and
> most visited *temenos* is the so-called *Hellênion*; it was set up by the
> joint effort of these poleis: of the Ionians Chios, Teos, Phokaia, and
> Klazomenai; of the Dorians Rhodes, Knidos, Halikarnassos, and
> Phaselis; and of the Aiolians Mytilene alone. It is to these poleis that
> the *temenos* belongs, and it is they who appoint the *prostatai* (magis-
> trates) of the *emporion*. Other cities which claim a share in the
> *Hellênion* do so without any justification; the Aeginetans, however,
> did set up separately a *temenos* of Zeus on their own initiative, the
> Samians one in honor of Hera, and the Milesians another in honor
> of Apollo.[105]

The site of Naukratis seems to have been settled for some sixty years
(since the time of Psammetichos I) before Amasis's "gift." What Herodotus is
describing appears to amount to a charter that concentrated and supervised all
Greek activity in Egypt at Naukratis[106] ca. 570 BC and especially the foundation
of the Hellênion.[107]

Amasis, an Egyptian pharaoh who was married to a Greek woman of
Cyrene,[108] is described here as a "friend to the Greeks." The term *philhellên*,
employed by Herodotus, supposedly provides an "Egyptian" point of view,
viewing all Greeks (Hellenes) as the object of Amasis's friendship. This is, of
course, a Greek perspective on how Egyptians saw Greeks, yet it testifies to a
Greek recognition of this type of perception. It conveys a generalized view of
Greeks by disregarding the salient differentiating characteristics that Greeks
might have considered more relevant, such as having a Chiote, a Samian, or
even an Ionian identity.

That this Egyptian point of view condensed all Greeks into a single entity is
implied in the term *alloglossoi* (mentioned earlier) and, more explicitly, in some
important parallels and analogies to the Hellênion. Amasis did not concern

---

105 Hdt. 2.178, translation adapted from Möller (2000), p. 183.
106 Cf. Möller (2000), pp. 188, 193.
107 Möller (2000), pp. 105–108 with Bowden (1996). Fantalkin (2008); cf. Fantalkin (2006), who interprets
Herodotus's words (2.179) that "long ago" (*to palaion*) Naukratis had a monopoly, as relating to the time *before*
Amasis's charter. Although possible, *strictu sensu*, this seems to stretch the meaning of *to palaion*. It is at least
equally likely that by Herodotus's time, after the Persian conquest, Naukratis no longer maintained its monopoly.
108 Hdt. 2.181.

himself only with Naukratis. He also moved the "camps" (*stratopeda*) of both Greeks (Ionians) and Karian mercenaries, who had originally come to Egypt at the time of Psammetichos I (664–610), to Memphis, where he settled them just north of the city proper in Karian and Greek quarters.[109] The Karian mercenaries at Memphis resided in a Karikon, the "Karian quarter," and worshipped in a Karikon, a "Karian temple."[110] In the Persian period the Karians came to be known as Karomemphitai, and their temple was still active in the fourth century.[111] We do not know enough about the internal differences among Karians, but we may assume they did not necessarily see themselves in terms of a monolithic identity. The Karikon at Memphis therefore seems to be analogous in its initial purpose to the Hellênion at Naukratis: a quarter and a temple common to the community and named after its ethnic identifier. Its name most probably originated from the external, Egyptian view of "Karians" as mercenaries. Herodotus seems to reflect this when he speaks of "Karians" and "Ionians"[112] and does not distinguish among the Ionians, something he does when he focuses on Naukratis.[113]

A general ethnic name that originated from military units may also be observed with regard to the Jewish mercenary community, known as "the Jewish (Judean) force," which was settled on the island at Elephantine. It, too, had a temple (built before the Persian invasion of 525), dedicated to Yahu (a form of Yahweh). Across the island from Elephantine, at Syene, other Semitic mercenaries, Aramaic speakers, and Phoenicians lived alongside each other and had no ethnic signifier for their unit, known as the "Syene force."[114] The Phoenicians are a case in point:[115] Phoenician mercenaries are mentioned by Herodotus as "Phoenicians from Tyre," residing in the "Camp (*stratopedon*) of the Tyrians."[116] This is quite specific and refers not just to "Phoenicians" but specifically to "Tyrians." In time however, origin distinctions among Phoenicians disappeared, and they all became "Phoenico-Egyptians" (Phoinikaigyptioi).

Greeks in Memphis underwent a similar generalization of their ethnicity and became Hellenomemphitai (Memphis Greeks). At Naukratis, crowding the Greeks together almost forced upon them the priority of Hellenic identity. This was expressed through the Hellênion, the Hellenic temple.[117] This is precisely

---

109 Hdt. 2.152–54. See Thompson (1988), p. 17.

110 The name may have signified both quarter and temple.

111 Aristagoras, quoted in Steph. Byz., s.v. "Hellenikon kai Karikon" and s.v. "Karikon" (*FGrHist* 608, frg. 9); cf. Polyaen. *Strat.* 7, 3 (*FGrHist* 665 frg. 200). See Thompson (1988), pp. 93–95; Lloyd (1975a), p. 17.

112 Hdt. 2.154.

113 Kaplan (2003), p. 14, says that Herodotus consistently calls the Greek soldiers in Egypt "Ionians" despite the fact that many came from the Dorian Dodecanese: "It enforces the possibility that collective identities such as 'Ionian' and 'Karian' emerged first in zones of cultural exchange."

114 Porten (1984), pp. 375–80, 385–93; Bresciani (1984), p. 368.

115 Thompson (1988), pp. 88–93.

116 Hdt. 2.112.

117 See Möller (2000), pp. 105–108, with reservations.

what happened at Memphis, where the Hellenomemphitai resided in a quarter also known as Hellênion and referred to their common temple as Hellênion.[118] Arsinoe, too, had a Hellênion.[119] The Memphis Hellênion also had magistrates with the same title as those in Naukratis, *timouchoi*.[120] Our evidence for the Hellênion in Memphis comes from the Hellenistic period, but there is no reason to suppose the Hellênion did not originate with the settlement by Amasis. Greeks needed to worship their gods in some combination of a *temenos* and an altar. Comparisons with *emporia*, such as Gravisca, indicate clearly that, even for a small minority of Greeks living among non-Greeks, temples were *de rigeur*.[121]

We see, therefore, that this wider perspective of foreign settlement in Egypt, some of it significantly contemporary with Naukratis's Hellênion, indicates an Egyptian practice of allowing either mercenaries or merchants to settle and establish common centers of worship, with no regard to differences among "Ionians" or other Greeks.

Unlike *philhellên*, which is Herodotus's own term for describing Amasis, the name of the Hellênion temple is an independent datum. It is significant both for how Egyptians viewed Greeks and how Greeks viewed themselves as Greeks. We are not told how the name Hellênion came into being. There are several possibilities, none of which entirely excludes the others. It may have been the name of the area assigned to Hellenes (Greeks were settled in Naukratis some sixty years before Amasis's charter), perhaps originally as a mercenary or a commercial area, similar to the Hellênion (the quarter) at Memphis (or its Karikon, if we take that to signify a quarter of Memphis). Egyptians probably did not bother too much with the fine-tuning of inter-Greek identities. "Hellenes" may have functioned for Egyptians as "Franks" did for Mameluks and the Arabs at the time of the Crusades (Frangi), a generalized name for all Christians arriving in the Levant.

In fact, ancient Egyptians probably referred to Greek identity in their own language as "WJNN, YAWANÎN, WEYENÎN,"[122] deriving from "Ionians"—a common term for "Greeks" in the ancient Near East. We need not be too schematic here. Some confusion and overlapping between the "Ionian" and "Greek" identities continued to reign. It is apparent that for Egyptians, any Greek mercenary, such as the Dorian "Telephos of Ialysos" from Rhodes, one of those who signed their name at Abu Simbel, was a "military WJNN (Ionian)" and hence a "Greek." Greeks must have understood what was meant by the context in which it was cited. By analogy, German speakers would

---

118 Swiderek (1961); Wilcken (1912), pp. 48–50, no. 30.
119 Bowden (1996), p. 23n26, as suggested by a papyrus from the second century CE.
120 Braun (1982), p. 43.
121 Boardman (1999), p. 206 with note 158; Torelli (1977).
122 Thompson (1988), p. 96; Ray (1988), p. 274.

automatically translate the name of their people to "Deutscher" when they hear them referred to as "Germans," "Allemands," or "Tedeschi." Hence the transition: Amasis the *philhelên* may have chartered Naukratis to the WJNN, but the Greeks made their temple not into a pan-WJNN or pan-Ionian temple, like the Panionion in Asia Minor or the pan-Ionian temple that the Phokaians attempted at Massalia,[123] but rather a "Greek" Hellênion.

Aside from the obvious external perspective, condensing all Greeks into a single entity, may we interpret the Hellênion as expressing some Panhellenic feeling on the part of its participants? We usually find Greeks eager to uphold their singular identity. However, at Naukratis they made a deliberate choice for the sake of the prerogative of belonging to the Hellenes.

The Nile-island communities we noted earlier ("Ephesos, Chios, Lesbos, Cyprus, and Samos") seem to have disappeared following Amasis's convergence charter for Naukratis. Lesbos (Mytilene), Chios, and Samos were integrated into a Hellenic framework of the *emporion* of Naukratis except that Samos entered with its own temple, as did Miletos and Aegina. Perhaps this was a result of an older commercial presence in Egypt.[124] The less important trading communities or the relative newcomers had to converge in the common Hellênion. In time, however, "all the sanctuaries were used by all the Greeks, as evidenced by the vase inscriptions and the pottery."[125]

Being a recognized Greek in Naukratis implied geographical exclusion from other trading sites in Egypt. But this was also likely their prerogative. Whereas from the Egyptian point of view the main concern had been to channel Greek commerce through Naukratis, for their part the Greek *prostatai* probably wished to prevent infiltration by non-Greeks (e.g., under cover of private deals made between Greek merchants and, say, Phoenician ones).[126] To some extent their task was analogous to that of the Hellanodikai at Olympia, whose function was not only to judge among Greeks but, apparently, also to decide who had the right to participate as a Greek.[127]

Whatever the Egyptian origins of the name of the *Hellênion* (a generalized ethnic, and/or a name of a place assigned for "Greek" settlement), Greeks certainly internalized the Panhellenic conception of their temple. This is made abundantly clear in numerous dedications from Naukratis "to the Gods of the Greeks."[128]

---

123 Strabo 4.1.4–5 C179–80 with Malkin (1987), pp. 69–72, and see pp. 175–182.

124 See Strabo 17.1.18 C801–802 on the Milesian presence at Milesian Teichos. For a good discussion of the role of Miletos see Möller (2005).

125 Möller (2000), p. 215.

126 Cf. Boardman (1999), p. 131.

127 Hdt. 5.22.2 with Hall (2002), pp. 129–30.

128 See Bowden (1996) for a critical evaluation of the site and the inscriptions. I see no reason to doubt that the *Hellenioi theoi* at Naukratis were understood as "Greek" gods.

How were these worshipped? This is not an idle question. City-states would normally have had well-defined *nomima*, the assemblage of elements such as terminology for magistracies, the names and number of "tribes," and especially the sacred calendar. In general, Dorian *nomima* differed from Ionian ones, but there were also many subdivisions and local particularities, especially with reference to mother cities and colonies where *nomima* of the latter were modeled on those of the former (see chapter 6). But what might have been the *nomima* of Naukratis, a Panhellenic settlement?

What is of significance here is the fact that Greeks of all kinds, Dorians, Ionians, and Aiolians, coming from a variety of poleis, needed to articulate and agree upon some common *nomima* if only for the sake of cults and divinely ensured communal existence. Perhaps the *timouchoi*, the officials in charge of the Prytaneion (council house) and its common hearth (*koinê hestia*), were also in charge of formulating, arbitrating, and supervising *nomima*. I have remarked elsewhere on the peculiar Hestia of Naukratis,[129] which could not have had the origins of its sacred fire from any specific mother city. As for the general *nomima*, I think it probable that they were using the *nomima* of Miletos right from the start since a second-century CE papyrus states that Antinoöpolis (which had a Milesian calendar) used the same law as Naukratis.[130] If Miletos's *nomima* came to be preferred, this was perhaps because of its precedence (the Milesian Teichos) in Egypt and the ease with which other Ionian Greeks could have adopted them.[131]

The very existence of the Hellênion, together with "the Gods of the Hellenes" as its common object of worship, implies a self-aware religious convergence. It was a *Greek* convergence that could happen only within a "colonial" context. The forces of rapid assimilation and co-optation seem to have depended on network dynamics that concentrated in and spread out from Naukratis. Network dynamics accelerated and foreshortened distances among the nodes of the Greek cities by means of the personal networks of traders (who did not necessarily follow city allegiance) and the more official network of city "representatives" running the *emporion*. The Hellênion now appears as the site of Panhellenic religious accommodation, expressly presenting itself as "Hellenic." The Hellênion was not a Panhellenic sanctuary in the same manner as Delphi and Olympia (i.e., centers of a Hellenic pilgrimage and convergence), the most explicit expressions of Hellenic networks. The Hellênion's patron gods were neither Apollo (Delphi) nor Zeus (Olympia) but rather "the Gods of the Hellenes"—all Hellenes.

Naukratis emerges as a laboratory of inter-Greek, even interethnic cooperation that results expressly and symbolically in presenting a "Hellenic" front to

---

129 Malkin (1987), pp. 129–31.
130 Ehrhardt (1983), p. 89; Bowden (1996), p. 26, notes 41–43.
131 The issue of Miletos's position is complicated and open to various interpretations. See Möller (2005).

the world. Not only do the intensity of contacts and the varied contents of exchange mesh well with the network terminology of nodes (contacts) and flows (contents), but their very existence and intensification seem to have been enhanced by the network nature of the Greek *emporion* in Egypt. We cannot quantify this but can reasonably imagine the traffic that took place between the merchants and their mediators, perhaps the *proxenoi*, and the various administrators of harbor and temple, all coming from a variety of Greek cities, all being treated by Egyptians not as Chiotes, Aeginetans, or Samians but simply as "Greeks." This must have had a significant impact.

In network-fractal terminology, what was happening to Lindos, Kameiros, and Ialysos, converging into "Rhodes" for the purpose of partnership in the Hellênion, was also happening to the "Dorians, Aiolians, and Ionians," who converged simply as Hellenic. If a fractal represents patterns that are basically a replication of much larger ones, then network fractals are the prism through which to view the functioning of this emergent Hellenicity. Pan-Rhodianism and Panhellenism replicated similar patterns of convergence, and only through the wide angle of Mediterranean networks can this be observed most clearly.

At Naukratis we find, then, a religious expression of Panhellenic identity in a single polis and *emporion*. It was both reflective and constitutive: Naukratis provided Greeks with a nonideological occasion to formally express their common Greekness and in so doing to articulate it more distinctly. The often-debated question, whether collective identity is defined by contrasts with some "Other" or by inward-looking processes, is in this instance superfluous. It was both. Rather, what matters is that the accumulation of particularized networks of commerce and services (notably mercenaries and managing officials) converged through a combination of network growth and ad hoc political circumstances (Amasis). Similar circumstances created comparable convergences in other periods (e.g., the Medieval and early modern Hansa cities or the "Europeans" in nineteenth-century China), yet with very different expressions, depending on context and human agency. Note, however, that the network dynamics remain similar. In Naukratis, once the new polis/*emporion* was in place, the convergence of different poleis also resulted in a religious and ethnic convergence of Panhellenism. They were worshipping Greek gods together as Greeks. The "overseas" context of trading networks and colonization appear yet again as a creative force for the rise of Hellenicity.

Endnote: Zeus Hellênios

As an official cult title, Zeus Hellênios should be distinguished from general, rhetorical mentions of Greek gods, as in the case of Aristagoras at Sparta, whose words in Herodotus are as follows (Hdt. 5.49): "I implore you by the gods of Hellas (*theôn tôn Hellêniôn*), save your Ionian kinsmen from slavery."

Similarly, the Athenians, in spite of the generous Persian offers, would not sin against Zeus, the god of Hellas, and think it shameful to betray Hellas (*dia Hellênion*). Aelian speaks of Aspasia of Phokaia, who, when taken with the force of Cyrus, called on the *theoi Hellênioi*.[132]

Curiously, we find *theoi Hellênioi* at Naukratis attested to in numerous inscriptions.[133] Hugh Bowden is troubled by the fact that "not one example contains parts of both the words *theois* and *Helêniois* or *Hellênon*."[134] Similarly, facing the numerous yet fragmentary formulae, Höckmann and Möller prefer, by way of conjecture, the formula "to the Gods, those of the Greeks."[135] In fact, out of the twenty-three probable cases of the formula, some seem rather straightforward, such as Bernard's number 594 [*TOIS ELLH*] or 604 [*OIS ELLH*]. Bowden is also unhappy with some of the inscriptions that refer to *theois tois Helêniois* (cult title: *Hellênioi theoi*), whereas others refer to *tois theois tôn Hellênôn*, meaning the same but suspiciously nonformulaic. However, this may be explained in several ways. Naukratis had been an exception in almost every respect. If Hera could be *Lakinia*, or Apollo *Pythios*, following (as was often the case) the name of the temple, why should it be so troubling to perceive the gods of the Hellênion as *Hellênioi theoi*? It is also likely that not all dedications were made by residents of Naukratis (as an *emporion* it is likely that many were passing through, including possibly many non-Greeks). The cult title was rare, and its formulation was probably internalized by non-Greeks, Egyptians mostly, with dedications to "their gods."

The possibility that the Zeus of Naukratis, at Aegina's temple, was "Hellênios" is puzzling but well worth a discussion. Aeginetan origins are possible, perhaps with some obscure connection with the Thessalian Hellenes.[136] Pindar explicitly mentions the god: "Island (Aegina) whose name is famous indeed, you live and rule in the Dorian sea, O shining star of Zeus Hellanios"[137] and he is referred to obliquely in other sources.[138] Perhaps the cult had been first linked with the Hellênion by the Aeginetans in Naukratis, but the case would need special pleading since Aegina had her own, independent temple there.[139]

The Greek Zeus, the Zeus of the Greeks—what could he signify? We must first distinguish between origins and impact: Whether or not it began as a cult

---

132 Aelian *VH* 12.1.

133 Bernand (1970), p. 696nn536–40, pp. 701–702nn594–604, p. 706nn644–47. Also Bowden (1996), p. 23n8.

134 Bowden (1996), p. 23.

135 Höckmann and Möller, (2006), pp. 13–15. I am grateful to Astrid Möller for allowing me to see the proofs of the article.

136 See Kowalzig (2007), pp. 201–19, esp. pp. 203–207, who presents a rich argument for the Panhellenic implications of the cult on the island of Aegina.

137 Pind. *Paian Ode* 6.123–26, trans. William H. Race in (1997b), p. 269.

138 Josephus *Ant.* 12.258–61. Cf. Hdt 5.49.1.

139 Fullest references in Raaflaub (2004), pp. 112–13. Raaflaub is mainly concerned with making the identification with Zeus as Eleutherios (contra Oliver [1960]) secondary and views the Panhellenic function as primary. Cf. Figueira (1981), pp. 257–58, with notes 58, 59.

title imported from Aegina, as some think, or whether Zeus acquired his epi-thet simply because of the name of the temple, the title Hellênios was recon-textualized in the common, non-Aeginetan temple. The older paradigm, that "origins" determine salient characteristics, needs to be replaced here with a network approach: Whatever "original" characteristics were there, the network context of Naukratis provided them with a different meaning. It is not the ori-gins that determine the significance but the new use made of the title. Moreo-ver, since it is clearly not Zeus but a whole pantheon of *Hellênioi theoi* that is expressly mentioned, this new use seems to have had an intentional, declara-tive force: These are "Greek" gods.

3

Sicily and the Greeks: Apollo Archêgetês and the Sikeliote Network

Thucydides describes the first arrival of Greeks in Sicily in terms that would seem almost appropriate to modern colonialism: Having landed in northeastern Sicily, Thoukles, a leader of Chalkidian migrants, founded the city of Naxos. He set up an altar to Apollo Archêgetês (founder, leader, beginner) and a few years later marched to war against the Sikels to found Leontinoi; he then proceeded to found Katana.[1] Thoukles thus appears as an *oikistês* (founder) of three cities, a founder of a little colonial empire. But his example would not be repeated. From this point on, throughout the history of Greek colonization discussed here (figure 3-1), while we may hear of one or even several oikists per colony, we never learn of several colonies per oikist.[2]

Greek colonization in the Mediterranean and the Black Sea developed rather as a network of "dots" that consisted of *poleis* and their adjacent, relatively small, hinterland territories. It was the reverse of what Thoukles had attempted, and this becomes apparent in Sicily right from the start. Katana rejected his hierarchical model: "The Katanians, however," says Thucydides, "chose for themselves Euarchos as founder."[3] Leontinoi, too, was soon independent.[4] Perhaps Thoukles wished to play the role of Cortez or Pizarro, but he was immediately downsized in a uniquely Greek fashion. Until the

---

1 Thuc. 6.3.1–3. Cf. Moggi (2009).
2 On the role of the oikist in general, see chapter III in Graham (1983), pp. 29–39.
3 Thuc. 6.3.3.
4 Thuc. 6.4.1.

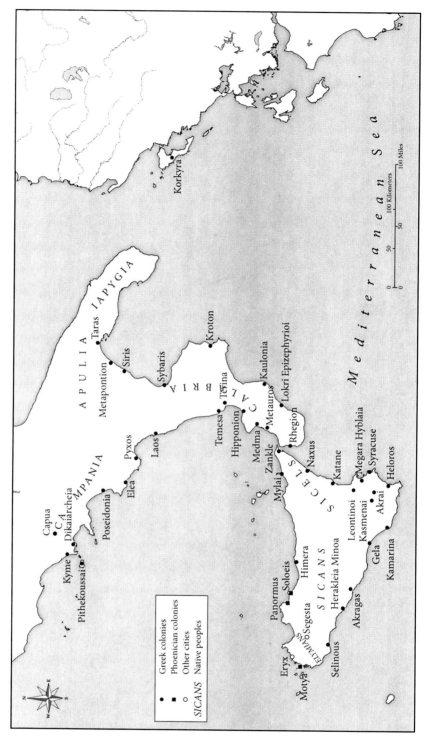

FIGURE 3.1. Sicily and southern Italy. After Graham (1982a).

age of the Sicilian tyrants (mostly during the fifth century), colonization would consist of founding mostly independent poleis, as well as independent daughter colonies, such as Selinous, which was settled from Megara Hyblaia.[5] By 580 BCE, when Pentathlos of Knidos failed to take Lilybaion in western Sicily, it was clear that the Elymians and Phoenicians would prevent the foundations of new Greek cities west of Selinous. This was the beginning of regional divisions in Sicily that were eventually marked in terms of Greeks and non-Greeks. This came to the foreground in 510/509, with the failure of Dorieus's invasion and his attempt to found Herakleia at Eryx in western Sicily, and especially in the early fifth century with the Phoenician and Carthaginian offensives against Greeks in Sicily.[6] The year 480 became emblematic as the year when Greeks were victorious against barbarians both at Salamis and at Himera[7] and the new emphasis on "oppositional Greek identity,"[8] defined *against* an outsider, appeared concurrently on both sides of the Mediterranean.

Rather than discussing this type of collective identity, we will see how the network of Sicilian Greek colonies also provided for a new, "positive" dimension of "Greek" collective identity. In the aftermath of Frederik Barth's research,[9] there has been too much emphasis on "boundaries" as defining ethnicity, with less attention paid to positive, deliberate, self-conscious practices aimed precisely at defining an overarching identity among Greeks.[10]

Jonathan Hall, in his two books on Greek ethnicity,[11] emphasizes the role of genealogy and ideas of kinship as articulating, before the rise of "oppositional" definitions, what he refers to as "aggregative" identity. Genealogies mattered, of course, both to gods and heroes, to the great aristocratic houses, and to some extent to entire communities. While genealogies may be prominent in the available sources, as noted (p. 61–62), I have some reservations as to how significant they really were since as an independent poetic discourse they possessed a textual life of their own, with poets probably alluding to each other but possibly divorced from common associations and definitions of collective identity. These often stressed common "historical" experiences as the "positive" content of collective identity. Both Tyrtaios and Mimnermos, for example, prefer to emphasize the *ktisis* (foundation

---

5 Thuc. 6.4.2. For Megara Hyblaia and Selinous, see De Angelis (2003). The significant exception is the short-distance settlements that were kept under the authority of their founder cities, such as Akrai and Kasmenai, dependencies of Syracuse. For the Sicilian tyrants see Luraghi (1994).

6 For an up-to-date discussion of Greek settlement in Sicily, see Domínguez (2006), pp. 253–357. On Dorieus see Malkin (1994b), pp. 192–218.

7 Pindar, *Pythian Ode* 1.70–80.

8 Jonathan Hall (1997), pp. 17–33, 34–51. Cf. Edith Hall (1989), pp. 3–13.

9 Barth's introduction in Barth (1969), pp. 9–38; See Jonathan Hall (1997), pp. 17–33, especially 24, 28, and (2002), pp. 9–10.

10 Malkin's introduction to Malkin (2001c), pp. 1–28.

11 Jonathan Hall (1997, 2002).

story) of Sparta and Kolophon, respectively, as the constitutive articulation of their respective political communities.[12] In fact, Tyrtaios seems to make a clear distinction between the genealogically defined Herakleidai, whose "return" provided Sparta with its charter myth, and "we the Spartans" who followed them: "For Zeus himself, the son of Kronos, the husband of fair-crowned Hera, gave this *polis* to the Herakleidai, *with whom we* left windy Erineos and came to broad Peloponnesos."[13]

The purpose of the foundation stories of both Sparta and Kolophon, while perceived as belonging to the wider dimension of Ionian or Dorian migrations, is to account for the individual polis. Of greater significance here is the impact of colonial circumstances on the articulation, through a regional network modality, of new types of Greek commonalities that transcended individual poleis or colonies. It is intriguing to find these articulations not in a genealogical but rather in a regional context that in turn elucidates their significance in network terms. This is not suggestive of an exclusive regional approach. Contrast with others, as well as an imaginary blood kinship, always had some role to play, depending on circumstances and time. It is rather the new kind of "colonial" regionalism that should be brought to the foreground, the better to observe it within a network context.

This chapter more closely examines how a regional type of identity was formed in Sicily, based on the notion of interconnectedness or "neighborhood," a generalized, bounded "island" identity that bypassed the Dorian-Ionian divide. Chapter 2 portrays the emergence of the island identity of Rhodes because Rhodians dispersed overseas, and the back-ripple effect condensed "Rhodes" at home. Now, in a reversed pattern, a regional Greek identity was created because Greeks from all over (including Rhodians) converged on Sicily. An awareness of being Sikeliôtai, Greeks living in Sicily, was constructed following a regional network and found its earliest expression in the altar of Apollo Archêgetês, the ritualized focus of a Greek-Sicilian network and accessible only to the Greek residents of Sicily.

---

12 Tyrtaios speaks of the foundation of Sparta: A late first- or early second-century BCE fragment from an Oxyrhynchus papyrus. See *P.Oxy.* xxxviii.2824, ed. Turner, as quoted in Gerber (1999a), pp. 37–38, frg. 2 (= 1a Prato). Cf. frg. 19, the myth concerning the origins of the Dorian tribes. See discussion in Malkin (1994b), pp. 33–43. Strabo (14.1.3–4 C633–4) quotes Mimnermos on the foundation of Kolophon: "Andraemon of Pylos founded Kolophon, as Mimnermos says in his *Nanno,*" and:

> Later, upon being expelled by the Aiolians, they [the Smyrnaians] fled to Kolophon, and upon attacking their own land with the Kolophonians they regained it, as Mimnermos states in his *Nanno,* after mentioning that Smyrna was always an object of contention: ". . . leaving Pylos, the city of Neleus, we came on our ships to longed-for Asia and with overwhelming force we settled in lovely Kolophon, the instigators of harsh aggression; and setting out from there, from the river . . . , by the will of the gods we captured Aiolian Smyrna."

See Gerber (1999a), frgs. 9 and 10. Cf. Malkin (1994b), p. 125.

13 Malkin (1994b), pp. 33–40, especially 38ff. Pindar could refer to Sparta as *he Dorida apoikian . . . Lakedai-moniôn* (*Isthmian Ode* 7.12–15), but this is descriptive, not constitutive. On the charter myth of Sparta in Pindar see Malkin (1994b), p. 41.

This network, articulated through pan-Greek-Sicilian ritual acts, was further enmeshed in the Panhellenic network of the Delphic oracle through the
multidirectional institution of the *theôria*. Whereas each polis had its own
direct channel with Delphi, either in connection with the oracle or with the
Pythian festival, the sacred embassies of Sicilian Greek cities would not depart
from the island without first sacrificing at the altar that was set up at the spot
where the very first Greeks landed in Sicily.

The Altar of Apollo Archêgetês

Some seven centuries after the first Greek landfall, at the time of the Roman
civil wars, Octavian arrived at the eastern coast of Sicily and landed at Tauromenion. Modern Taormina is located up on the mountain just under the
ancient acropolis, where it commands an arresting vantage point and overlooks the promontory of Giardini Naxos to the south. That is where the first
Greeks to have colonized in Sicily landed in 734 BC.[14] Octavian moored his
ships by the shrine of the Archêgetês, situated, obviously, on the shore. Appian,
who is our source, goes on to say that the shrine contained a small statue of
Apollo Archêgetês that had been set up by the founders of Naxos.[15] At that time
the city of Naxos had been in ruins since 402/403 BCE, when Dionysios I oblit-
erated it and transferred its population to Tauromenion.[16] Apparently, the sanctuary was too sacred, too pan-Sikeliote, and therefore remained in place for
centuries after the destruction of Naxos. Its history is fascinating and relevant.

We first hear of it in Thucydides' account of Greek settlement in Sicily.
"The first Greeks to sail over to Sicily," he says, "were some Chalkidians from
Euboia who settled Naxos with Theokles as founder and set up an altar in honor
of Apollo Archêgetês. This is now [or 'which is still standing']" [17] outside the city,
and on it sacred *theôroi*, whenever they sail from Sicily, first offer sacrifice."[18]

Jonathan Hall raises doubts about the antiquity and even existence of
the altar,[19] as archaeologists have never located it. Nonetheless, the grounds
of Giardini Naxos are rather extensive and were not all excavated, rendering

14 Blackman (2004).

15 Appian *Bellum Civile* 5.109. Cf. Paus. 1.42.5 for an Aiginetan-type statue of Apollo Archêgetês at Megara,
apparently a small statue made of ebony.

16 Athenians identified Dionysios I as "the ruler of Sicily," τὸν Σικελίαν ἄρχοντα. See Rhodes and
Osborne (2003), 10.6–7, 33.19–20 and 34.7–8, corresponding to Tod (1946), 108.6, 133.19–20, and 136.8, respec-
tively. Reger (1997), p. 474. On the destruction of Naxos, see Diod. *Sic.* 14.15; Freeman (1891), pp. 35–38n1; on
Dionysios I, see Caven (1990).

17 Hornblower (2008) ad loc.

18 Thucydides 6.3.1, ἐφ᾽ ᾧ, ὅταν ἐκ Σικελίας θεωροὶ πλέωσι, πρῶτον θύουσιν.

Translation (modified) from Charles F. Smith (1921), p. 187. Thoukles is a variant of the founder's name in
other sources.

19 Jonathan Hall (2002), p. 122.

the premise of this doubt invalid.[20] However, neither Carla Antonaccio, who shares these doubts, nor Jonathan Hall has analyzed the evidence of Appian,[21] who clearly points not only to the existence of the altar but especially to its impressive continuity, which stretches over a few centuries. It must therefore have continued its ritual function long after the city that established it lay in ruins.

I should mention here a major point of source methodology regarding the almost automatic suspicion of any evidence from the Classical period concerning the Archaic period. When Thucydides provides us with a *story* about Thoukles, he is using one kind of source, but when he speaks of the altar and the *theôria* associated with it, we need to measure this evidence with a different yardstick for the simple reason that it concerns the *practice* in which entire societies were engaged. For the first, historiography is the immediate tool of analysis, as in "did Thucydides draw this information from Antiochos of Syracuse?"[22] Or "Who might have been interested in this image of Thoukles"? However, the mention of the altar (together with the evidence of its longevity) and the *theôria* refer not to another text or tradition but to a living reality, an actual, recurring practice shared by a large community over time. It is an issue of participation and practice: Although cults could be used or even instituted ideologically, their existence, especially beyond the ad hoc occasion of their establishment, implies a living social reality and certainly a *datum* independent of the historian writing about it. We are all familiar with *aitia* that explain the unknown origins of cults. It would be rare indeed to find the reverse.

Thucydides is no doubt aware that the altar is "now" situated outside the city, thus making it clear that he regards it as an ancient, sacred, unmovable point. Considering the *longue durée* of its existence in the centuries following Thucydides, the question remains as to what extent Thucydides was in error about the antiquity of the altar. Is there any a priori reason not to believe that it was set up in the context in which he says it had been? Except for an impressionistic reaction, "it's too early for comfort," which some historians strangely regard as a legitimate argument, it is as good as the use of "common sense," a fallacious notion at best, as common sense depends on the culture that makes it common. I find no such a priori reason.

Moreover, there is a ritual reason that may support the notion of an altar to Apollo that was set up precisely at the moment of landing. When we consider

---

20 Pelagatti (2004); Blackman (2004). The importance of the seacoast of Naxos has been brought to light by the discovery of ship sheds large enough to hold triremes, possibly dating to the end of the sixth century and lasting until Naxos's destruction. See Blackman and Lentini (2003); Lentini (2009), p. 49. I wish to thank Lieve Donnellan for help on this point and for allowing me to read her work in progress.

21 Antonaccio (2001), p. 134 and note 21. Cf. Antonaccio (2007), pp. 272–73.

22 On Antiochos as a source of Thucydides see Dover's commentary in Gomme, Andrewes, and Dover (1970), pp. 198–202; Luraghi (1991); Hornblower (2008), pp. 272–73.

that altars to maritime Apollo, even temporary ones, were established on beaches to Apollo *ekbasios* as the god of disembarkation from ships[23] or, as in the *Homeric Hymn to Apollo*, to Apollo Delphinios,[24] it is quite possible that such an altar was transformed into that of Apollo Archêgetês within the first generation. It happened precisely because of its locality: Naxos, the first point of landing in Sicily.

Thus, we see an altar and a shrine that probably existed since the last third of the eighth century until at least the first century BCE. This was obviously not a major sanctuary but a sacred spot whose symbolism radiated to all the Greeks living in Sicily. It was a "Mayflower" altar, commemorating the first landing of Greeks who came to *stay*. In the centuries to come it probably reminded Greeks arriving at Sicily of that first Greek landfall. There was also a valid, practical reason for this function, probably the one that determined the choice of the site of Naxos in the first place: Landing in Naxos provides a maritime advantage for people sailing from Greece through Corcyra with the northeasterly winds.[25] The Corinthians must have been aware of this route when they founded both Corcyra and Syracuse. The Athenian navy also followed this route in the fifth century on its way to the siege of Syracuse.

The overall colonial activity, particularly that of the first Greeks in Sicily, was rapid and intense. Within approximately fifty years, since the 730s of the eighth century, quite a few colonies were founded.[26] Apollo became the Archêgetês of the Greeks in Sicily soon after 734, the Thucydidean date for the foundation of Naxos, and probably by the end of the eighth century, when various other colonial groups were establishing themselves in eastern Sicily. This is, of course, an assessment of probability. When Thucydides, probably following Antiochos of Syracuse, insists that Naxos had been founded one year prior to Syracuse, he seems to hint at a discourse of "who was first?"—a one-upmanship of colonial history, especially since a year's difference in colonial terms may be comparable to identical twins arguing about primogeniture. Yet, as with Jacob and Esaw or Romulus and Remus, the point is symbolic and important. Had Syracuse dominated the historiographical discourse, we might have suspected this powerful city (which eventually destroyed Naxos) of manipulation, especially in a history written by a Syracusan (Antiochos).[27] In fact, the reverse is true: Naxos managed to retain its

---

23 Malkin (1986a). On Apollo Embasios and Apollo Ekbasios see Detienne (1998), pp. 138–39, 250n119, 294nn22–24.

24 *Homeric Hymn to Apollo*, 487–96. Malkin (2000).

25 On maritime routes to the west from Greek ports, see Heikell (2006).

26 See Graham (1982a), pp. 160–62, for a full list of all Greek colonies with both literary foundation dates and approximate dates of earliest archaeological finds. Also Tsetskhladze (2006a), pp. lxvii–lxxiii.

27 Sjöqvist (1973), p. 18, for example, argues that conflicting foundation dates given in the accounts of Thucydides, on the one hand, and Diodorus, Ephorus, Timaeus, and Strabo, on the other hand, are the result of the usage of Dorian sources by the former and Ionian sources for the latter, each emphasizing the foundation of their Sicilian colonies. However, no Dorian colony ever claimed primacy and translated it into a common Sikeliote ritual.

primacy both in collective Sikeliote memory and in cult practice, indicating a fortiori that in spite of Syracuse's predominance in the Classical era, Sikeliote Greeks took Naxos's primacy seriously.

It is a fair assumption that powerful co-optative or assimilative forces, which are typical of colonial situations, came into play to form a generalized Greek, regional identity within the first fifty years of Greek arrival in Sicily. In migratory societies such assimilative forces are characteristic of a process by which people "even out" differences to adjust and realign themselves and their identity to a new situation and its defining characteristics. These may include language, holy days, values, and customs that are rapidly adopted both as the common grounds for living together and as signs of successful integrations. However, here we do not have a "country" into which migrants arrive, with its "inner" cohesive forces at play, but a "land" (Sicily) in which various city-states were founded. The assimilative forces within each of those could possibly be comparable to modern societies' "absorption" of immigrants. However, the dynamics of identity formation *among* the newly founded cities (while influencing also the "inner" identity of each one) may better be understood in network terms: rapid connectivity, a sense of common identity in relation to itself (Sikeliote) and to other Greeks through ritual articulation in relation to Apollo Archêgetês, their "connector" to the wider Greek web.

In ancient Greek colonies, *nomima* were the most effective means of collective integration within a polis. However, as we are not dealing with mediating various individuals or discrete groups to the new polis but with the relationship of all new poleis in Sicily to each other, we may need to find common *nomima*. The altar of Apollo Archêgetês and its *theôria*, predicated on the network of Greek cities in Sicily, constituted precisely this: Sikeliote *nomima*.

Through a process of imaginary socialization, settlers in Sicily most likely regarded Naxos as the place where "more people like us" (that is, other Greeks) have touched land. I will soon deal with the problematic term *Sikeliôtes*, but let me say for the moment that it seems that the first Greeks in Sicily probably became *Sikeliôtai*, "Greeks of Sicily," perhaps initially in a narrower ritualistic sense, by co-opting the altar as their common point of reference for collective identity. It seems probable that this took place within the first generation, say forty years,[28] of colonization in Sicily, when those arriving in the new world were probably arriving via Naxos due to the maritime advantages of the route. It is during the first generation that ritual actions must have been particularly important for them, and new frameworks were forged at a particularly rapid pace.

---

28 "Foundation" signifies the entire period of the oikist's mature life, from arrival at the site to his death, ritually commemorated by burial in the *agora* and a continuous communal cult, thus providing the foundation with a closure. See p. 23 with Malkin (2009).

While Greek commonalities are often expressed through cult and ritual, here there is an expressly *regional* commonality. Neither "Ionian-Chalkidic" Zankle nor "Dorian-Corinthian" Syracuse but "Sicily" is what primarily defined the *theôria* that used to sail from the altar. The more common scholarly discourse approaches the Greeks in Sicily either in terms of their mother cities, interpolis rivalry, or Chalkidian-Ionian vs. Dorian colonies (accepting or denying any of the above) or in discussing the dichotomy of "Greeks and native populations." It may take a special effort to switch the perspective to a regional-network mode, but this may be necessary if we are to appreciate the new kind of *Hellenic* network that was being created in Sicily. Sikeliote-Hellenic identity was not exclusive of other Greek identities while still excluding all non-Greeks. No Syracusans needed to prefer it over, say, their Syracusan, Corinthian, or Dorian circles of identity. Sikeliote identity existed as a parallel alternative, which, in times of peace, was articulated in ritual and, in times of external danger (e.g. during the Athenian invasion), capitalized upon it as a Sikeliote rallying cry (figure 1-6).

The Dorian-Ionian division sometimes overshadows our appreciation of Greek Sicily. Scholars like E. Sjöqvist have attributed a different "nature" to the "peaceful" Ionian and the "bellicose" Dorian colonies[29] in spite of the fact that sites such as that of Chalkidian Leontinoi were conquered by force, whereas Dorian Megara was overtaken by means of a peaceful invitation from a local king. The Dorian-Ionian division is familiar from fifth-century rhetoric and, with regard to Sicily, through the treatment of Thucydides.[30] However, this division in Sicily is neither earlier nor better attested to than the evidence for Apollo Archêgetês, apart from one major difference: The Ionian-Dorian distinction is evidenced mainly through rhetorical compositions, whereas Apollo Archêgetês relates to cult, a *recurring practice*. It involved entire communities and their representatives, the *theôroi*. Moreover, the express content of this ritual practice was Panhellenic, the Panhellenic sacred truce within which the institution of the *theôria* operated.[31] This evidence is very different from what ancient authors report on political or military speeches during emergencies.

The altar may have signified the opening up of a new land for Greek settlement. In chapters 5 and 6 we note a parallel development in Massalia about 600 and again after 545, where the Phokaian colonists established a cult to Apollo Delphinios, to be common to all Ionian Greeks. Like Naxos, Massalia was the first Greek city in a new country where no other Greek had

29 Sjöqvist (1973), pp. 37–39. The Ionian colonies, says Sjöqvist, were primarily the "free enterprises of private citizens in quest for a better and freer form of life." The foundation of the Dorian colonies in Sicily, however, was militant in character and resulted in constant clashes with the native Sicels.

30 See Alty (1982).

31 On the *theôroi*, official pilgrimage, and sacred truces see Dillon (1997), pp. 1–26. Cf. Elsner and Rutherford (2005b).

settled before. Although this is a case of a single mother city (Phokaia) in contrast to the numerous mother cities active in Sicily, at the time this was taking place, with the fall of the Assyrians, the pressure of the Lydians, and eventually the rise of the Persians, many other Ionians might have been expected to rush westward. Precisely because of the great distances, settlers of Massalia probably felt a need to assert, in a "new" land with no Greek poleis preceding them, a collective identity that transcended the limited Phokaian connection.

It appears as though, upon arrival, Greek settlers felt some need to assert a belonging to a wider "Greek" network. As noted (p. 57), the implication that, in the early periods of colonization, Greek settlers somehow had a concept of "Hellenicity" articulated in the face of lands with no Hellenic precedence in them—in fact, that they had such a concept because of colonization—may seem far fetched. However, the ritual consistency seems indicative of a wider Greek network, as we have seen in the case of Cyrenaica, where the cult of Apollo Karneios, a Dorian god of migration, served to express integration and appropriation. In Cyrenaica, too, we noted the cult of the "local" (Zeus) Ammon, for whom Libya in its entirety was his "precinct" (*temenos*) and whence his cult and the fame of his oracle poured over to Greece.[32] Zeus Ammon, traveling from Cyrene to Thebes (Pindar's city), illustrates again the back-ripple effect of Greek networks. Moreover, we saw how, during the second phase of immigration to and settlement in Cyrenaica, an oracle was procured to encourage settlement, stressing a Panhellenic colonial vision. The first such oracle ever recorded was addressed to "all Hellenes" (*Hellenas pantas*),[33] precisely within the wider context of colonization. Finally we noted the regional-maritime cult of Achilles Pontarches for Black Sea colonies, a hero-god whose presence was felt over the water and in the narrow coastal strips of the Greek colonies. Like *lingua franca* (see p. 58), that sailors' language spoken only on board ships and in ports, such Greek maritime cults illustrate how networks of cults expressed the "tying in" of the coasts with the sea as a virtual center.

Such "new" cults in "new" lands (compare, too, the Hellênion in Naukratis) have significant implications for the history of Greek civilization, Greek collective identities, and the ways in which they came to be constructed: through a network of cults that articulated belonging and connectedness and provided a link with the new spaces (both maritime and terrestrial) of Greek settlement and presence. The network is not merely reflective but also dynamic: The interconnectivity implied in colonization pushes Panhellenic aspects to the foreground in "new" lands (Massalia, Cyrene, Sicily, Egypt, the Black Sea) while concurrently articulating more locally specific, regional (Greek) identities.

---

32 For the cults of Apollo Karneios and Zeus Ammon, Malkin (1994b), pp. 143–68.
33 Hdt. 4.159.

The "Greeks Living in Sicily"

Thucydides employs the term "Sikeliôtai" in the sense of "Greeks living in Sicily," emphasizing a kind of Hellenic identity predicated neither on subethnic identity nor on the polis but on geography: a shared region. Carla Antonaccio meticulously reviews his use of the term and observes that in the extant sources Thucydides is the first to employ it.[34] Here I do not cover the same ground except where I wish to emphasize some additional or alternative angles. First let us examine again Thucydides' words about Apollo Archêgetês: "[T]he first Greeks to sail over to Sicily were some Chalkidians from Euboia, who settled Naxos with Theokles as founder . . . and set up an altar in honor of Apollo Archêgetês."[35]

It is the "first Greeks," *hellênôn de prôtoi*, who set up the altar (*hidrusanto* in the plural), not their leader.[36] In Greek, the sentence also contains a juxtaposition of "Greeks" vs. others, expressed through the particle *"de,"* which I have purposefully glossed over in the initial translation.[37] At this point Thucydides has just finished describing the non-Greek settlement and ethnography of Sicily (Sikels, Sikans, Elymians, and Phoenicians), and now he turns to "the Greeks" as a generalized opposition: "But, [in contrast to the Barbarians] *the first of the Greeks* to sail over to Sicily were some Chalkidians from Euboia . . ." This clarifies his historiographical perspective in his description of the island (barbarians vs. Greeks in Sicily) and leads him immediately to mention the altar of Apollo Archêgetês precisely as a common altar of all of the Greeks of Sicily.[38] The first of the Greeks, he seems to be saying, founded both the city of Naxos *and* a common Greek altar. Clearly then, from his point of view, he seems to take for granted the altar's pan-Sikeliote attribute when he says that *theôroi* sailing from Sicily would first stop there.

He is also speaking of a general custom. He does not use a definite article, "the" *theôroi*, which would imply in context Naxian *theôroi*, but all *theôroi* sailing from all of Sicily. Moreover, he is speaking of a recurring practice ("whenever" [*hotan*]), and he refers to setting out "from Sicily" (*ek Sikelias*) rather than "from Naxos."

In short, there can be little doubt that for this fifth-century historian all Greeks living in Sicily had a shared Greek quality to distinguish them from non-Greeks. He understood this shared Hellenicity as historically defined by colonization and by means of contrast with the non-Greek Sicilian populations. Moreover, Hellenicity was recurrently and positively expressed (that is, not through contrast) through ritual at the common Greek altar to Apollo Archêgetês.

---

34 Antonaccio (2001), pp. 116–22.
35 Thuc. 6.3.1.
36 Antonaccio (2001), p. 134, translates as if Thoukles himself is the subject of the sentence, although, of course, he is implied.
37 Ἑλλήνων δὲ πρῶτοι. See Hornblower (2008), p. 278.
38 Thuc. 6.3.1.

We do not know how long before Thucydides the term "Sikeliôtai" was employed. Carla Antonaccio has come to the conclusion that it was a fifth-century neologism, but given the absence of any evidence either way it remains an inference derived from silence, and considering the state of our sources, this signifies little. However, a comparison with other generalized island identities in Archaic Greece would have demonstrated that the construction "Sikeliôtai" was perhaps more common than exceptional and had been so even in the Archaic period. Sicily was surely perceived by Greeks as an island long before the famous speech to the Athenians by Nikias, who suggested letting the *Sikeliôtai* exist within their maritime *horoi* (boundaries).[39]

As we have seen in the discussion of Rhodes (chapter 2), some fascinating expressions of regional, "island identities" come to the foreground. The list of examples studied by Gary Reger[40] and Christy Constantakopoulou[41] constitutes a sufficient case for *expecting* the form "Sikeliôtes" to have been around before Thucydides, both from an inner Sicilian perspective and from that of other Greeks.

Paradoxically, it is the hostile speech of Alkibiades, "denying [the mixed lot of the] *Sikeliôtai* a land (*gê*) of their own"[42] and reminiscent of Herodotus's prejudicial distinction between the pure and the mixed Ionians[43] that points to something authentic in the colonial experience in Sicily. Against the background of initial colonization and that of the later reshuffling of populations and cities by the tyrants, the Greeks in Sicily are characterized as populated by a "mixed rabble" (*ochlois te gar xummeiktois poluandrousin*). The prejudice, in and of itself, is less relevant here; many Greek settlers in Sicily were apparently *symmeiktoi*, a "mixed lot," from the outset, joining distinct nuclei, such as those *panhellenes* of Archilochos, who joined the Parian foundation of Thasos, or the "Hellenes," who joined Cyrene in the second wave of colonization.[44] They quickly integrated into their new Corinthian-Syracusan, Parian-Thasian, and even Cyrenaian identities, thus providing the impression of homogenous colonies. Settlers assimilated and co-opted with the identity and *nomima* of the founding nucleus.[45] By the early Classical period, after the frightening scale of the tyrants' activities, the destruction of some cities, the refounding of others, and the relocation of populations, the mixed nature of Sicilian Greeks came to the foreground in a different way to be used, demagogically, in the speech of Alkibiades.

It is important to contextualize the two rhetorical strategies found in Thucydides with regard to what separates and what connects Sikeliote Greeks. One

39 Thuc. 6.13.1.
40 Reger (1997), pp. 450–92.
41 Constantakopoulou (2005).
42 Antonaccio (2001), p. 120, on Thuc. 6.17.2–3.
43 Hdt. 1.146.
44 Archilochos, frg. 102 in Gerber (1999b), p. 142; see pp. 55–59.
45 Malkin (2002b) and see pp. 54–55; 189–197.

calls for loyalty along the Dorian-Ionian division, while the other, especially in the speeches of the Syracusan general and politician Hermokrates, elevates the Sikeliôtai as an entity that needs to bypass such divisions. Both must have been exaggerated, yet their rhetorical use implies an expectation of response in terms already familiar to their audiences and not invented for this purpose. Evidence for ad hoc use of a concept applying to collective identity is not evidence for its invention, although it is true that when people articulate such concepts they also renegotiate or redefine them.[46] Identity is not something that constantly occupies us unless we are faced with a challenge. It is hard to imagine that Thucydides *invented* the term "Sikeliôtai" if it were intended to carry the burden of the speech of Hermokrates.

Thucydides has Hermokrates saying (Antonaccio's translation):

> There is nothing to be ashamed of for those living together (*oikeious*) to submit to each other, a Dorian to a Dorian or a Chalkidian to another of his own kin (*sungenôn*), and, taken all together, we are all of us neighbors (*geitonas*) and live together (*synoikous*) in one country (*chôra*), in the midst of the sea, all called by one name Sicilians (*Sikeliôtai*).[47]

"Sikeliôtai" in this speech is not contrasted with barbarians. It is a positive definition that relates to all Sicilian Greeks. Antonaccio is quite right to emphasize the rhetorical attributes of such speeches, yet she fairly notes, too, that Thucydides himself uses generalized terms for Sicily and Sikeliôtai. In fact, a comprehensive vision of Sicily and Sikeliôtai is provided in his own words, for example: "That summer [426 BCE] war was being waged in Sicily not just by other people (*alloi*), according to the circumstances of each, but also by the *Sikeliôtai* themselves."[48] This rather neutral and matter-of-fact application of the term seems to argue for its independent existence. Closer in time to the rhetorical context of the congress of Gela in 424, Thucydides speaks of "Kamarinians, Geloans, and the other *Sikeliôtai*."[49] Herodotus already speaks of the Greeks "residing in Sicily," but he also speaks of the "land of the Italiotes,"[50] referring to Italiôtai as the Greeks living in Italy. Considering that Italiote Greeks also had a common sanctuary at least from the fifth century (at the temple of Hera Lakinia near Kroton),[51] it strengthens the impression of *regional* colonial identities named after a "region," Italiôtai, Sikeliôtai, with fluctuating uses.

---

46 Malkin (2001b).

47 Thuc. 4.64.3.

48 Thuc. 3.90.1.

49 Thuc. 4.58.1. Note that in 7.33 Thucydides says that of "all of Sicily" (*pasa he sikelia*), meaning Greek Sicily, was aiding the Syracusans against the Athenians, in contrast to the disaster that befell the Syracusans among the Sikels (or "in the country of the Sikels" [*en tois sikelois*]).

50 Hdt. 7.165 τάδε ὑπὸ τῶν ἐν τῇ Σικελίῃ οἰκημένων; 4.15.2 Ἰταλιωτέων . . . τὴν χώρην. Note that when the Athenians try to get Rhegion to support the likewise "Chalkidian" Leontinoi, Rhegion refuses, waiting to see what the other "Italiotes" will decide. This is another illustration of the overriding importance of regional identity. See Thuc. 6.44.

51 Spadea (1996).

There are two other significant rhetorical uses, this time expressed by Athenians. In arguing against the Athenian invasion, Nikias advises the Athenians to let the Sikeliôtai remain within their boundaries (*horoi*), which are defined by the surrounding seas.[52] He mentions the Ionian Sea and the *Sikelikos kolpos*—another generalized regional view with regard to Sicily. The case is not quite neutral since Thucydides insists that all of Sicily was Athens's real purpose, and thus there is an interest in a comprehensive, Athenian regard toward all Sikeliôtai.

We saw how, at Olympia, a Greek declaring his identity to the Greek world called himself a "Rhodios." Gillian Shepherd stresses the investment of western colonial Greeks in Olympia rather than in dedications in their mother cities.[53] Through Olympia they were staking a Panhellenic claim, and at Olympia they were engaged in competitive emulation in relation to each other. The sanctuary of Apollo Archêgetês was nothing like Olympia or Delphi, a point that convinces Carla Antonaccio of its negligible role in articulating Greek Sikeliote identity. However, its purpose was not to be Panhellenic but pan-Sikeliote, namely, an overarching Hellenic identity defined in regional terms. Nor did it function as the pan-Ionion in Ionia. It served a different purpose and a different function and operated in a different ritual context.

Following Gillian Shepherd's line of thought, Olympia and Delphi were indeed important for Greek Sikeliotes as their display arena for competitive emulation in a "convergence" context that is obviously network oriented. Having a common, Sikeliote, point of ritual departure from Sicily *to* those great sanctuaries only emphasizes the interactions of the circles of overarching identities. Instead of allowing the great Panhellenic centers to overshadow the "periphery," we may understand it in network terms: The *pan-Sicilian network*, converging at Naxos, was ritually connected not with any particular mother city but with the *Panhellenic network* of the great sanctuaries through the ritual intermediary of the Sikeliote *theôroi*. The altar of Apollo Archêgetês thus appears as a "connecting hub," a Sikeliote hub, of the Greek Wide Web.

Colonization encouraged such modalities of definition, based on the new mixtures created in colonial lands and created along regional network lines. Dieter Mertens speaks not of colonial style in architecture but of typical mixtures of styles that do not draw on the traditions of any particular mother city.[54] Similarly, Gillian Shepherd has studied colonial burial practices that are more similar to each other than to those between a particular mother city and colony. The imported material culture, arriving from various Greek origins east of Sicily, as well as the "colonial" development of taste for certain

---

52 Thuc. 6.13.1.
53 Shepherd (2000).
54 Mertens (1996).

types of pottery (e.g., "Thapsos cups," produced by Corinth for export, or Phoenician-style plates, uncommon in "the Greek homeland"),[55] also contributed to the "mixed" image Sikeliotes may have had of themselves. Combined with the later mass relocations by the tyrants, this image is reflected in rhetorical *topoi*, such as the speech of Alkibiades, who denounced Sicilian Greeks as a mixed lot, easily relocating.[56] Thus, ritually, materially, and conceptually, Sikeliôtai are distinct in terms of practice, self-awareness, and the regard of others.

There would be little point in asking whether Sikeliote identity constituted either a Panhellenic or a discrete ethnic identity and, when discovering it was neither, discarding its importance. "Perhaps the most telling objection," says Jonathan Hall, ". . . against an early Hellenic consciousness in Sicily is the fact that it never seems to have been a particularly salient level of identification in subsequent periods."[57] Similarly, citing Pindar (*Pythian Ode* 1.72–80), who "likens the Syracusan victory over a Phoenician and Etruscan fleet off Kyme (Cumae) to the battles of Salamis and Plataia . . . the possibility was *not capitalized upon*" (my emphasis). "Sikeliôtai" for Hall is "a regional term which is not predicated on common descent but on the fact that they are neighbors inhabiting the same island (Thuc. 4.64.3)."

But what exactly should "capitalize" mean? Ritual and religious practice that seemed important to Sikeliote Greeks was probably irrelevant to that kind of "capitalization." My point is precisely this: Yes, Sikeliôtai is a regional term, and yes, Hall is right that it is not predicated on descent but rather on "neighborhood," except that he does not consider that to be of sufficient importance. Still, it is precisely in the regional ("neighborhood") network that the novelty lies. Once we set aside the genealogical "tree" model or various political constructions and apply a network perspective, we also escape the trap of descent-oriented definitions of ethnicity that are ill fitting for the new colonial situation. In other words, we need to get out of the circle inside which descent definitions of collective identities still enclose us. Hall insists on descent as the salient definition of ethnic collective identity, yet once he encounters a collective Greek identity that is predicated not on descent definition but on region and ritual, he denies its existence because it is not descent oriented.

The Sikeliôtai should be understood as a network of Greek cities in Sicily whose common denominator was regional. Sicily was not a territory in a political sense, nor was it a common homeland (a territorial trait of ethnicity, according to Anthony Smith),[58] although it could offer a platform of similar historical

55 Coldstream (2004).
56 Thuc. 6.17.2–3.
57 Hall (2002), pp. 122–23.
58 Smith (1986).

experience (colonization). Rather, the common ritual at Naxos relates specifically to conceptualizing *Greek* Sicily as a whole. Eriksen distinguishes between
an "us identity,"[59] namely an identity that depends on how others see us, a collective identity that is an *object*, and a "we identity," a subject, the "we," which is
the active agent whose actions, practices, and historical memories define it.
Thus, the subjectified, assertive "we identity" of the Archaic period was at once
all-encompassing in relation to Sicily and at the same time merging into the
network of the great Panhellenic sanctuaries. Because it was shared only
among Greek cities, we ought to view it as something parallel to the Hellênion
in Naukratis: not in the Hellênion's specific function but in the articulation of
Greekness taking place precisely because of the colonial context and the network nature of the association.

The criterion for participation in the network was being Greek: Greek cities
in relation to each other; Greek cities in their definition as "not Sikel," "not
Elymian," and so on; and Greek cities in relation to Olympia or Delphi. It was
mostly a question of practice, not ideology. However, once in place, in later
periods it could be used in ideologically rhetorical strategies. The latter ought
not to color our appreciation of the former. The comprehensive creation of
Greek units based on region and resulting from colonization and the network
dynamics of interstate rituals transcended the mediation of kinship criteria. It
was a network of the collective identity of Sikeliôtai, enmeshed with the greater
Greek world while redefining it in the process since the Panhellenic sanctuaries now enjoyed far wider horizons. Apollo Archêgetês at Sicilian Naxos was the
"frog" node, across the water, of Apollo Pythios, the Delphic god of Greek colonization. He was also the gateway to Panhellenism and its expression, the festivals. The network would function in multiple directions, as the institution of
the *theôria* illustrates.

Delphi and the *Theôria*: A Multidirectional Network

There can be little doubt that Apollo Archêgetês was a god of colonization,
overlapping in many respects with the Pythian Apollo of Delphi.[60] For example,
it was the Pythian Apollo who provided Cyrene with its foundation oracle, and
it was as Apollo Archêgetês that he was worshipped in Cyrene in the same context as the commemoration of Apollo's oracular foundation prophecy.[61]

The time frame for Delphi's rise to Panhellenic significance coincides with,
and to a major extent was also probably the result of, colonization (discussed
later). The town of Delphi seems to have been reestablished around 800 BC, and

59 Eriksen (1993).
60 Malkin (1987); Detienne (1998).
61 Meiggs and Lewis (1989), ch. 5: The Foundation of Cyrene; Rhodes and Osborne (2003), no. 97: Sacred
Law from Cyrene.

the Pythian oracle shows a range of dedications transcending its immediate region soon after 750, with a growing circle of participants after 725.[62] The Delphic network encompassed both the twelve members of the Amphiktyony and all others who wished to have access to the oracle.[63] Over the centuries, these included regime reformers, such as the quasi-historical person known to us as Lycurgus at Sparta, Kleisthenes of Sikyon, the Athenians Solon and Kleisthenes, the founders of colonies, and quite a few tyrants seeking Delphic legitimation as refounders of the social order.[64] It may be important to reiterate the distinction between the sanctuary (the site of the Pythian festival) and the oracle at Delphi. Catherine Morgan makes the important claim that the twelve peoples constituting the Amphiktyony were interested mainly in the sanctuary, whereas those interested in the oracle were rather the emerging *poleis*.[65] Moreover, Christiane Sourvinou Inwood rightly emphasizes that the order of oracular consultation was determined according to *poleis*, although most members of the Amphiktyony were *ethnê*. That distinction would also help to explain the particular role of Delphi in the founding of colonies, most of which became *poleis* and none an *ethnos*.[66]

Concurrent with this development had been the rise of Olympia and, at some point, its institution of the judges of the Greeks, the Hellanodikai. These judged among Greek competitors but in certain circumstances also seem to have judged the eligibility of participation in terms of who was a Greek since only Hellenes were qualified to participate.[67] Thus, we see that the category of Hellenes became more closely connected with the notion of *access* to Panhellenic sanctuaries.

Elsewhere I have studied the role of Apollo and Delphi in Greek colonization while emphasizing the role of the *oikistês*, the founder, to whom oracular prophecies were given personally and who was addressed in the second-person singular. This emphasis on the *oikistês* was a political and symbolic compromise. The oracular prophecies could not have been given to the mother city since the new polis was not to be hers, and it could not have been given to the *apoikia* (namely, to the group of people setting out) because its members have not yet come into being as an entity. The *oikistês* embodied the potential and the actual and occupied the intermediate position of both a representative of mother city and colony. Hence, it was to him alone that a founder's cult was instituted after his death, the first cult that, by definition, was explicitly the colony's own and not imported from the *metropolis*.[68]

62 Morgan (1990), passim and pp. 184–85.

63 Tausend (1992).

64 I have discussed the common denominator (in relation to Delphi) among reformers, founders, and tyrants in Malkin (1989). Cf. Jacquemin (1993).

65 Morgan (1990), pp. 184–85.

66 Sourvinou-Inwood (2000). Cf. Morgan (2003).

67 This seems to be implied in Hdt. 5.22.1–2. See Jonathan Hall (2002), p. 130. Cf. Paus. 5.9.5 with Lévy (1991), p. 66.

68 Malkin (1987), pp. 17–91, 184–266.

Hence, a colony would have something its mother city did not have, namely, a double origin: an *apoikia* from home and an oikist "from Delphi." Later on the pattern of an oracular consultation by a founder became a universal expectation and a *topos* of foundation narratives. It came to be attached also to the older Greek world, with numerous foundation stories invented along the lines of actual colonial practices, which could not have existed before the eighth century and the rise of Delphi. The Greek world thus came to be enmeshed in a mental network whose hub was the Delphic oracle. In other words, the *direction* and diffusion of this mental pattern was from the more distant shores of the Mediterranean toward mainland Greece and the Aegean (the back-ripple effect), with a virtual center situated at Delphi.

What most also had in common was Delphi, both in its role as the oracle that had prophesied their foundation and as the ritual destination of their sacred embassies. In Sicily, all Sikeliote foundations related to Delphi in the same way regardless of whether a city's circle of collective identity had been, say, Syracusan-Corinthian-Dorian or Zanklian-Chalkidian-Ionian. Moreover, Delphic origins provided Greeks who came from no *polis*, such as those ambiguous "Cretans" who cofounded Gela with the Rhodians, with a focused origin. Delphi was probably particularly important for those settlers who would join an original nucleus around an oikist, as those desperate Megarians who were picked up by Archias en route to Syracuse,[69] thus probably facilitating integration in a land with less of an emphasis on origins from a particular mother city. There are even mentions of ritually discrete groups (as seems to have been the case at Rhegion), when colonization actually involved going to Delphi and setting out *from* there.[70]

Delphi was thus particularly important especially in the context of general mobility. The double origins must have made assimilation with the original nucleus much easier. We see, then, a triple mediation: Delphi, both in terms of practice and as a mental framework, mediated the internal identities of each new polis; in Sicily (and elsewhere) it mediated the network of new poleis among themselves; and, finally, it mediated between this Sikeliote network and the entire Greek world.

In short, each colony had its own mother city to distinguish itself from others but had Delphi to emphasize its commonalities with the entire world of new foundations. The characteristic tension in the history of Hellenism between the particularistic and the Panhellenic thus finds articulation in the double "Delphi-*metropolis*" origins.

What is noteworthy about the altar of Apollo Archêgetês at Sicilian Naxos is that it seems to have been common or at least accessible to *all sacred ambassadors*, or "pilgrim *theôroi*," sailing away from Sicily. Not enough attention has

---

69 References in Malkin (1987), pp. 93–97, 210.
70 Malkin (1987), pp. 31–41.

been paid to the pan-Sikeliote implication of these *theôroi*. What do they signify? Let us recall the two-way nature of the institution of *theôria*.[71] At Delphi, for example, before the Pythian games, there would be an official pronouncement followed by a delegation (*epangelia*), with announcer-*theôroi* proclaiming the sacred truce, *ekecheiria*, and invitations to Greeks to participate. In response, the sacred deputies sent over were also called *theôroi*, who may be distinguished from the announcer-*theôroi* as pilgrim-*theôroi*. Those hosting the announcer-*theôroi* were called *theôrodokoi*, and extensive lists of such persons are known from inscriptions, beginning mostly at the end of the fifth century.[72] Similarly, those hosting pilgrim-*theôroi* were also called *theôrodokoi*, whom Paula Perlman labels "*theôrodokoi* type II."[73] The organization of the lists of *theôrodokoi* tends to reflect the routes followed by the announcer-*theôroi*, and they are grouped according to geographical regions rather than *poleis* since the same announcer-*theôros* visits all *theôrodokoi* in a particular region.

There is also a reverse direction of *theôria*: not from Delphi to the Greek world but from Greek communities to Delphi. *Theôroi* in this sense are representatives of their communities, sent to Delphi to "see and observe," to sacrifice, and perhaps to consult the oracle.[74] Thus, the institution of the *theôria* crisscrosses the Greek world in a multidirectional network that consists of announcer- and pilgrim-*theôroi* and their hosts, *theôrodokoi* types I and II but—depending on the nature of the particular circumstances—also consisting of sending *hiera*, sacrifices, and choruses. In her study of the *theôria* in later periods Barbara Kowalzig rightly emphasizes the institution as a social organization that often competes with or bypasses political and ethnic groupings. *Theoric* cult breaks up local boundaries and allows new ways of relating to other communities, which is precisely what I am claiming for Sicily in the late eighth and early seventh century.

Regionalism also finds its expression in the manner in which the itineraries of announcer-*theôroi* sometimes appear on inscriptions, where the *theorodokoi* are listed in inscriptions according to regions.[75] Originating perhaps from practical reasons, such a geographical definition circumvented implied hierarchies among the communities visited. Ian Rutherford has studied a case of a *phiale* dedicated at Delos by "the Amphikleidai from Naxos from Sicily" (*Naxou ek Sikelias*)[76] although here "Sicily" may simply distinguish Sicilian

71 In this chapter I concentrate only on the Delphic *theôria* as it seems most pertinent to Apollo. Generally on *theôria*, see Rutherford (2002, 2007); Perlman (2000), pp. 13–35; cf. Boesch (1908); Dillon (1997) on the institution of the *theôria*: chapter 1, 1–26; cf. Elsner and Rutherford (2005b); Kowalzig (2007), especially chapters 2–4. I wish to thank Barbara Kowalzig for allowing me to read the manuscript of her (now published) article, Kowalzig (2005). See also Constantakopoulou (2007), pp. 29–60.

72 See Perlman (2000), pp. 14, 47, 121, also on θεωρός and δέχεσθαι.

73 Perlman (2000), p. 17ff.

74 I say "representatives" with caution: Paula Perlman (2000, p. 27) stresses that, although similar to the institution of *proxenia*, *theôroi* represent the gods, the sanctuaries, and their administration, in contrast to *proxenoi*, who represent *poleis*.

75 Perlman (2000), p. 31.

76 Rutherford (1998).

Naxos from its Aegean namesake. However, the words of Thucydides—*hotan ek Sikelias theôroi pleôsi* [whenever *theôroi* sail from Sicily][77]—seem to go beyond that, acquiring a formulaic, religious significance, especially when we note that "Sicily" and "Italy" exist in the various lists of *theôrodokoi* in relation to the itineraries of the announcer-*theôroi*.[78] Thucydides himself attended such Panhellenic festivals and was familiar with them both in terms of the general significance of *theôroi* and specifically those of Sicily, who were prominent and frequent visitors. He may even have heard about the special pan-Sikeliote significance of Apollo Archêgetês at such occasions.[79]

The implication from his text is that, in time, Sicilian *theôroi* would sail *as a group*, perhaps also for practical reasons, such as security. Sailing together from Sicily to the great Panhellenic events was a practical measure and afforded safety from pirates and especially from other Greeks since the nature of sailing under a Panhellenic sacred truce would be more apparent when sailing in what amounted to a "sacred ship." It is analogous perhaps to the practice of Hellenistic *theôroi* from various islands in the Dodekanesos, who met together at a festival on Kos before traveling *together* to Delos.[80]

In time, the ritualistic expression of Sikeliote identity by setting out by *theôroi* from the altar of Apollo Archêgetês depended less on the altar itself than on its connectedness with Delphi and Olympia in particular. The link matters more than the originating point, which is what a network is all about. The multidirectional "traffic" of announcer- and pilgrim-*theôria* is the important phenomenon. This perhaps explains why the sanctuary to Apollo Archêgetês always remained minor, albeit with a centuries-long life. Along the connecting lines of the network, both announcer-*theôroi* and pilgrim-*theôroi* would be traveling back and forth, revitalizing the strands of the network and emphasizing through their ritual action their common Sikeliote origins.

It is also important to reflect on the fact that before the beginning of the sixth century, or the date assigned to the First Sacred War and the reorganization of the Pythian games, the Pythian festival consisted mainly of poetic (hymns) and musical competitions honoring Apollo.[81] The character of the pre-sixth-century *theôria* was therefore concerned much more with Apollo as such rather than with prestigious aristocratic *athla* that at Delphi were a later development.

Delphi and the altar of Apollo Archêgetês provided a positive, *self-referring* content of a new type of regional Greekness that transcended polis and ethnic divisions among Greeks. An imaginary process of conceptualizing "foundation"

---

77 Thuc. 6.3.1, see note 18.
78 Perlman (2000), p. 31.
79 For Thucydides in Olympia see Clark (1999), pp. 115–31.
80 Sokolowski (1969), pp. 272–76n156b. One wonders, too, whether at some point a Sikeliote chorus might have been on such a ship (Elsner and Rutherford 2005a). For the relations between *theôria* and collective identity, see the excellent discussion of Barbara Kowalzig (2005).
81 Parke and Wormell (1956), p. 108.

probably followed closely on the heels of the first settlers.[82] This regional, Panhellenic, Sikeliote identity with its common symbol, the altar of Apollo Archêgetês, developed in tandem with the enormous rise of Delphi's own Panhellenic status since the last third of the eighth century BC.[83] Its influence had become prominent especially in Greece and the western Mediterranean, extending a network of Panhellenism and consciously reiterating its famous perception as "the navel of the earth" (omphalos).

Similarly, the development of Delphic theôria itineraries must have followed closely in the wake of colonization. Paula Perlman assumes that the early theôroi lists did not include the colonies,[84] and thus new lists needed to be created. It is precisely in such a context that the altar would have gained in importance. In other words, we can thus identify not only a regional Sikeliote interest and symbolism but also an external demand for pilgrim-theôroi in a way that helped conceptualize Greek Sicily as a discrete entity.

It is in this manner that we may envisage the intermeshing of networks: Delphi as a hub with its own radiating itineraries of announcer-theôroi and local theôrodokoi, organized regionally and mainly concerned with the Pythian games; Delphi as an oracle, with its direct, unmediated connection with each polis; the theôrodokoi type II, hosting pilgrim theôroi; and the "Sikeliote" theôria, pulling the Sicilian strands of the colonial network at Naxos to connect with Delphi or whatever other sanctuary it was about to visit. Greek Sikeliôtai acquired a new kind of Hellenic identity in the process. Hubs and networks continued to feed into and be fed by the Panhellenic networks that we call Greek civilization.

Endnote: Palikoi

The emergence of Greek-Sikeliote regionalism is paralleled by the appearance, in the fifth century, of a non-Greek, regional-ethnic identity, that of the Sikels. The career of the Sikel leader Douketios was modeled on that of a Greek tyrant-founder. He collaborated with Syracuse against Katane, relocated his native city of Menai, and refounded it as Menaion. He also founded the city of Palike and seems to have centered his newly founded koinon tôn Sikelôn [Union of the Sikels] around the sanctuary of the Palikoi, native Sikel deities.[85] When he was later defeated, he found refuge in Syracuse, was exiled to Corinth, and returned to Sicily as founder of Kale Akte, a desirable spot that the Samians had once tried to settle.

What is striking in all this is the sense of a mirror image: As others have observed, everything about Douketios implies being Greek except that he

---

82 Cf. Braund (1998).
83 Forrest (1957).
84 Perlman (2000), p. 59.
85 Maniscalco and McConnell (2003); cf. Hodos (2006), p. 121.

apparently signified an assertion of collective Sikel identity in contrast to Greeks. Although he chose for his *koinon* "the cities of the same ethnicity" (*tas homoethneis*),[86] it was basically a regional cult. It is not clear how many Sikans, for example, could join in.

It looks as if "Sikels" and "Sikeliôtai" were at once complimentary and adversarial. Both denoted something far larger than a city identity. To the extent that Sikels had had any sense of being Sikels before Greek colonization, by the fifth century they certainly did: The development of antagonism and armed conflict between the larger groups on the island (including the Elymians and Phoenicians) probably gave rise to oppositional types of collective identity. In sum, the mirror reflects in both directions: The shrine of Apollo Archêgetês and that of the Palikoi functioned differently and signified a wide spectrum of associations. But they had this in common: Ritually and mentally they served as the focus of the new collective identities that emerged in Sicily.

---

86 Diod. Sic. 11.88.6–9.

4

Herakles and Melqart: Networking Heroes

As the Greeks and Phoenicians of the Archaic period explored maritime routes, traded, and established *emporia* and territorial colonies, cultural borrowings among themselves and the native populations soon transcended any particular point of trade or settlement to create a network that crisscrossed the spaces of the ancient Mediterranean. These borrowings were the result neither of cultural imperialism nor of any program to create Greek or Phoenician colonial empires. Most of the new settlements were relatively small, independent entities, and even the largest among them controlled only a small portion of the hinterland. This was the context for the emergence of a colonial middle ground that greatly facilitated cultural exchange, especially within regional networks.

This exchange was expressed both materially, for example in architecture, art, or pottery, and in cults, myths, and filters of perception. The network of myths and cults in particular could be used to facilitate coexistence or to peacefully mediate among ethnic groups and their territorial claims. Conversely, the same mythic and cultic network could justify antagonism and appropriation. As we will see, cultic and mythic filters of perception formed an "accommodating" middle ground for both native populations and the Greek and Phoenician colonists but could also function as charters, based on appropriated identities, for conquest and settlement. Once in place, the networks both reflected and created structures of interactions. However, with changing historical circumstances, the interpretation of such structures was left to the participants. This chapter focuses on the ancient western Mediterranean and specifically on Sicily, where Melqart the Phoenician and Herakles the Greek illustrate the full spectrum, within the same network, from mediation to appropriation.

Both the Phoenician Melqart and the Greek Herakles provided frameworks of identity and foci of belonging to a place. Among Greeks, Herakles was first and foremost a "culture hero." Through his precedent-setting acts of clearing the land of monsters, such as Antaios in Libya, he opened the way for human civilization to follow.[1] In the more specific historical contexts of new foundations his mythic precedents could also serve to articulate a notion of "place." Euhesperides in western Libya, for example, could be conceptualized as the site of Herakles' adventure with the golden apples of the Hesperides.[2] However, not everything is political, and not every mythic articulation is ideological or legitimating. A distinction between, on the one hand, "myths of land" and on the other, "myths of territory," should be kept in mind. Antaios was not killed in order to legitimate the settlement of any specific community. To transform such myths into justification for territorial appropriation, a "charter" aspect was added: a promise, made explicit in various mythic narratives, of an inherited "right" to the territory to be claimed by a future descendant of the hero, and the basis for founding a political community.

The Herakles of the Archaic period was usually not a colonizing hero. He rarely stayed in one place long enough to establish anything. He was rather the great traveler, wandering a world of human beings and phantasmagorical creatures. Sometimes he even reached the edges of the earth, where no colonial charter was conceivable. Nor was he ever a truly maritime hero like the heroes of the Nostoi, such as Odysseus, returning from Troy. It is their perspective, from ship to shore, which is the salient characteristic of the initial periods of historical Greek colonization (see pp. 48–50). In contrast, Herakles was a quintessentially terrestrial hero, eliminated from the Argonauts' roster in the initial stage of his only major maritime adventure.

The colonial Herakles is typical of the *later* colonial experience. At the end of the sixth century Dorieus made political use of his myth. By then most of Sicily's coastal areas had been occupied. Herakles tends not to appear as a founder, *ktistes*, before the fifth century. The case of Kroton is symptomatic. Although Herakles is characterized as *ktistes* on the colony's coins, the myth associated with Herakles relates a precedent and a prophecy rather than an actual foundation. Mourning his young friend Kroton, whom he had accidentally killed, Herakles prophesies the foundation of a city to be named "Kroton." But Kroton had a historical founder, a certain Myskellos of Rhypai.[3] Why,

---

1 Burkert (1979), pp. 78–98.
2 Malkin (1994b), pp. 186–87.
3 Giangiulio (1989); Jourdain-Annequin (1989a), p. 35.

then, was Herakles considered a *ktistes*? Greek cities in the western Mediterranean of Classical times began to appropriate mythic origins in response to the challenge of their national youthfulness, apparently wishing to have ancestries as venerable and as ancient as those of their mother cities. An association with Herakles, a hero whose time preceded even the Trojan War, could serve this purpose.

This use of Herakles helped integrate the new colonies into Panhellenic networks of myth, thus enhancing the Greekness of those colonies. Conversely, "older" cities, such as Corinth, Sparta, and Miletos, adopted the "colonial" framework (e.g., with Delphic prophecies and stories of founders) to explain their own origins. Colonies of the Archaic period shared certain practices of foundation, and the resulting network of Archaic colonies probably also facilitated the systematization of the necessary elements of foundation stories. A curious formation of mental networks developed. It appears that once the discourse of "origins" had been established, cities of "old Greece" began telling themselves similar stories, with mythical founders who were more venerable than the obscure historical founders of the Archaic period. Finally, a city such as Kroton also acquired similarly respectable origins by pushing back its foundation and attributing it to Herakles. We have come full circle. The more ancient cities adopted the colonial foundation frameworks but with heroes as founders, which were in turn adopted by colonies. This is a nice illustration of the self-emergent process of the creation of mythical, quasi-historical, and historical networks of collective imagination, with both imitation and "competition" among the actors in the network.

Herakles could be turned to face the "natives," sometimes as their own ancestor or founder, as was Odysseus for the Etruscans (Utuzde).[4] While foundation might imply conflict, a hero who preceded the historical date of foundation and was somehow "shared" by Greeks and non-Greeks could thus mediate relationships. Both Greeks and natives would come to participate in a universal mythic network for conceptualizing the progenitors of various ethnicities.

In network terms "founders" could function as "ties" by connecting a variety of "actors" or "nodes." Herakles and his descendants (the Herakleidai) were particularly apt for this role. The concept of "founder" relates, of course, not only to political communities but also to aristocratic and royal dynasties that may also form the basis for collective identities. The Spartan Herakleidai are the best known. As early as the seventh century Tyrtaios makes it explicit that the Herakleidai were the leaders to whom Zeus donated the *polis*, explicitly distinguishing them from those whom they were leading.[5] This is a charter

---

4 Malkin (1998), pp. 156–209.
5 Tyrtaios frg. 1a, in Prato (1968). For a possibly more extended use of "Herakleidai" and for the issue of legitimating myths implied in Zeus's "gift" see Malkin (1994), pp. 33–45.

myth as explicit as that of the Promised Land in the Old Testament. Historical Herakleidai, such as the Corinthian founders of Corcyra (Chersikrates) and Syracuse (Archias), functioned particularly among Dorian Greeks as founders. In Sparta in particular, the Herakleidai's function related not only to the origins of Dorian Sparta and its claim to the land but also to the definition and legitimation of its royal houses. All were descendants of Herakles, and, as a result, all were justified in their royal status. The Archaic term *archêgetai*, the official appellation of the early kings, conveys the double meaning of "founders" and "leaders." As founders they are responsible for both the Spartan state and the Spartan kingship, and they function as leaders "to this day."[6]

The distinction between the collective articulation of identity (that of "the nation") and self-definition in terms of aristocratic bloodlines, has a long history in Europe and reverberates even today. With the rise of the *polis*, a new need to articulate identity in more collective terms had emerged. The tension between the collective and the genealogical was enhanced because, whereas Sparta could define itself through its Herakleid kings, most *poleis* had no kings. This was also true of new foundations. Archias was the founder of Syracuse and was probably worshipped as a hero after his death, but no descendants of Archias ever ruled the Syracusans.[7] With the exception of Sparta and its "granddaughter" colony Cyrene (Sparta-Thera-Cyrene), neither new colonies nor older *poleis* allowed the historical aristocracy to define their collective identities.

Sparta did retain personal-genealogical lineages as elements of its political and religious life (the Herakleid kings were also the priests of Zeus).[8] The Herakleid myth provided not only a charter for the possession of its territory and for the legitimacy and continuity of its royal houses but also a prism for perception of the world in specific historical contexts, thereby reinforcing its claims of dynasty and territory in other areas of the Mediterranean, especially western Sicily.

What is remarkable is that the grafting of Herakles onto specific sites of intended colonization followed preexisting networks established not by Greeks but by Phoenicians. Sections of Herakles' mythic itineraries, as well as colonizing claims emanating from them, overlapped in Sicily and in the western Mediterranean with areas in which the cult of the Phoenician god Melqart, whom Greeks identified with Herakles, was established. If the "Mediterranean is exchange," as Fernand Braudel has said,[9] western Sicily was the scene of a great cultural borrowing. Beginning neutrally, if not amicably, the syncretistic interactions of Melqart and Herakles reversed the established order and the use

---

6 Cartledge (2001), pp. 62–64.
7 On founders and posterity, see Malkin (1987), pp. 241–54.
8 Parker (1989), pp. 143, 152–53.
9 See pp. 43–44 (= introduction, note 118).

of the Herakles myth as a charter for the founding of a new *polis*, a new "Her-akleia." (For Sicily see figure 3-1).

Just as some colonial sites were chosen because they fitted into a preexist-ing pattern of maritime networks of commerce, so, too, did cultic and mythical associations inasmuch as they served the purpose of either mediation or con-flict. Crisscrossing the Mediterranean, mythical itineraries formed a mental network that could serve Greeks in different contexts. Two Herakleidai, one from Knidos and the other from Sparta, sought to colonize western Sicily, where Phoenicians had settled since the eighth century. Around 580 BCE, Pen-tathlos attempted to conquer Lilybaion in western Sicily, where he confronted the Phoenicians and their colony on the offshore island of Motya. When he joined Greek Selinous in its war against the Elymians of Egesta, he died in bat-tle at the hands of the Elymians and the Phoenicians. The colony at Lilybaion was abandoned, and his followers went on to settle in the Aiolian Islands north of Sicily, where they preyed on shipping in the Straits of Messina and stirred up trouble, especially for the Etruscans. Pentathlos apparently invoked the Herak-leid charter myth, which recalled that Herakles, during his travels in Sicily with the cattle of Geryon, had won Eryx and left it in the hands of the natives until the day when one of his descendants would return to claim it. Writing in the mid-sixth century, the myth served Stesichoros of Sicilian Himera, who was perhaps prompted by Pentathlos's attempt.[10]

Around 509 BCE, the Spartan Dorieus—another descendant of Herakles and a relative of Pentathlos—aimed for Eryx (Erice) in western Sicily, the site of a famous temple of Astarte (and probably Melqart). Dorieus must have known about the Phoenicians when he arrived there and was probably aware of the wider dimensions of the Mediterranean, which included Greeks, Etruscans, Phoenicians, and even Romans. He went to Italy (Kroton) and then to Sicily after having failed to establish a colony in Libya, where a coalition of Phoeni-cians (Carthaginians) and local inhabitants had driven him out. When he stopped in Italy, it was around the time (509 BC) when Rome and Carthage were forging their first treaty, which related to maritime influence zones. In Sicily he made use of the charter myth of Herakles' right to western Sicily. It is no wonder that the Phoenicians, both those in Carthage and those in western Sicily (some 170 kilometers away), were concerned.[11]

Why would the Herakleid claim to western Sicily have been taken seri-ously? Why was it convincing both to the Spartan followers of Dorieus and to non-Dorian Greeks such as Philippos of Kroton, who joined him with his own fighting men and private ship? Perhaps more intriguing is the question as to

---

10 I study these issues in detail in Malkin (1994b), chapter 7. The emphasis here is rather on the overlap-ping of Herakles and Melqart and the colonial middle grounds in which both played a significant role. For Her-akles in the west, see Jourdain-Annequin (1989b) with Mastrocinque (1993a). For the use of his myth in southern France, see Dion (1962), pp. 527–33. For the Aiolian Islands, see Castagnino Berlinghieri (2003).

11 Whether concerned together or discretely is an open question. Cf. Malkin (1994b), pp. 203–18.

why the myth was *expected* to be grafted onto this particular terrain. It is a mistake to see such charter myths as merely cynical or one sided. An invading
power with an explicit justification engraved on its banner somehow expects it
to be accepted. The charter myth was probably rife with significance both for
the people who followed Dorieus and for those threatened by him. Paradoxically, the myth was a powerful tool because it had been the threatened Phoenicians themselves who were initially responsible for the localization of Herakles
in Sicily. It was apparently the Phoenician cult of Melqart in western Sicily that
was responsible for the translation of the mythic geography of Herakles'
adventure with Geryon into concrete, colonial site topography.[12] A network of
a middle ground type, involving both Herakles and Melqart, may provide the
right perspective.

However, it will not be sufficient to identify the cult of Melqart in western
Sicily. We need to understand what it was in the figure of Melqart, specifically
in the context of Greek colonization, that made him the *archêgetês* of settlement, a focus of territorial and collective identity. Why was he so flexibly
translatable between the two maritime, colonizing civilizations of the ancient
Mediterranean? Once we understand the attributes that allowed this "translation," we may also understand how both could belong to the "same" network
with varying implications making their appearance relative to particular historical circumstances.

Beginning in the eleventh or the tenth century BCE, on the Levantine
coast of what are today Israel, Lebanon, and Syria, we find autonomous city-
states that were known to ancient Greeks as Phoenician. Instead of the polytheistic *koinê*, which seems to have been the rule in this area in the second half of
the second millennium BCE, each city now emphasized its own pair of protecting gods. Baalat Gebal בעלת גבל (Lady of Byblos), for example, was paired with
Baal Shamen, and in Sidon we find Astarte and Eshmun. In Tyre it was Melqart
who was dominant, yet associated in cult with Astarte,[13] and it is on Tyre, with
its unique god Melqart, not on "Phoenicians" in general, that we should
focus.[14] "Phoenicians" is a Greek generalization; Herodotus knew how to distinguish Tyrians from Phoenicians.[15] Although he spoke of Herakles in Thasos
and of the "Phoenicians" who founded Thasos and dug the "Phoenician
mines,"[16] he must have been referring to Tyrians. It was only in Tyre that

12 Jourdain-Annequin (1989b), p. 167.

13 Aubet (2001), p. 152; for an overview of the reassessment of Phoenician religion (replacing the old idea
of triads of deities), see Markoe (2000), pp. 115–42, and Ribichini (2001), pp. 120–44. For a detailed study see
Lipinski (1995).

14 Katzenstein (1997), Bunnens (1983); see also Sommer (2000). Again, as with "Milesians," "Chalkidians," and so on we may assume that other Phoenicians joined in trading and colonial enterprises. See Fletcher
(2004); contra: Descœudres (2008), pp. 310–11.

15 For example, Hdt. 2.112.

16 Hdt. 2.112; 6.46–47 and note 66.

Melqart attained any prominence, and Sidon was destroyed ca. 677, about the time Thasos was founded.

Neighbors closer than the Greeks, ancient Israelites such as Isaiah (chapter 23) and Ezekiel (chapters 27, 28),[17] addressed their prophecies of doom to particular cities, whether Ṣor (Tyre) or Ṣidon (Sidon), with "Canaan" sometimes approaching a *regional* term of reference. It was Tyre that colonized Carthage, Malta, Sardinia, and Gadir in Spain, often with prominent state temples to Melqart.[18] It was Tyre, therefore, that dominated Phoenician commerce and colonization in the Mediterranean during the Archaic period, and Tyrian patterns dominated in the spread of the cult of Melqart. Apparently Tyre had been deliberately using the cult of Melqart as an instrument of commercial and colonial policy.[19]

Ezekiel's words merit further analysis in our context, but for now the network aspects of his statements are sufficient. Note that in Ezekiel's prophecy Tyre is treated differently from the other subject nations. The rule of the Assyrians and Babylonian empires is represented as *'ol* [literally, yoke] imposed upon subject terrestrial nations. The imposition of the *'ol* is reason for mourning, and release from it is cause for joy. However, these are not the terms used with regard to the loss of the *rochel* (commercial) partners (28.19), accompanied by a sense of amazement, sorrow, and anger. Ezekiel (28.4–5) stresses the wisdom of Tyre in its commercial successes. It is the "trader of nations, of many islands." He employs technical commercial terms (*mdarav, izavon*), which imply a discrete yet familiar category of commerce. *Rochel* is applied to Tyre's commerce with Yawan (Greece), Tuval, Meshech (28.12), Dadan (28.15), and Judaea and Israel (28.28). In contrast to the joy about the release from the *'ol* of an empire, Tyre's partners will mourn since Tyre's fall signifies not another subjected nation but the sinking of a major hub of the network even for those not directly affected (Yawan).[20] In short, Ezekiel illustrates the contrast between the Middle Eastern type of empire and its *'ol*, and the commercial, often subject-free network of Mediterranean maritime civilizations.

---

17 Alfonso (2002); Kasher (2004).

18 For the reevaluation of the earlier date of the beginnings of Carthage, see Docter, Chelbi, and Telmini (2003); Docter, Niemeyer, Nijboer, and van der Plicht (2005 [2004]). Cf. Lancel (1995). In other places in the Mediterranean, such as Cyprus (especially at Kition, rendered KITTIM in the Hebrew prophecies), Crete, or Kythera or even with regard to various Phoenician enclaves, as in Rhodes or Pithekoussai, the organized role of Tyre is less clear. See Gras, Rouillard, and Teixidor (1989), pp. 53–78; Fletcher (2004); Elayi (2000). For relations between Tyre and Phoenician colonies see Ferjaoui (1993).

19 Aubet (2001), p. 150.

20 Tyre is רוכלת העמים, אל-איים רבים (merchant of peoples, looking to islands [or coasts]). Judea appears as a hinterland supplying Tyre with agricultural and elite commodities (including honey, oil, and perfume plants, if we understand correctly חטי מנית ופנג ודבש ושמן וצרי). Compare the twenty hinterland "cities" King Solomon gave Hiram who was not happy with their quality. Kings I 9.12–14. I wish to thank Matan Kaminer for drawing my attention to the significance of *'ol*.

Melqart was a new god. Unlike Baal, he is never mentioned in earlier second-millennium inscriptions. Josephus, quoting Menander of Ephesos, recounts that King Hiram (tenth century) destroyed older temples and built a new, joint temple to Melqart and Astarte.[21] His name clearly points to "urban" roots (QRT, city; cf. Hebrew Qiryah), thus linking him closely with the new phenomenon of the distinct Phoenician city-state. He was similarly prominent in the Tyrian foundation of Carthage, the "new city" (QRT ḤDŠṬ). Our meager sources provide no independent Phoenician mythology of Melqart, and the available Greek sources make Melqart part of Tyre's own foundation.[22] At Gadir, the Tyrian colony in Spain, the temple was built before the city itself, perhaps implying that for Tyrians the foundation of a colony began with the establishment of a temple to Melqart.[23] Eventually, such use probably heightened Greek awareness of Herakles, whom they identified with Melqart, as a hero associated with, or even justifying, colonization.

Melqart's role in Tyre was that of founder of both the city and the dynasty.[24] In this respect he functioned similarly to Herakles at Sparta, where Herakles acquired the right to the land and his descendants, the Herakleidai, founded both Dorian Sparta and its royal houses. Thus, kingship not only had divine origins but was coterminous with the essence of the state.[25] It is noteworthy that, whereas at Tyre the king was also the priest of Melqart, we hear of no such kings in Tyrian colonies. This is perhaps because the idea of kingship was so tied up with the king of Tyre[26] and with Melqart as founder of both city and royal dynasty that to have had other such kings seemed a contradiction in terms.

It is noteworthy that during the political debates that preceded Alexander's siege of Tyre, a delegation of Carthaginians was on hand to intervene.[27] It happened to be in Tyre on official religious business between mother city and colony, probably having arrived in the sacred Carthaginian boat that brought offerings to Melqart in Tyre. The delegation from Carthage encouraged its mother city to resist Alexander and promised aid that it was never to provide.[28]

All ties between a mother city and a colony embodied the contrasting poles of, on the one hand, an independent identity and, on the other, dependence on a source that provided for that identity. To have had "origins," a mother

---

21 Josephus AJ 8.3.145–46; cf. c. Apion. 1.117–19.

22 Arrian 2.15.7–2.16.7 and Josephus (see note 21, this chapter).

23 Aubet (2001), pp. 156, 195; for an excellent, detailed study of Melqart, to which this chapter owes much, see Bonnet (1988).

24 Bonnet (1988), p. 97; cf. Elayi (1986), p. 251, who suggests that Melqart was more a "poliad" deity than a dynastic one.

25 For other Phoenician-Spartan comparanda, see Drews (1979).

26 Aubet (2001), p. 147; cf. Bonnet (2011), p. 383. Herodotus (7.165–66) and Diodorus Sic. (13.43.5; 14.34.5) perhaps misrepresent the Carthaginian sôftim.

27 Quintus Curtius Rufus, Hist. Alex. Mag. 4.2–4. Cf. Amitay (2008).

28 Polybius (31.12) speaks of a sacred Carthaginian boat designed to send offerings to Melqart. Diod. Sic. 20.14.1–2; Arrian 2.24. 5; Quintus Curtius Rufus, Hist. Alex. Mag. 4.2,10).

city was imperative for both Greek and Phoenician colonies. However, Greek colonies emphasized their independent new identity around the cult of the founder, the one cult that could not have been imported from the mother city. Moreover, other religious cults in the Greek colonies, while imported, were not considered "branches" of the "central" cult in the mother city.[29] This is precisely what appears to have been the case in Tyrian colonies. The ritual delegation of Carthage appears to confirm this attitude inasmuch as it points to religious ties between a mother city and a colony that were even more expressive, continuous, and formal than those among Greek *metropoleis* and *apoikiai*. Phoenician ideas, so rarely glimpsed in our meager sources, now came to the foreground. The Phoenicians apparently believed that the Mediterranean contained several Phoenician-Tyrian colonies, all aware of their origin and all of them probably perpetuating the ties of their network by means of the practices of annual rituals.

The *MLK* element in the name of Melqart (Melkqrt) is usually translated as "god," mainly because it is found in contexts in which there can be no doubt that it relates to some "Baal." However, Melqart had some of the characteristics that are typical of a Greek hero, and *MLK* could oscillate between the divine and the human.[30] The king of Tyre was obviously a mortal. However, his neighbor, the Hebrew prophet Ezekiel, derisively accuses him of pretending to be a god. In biblical Hebrew the word *MLK* (the word *melek*, formed on the same root *MLK*) usually signifies "king," not "god," although it may combine with the idea of "god" as an epithet.[31] This "human" meaning of *MLK* helps to explain how Melqart could be perceived by another foreigner, Herodotus, as having had the dual nature of god and hero,[32] a distinction that the Phoenicians probably never had to acknowledge. Melqart was therefore a kind of supreme ruler closely linked with the king of Tyre, his priest. He embodied the principle of the sovereignty of kingship and the state and was responsible for the foundation and preservation of both.

The god-hero duality is not simply a question of ritual, a point that was of particular interest to Herodotus when he traveled to Tyre and Thasos to follow the cult of Herakles. The distinction was also political and related to the mutually reflective natures of human kingship and the idea of Melqart. The two parts of Ezekiel's prophecy on Tyre illustrate this distinction. In the first, the human king of Tyre is addressed as "Neggid Ṣor," rebuking his pretense to be a god, and in the second, where the king's earthly domain and commercial riches are described, he is called "king [*melek*, root: *MLK*] of Ṣor." The *Septuagint* follows the distinction with *archon* for *neggid* and *basileus* for *melek*.

29 Malkin (1991) with Rolley (1997).
30 Bonnet (1988), pp. 76, 108.
31 Bonnet (1988), p. 45. For a detailed commentary, Kasher (2004).
32 Hdt. 2.43. 44.

Apparently, some differentiation concerning the dual aspect of the concept of Melqart and the role of the king was misunderstood (or misrepresented) by Ezekiel.[33] *Neggid* may refer to the divine powers claimed by the ruler of Tyre and *MLK* to his human aspect of "king." For Greeks, who did not have god-kings, the distinction probably seemed comparable to what they knew as a differentiation between god and hero. Herakles, whose apotheosis was already known to Homer,[34] was the only Greek hero with both qualities. However, the Homeric Herakles was a wild hero, not a city founder. It is probable that the Greek-Phoenician colonial interactions in the Mediterranean, combined with the Phoenician emphasis on QRT [city], opened the way for the Greek Herakles to become *archêgetês* not just of dynasties but also of cities.[35]

I am suggesting here that the conventional term "syncretism" (Herakles = Melqart) be viewed through the network perspective, as we are not dealing with specific ritual and cult but rather with the "city founding and land possessing" associations of the god-hero. These issues were common to both Greeks and Phoenicians along various Mediterranean shores. The use of the term "archêgetês," in a (bilingual) Greek-Phoenician inscription from Malta dating to the second century BCE, may shed further light on the acceptance of Melqart as Herakles in the context of colonization.[36] The Phoenician text reads as follows: "To our Lord, to Melqart, Baal of Tyre: [This is] what vowed Your servant *'bd śr* and his brother *'śrsmr*, the two sons of *'śrsmr*, son of *'bd 'śr*, because he heard Their voice. Let him bless them." The Greek text reads: "Dionysios and Serapeion, the [sons] of Serapeion, Tyrians; to Herakles Archêgetês." Clearly, the Greek inscription is intended to convey the essence of the Phoenician one rather than to provide an accurate translation. The differences are telling. In the Greek text there is an explicit self-identification as "Tyrians," whereas in the Phoenician text Tyre is implied in "Melqart, Baal of Tyre," which is rendered as *archêgetês* in Greek. Moreover, as Corinne Bonnet argues, the term "archêgetês" itself implies this, as it is meaningful only for those who share their community of origin with the god, namely Tyre. *Archêgetês* as a title of Melqart also appears in a late Delian inscription of a corporation called the Herakleidai of Tyre.[37] Finally, Dio Chrysostom calls Herakles of Tarsos *archêgos*.[38] It would appear, then, that the Phoenician term "Melqart, [the] Baal of Tyre," in the possessive and in relation to a city, was interchangeable with "Herakles, [the] *archêgetês*."

33 מֶלֶךְ צוֹר 27.1; נְגִיד צֹר 23.11; Aubet (2001), pp. 147–48 and appendix ii.

34 *Odyssey* 11.601–604 (but see *Iliad* 18.117–19, where Herakles seems to be simply dead); see Gantz (1993), pp. 460–63.

35 Jourdain-Annequin (1989b) provides a detailed study of this role of Melqart-Herakles in the West, especially in Gadir and Lixos (95–135).

36 Bonnet (1988), p. 245.

37 *ID* 1519 (153/152 BCE).

38 *Orationes* 33.47.

Some form of duality is implied in "Melqart, [the] Baal [of] Tyre," a duality
that the kings of Tyre employed when officiating in the cult for the god Melqart,
founder and lord of their city and dynasty. When we observe the functioning of
the term "archêgetês" in Greek, we note a comparable duality in the exceptional case of the Spartan kingship. The Spartan kings used to be called
archêgetês,[39] perhaps relating to the notion of the Herakleid double foundation
of the city and the two dynasties. Herakles himself was worshipped in Sparta
as archêgetês.[40] Battos of Thera (itself believed to have been a colony of Sparta),
who was the founder of Cyrene, was also officially designated by the home
community as "archêgetês and basileus" (which Herodotus renders as hegemôn
and basileus). A sacred law of Cyrene mentions Battos as enjoying a founder's
cult as archêgetês.[41]

In Greek the word archêgetês has as its primary connotation the idea of
"beginning" and "origins" (archê), as well as "leadership" (agein). It may be a
god's epithet (as in Apollo Archêgetês) or synonymous with the human
founder but perhaps with genealogical connotations that the oikistês never
acquired.[42] Ephorus, for example, says that although Eurysthenes and Prokles
were both oikistai (founders) of the Spartan state and of its two royal dynasties,
neither was recognized as archêgetês, and their descendants were not named
after them.[43] Here the concept of archêgetês as founder, progenitor, and king
becomes explicit.

Why, when searching for an equivalent for "Baal of Tyre," was archêgetês
the term that came to mind for the two Phoenicians? To answer this question
we need to appreciate the modalities of the syncretism of Herakles and Melqart.
It is important to bear in mind that we are not dealing with a one-sided phenomenon or one with readily identifiable Greek and Phoenician "layers." The
joining of Herakles and Melqart was influenced by the fluctuating dynamics of
mutual perceptions. "On est confronté ici à un phénomène cumulatif et réciproque
d'assimilation profonde" [Here one is faced with a phenomenon of deep assimilation which is both cumulative and reciprocal], as Corinne Bonnet puts it.[44] As
we shall see, what Greeks made of Herakles, especially when they called upon
him to justify violent conflict, probably influenced Phoenician perceptions of
their own god. This is true also of iconography. The lion attributes of Herakles
apparently influenced sixth-century representations of Melqart in both Cyprus
and Tyre.[45]

---

39 Plut. Lyc. 6.
40 Xen. Hell. 6.3.6.
41 Meiggs and Lewis (1989), no. 5; Hdt. 4.153; Rhodes and Osborne (2003), no. 97, line 22; Malkin (1987),
pp. 204–16.
42 Malkin (1987), pp. 241–50.
43 Ephorus FGrHist 70 F 118.
44 Bonnet (1988), p. 401.
45 Bonnet (1988), pp. 410–12; Demetriou (2001), pp. 138–39.

Several modalities of syncretism between Greeks and Phoenicians seem to have existed. First, there was the Mediterranean network in which the ports and shores relate to each other[46] in a maritime network of connections that was present from the eighth century on and prominent by the sixth. Second, Greeks and Phoenicians developed, more or less simultaneously, a political culture of city-states. Third, they had similar experiences of founding new, mostly maritime city-states in new, sometimes overseas lands. Finally, they had in common the malleable and interchangeable context of polytheistic religion. It is among these networks, both material and mental, when superimposed onto one another, that we can best locate the dynamics that led to the mutual suppositions about the "identity" of Herakles-Melqart. What people did about such suppositions needs to be distinguished from the dynamics that led to their formation.

The colonial experiences of Greeks and Phoenicians contained many similarities. Their presence in the Mediterranean used to be described in terms of rivalry, perhaps by analogy with the rush of European colonial empires to carve up the world. In fact, Greeks and Phoenicians were contemporary colonizers, sometimes rivals, as was perhaps the case in late sixth-century Sicily, and sometimes intertwined in varying degrees of mixtures of cohabitation, as happened earlier at Pithekoussai.[47] It is no longer possible to characterize Greek and Phoenician colonization using modern typologies of colonialism. The overall perception used to be that there were far fewer Phoenicians than Greeks (which still seems true) and that Phoenicians preferred small trading stations (*emporia*), whereas Greeks opted for the agriculturally supported colony (*apoikia*). This assessment has changed radically, especially with the new chronology attributed to early Carthage and the discovery of a widespread Phoenician presence in Spain, where "agricultural" colonies no longer seem exceptional.[48]

It is worth recalling (see p. 22) the Mediterranean *longue-durée* perspective on the similarity of the political culture of the city-state, which also facilitated syncretism between them. As noted in the introduction, the eighth century BCE witnessed the emergence of a new, alternative political culture. Whereas in the Near East huge multiethnic empires were the norm until the fall of the Ottoman Empire in the twentieth century, Mediterranean peoples (Greeks, Etruscans, Phoenicians, Latins) preferred the small, close-knit, homogeneous political community, which eventually made room (in Greece at least) for the concepts of *koinonia* (partnership and rotation) and of the citizen (*politês*) to emerge. It is precisely because of the emergence of the political community in Mediterranean lands that communal-type heroes, *archêgetai*, were needed,

---

46 See pp. 42–44.
47 Ridgway (1992), pp. 111–18. Cf. Docter and Niemeyer (1994).
48 Aside for the overviews by Aubet and Marcoe, see, for example, Coldstream (1982), Niemeyer (1990), and Negbi (1992).

merging the vertical blood principle of aristocracy with the horizontal definition of society.

The shared network of these Mediterranean peoples was also religious,
revealing a common polytheistic *mentalité*. "Conversion" was never the issue
as it came to be in the colonization of the New World. Both the Greeks and the
Phoenicians maintained polytheistic systems of religion, the dominant principle of which was that "all is full of gods" (to quote the famous dictum of Thales
of Miletos).[49] The gods of "others" were either unfamiliar ("new gods") or simply the same but known by different names and characteristics. Herodotus in
particular was sensitive to the distinction between the gods and their
names.[50] Religion was *langue*; the names of the gods and their particular cults
were *parole*. For example, in third-century Rhodes, a Phoenician (Sidonian)
woman made a dedication to Herakles as the consort of Athena, implying a
syncretistic identification of Athena as a Phoenician goddess.[51] Conversely,
when Herodotus provides us with the Egyptian name of Zeus, he sees a "Zeus"
in the Egyptian deity (*langue*) even though his name, cult, and even status may
be peculiarly Egyptian (*parole*). It is as if he were saying, "That is how you say
'Zeus' in Egyptian."

"The law [*nomos*] of the Greeks," says Thucydides, "was that whoever had
power over any land, whether larger or smaller, to them also the sanctuaries [*ta
hiera*] should always belong, to be served as far as possible by the rites that were
customary before that time."[52] There was a sound religious reason for this
approach. Gods and heroes were perceived as "holding the land" [*echein tên
gên*], regardless of which polis had control over it. Thus, when the Argonauts
arrived at the banks of the Phasis they poured libations "to Earth, to the gods of
the land [*epichorioi theoi*], and to the souls of its dead heroes."[53] We may note,
too, how, before the battle of Plataia we find the Greeks sacrificing to the seven
hero-*archêgetai* who possessed the land of the battlefield.[54] In short, when arriving in a new land, reverence for the "local gods," particularly if these were
somehow perceived as *archêgetai*, was expected.

Whereas the Argonauts came only to visit, settlers needed a lasting peace
with the gods. It was therefore important to know who these were, if only for
the sake of proper ritual, and it was best if the local divinities and heroes could
be identified with their Greek "namesakes." For a Greek speaking the language
of polytheism, if Herakles was already "holding the land," even if known by the
Phoenician name of Melqart, the application of the Herakles myth could easily

---

49 Ascribed to him by Aristotle in *De An. I*, 411a7. Thales was probably not making a point about polytheism, but the dictum he seems to be quoting for his own purpose is sufficiently illustrative.

50 For example, Hdt. 2.50, 53.

51 Baslez (1986), p. 291.

52 Thuc. 4.98.2.

53 Apollonius of Rhodes, *Argonautica* 2.1271ff.

54 Plut. *Aristid.* 11.3.

follow. It is in this context that we should understand Plutarch's general statement about the activity of founders who received religious authorization at Delphi and were provided with "signs for recognizing places, the times of activities, the shrines of the gods across the sea, the secret burial places of heroes, hard to find for men setting forth on a distant voyage from Greece."[55]

When we turn to the convergence of Herakles and Melqart, a preliminary problem arises in identifying the components of "sameness." Of Melqart we know little. "Herakles," too, is not a person but a mythic hero, whose images and roles have had their own, cumulative history. The "twelve labors" and the ancillary adventures merely reflect an order imposed by mythographers on an enormous variety of Herakles-related myths. From the Homeric wild man and arrogant warrior,[56] he shifts in later periods to a civilizing hero and founder. Which "Herakles," then, was "syncretized" in the Mediterranean?

Scholars disagree on why the two were so readily identified. Perhaps, because Greek-type heroes are exceptional in other ancient polytheistic systems, what appeared to Greeks as heroic attributes of Melqart (who was mostly a god for Phoenicians) and had been almost unparalleled in the Near East (Gilgamesh, two-thirds a god, is a much earlier exception) made him appealing to them, especially as Herakles, too, was *heros-theos*.[57] Teixidor stresses the heroic commonalties as the basis for the syncretism,[58] but this is only a partial explanation. Greeks may have also linked the annual death and rejuvenation of Melqart with the ambiguous nature of Herakles' own death and apotheosis, a hero turned into a god. Most significant is Herakles' function as *archêgetês* of both kings and Herakleid city founders, which may have appeared remarkably similar to the relation of Melqart to the king and city of Tyre and to Tyrian colonies such as Carthage and Gadir. In short, both Herakles and Melqart could be perceived as heroes and gods, and both were *archêgetai* of heroic genealogical lines—of royalty and of city founders—implying the rightful possession of territories.

In his major study of the cult of Herakles-Melqart on Thasos, van Berchem points to Melqart's qualities as protector and guarantor of new foundations, his responsibility for contacts with the metropolis, and his role as mediator of cultural and economic ties with the indigenes.[59] He also stresses the ban on the participation of women and the "Semitic" prohibition of pig sacrifice[60] and notes that the Thasian festival of Herakles Sôter took place at the same time as

55 Plut. *Mor.* 407f–408a.
56 *Iliad* 2.657; 5.392–404; 638–42; 11.690–91; 14.249–56; 15.24–30; 18.117–19; 19.95–133; *Odyssey* 8.224 with Lacroix (1974), Bonnet (1988), p. 405; cf. Brommer (1986).
57 Pindar, *Nem.* 3.22.
58 Teixidor (1983), pp. 247–51.
59 Van Berchem (1967), pp. 88–109.
60 Van Berchem (1967), pp. 92–94, 97.

that of Melqart in Tyre.[61] His model is that of Phoenicians' living together with Thracians in Thasos, and he notes a similar pattern in the Aegean, at Lemnos,[62] and at Erythrai, where Pausanias tells us that the image of Herakles was Egyptian, having arrived on a raft from Tyre.[63] Only Thracian women were allowed to enter the sanctuary. At Kos the priest of Herakles would wear women's clothing to perform the sacrifice, a custom similar to that in both Gades and Rome.[64]

The famous temple to "Thasian Herakles," as he is called in inscriptions,[65] was clearly dedicated to the city's major god. In Paros, the mother city, Herakles had no special standing and thus his status at Thasos cannot be explained in terms of origins in the mother city. Herodotus visited Thasos and described Phoenician colonizing and mining activity there.[66] Thus, in Thasos at least, Phoenician priority seems evident, and it appears likely that Melqart's aspects of city foundation and territorial possession began gradually to be attached to Herakles and not the other way around.[67] What is noteworthy is that what happened in Sicily in the sixth century in relation to Melqart took place a century and a half earlier, when Paros colonized Thasos. Perhaps it was there that the city-related syncretism between Herakles and Melqart received strong emphasis.[68]

The cult at Thasos is important. To reemphasize the point made earlier (chapter 3): For a social *histoire de mentalité*, cult is more significant than myth. This seems counterintuitive, for one might think that myth, usually expressed not in ritual acts but in words, would be the more revealing of the two. However, a myth, explicit as it may be, might reflect only the concerns of erudite circles, poets, and mythographers. By contrast, cult signifies a living reality relevant to the community at large. Hence, the importance of the cult in Thasos: A new colony is established, incorporating into the city pantheon the cult of Melqart in the form of Herakles.

Whereas Thasos was a successful Greek settlement, in Sicily it was the failure of colonization that explicitly brought forth the territorial charter myth of Herakles. When Dorieus returned from Libya, he was advised by a seer to "found Herakleia, the one in Sicily . . . For Herakles himself, said Antichares,

---

61 Van Berchem (1967), p. 102, cf. 37.
62 With Homer, *Iliad* 23.745, and see Coldstream (1982).
63 Paus. 7.5.5–8.
64 Van Berchem (1967), pp. 108, 86, 31ff.
65 Bonnet (1988), p. 359.
66 Herodotus 2.44 with Paus. 5.25.12. For the mines, see Holtzmann (1979), who suggests that Herodotus may have been referring to the mainland; Muller (1979) for the mine on the acropolis of Thasos; des Courtils, Koželj, and Muller (1982). Cf. Morris (1992), pp. 143–46.
67 Van Berchem (1967), especially pp. 88–109; see also Launey (1944), Pouilloux (1974) [following Pouilloux (1954)], Bergquist (1973), Graham (1978), pp. 212–17.
68 Teixidor (1983), pp. 245–51. For Cyprus as a candidate for Greek-Phoenician acculturation see, for example, Jourdain-Annequin (1989b), pp. 144–57, 163–69. In general, Masson and Sznycer (1972).

had acquired all the country of Eryx to belong to his descendants."[69] He was about to reenact the myth of the return of the Herakleidai, now applied not to the Peloponnese but to western Sicily. Unlike a Delphic foundation oracle, this one was not addressed in the second person to Dorieus. Any Herakleid would have done, and Pentathlos probably had already employed Herakles seventy years before. The charter myth was circulating in the Greek world and was accepted by an Aiolian seer, an "Achaian" (Philippos) from Kroton (who joined Dorieus with his own ship), and Dorieus's own Dorian-Spartan followers. It was therefore firmly entrenched as Panhellenic. The Spartans, for their part, must have been particularly receptive to this type of legitimation inasmuch as they combined the personal-genealogical right of a Herakleid leader with a communal-political possession of new lands, the foundation of a new state, and the forging of a new identity. Was this not how Sparta itself had been founded? Herakles brought Tyndareos back from exile and placed him on the throne as a guardian. His descendants, the Herakleidai, "returned," leading a host of Dorians, and actualized their legacy. Now another Herakleid was setting out to do precisely the same thing.[70]

What, then, happened in Sicily? According to Thucydides:

> Phoenicians too lived all around Sicily, on promontories along the sea coast, which they walled off, and on the adjacent islets, for the sake of trade with the Sikels. But when the Greeks also began arriving by sea in significant numbers, the Phoenicians left most of these places and, settling together, lived in Motya, Soloeis, and Panormos near the Elymians, partly because they trusted their alliance with them and partly because the sea voyage from Sicily to Carthage was the shortest one.[71]

However, this description of the eighth-century encounters of Greeks and Phoenicians in what both saw as a trading and colonial land may be anachronistic. Those Phoenicians who abandoned the *emporia* ("for the sake of commerce," *emporias heneken*) around Sicily could not have been happy with this loss, and we may assume that violence occurred at specific points in time,

---

69 Hdt. 5.43.

70 Malkin (1994b), pp. 15–43.

71 Thuc. 6.2.6. Translation (modified) by C. F. Smith (1921). Cf. Moscati (1985); Tusa (1986). It has been suggested to me by an anonymous reader of this book (while still in manuscript form) that the prefix *ep-* in *epesepleon* ought to be translated as "when the Greeks started to sail in and attack them (the Phoenicians)," thus rendering the nature of first Greek arrival as aggressive. However, the meaning here seems "in addition," *insuper*, as Poppo/Stahl have it, followed by later commentators such as Classen/Steup and Marchant. Charles F. Smith, in his 1913 single-volume commentary, is explicit: "sailed in afterwards, i.e., after the Phoenicians." The Budé edition similarly has *à leur tour*. Bétant (1969, p. 358), who spells the word *epeisplein* renders it also as *supervenire (de navibus)* (i.e., in a temporal sense). In addition, LSJ (9th ed.) gives the present passage for the meaning "sail in after" and then lists Thuc. 4.13.3 under sense II for the meaning "sail against, attack." I wish to thank Simon Hornblower for a much longer, detailed clarification, although he bears no responsibility for how I present this.

although not as an overall Greek-Phoenician conflict.[72] Losing *emporia* is something that happened now and then; the Spartans, for example, lost their *emporia* in north Africa at the end of the sixth century.[73] "The Phoenicians" here are Thucydides' own generalization, more appropriately applied to them in Sicily when they converged into larger entities in three cities because of the arrival of Greeks.

The Phoenician presence (Thucydides uses the verb "to reside," *oikeô*, not "settle/found," *oikizô*) around Sicily before the arrival by Greeks had more in common with the floating *emporion* on a Phoenician ship, as described in the *Odyssey*: trading for a year with the natives of Sicily rather than with a fortified settlement.[74] Note that archaeologically, the "walled-off" sites appear much later than the eighth century. Motya's wall, for example, was built only after Pentathlos's invasion of Lilybaion (across from Motya) ca. 580.[75] The connection to Carthage, which Thucydides mentions as Motya's advantage, was probably more significant around 600, when we also hear of sea battles between Carthaginians and Massaliots (chapter 5). In short, whereas Thucydides implied resistance and conflict right from the start, this should not be read as a clash between two ethnicities, Phoenicians and Greeks. In fact, the initial situation in Sicily was more fluid, reciprocal, and transitory. Aside from Motya (see later), the two "Phoenician" cities, Soloeis and Panormos (with its Greek name), seem to have had mixed populations.

By the time Pentathlos of Knidos and Dorieus of Sparta, Herakleidai both, came to Sicily, the island had become "full" and conflicts appeared more generalized. The only area relatively free of Greeks was western Sicily—but the Phoenicians and the Elymians successfully resisted the Greeks, and both Pentathlos and Dorieus met their death there. It was in that area that the most explicit—indeed extreme—use of a charter myth became rooted: Herakles won the land from an eponymous hero and left it as an inheritance to his Herakleidai descendants.

In general, political and territorial myths become explicit in direct proportion to the threat posed to their realization. Situations of this nature arose specifically in the Spartan Mediterranean, perhaps as a legacy of Sparta's own Messenian Wars. The first expression of this is hinted at in relation to Taras in southern Italy, founded from Sparta right after the First Messenian

---

72 Moscati (1985); Luraghi (1991), pp. 46ff. Cf. Bonnet (2009), who tends to see this as a historiographical construct. Could Thucydides have had on his mind Carthage and its later attempts of conquests in Sicily? He mentions the distance from Motya to Carthage as a significant factor. However, Carthage's real involvement in Sicily came about shortly after the failed attempts of Dorieus at the end of the sixth century. See Hans (1983).

73 Hdt. 4.198 with Malkin (1994b), pp. 201–202.

74 Homer, *Odyssey* 15.403–84.

75 Graham (1982b), p. 187, Giangiulio (1983), pp. 793–94. For Motya, see also Longo (1999); Falsone (1988).

War (ca. 708), where we find an oracle commanding the settlers to "be a plague to the Iapygians." No comparable colonial prophecy exists.[76]

When Dorieus arrived in Sicily, the mythical itinerary of Herakles was already familiar in the region. Aside from Stesichoros, Hekataios of Miletos links Herakles with the eponymous nymph of Phoenician Motya.[77] In Motya itself mixture and hybridity existed side by side with the supposedly clear ethnic divide. For example, there were in Motya "temples revered by the Greeks."[78] It is likely that one of those had been a Melqart sanctuary. There is also the now famous statue of the "Youth of Motya," sculptured *à la grecque* but with the long, evocatively feminine dress that may represent the dress of the priests of Melqart.[79]

Soloeis, according to Thucydides, was a Phoenician city, but the archaeological evidence seems to indicate a mixed settlement, possibly a biethnic community. Herakles appears on the fifth- and fourth-century coins of Soloeis. More significantly, Hekataios indicates for Soloeis a charter myth along the same lines as those that we will soon observe for Eryx: winning the land from the eponymous Solous and leaving it in escrow for his descendants.[80]

Finally, Selinous, the westernmost Greek colony (founded in 628 BCE from Megara Hyblaia), oscillated among Phoenician, Elymian, and Greek poles and exemplifies the fluidity of Greek and Phoenician religious and political relationships. Regional networks came to matter more than the Greek-barbarian divide. Loyalties and alliances in the Greek colonial world did not necessarily follow ethnic lines, and much depended on ad hoc politics played out along regional network lines. Pentathlos found Selinous at war with the Elymians in 580, a war it lost despite his help and in which he himself died. Some unknown war between Selinous and Motya is implied by an epitaph dated to around 550, which reads: "I am the stele of Aristogeitos, son of Arkadion, who died by the walls of Motya."[81] Selinous sided with Carthage at the battle of Himera in 480, fought wars and made alliances with the Elymians, and was conquered by Carthage in 409. Before the Athenian invasion of Sicily, Selinous had a dispute with the Elymians of Segesta over some territory and marriage rights (which indicate, in and of themselves, the cross-ethnic, regional relationships).[82] To trick the Athenian envoys into thinking they had the means to pay for the war, the Elymians borrowed cups of gold and silver from *both* Greek and Phoenician

---

76 Malkin (1994b), pp. 115–27.

77 Hekataios, *FGrHist* 1 F 76.

78 Diod. *Sic.* 14.53.2.

79 Cf. Bonnet (1988), p. 275, who notes that sometimes we find the name *"bdMLQrt,"* for example, on stelae of the sixth and fifth centuries in the Tophet of Motya. For the various interpretations of the "Youth of Motya," see Bell (1995), pp. 1–4 with notes. See also the articles in Bonacasa and Buttitta (1988) dedicated wholly to the study of the statue.

80 Hekataios *FGrHist* 1 F 71–72; cf. Giangiulio (1983), p. 795.

81 Dubois (1989), pp. 71–72, no. 73.

82 Thuc. 6.6.2.

cities.[83] These incidents imply various modalities of mutual contacts. Dorieus perhaps relied on Selinous, but the leader who replaced him, Euryleon, attempted to take control over Selinous. There was also the anticipated blend: The Malophoros Sanctuary at Selinous contained a sacred area for Phoenicians, and the area near Temple C is full of Phoenician inscriptions (but mostly from after Carthage's domination).[84]

The Elymians inhabited and, one suspects, also mediated intergroup relations in an area in which Greeks and Phoenicians were close neighbors. Somehow they came to be regarded as originally "Trojans" and thus entered the Greek discourse of the heroes of Nostoi (return stories of the heroes of the Trojan war) and their ancestry of peoples in the western Mediterranean.[85] Formal Greek influences are evident, notably in the late fifth-century Doric temple at Egesta (Segesta). But such "Hellenization" did not mean pacification. We often find Elymians resisting and aggressively fighting Greeks. Egesta could also pit some Greeks against others. By the later fifth century its leaders were sufficiently astute as to convince the Athenians to invade Sicily.[86]

Western Sicily thus appears as a middle ground of cultural exchange, the kind we will also see in chapter 5. Characteristic of colonial regions, says Richard White, is precisely this sort of "middle-ground" acculturation (see pp. 45–48). But acculturation is not wholesale adoption. It is based, he says, on a "mutual, creative misunderstanding" in which each side draws a picture of itself according to the way it imagines the other sees it. The result, says White, is a new cultural terrain, accessible to both the indigenous and the newly arrived.[87] Sadly, because of the state of our sources, we will never know the precise significance that each "side" attributed to its "Herakles-Melqart." It is plausible that each explicit use of the hero would provoke a change in his "nature," for example, drawing his contours as city protector ever more sharply. Perhaps this was the reason Motya, in the aftermath of Pentathlos's invasion, raised its first-ever defensive wall and an anonymous Motyan dedicated a skyphos with the inscription . . . *lqrt*.[88]

Herakles first appears in Selinous on the famous Archaic metopes of Temple C, interpreted by some as "a colonial symbol of civilizing power grappling with wild beings" or a "frontiersman."[89] He had been one of the city's protectors,[90] and he appears on the city's fifth-century coinage. A statue found

83 Thuc. 6.46.

84 Bonnet (1988), pp. 276–78.

85 Thuc. 6.2.3; Hellanikos *FGrHist* 4 F 79b (= Dion. Hal. *Ant. Rom.* 1.22.3). On Nostoi: Malkin (1998).

86 For a history of the Elymians, see De Vido (1997). See also Nenci, Tusa, and Tusa (1988–1989).

87 White (1991), introduction.

88 Bonnet (1988), pp. 267, 276–78.

89 Asheri (1988), p. 755. Cf. Martin (1979), p. 13, with references to the metopes at the Heraion of Silaris and Poseidonia. See also Giangiulio (1983), pp. 805–806, and Marconi (2007).

90 As he is referred to in an inscription from Temple G, where he is worshipped together with Zeus, Hera, and the Malophoros. Bonnet (1988), pp. 276–78.

in the sea not far from Selinous is of the "smiting god" type and has been identified as Melqart, although it could represent another Phoenician deity such as Reshep.[91] Of special significance is an Archaic inscription in the Dorian dialect (Megarian) and the Selinuntine alphabet with a dedication in Greek to Herakles.[92] It was discovered at Poggioreale, a frontier site either in the *chôra* of Selinous or in Elymian territory and is variously dated to the late seventh or the early sixth century. The debate over its significance covers the spectrum of Herakles' presence in western Sicily. Some regard it as Greek, while others view it as an Elymian dedication influenced by the Greeks of Selinous or as a "Dorian conqueror." Still others attribute liminal significance to the "Herakles sanctuary" at Poggioreale, situated on the "border" between two rival cities, Selinous and Egesta.[93] For our purposes, however, the Poggioreale inscription firmly establishes the presence of Herakles, under his Greek name, about the time when Pentathlos invaded western Sicily. It was located in the middle ground (now in a more literal sense) between the Elymians, the possessors of Eryx, and the Selinuntines. Was this an extension of a Greek Herakles from Selinous, or was it a Melqart (written in Greek as "Herakles") protecting his territory relative to the Greeks? Or was it perhaps both—a mediating figure acceptable to everyone, Elymians, Greeks, and Phoenicians?

After Dorieus's death, the surviving cofounder, Euryleon, captured the Selinuntine colony Minoa and then attacked Peithagoras, the tyrant of Selinous. Then, having himself attempted tyranny, he, too, was killed.[94] Dorieus's purpose had been to "found Herakleia, the one in Sicily"; it seems a plausible inference that Euryleon attempted a refounding of Minoa as "Herakleia," thus perhaps accomplishing Dorieus's purpose.

Why "Herakleia" for "Minoa"? Our source for the name is mainly Diodorus,[95] who mentions Minoa as Herakleia for the first time in relation to the year 314, when the town was turned over to the Carthaginians. It seems that the site served competing mythological associations: The Seluntines recaptured their colony (probably reverting to the name "Minoa"), then lost it to Akragas, whose ruler Theron removed from there the bones of the mythical King Minos of Crete (who had chased Daidalos to Sicily only to be murdered in his bath by King Kokalos).[96] The Minoan association appears twice in Diodorus's mentions of the site, which may explain why he speaks of "Minoa" again for the year 357,

91 Bonnet (1988), p. 266. Cf. Morris (1992), pp. 208–11.

92 *SEG* 19 no. 615 with De Vido (1997), pp. 129–33.

93 Dubois (1989), pp. 84–85 no. 84; Manni-Piraino (1959), pp. 159–73; de la Genière (1978), pp. 33–48; Martin (1979), p. 12; Giangiulio (1983), pp. 796–97 with note 34; Domínguez (1989), pp. 400–403; De Vido (1997), pp. 129ff; De Angelis (2003), pp. 152–54.

94 Hdt. 5.46.

95 Diod. *Sic.* 4.79; 16.9.4; 19.71.7.

96 Diod. *Sic.* 4.79.3–4; see Dunbabin (1948b); D'Asaro (1991). Hornblower (2008), p. 292, says that it is possible, too, that Minoa reflects the "granddaughter" relationship with Megara Nisaia, with Thuc. 3.51.1.

as a harbor belonging to Akragas, while emphasizing again its origins in rela-tion to the myth of Minos.[97]

That Diodorus speaks of Minoa as "Herakleia" in a context where the site is turned over to Carthage is significant since Minoa seems to have had a Phoenician name, Makara,[98] expressing the presence there of Phoenicians and probably of Melqart. There is also a Phoenician coin from Herakleia Minoa with the legend "RŠ MLQRT," the promontory of Melqart,[99] but as we are not sure of the location of its mint its implications are limited. In any case, the Phoenician associations and presence in these areas before they were taken over by Selinous are clear: Neighboring Mazara was perhaps once another Phoenician *emporion*.[100] In 409 it was Hannibal Mago who chose it as a base in his offensive against the Greek cities. Therefore, it seems that the name "Herakleia" (for Minoa) was no arbitrary imposition. It was proba-bly the result of localizing syncretism, and its choice no doubt rested on the expectation that a preexisting frame of reference of Melqart-Herakles would facilitate its superimposition.

Euryleon's action may, on first impression, seem aggressively similar to Dorieus's. The name "Herakleia" seems to signify direct continuity by express-ing both a fulfillment of the foundation prophecy and the Herakleid charter myth. Nonetheless, it was founded in a different location, following a defeat at the hands of the Elymians and the Phoenicians, and the action now—wresting Minoa from Selinous and renaming it "Herakleia"—was against other Greeks. If this reconstruction is correct, the name "Herakleia" could also signify a reverse policy, that of mediation with Elymians and Phoenicians.

The Melqart-Herakles aspect of Makara (Minoa) probably helped Euryleon to identify the "Herakleia, the one in Sicily," which the Spartans had set out to found. Perhaps he was regarded as having been provided with what Plutarch called "signs for recognizing places." Generally, it was possible to redirect foun-dation oracles, often admitting some initial mistake; for example, the Phokai-ans abandoned Corsica (Kyrnos) and founded Hyele (Velia), having been told that the oracle was referring to the hero Kyrnos and not the island of that name.[101] Euryleon may have told the colonists that Makara, not Eryx, was the intended "Herakleia."

---

97 Diod. *Sic.* 16.9.4. The reference is misrepresented by Dunbabin (1948a), p. 353n5), who overlooks the "Minos" connection in this passage.

98 Herakleid. Pont. frg. 29 = *FHG* vol. 2, 220.

99 Bonnet (1988), p. 267. Kraay (1976), pp. 233–35, discusses the possible locations of the mint (Kepha-lodion, Herakleia Minoa). His argument against minor and distant Kephalodion as the mint is convincing. How-ever, his claim against Herakleia Minoa as the mint because it was "on the Greek side" (vs. Carthage) of the Halykos River seems irrelevant in view of the middle ground approach suggested here. I thank William S. Bubel-lis for help on this issue.

100 Morris (1992), pp. 204–208, on the possibility of earlier Phoenician presence.

101 Hdt. 1.167.

The choice of Herakles as eponym for Herakleia was probably perceived as authentic. It rested on a strong regional Melqart association and may have been expected to mediate relations among Greeks, Phoenicians, and Elymians. At the same time, it was turned against another Greek city, Selinous, whose colony, Minoa, had been replaced by "Herakleia." Instead of the superimposed Selinuntine "Minos" myth, Euryleon emphasized the "local" Melqart. This all unfolds among the same nodes: A "Herakles" is bounced back and forth (sometimes as Melqart) along the same trajectories but with varying meaning. What first Dorieus, then in his own way Euryleon attempted to do was to anchor the bouncing Herakles on the ground in the form of a Herakleia. This was a move from a relational role of Herakles to an irredentist one, legitimating not mediation but fixity. The Herakleia as a compromise (see later) was only a Greek type of compromise and not something accepted by others.

To the Elymians and the Phoenicians the change of names could have signified a welcome return to the older name of the colony (Makara = Herakleia) before the Selinuntines seized it and named it "Minoa."[102] For the colonists it retained its Greek character in the figure of Herakles. The hero is known for mediating compromises in the Greek colonial world, perhaps because of his Panhellenic status, both in the case of colonies of mixed origins (e.g., Herakleia Pontike) and in the world of Spartan colonization, where Taras founded Herakleia (a compromise with Thourioi) and Sparta founded Herakleia Trachinia with a mixed population.[103]

We see, therefore, how flexible the Herakles myth could be. Only myth, as a convincing package of logical contradictions, can evoke images of acceptable middle grounds. In the fourth century Plato would use myth to articulate what was beyond logical constructions, but this had always been the salient quality of social and political myths. Here an irredentist Herakles could easily be identified with Eryx because of the Phoenician cultic infrastructure of Melqart. He could still seem irredentist to the followers of Euryleon and at the same time be viewed as a pacifying and mediating hero-god to the Elymians and Phoenicians around Herakleia Minoa.

In short, in this area of mutual syncretistic influences—where Elymians could both fight Greeks and build a Greek temple, write their language in a Greek alphabet, and intermarry with and borrow expensive cups from both Greeks and Phoenicians; where artisans catered to both Phoenician and Greek tastes; where the cult of the goddess on Mount Eryx could have been regarded as either Elymian, Phoenician (Astarte), Greek (Aphrodite), or Roman (Venus Erycina); and where what was Herakles to some was Melqart to others—what mattered was the shifting middle ground that could allow the Herakles myth to

---

102 D'Asaro (1991), pp. 91–95. See Thuc. 3.51.1 for a Minos-associated name at Megara Nisaia, mother city of Megara Hyblaia and grandmother city of Selinous.

103 Malkin (1994b), p. 235.

be superimposed on the western Mediterranean and pinpointed at sites of the Phoenician Melqart.

If, as some historians believe, the Phoenician Melqart also functioned as a god of promontories for Phoenician sailors (note again, *RŠ MLQRT*), this would help to explain how the quintessentially terrestrial Herakles became associated (for Greeks) with the world of maritime colonization.[104] In other words, the maritime and city-founding attributes of the Greek Herakles may have first appeared among Phoenicians. What happened when the mythological, Mediterranean Wide Web was redirected to the regional network of western Sicily?

With Pentathlos the Herakleid from Knidos and with Dorieus the Herakleid from Sparta, Herakles' Sicilian section of his itinerary acquired irredentist aspects by serving as a charter myth for conquest, a replay of the return of the Herakleidai. A Phoenician Melqart was borrowed as "Herakles" to justify the appropriation of the land that had been under Melqart's protection. This was first and foremost a territorial appropriation, resting on a Herakleid justification that, at Sparta at least, there had been the basis of both dynastic legitimacy and collective identity. Colonization signified a new collective identity—not in ethnic terms as "Greek" but certainly as Herakleid and Dorian (Dorieus's own name is probably evocative). Had Dorieus succeeded, it is probable that the Spartan Herakleid charter myth would have functioned similarly in Sicily, creating a new political community whose core, as at Sparta, was ethnically and ideologically Dorian Greek, antagonistically positioned against the local inhabitants. In contrast to the Messenians of the Peloponnese, however, the Phoenicians of Sicily had already provided, through Melqart, the territorial connection between Herakles and the land.

However, both Pentathlos and Dorieus were killed. Euryleon founded a very different kind of Herakleia from the one intended for Eryx, positioned not against Phoenicians and Elymians but against a Greek city, Selinous, which he attempted to conquer. Minos was replaced by Herakles, conforming to a mediating and perhaps pacifying middle ground in which Makara, a city of Melqart, was one of the "signs for recognizing places" identified with "Herakleia," its equivalent. Thus, from the general Mediterranean networks of trade and colonization, where both Greeks and Phoenicians sometimes overlapped and where the polytheistic frameworks of religion enabled syncretism, we have closely examined the regional middle ground in western Sicily and the fluctuating roles of Melqart and Herakles. It is almost impossible to imagine the one without the other.

---

104 Brody (1998), pp. 33–37. Aubet (2001), p. 278, claims that Melqart protected commercial undertakings, with reference to Avienus (*OM* 358), who says that Phoenician seafarers would dedicate to Melqart.

5

Networks and Middle Grounds in the Western Mediterranean

The extent of the Phokaian network during the seventh and sixth centuries is staggering (figure 5-1). We find Phokaians in their home polis, Phokaia in Asia Minor, Amisos and Antheia in the Black Sea, Lampsakos in the Dardanelles, Naukratis in Egypt, along the trade routes beyond Gibraltar, in the Adriatic, and in the colonies of Alalia in Corsica and Massalia in southern France, along with various types of settlements. Some were mixed settlements (at Saint Blaise, for example), some probably *emporia*, some settled from Massalia, and others directly by Phokaians. Further settlements at Emporion, Hemeroskopeion, and Mainake bring us to Iberia. Elea in southern Italy (and possibly Leontinoi in Sicily)[1] closes the Mediterranean circle together with less direct Italian networks (Rome, Poseidonia, Sybaris).[2]

Herodotus provides a framework for the Phokaians in the Mediterranean, illustrating a general belief that the Phokaians had sailed farther than any other Greeks: "The Phokaians had been the first of the Greeks to practice long sea voyages (*hoi de phokaiees houtoi nautiliêisi makrêisi protoi Hellenôn echrêsanto*) and it was they who opened up the Adriatic and Etruria and Iberia and Tartessos. They sailed to these places not in rounded boats but in pentekonters [fifty-oared warships]."[3] At Tartessos, he says, they declined the offer of King Arganthonios to

---

1 Thucydides (5.4.4) mentions an area in Leontinoi called Phokaia.

2 Morel (1992, 1997), with references also to Eustathius ad *Il.* 2.561 on *Italia massaliôtiké* and Steph. Byz. on Troizen (s.v.), existing *en Massalia tês Italias*. Antonelli (2008) appeared too late for me to consult it.

3 Hdt. 1. 163 (trans. D. Grene): οἱ δὲ Φωκαιέες οὗτοι ναυτιλίῃσι μακρῇσι πρῶτοι Ἑλλήνων ἐχρήσαντο.

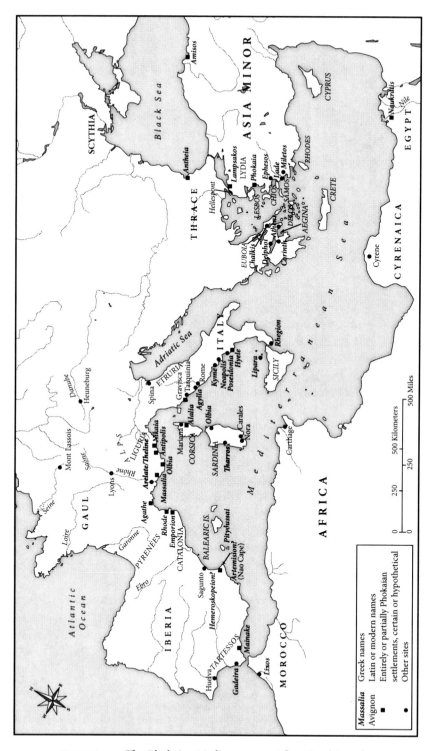

FIGURE 5.1. The Phokaian Mediterranean. After Morel (2006).

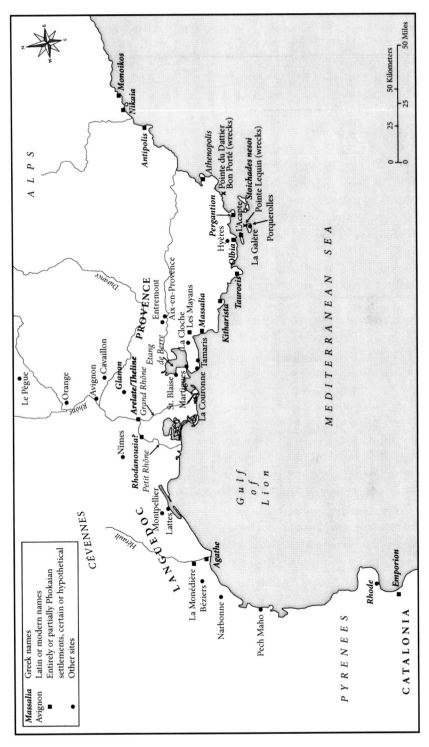

FIGURE 5.2. Mediterranean Gaul and the Gulf of Lion. After Morel (2006).

settle around the Gualalquivir (beyond Gibraltar), yet struck it rich. Excavations at Phokaia revealed the remains of its defensive wall, dating to around 580 and which Herodotus says was paid for by Arganthonios.[4] In 545, facing Harpagos, a major part of the Phokaian population fled to the west, carrying their *hiera* (sacred cult objects) with them, joined the Phokaian settlers at Alalia in Corsica (who had arrived there twenty years earlier), and built temples (*kai hira enidrusanto*), a sign of permanence. During the next five years they harassed and plundered their neighbors (*perioikoi*), and after a naval battle with Carthaginians and Etruscans, they abandoned the site, turned to Rhegion, and were redirected to southwest Italy, where they established themselves at Hylele = Elea.[5] There is no mention here of Massalia, although it is inferred, following the discovery of a significant increase in Greek material at Massalia itself around that time, that many Phokaians had arrived there as well.[6]

Maritime Perspectives, Maritime Networks

Before observing Massalia, let us observe an illustration of the Phokaian network in the Mediterranean *longue durée*. In the year 196 BCE, when Lampsakos was threatened by Antiochos III[7] and with its maritime and immediate terrestrial commerce disrupted, the people of Lampsakos sent someone known as Hegesias as ambassador to Massalia in order to further their alliance with Rome.[8] The people of Massalia and Lampsakos were "brothers" and justifiably so: Both had the same mother city, Phokaia. Moreover, Lampsakos apparently had disputes with its neighboring Gauls of Asia Minor that somehow were to be aided by Massalia. The Massaliots were inclined to assist. Their leading body, the "Six Hundred," provided Hegesias with a letter to the Tolostoagian Gauls. Apparently the Gauls, who were neighbors of Massalia, had relatives in Asia Minor.

This takes place in the Hellenistic period, centuries after the foundation of both Massalia and Lampsakos. It was a time when states took advantage of any kinship claim (Lampsakos also claimed to be related to Rome via its own purported relation to Ilion, or Troy, an ancestor of Rome). However, inventions were based on conventions, and some of these were more authentic than others. The ancient colonial network (Phokaia, Massalia, Lamspakos) was indeed centuries old.

The episode illustrates the *longue durée*, over centuries, of mental networks of affinity, with intermittent expressions. Schematically there are six nodes:

4 Akurgal (1956), pp. 4–11, especially p. 8; Özyigit (1994).
5 For a discussion of the various accounts of the Phokaians' arrival at Massalia, see Woodbury (1961).
6 Hermary, Hesnard, and Tréziny (1999), p. 51ff; Bats (1992), pp. 268–71.
7 Livy 33.30–34.
8 Frisch (1978); translated in Bagnall and Derow (2004), no. 35, pp. 70–73. I wish to warmly thank Ian S. Moyer for drawing my attention to the inscription and its significance.

Phokaia as a mother city, which is not mentioned explicitly; Rome, to which the combined embassy of Massaliots and Lampsakenes is eventually sent; Massalia, Lampsakos, and the Gauls of both Asia Minor and southern France. In network terms the episode illustrates how nodes physically distant from each other (time and again Hegesias's journey to Massalia is presented as long and dangerous) were more rapidly connected than nodes physically close to each other. To speak to Rome in the central Mediterranean, Lampsakos, in the eastern Mediterranean, needed Massalia, in the far-western Mediterranean as a connector. It also needed Massalia for influence over Massalia's own neighbors (the Gauls of southern France) in order to have influence with the Gauls of Asia Minor, the neighbors of Lampsakos. Time and space intermingled. The colonial network with its centuries-long existence operated spatially at any given moment, with the dynamics of short paths traveling by means of long-distance links.

Let us now return to the early history of the Phokaian network. Although some ancient sources identify the date of the Phokaian flight from the Persians in 545 BCE with the date of Massalia's foundation, it seems clear it was already founded around 600, a date supported by archaeological evidence (see figures 5-2 and 5-3).[9] Massalia was founded at a site whose position resembled that of Phokaia: a promontory between two ports. Massalia appears to have been founded with a view to both long-distance maritime commerce and the probable inland routes up the Rhône River. Yet the port itself, more than its exact position (which is not close to the river), seems to have been the determining factor for choosing the site, especially when taking into account that the *chôra* of Massalia was small and mediocre to begin with (it remained small until the second century BCE). In other words, the maritime perspective was more important than the hinterland one.[10] Initially, it could not have been entirely self-sufficient. Jean-Paul Morel rightly observes that "it survived through its membership of a Phokaian commercial network encompassing the Mediterranean as a whole."[11]

In contrast, ancient Arles was in a far superior position to control the Rhône, but a much less favorable one with regard to access to the sea, as it was some thirty kilometers away from it. The two communities, Massalia and Arles, immediately indicate the further complexities of the region: Whereas "hinterland" Arles seems to have been a mixed Greek-Celtic settlement,[12] maritime Massalia was a foundational colony, a Greek polis.

---

9 A convenient general overview: Hermary, Hesnard, and Tréziny (1999). See Tréziny (1997). For the literary sources, see the overview by Guyot-Rougemont and Rougemont (1992) and especially Raviola (2000). Note especially Ps. Skymnos, verses 211–14 (120 years before the battle of Salamis, i.e., about 600 BCE); Aristotle *ap.* Athenaeus, 13.576a; Justin *ap.* Trogus-Pompey, 43.3.4; Eusebius, *Chronikon*; St. Jerome, *Chronikon.* Connected with Harpagos's attack in 545: Herodotus, 1.164; Strabo, 6.1.1 C252; Thucydides, 1.13–14; Pausanias, 10.8.6; Isocrates, *Archidamos,* 84; Aristoxenos, *FHGr.* 23 II. P. 279; Ammianus Marcellinus, 15.9; Aulus Gellius, 10.7; Seneca, 7.8; Solinus 2.52; Isidore of Seville, *Orig.* 15.1; Agathias, *Hist.* 1.2. See also Gantès (1992).
10 Graham (1982a), pp. 140–41. Morel (2006), p. 381, with comparisons to Phokaia and Hyele.
11 Morel (2006), p. 366.
12 Hodge (1998), p. 160, and Rouillard (1992), p. 183; Morel (2006), p. 392.

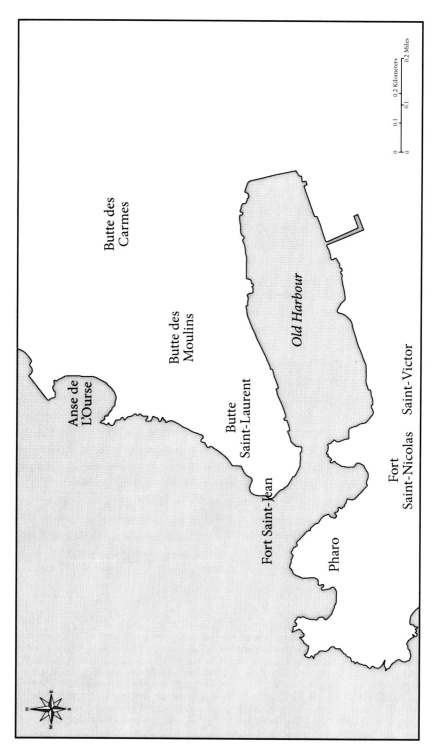

FIGURE 5.3. The site of Massalia. After Morel (2006).

The choice of the excellent harbor, "washed by sea around three sides of the town,"[13] is comparable to similar choices of Greeks in the Mediterranean, such as Taras, Byzantion, and Syracuse. Harbor choices illustrate the Greek maritime perspective: from ship to shore, observing lands and the options they offer as seen from the sea toward the hinterland. It was first and foremost a "backward" perspective, from the coasts "back to the sea," relating to it as a shared space of cultural and commercial connectivity. Ever since the Ionian migrations, Greeks continued to accumulate the experience of choosing the same kind of maritime sites: offshore islands, coasts by river mouths, and promontories.[14] By 600, Greeks in the "far"-western Mediterranean were also building on the accumulated experience of applying these settlement patterns, attached to the foundation of new colonies, to mixed settlements, and to sub-colonies. The latter were established mostly in the coastal microregions, advancing relatively little inland and also serving regional, short-distance coastal navigation.

It is not enough to draw a few points on the map, identify them as "Phoka-ian," and come up with a diagram of a Phokaian network. Alalia, founded in 565 BCE on the island of Corsica, is an excellent example of a contingency-dependent node (i.e., a historically contextual rather than a mathematical node), where we can estimate the difference between its intended role and the resulting historical functions. Alalia was founded by Phokaians, was connected to three networks, and probably served as some kind of link among them. It belonged to the more strictly regional network, involving its neighbors and the Etruscans. It came to be involved in a non-Greek, long-distance network with Etruscans and Carthaginians, and it probably served Phokaian long-distance navigation.

The choice of the site for the Phokaian foundation was not the best place to anchor a ship. In fact, the Phokaian settlement at Alalia could be said to be the worst on the island, compared, for example, with Bonifacio in the south.[15] But Alalia had two advantages: It possessed the best agricultural hinterland and a position facing Etruria. Michel Gras calculates that the *chôra* could support a population equivalent to that of Phokaia itself. He also considers that it was meant to absorb the many Phokaians who already had forebodings about their future in Asia Minor, especially in relation to Lydian aggressiveness and the rise of the Persians.[16]

According to Herodotus's account, the agricultural potential to support a large population was not realized at first. Perhaps that is why we hear of no opposition to Alalia during the first twenty years of its life, yet once the Phokaian refugees arrived there en masse, Alalia became a base for piracy. That a critical

---

13 Caesar *BC* 2,1; Strabo (4.1.4 C179) compares it to a theater. On the difference, see Hodge (1998), pp. 73–74.

14 Graham (1971).

15 Hodge (1998), p. 64.

16 On the demography of Alalia, see Gras (1985), pp. 393–442.

mass of Phokaians signified an awareness of something new is symbolized by the building of new temples (mentioned expressly by Herodotus). Temple founding turns a transitory presence into a permanent one, although it does not necessarily signify a new sovereign polis, as we can see at the Greek *emporion* at Etruscan Gravisca, where the temples served the local community and probably visitors as well.[17] Yet it is particularly significant in the context of foundation, as an intentional, self-aware ritual event, symbolically thought out. It has been observed at Megara Hyblaia as far back as the last third of the eighth century BCE.[18] Granting the right to build sanctuaries was obviously the major thrust of the charter of Amasis to the Greeks in Egypt (see pp. 81–93). Since the new temples at Alalia functioned up to the battle of Alalia (namely, not longer than five years), the symbolic value of such intentional action comes to the foreground since Herodotus's apparent point is to contrast the mere five years with the long-term plans for a permanent settlement in Corsica.[19] There had probably been some sacred precincts (*temenê*) already in existence that could have been used for the new temples. The newly arrived Phokaians, carrying with them *hiera* from their country, were perhaps re-creating their home temples on a more symbolic scale.

Let us observe what happened after the famous battle against the Carthaginians and Etruscans. In spite of the impression of total abandonment given by Herodotus, Alalia continued to exist but no longer as Phokaian. Strictly speaking, the text does not speak of abandonment but only of the "departure of the Phokaians," perhaps relating only to those Phokaians who arrived in 545 and not to the original Phokaian colonists. In any case, Alalia now became a mixed settlement of Etruscans, Phoenicians, natives, and Greeks.[20] Perhaps it had come to resemble the way it had been before the Phokaian refugees arrived, an unthreatening settlement amid other players.

During the sixth century, while Phoenicians, and more specifically Carthaginians, were extending their Mediterranean involvement, especially to Sardinia, Greek piracy in the western Mediterranean was becoming a difficult issue. It probably began with the remains of Pentathlos's army, which failed to conquer Lilybaion in western Sicily around 580, settled in Lipara, and harassed Etruscan navigation north of the Straits of Messina (see p. 80).[21] The settlers are described as sharing the booty and reallocating their lands every twenty years, so it was therefore a long-term problem. This was probably still continuing

---

17 Torelli (1971a), pp. 196–241; cf. Ridgway (1973–1974), pp. 49–51; Frau (1982); Torelli (1971b). Torelli (1982), pp. 309–15 (a special issue: *I Focei dall'Anatolia all' Oceano*), stresses the role of Phokaian visitors.

18 Vallet, Villard, and Auberson (1976); Gras, Tréziny, and Broise (2004); De Angelis (2003).

19 It is doubtful that entire temple buildings were completed during such a short span of time. What happened perhaps was that the new arrivals carved ambitious *temenê*, dedicated new altars, and in general proclaimed their ambitious building plans.

20 Jehasse and Jehasse (1991), p. 18; Hodge (1998), p. 141.

21 Diodorus 5.9 (probably following Timaios *FGrHist* 566 F 164; and Paus. 10.11.3. The latter is based on the authority of Antiochos (*FGrHist* 555 F 1). Cf. Domínguez (1989), pp. 551–52.

when, some thirty-five years later, the Phokaians, who were coming to Alalia from Asia Minor, began preying on both Carthaginian and Etruscan ships. The equilibrium of the mixed Mediterranean network (Greeks, Phoenicians, and Etruscans) was now disturbed, and with the precedent of Lipara, the Carthaginians and Etruscans took no chances and went to war.

Most of the Phokaians were forced to leave Alalia, and some of their prisoners were stoned to death by the Etruscans,[22] but in 565 the founders of Alalia were in no position to know that that would happen. Although the majority of Phokaians had not left for Alalia before the Persian conquest, it appears as if the original intention had been to establish a substantial foundational colony at Alalia. Phokaia turned to Delphi for a foundation oracle (thus placing the foundation in a Panhellenic framework)[23] and chose a site that could support a large population. However, as ambitious temples began to be constructed only twenty years after the original settlement, this implies that the beginnings were in fact modest and that the original nature of the settlements resembles more of what it later became, namely a smaller, probably mixed, settlement.

The Delphic foundation oracle, "to found Kyrnos," is interesting: It is a useful oracle for historians precisely because it was not fulfilled but excused and hence needs to be regarded as authentic (i.e., it was not invented after the fact, as in many cases). The apology signified that Delphi meant for the Phokaians to found a cult to a hero named Kyrnos, not the island Kyrnos.[24] That such an excuse had been necessary also points to the importance attached to the precise words of the Pythia in foundation oracles.[25] *Post eventum*, the Pythia appears to have been saying all along: Who asked you to take *all* of Corsica? Have respect for the hero of the land as its mediator, not as the justification for its conquest.

A delicate relationship existed between a network and the critical mass at its nodes. As long as Alalia was sufficiently small, involved in local-regional commerce, and probably serving as a station for the long-distance trade, it was integrated with the regional network, and its function was probably not very different from that of many other settlement projects in the area that roused no opposition, such as Gravisca. However, once the Phokaians arrived with their women and children, built new temples, and started preying on navigation, the critical mass shifted, interfering with the balance of the multiethnic Mediterranean network and provoking a pan-Mediterranean war that involved Greeks, Etruscans, and Carthaginians.

Unfortunately, we know far too little about the general context of the disturbances of the western Mediterranean network. Our sources (especially Herodotus) say nothing about an involvement of Massalia at Alalia,[26] although if it had not participated in this particular battle, it did fight wars with Carthage.

22 Hdt. 1.166–1.167.1.
23 Herodotus (Hdt. 1.167.4) explicitly mentions the Pythia. See pp. 203–204.
24 Hdt. 1.165.1, 167.3–4.
25 Malkin (1987), pp. 23, 72–73.
26 Bats (1994).

Thucydides says that "The Phokaians, when they were colonizing Massalia, conquered the Carthaginians in a sea fight."[27] It is not clear whether Thucydides was referring to the foundation of ca. 600 or, like other authors, conflated this with the flight from Harpagos in 545.[28] It is clear in any case that there had been at least one major battle between Massalia and Carthage, following which the Massaliots dedicated an image of Apollo "as first fruits of their naval victory over the Carthaginians."[29] Probably more than one such battle took place. In mentioning another impressively costly dedication at Delphi (a statue of Athena that was larger than the one in the Pronaia temple) Pausanias recounts that the Massaliots were colonists of Phokaia and adds, "They proved superior to the Carthaginians in a sea war, acquired the territory they now hold, and reached great prosperity."[30] It appears that naval wars were a preoccupation of Archaic and Classical Massalia and perhaps also involved Spain. Some scholars have stated that Carthage destroyed Mainake ca. 500, but there does not seem to be sufficient evidence for this.[31] In fact, numerous memorials were set up in Massalia for the victory over "those unjustly disputing the sea," as Strabo has written,[32] but little more is known about their circumstances.

Long-Distance Voyaging

It is impossible to discuss Greek colonization without having some idea of its role in the ancient Mediterranean economy. Interpretations of ancient economies oscillate between the primitivist model of an unalienated economy, whose priorities are embedded in social values, and the modernist case for applying universal criteria of profit strategies and control of trade routes, perhaps similar to those of the modern colonial age. Whatever position is adopted, it is difficult to deny that the ancient economy was also carried on board ships and that

27 De Wever (1968).

28 Thuc. 1.13.6. Some have emended Massalia in his text to Alalia, whereas others have noted that some manuscripts have "*Messalian*," thus perhaps a place in Africa. None of this is needed; we know so little of Massalia's history that we need not fall into the trap of making connections only between the few facts we do know. See Hornblower (1991), p. 46. On the text of Thucydides and its possible readings (e.g., one battle with Massalia or many), see Luraghi (2000), pp. 237–38.

29 Paus. 10.18.7.

30 Paus. 10.8.6; see also Bommelaer (1991), pp. 62–63.

31 For Mainake, the precise location of which is unknown, see Avienus, *Ora Maritima* 425–31; Ps. Skymnos 146–57 (*polis massaliôtikê*), claims it is the remotest Greek polis in Europe. Strabo (3.4.2 C156), calls it the westernmost Phokaian [*sic*] foundation and, arguing for the precise location of the long-destroyed Mainake, says that "the city of Mainake is farther away from Kalpe and is now in ruins (though it still preserves the traces of a Greek city)." Cf. Bats (2009), p. 203. Hodge (1998), pp. 31, 165–68, speaks of "Mainake, destroyed around the end of the century by the Carthaginians" (p. 165) and later says that "Mainake was destroyed by Carthage around 500 BC" (p. 167). He gives the reference to Avienus, but all Avienus says is that "Next to these there is soon the Barbetian ridge and the river Malacha with a city of that same name. Formerly it was called Menace" (trans. Murphy [1977]). Hodge may be following the statement in the article in the *RE* 1928: "Um 500 v. Chr. von den Karthagern zerstört, die Ruinen sah um 100 v. Chr. Artemidor (Strab. p. 156), später mit Malaca verwechselt (Avien. 427, Strab. p. 155) wie Tartessos mit Gades"; see Schulten (1928).

32 Strabo 4.1.5 C180. Cf. Justin 43.5.2 with Hodge (1998), p. 31n44.

strategic maritime sites were clearly on the minds of those choosing the places in which to settle. Some modernist approaches interpret these in terms of maritime international "zones of influence" (Phoenicians and Greeks), "sea lanes," and long-distance routes (see pp. 40–41).[33] Understanding the relationship between routes and settlement sites is crucial to both approaches. Georges Vallet[34] and Jean-Paul Morel insist on a modernist perspective, especially with regard to "straits colonies," beginning with Vallet's major work on Rhegion and Zankle. Pairs of Greek colonies were consistently founded across from each other on maritime straits, often within a generation, notably Rhegion and Zankle at the straits of Messina, Byzantion, and Chalkedon on the Bosporos (together with Herakleia and Kallatis) and Pantikapaion and Phanagoreia in the Crimean Bosporos. Similarly, the Phoenicians and Carthaginians settled in Carthage and western Sicily, as well as Gades and Lixus around Gibraltar.[35]

This is a convincing argument, and it seems almost self-evident that both Greeks and Phoenicians were well aware of the role of such straits relative to long-distance voyages. However, it need not be viewed as an overriding determinant of ancient Mediterranean *réseaux*, as Jean-Paul Morel thinks.[36] In his view, long-distance routes define the networks and explain the choice of sites for Phokaian colonization: His concept of *réseaux* is traffic oriented, and he claims that a *réseau* of settlements exists *pour assurer des traffics au long cours* [to guarantee long-distance voyaging].[37] He sees Greeks defining distant goals and, once determined, establishing new settlements to ensure the routes to these settlements. This type of claim had been made with regard to Pithekoussai, noting that the first Greek settlement in the west was also the farthest. I have my doubts on this point: first, since the nature of Pithekoussai itself is not clear, and second, because Eretrian colonization at Corcyra seems to be contemporary with Pithekoussai, thus rendering the pattern of "first = farthest" inconsistent.[38] Moreover, "distance" as such is not a simple concept. It does not depend merely on a ship crossing the sea from east to west but may also involve the interplay of several networks and nodes that can significantly foreshorten distances. Such foreshortening is an attribute of networks even though the agents involved may not have been aware of their accelerating dynamics.

---

33 Finley (1999 [1973]); Finley (1983) places little emphasis on markets and economic motivation and focuses his perception of ancient economies on the role of status and civic ideology; for a reevaluation of Finley's position, see Greene (2000). Also Polanyi (1977), who followed up on Finley's views, with Figueira (1984) on Polanyi and the ancient port of trade. For surveys of the various approaches to ancient economy, see Garnsey, Hopkins, and Whittaker (1983); Silver (1995); and more recently Cartledge, Cohen, and Foxhall (2002); Scheidel and von Reden (2002) and Manning and Morris (2005). See also Stager (2001) on maritime trade and hinterland production in the Bronze Age and Hasebroek (1965) on trade and politics in ancient Greece.

34 Vallet (1958).

35 Vallet (1958); Morel (1984, 1997). Less certain is Morel's notion that other early colonies were perceived a priori as couples: Pithekoussai and Cumae; Palaiopolis and Neapolis at Emporion; Catane and Leontinoi, Zancle and Mylai, Mylai and Metauros—all in Sicily. Phokaians: Massalia and Emporion.

36 Morel (1997).

37 Morel (1997), p. 60.

38 Malkin (1994a).

The issue of long-distance maritime traffic has dominated the perspective of research for a long time, and scholars have often discussed the Mediterranean as if it contained definite sea "lanes" and "routes," the mastery of which must have been of prime importance in antiquity as they were after the invention of the steam engine. In contrast, the category of long-distance maritime traffic is discussed in restrictive terms in *The Corrupting Sea* and with good reason. Horden and Purcell illustrate, for example, how many alternatives might have existed around the general outlines of any Mediterranean sea lane that served the reputed long-voyage category. Moreover, for significant parts of the Mediterranean, they offered the alternative model of *cabotage*, short-distance maritime traffic, which formed microregional networks that interconnected among themselves. Trade then moves from one microregion to the next.[39] Whereas Horden and Purcell seem disinclined to maintain both *cabotage* and long-distance categories, I find that the network approach allows for both: When conceived in terms of just a few links that connect regional, "thick" clusters, the effect is to foreshorten the connectivity of the entire network. We will see examples of microregional networks when discussing Emporion.

Some scholars, such as Wallinga, consider the metal trade as determining the goals of Phokaians at Spanish Tartessos.[40] Herodotus appears to make this explicit,[41] but then he is the one who relates that they refused the invitation to settle there. With regard to Massalia, Wallinga views it at the end of the tin road from Armorica and southern England. Similarly, Alalia lies near Etruscan iron and other metal deposits. Amisos could have served as a station on the road to Chalybes (Asia Minor), and Emporion is situated near the northern Spanish mines. Many have observed the probable role of the prehistoric tin routes from Brittany and Cornwall reaching Spain and Gaul through the Rhône valley.[42] This route applies, of course, not only to Greeks. In general, we may see Etruscan, Phoenician, and Phokaian activity and settlements channeled, like rainwater draining into riverbeds, into preexisting trade networks (see also pp. 21–25). Those preexisting networks of maritime, overland, and river routes could determine the choice of particular sites, indicating a trust in the continuing existence of the network. Whether *emporia* or colonies, new settlements then gave this prehistoric network a new dynamism and enhanced its range of connectivity.

Awareness and the use of long-distance routes may also explain specific network behaviors and choices made by ancient Phokaians, illustrating the role of human agency within a network context. They were following existing network patterns. After the Phokaian naval disaster at Alalia, they did not found Hyele (Elea) directly but first bypassed it and stopped farther south at Rhegion,

---

39 Horden and Purcell (2000), pp. 137–43.
40 Wallinga (1993), p. 70.
41 Hdt. 4.162.
42 Cf. Hodge (1998), pp. 57–58. Perhaps too much has been made of the Rhône valley as a Greek conduit during the Archaic period. See the perceptive assessments of Dietler (1997, 1998, 2005).

by the straits of Messina. It was only with the help and encouragement of Rhegion that they continued to found Hyele. Rhegion had been important on the route from Massalia via Alalia to Phokaia and especially for the trade in the Tyrrhenian Sea. Vallet goes so far as to speak of Phokaian-Chalkidian alliances[43]— but at this point I would shy away from this type of geopolitical explanation. Rhegion was perhaps interested in finding an ad hoc solution to the (Greek) piracy from the Aiolian islands, and a strong maritime "neighbor" at Hyele would have been welcome.

The question then remains, to what extent had there been a consistent Greek awareness of long-distance voyaging? There clearly was one, as spelled out in so many words by Herodotus (quoted earlier): "The Phokaians had been the first of the Greeks to practice long sea voyages." The recognition of the category is what is noteworthy even though the claim that the Phokaians had been first is dubious. It is interesting that Herodotus does not mention the earlier Euboian maritime, commercial, and settlement activities that reached both the Levant and Italy. In the *Odyssey*, when King Alkinoös speaks of the farthest land known to the Phaiakian sailors, he mentions Euboia: a Phaiakian illustration of long-distance voyaging.[44] The merchant Mentes in the *Odyssey* also suggests long-distance trade with the copper he buys in Temessa (whether identified in Italian Bruttium or in Cyprus).[45] However, Euboian Chalkis and Eretria sharply declined after 700, possibly because of the Lelantine war. By the time of Herodotus, what had been "long distance" in the eighth century had shrunk to "mid-distance" in comparison with the long-distance voyage to Gibraltar. Long-distance voyaging was not a one-time affair. It had to be purposeful to be meaningful, and Herodotus understood the difference. He tells of Kolaios of Samos, who also made a profitable long-distance voyage but as a result of a freak accident.[46] In contrast, the Phokaians knew what they were doing and kept doing it.

Their activity involved both *emporia*, some of which were mixed settlements, and foundational cities, or colonies. The *emporia* in particular served context-related purposes. They could relate to long-distance voyages as service stations or as termini, but they appeared for the most part to be active in the microregions, where they probably served short-distance mediations along the coasts in terms of the *cabotage* model and toward the hinterland as mediators of commerce with what some call local "gateway communities" (see p. 164). In contrast, Massalia was founded as a colony, continued to found new settlements, and was active in both the immediate microregion, in the middle regions of the western Mediterranean (Iberia, Italy), and in terms of long-distance voyaging

---

43 Cf. Vallet and Villard (1966).
44 Homer, *Od.* 7.319–24.
45 Homer, *Od.* 1.182–84. For the various identifications of Temessa, see Heubeck, West, and Hainsworth (1988), p. 100, and Stanford (1984), pp. 223–24.
46 Hdt 4.152.1–2.

and contacts with Asia Minor. I am therefore arguing for accepting all of these, the long-, mid-, and microdistance voyaging, with a few significant overlaps among all three. The overlaps functioned as links by connecting all three circles, thus enhancing the prominence of places such as Massalia and Emporion. Short-distance networks fed into the long-distance ones.

Emporia

I have so far been using the term *emporia* as self-evident, without attempting a definition. The debate about the nature of ancient *emporia* has acquired more prominence in recent years, when it has concentrated on problems of definition, assessment of aims, and issues of permanence and long duration. The latter were factors that could turn an *emporion* into a polis, as at Egyptian Naukratis. "Emporion" carries with it provisional or tentative associations. The most transient *emporion* is that of the Phoenician ship in the *Odyssey* that remains, perhaps in Sicily, for one year, trades with the locals, and then departs.[47] Some *emporia* probably did start that way, and once maritime routes became more frequented, such *emporia* served them en route and grew in proportion to the increasing volume of trade and traffic. This seems particularly apt for the long voyages along the Italian and French coasts, especially if we take into consideration the currents and winds that made long stretches of coastal voyages difficult.[48] Thus, the *emporion* played a role both on a microregional level and in serving long-distance routes at the same time. It is important to note that, most notably at Gravisca, a Greek *emporion* may consist of a community with some degree of permanence, living among a non-Greek majority—in this case, Etruscans, yet with symbols of continuity and community, such as temples.[49] Nicholas Coldstream has analyzed Phoenician enclave *emporia* in the Mediterranean along similar lines.[50] The issue of enclave *emporia* is important as it points to the complexities of Mediterranean communities and avoids simplistic archaeological interpretations rendering this or that site exclusively "Greek" or "Phoenician."

Not all *emporia* evolved. Some were founded. The variety of *emporia* studied by Pierre Rouillard, Alain Bresson, and Michel Gras and others is impressive and leads to the conclusion that *emporia* could be independent settlements, not merely protocolonies, or they could be enclaves inside other settlements, as at Gravisca, or settlements in the service of a *polis*.[51] In a more organized way they could perhaps also be purchased. The Phokaians, a people perhaps particularly

---

47 Homer, *Od.* 15.445. The identification of the island Syros with Sicily is debatable. See Heubeck, West, and Hainsworth (1988), p. 257; also Stanford (1984), pp. 256–57. See pp. 22–23.
48 Hodge (1998), pp. 22–29.
49 Gravisca: Torelli (1971b, 1977, 1982, 1988); Frau (1982); Solin (1981).
50 Coldstream (1982).
51 Bresson and Rouillard (1993); Hansen (1997a). For an insightful, comparativist study of *emporia*, see Curtin (1984).

fond of this type of settlement, as Ettore Lepore suggests,[52] tried to do precisely that when they failed to buy the Oinoussai from Chios.[53] Perhaps this is what happened at Hyele-Elea, which may explain the strange statement in Herodotus (1.167) about the way it was settled by Phokaians. He says that "they *took possession* (*ektesanto*) of that Oinotrian city, which is now called Hyele; [then] they *founded* (*ektisan*) it." Archaeologically, there is no evidence for such presettlement during the first half of the sixth century, so the idea must remain tentative. Hyele probably functioned within the context of commercial networks in the Tyrrhenian Sea and likely relied on Rhegion at the Messina Straits, which might explain why the Phokaians could turn to Rhegion and expect help, which did in fact come their way. Herodotus may have been describing the moment of transition at Hyele from an *emporion* to an *apoikia*, making it clear that this is where his story of the Phokaian flight from Asia Minor, carrying their *hiera* with them, finally ends.

From "Many-to-Many" to "Hub" Networks

During the late seventh and the early sixth century, the Phokaian maritime network was mediated neither by Phokaia nor by Massalia but was a "many-to-many" network that radiated from each node to the Mediterranean at large. In this way the variety of settlements and their applied connectivity enhanced the actual network of contact, of both commercial and cultural exchange, as well as the mental perception of the sea as the virtual center. It is difficult to assess the exact nature of Phokaian activity in the far western Mediterranean. A site such as Saint Blaise, whose ancient name is not known, existed at least since the time of Massalia's foundation (ca. 600).[54] It is a hill site in a land surrounded by lakes and not too distant from the sea and the Étang de Berre, where we also find Martigues on a small island connecting the Étang de Berre and the sea.[55] Saint Blaise is characteristic of the regional middle ground networks. Apparently Saint Blaise was a mixed settlement, a kind of international *emporion*, where we find local populations, Etruscans and Greeks. Around 500 it came under the influence of Massalia. In other words, whereas Massalia itself should be regarded as a foundation, other contemporary settlements may have begun as *emporia*, often with mixed populations, with no necessary direct links to either Phokaia in Asia Minor or to Massalia. Perhaps such dispersed settlement in small groups was more typical of Phokaian activity, as this seems to have been the case also in the Adriatic with the difference that no Massalia had been

52 Lepore (1970).
53 Hdt. 1.165.
54 Hodge (1998), pp. 143–48. For the Saint Blaise archaeological reports, see Rolland (1951, 1956) as well as Bouloumié (1979, 1982a, 1992); Sourisseau (1997, 2003). See also Bouloumié (1982b, 1984).
55 Chausserie-Laprée (1990).

founded there. At the Po delta, for example, Greeks, Etruscans, Umbrians, and Veneti cohabited from the end of the sixth century to the fourth.[56]

What happened to Saint Blaise and to several other points of settlement along the shores of southern France[57] seems to be characteristic of an overall process of what may be called *network homogenization*, following Albert-László Barabási's analysis of hub formations (see pp. 38–41). Colonial middle grounds appear first as rich and variable, extending geographically and spatially for long periods with an apparent equilibrium consisting of the activities of individuals, small groups, locals, Greeks, Phoenicians, and Etruscans.[58] No single power assumes control. Then, gradually, on a regional level, Massalia takes over some *emporia* and founds new subcolonies, thereby turning southern France into a Massaliot area. The nature of the regional network transforms itself from equivalent ties between its nodes to a more hub-oriented one with greater centralization in a single regional power (Massalia). With this interpretative approach, introducing a temporal dimension to the development of networks, a transition over two or three centuries from free, many-to-many connectivity to connections via hubs, we are no longer forced to choose between colonization on a centralized model and a chaotic free-for-all.

The network model thus also allows for a compromise between the modernist and primitivist approaches as it includes elements of both with varying emphases depending on the period and the extent to which the network functioned either as a middle ground or around a centralized hub. The regional homogenization noted for southern France was but a fractal of similar processes taking place in the wider expanses of the Mediterranean, culminating in the sixth century with the relative disappearance of Phoenicians from southern France, of Phokaians from southern Spain, and of Etruscans from both.

After the abandonment of Alalia (and possibly the destruction of Mainake), Greeks seem to have avoided the seas around Corsica and Sardinia, Etruscans seem to have reoriented themselves northward, and Phoenicians consolidated their *emporia* and colonies in north Africa and Iberia. Within a wider perspective, all this occurred when a general consolidation of what we call Greek civilization took place, a result both of the increased volume of the network and of the diminishing varieties of its agents of exchange.

Thus, the long duration of such processes allows for the mixed-bag character of the primitivist model of microregional and multiethnic settlement and trade, to coexist and evolve into a division that appears similar to the modernist approach of maritime zones. The traces of some influences persisted, for example, in the spread of the alphabet: Celts continued to use a Greek-type alphabet, and in the seventh century the Iberians of northern Spain adopted a Phoenician-related alphabet yet

---

56 See D'Ercole (2005), p. 167. Cf. the small Greek community at Tor Pisana (near Brindisi) from the second quarter of the seventh century. D'Andria (1988), p. 659.

57 Bats (1992).

58 Bats (1992), pp. 268–71, indicates the temporal framework: From the end of the seventh century to ca. 540, maritime traffic was split among Phokaians, Etruscans, and Phoenicians.

developed a semisyllabic script. In the east the Ligurians sometimes used the Etruscan alphabet (whose origins were Greek). Between these two frontier zones the
Ionian-Greek alphabet was more common.[59]

Mediating between the earlier, less regulated networks and the "hub-influence
zones" are the middle-ground networks, which function especially when some
form of equilibrium exists between numerous agents. That is how Richard White
views the North American middle ground, where for almost two centuries the
whites were another "nation" like the Iroquois or the Hurons. Similarly, from the
seventh until about the late sixth century, such equilibrium existed in the western
Mediterranean and allowed for the existence of *emporia* side by side with foundational colonies. The *emporia* in particular permitted very mixed groups to operate
on both regional and long-distance levels.

However, after the mid-sixth century the domino effect of the Persian invasion in the east brought about the influx of Phokaians to the west, culminating
in the battle of Alalia in 540 between Greeks, Etruscans, and Carthaginians.
For its part, Carthage was expanding its role in the western Mediterranean in a
manner analogous to that of Massalia, especially in Spain. A more modernist
realignment of networks now began to take shape: The Roman-Carthaginian
treaty of 509 already implied a clear vision of maritime zones regardless of how
seriously it was actually implemented.[60] If Carthage destroyed Phokaian Mainake in southern Spain just about that time (ca. 500), that would also lend support to the zoning nature of the grand-scale networks; the battle of Cumae
(Kyme) in 474, when Hieron defeated the Etruscans, saw Sicilian Greeks
involved in northern waters and a further shrinking of Etruscan maritime presence. But we also need to be wary of oversimplification: The zoning engen-
dered some traumatic events, such as the battles just mentioned, as well as
those mysterious battles between Massalia and Carthage, but it was also a very
slow process, one that allowed for both types of approaches not merely to
replace each other but to overlap for considerable periods and over significant
areas. Ancient Arles, for example, seems to have existed as an independent
mixed community for a long time,[61] and Massalia founded some of its major

59 Bats (1988), especially pp. 129–33. Strabo (4.1.5 C181), for example, says that most Gauls wrote their
contracts *hellenisti* (a Greek alphabet?) in Greek, as the Pech Maho tablet seems to indicate. Lambert (1992),
especially p. 291, for *hellenisti* "à la manière grecque."

60 For the Roman-Carthaginian treaty, see Polyb. 3.22–23. Walbank (1999), p. 341, gives a concise account:
"[T]he Romans 1) shall not pass the Fair Promontory and anyone driven thither by storm shall conform to certain
regulations, 2) shall trade in Libya and Sardinia only on certain conditions, 3) shall be free to trade in the Carthaginian province of Sicily on the same terms as anyone else. The Carthaginians 1) shall do no wrong to certain
specified Latin towns subject to Rome; 2) shall not touch any other Latin city; or if they do, they shall hand it over
to Rome, 3) shall make any stay in Latium conform to certain rules." For a discussion of the treaty and the various
identifications offered for the Fair Promontory, see Walbank (1999), pp. 341–45.

61 Rouillard (1992), p. 183. For the (mostly Roman) archaeological site see the "Informations archéologiques" series of publications in *Gallia* 1960, 18: 303–305; 1964, 22: 574–76; 1967, 25: 398–402; 1972, 30:
514–17; 1974, 32: 505–509; 1977, 35: 513–17; 1986, 44: 388–402. See also *Gallia Informations* 1987–1988 II:
229–39; 1990 I–II: 141–53. Although focused on Roman and Gallic Arles, Constans (1921); Rouquette and Sintès
(1989), pp. 11–16; Sintès (1996), pp. 23–37, contain short sections concerned with the pre-Roman settlement.
Also Arcelin (1995).

colonies in the south of France, such as Olbia, rather late—in the mid-fourth century—and some others much later on.[62]

Modernist claims about zoning should be appreciated within a context of networks operating within long periods of middle-ground coexistence. Accepting the equilibrium of Mediterranean networks down to the sixth century allows us to better observe both the coexistence and the shifting balances among a variety of networks: regional, long distance, and ethnic. For example, Enric Sanmarti-Grego advances the notion of "geographical zones of influence" and claims that Massalia's range of influence extended up to the Pyrenees in the west and the Adriatic in the east, whereas Iberian Emporion was oriented more toward the Iberian hinterland and the coasts down to the south of Spain. He believes that Emporion itself, until the mid-sixth century, was more Phokaian than Massaliot. Whereas the novelty of the idea consists in placing a different emphasis on Emporion's role, the vision is still monolithic and potentially static (Massaliot vs. Emporiot zones).

Assigning colonizing agency to either Massalia or Emporion raises a more basic question, one that emerges from our late sources, which confusedly shift between calling this or that settlement "Phokaian" or "Massaliot." The issue has direct relevance to the question of networks. "Massaliot" signifies a hierarchical mother city–colony relationship, a regional center–periphery control (short-distance colonies, founded not overseas but near mother cities, such as Akrai and Kasmenai, which were dependent on Syracuse and were not autonomous poleis). In contrast, "Phokaian" points to less systemized and more diverse types of colonies by Greeks (probably under the leadership of Phokaians),[63] who settled in a variety of ways and probably accepted a Massaliot identity, especially after the fourth century BCE, when Massalia extended its influence over existing settlements and founded new ones.

Most of the sources that enumerate the many cities on the coasts of France and Spain tend to refer to them as either "Phokaian" or "Massaliot." There is a clear danger here that any settlement that appeared somehow Greek was ethnically labeled, with historiographical hindsight, as "Phokaian" and politically labeled as a "Massaliot" foundation. It is to be expected that, similar to the "Ionians" in the east, "Phokaian" became equivalent in various native eyes to "Greek."[64] Similarly, "Chalkidic" colonies in Sicily came to be synonymous with either "Euboian" or "Ionian."[65] Although the scholarship is almost unanimous in accepting that Phokaians (and then also Massaliots) alone operated in the far west, it is important to remember that our knowledge is limited and

62 Hodge (1998), pp. 174–77. For more on Olbia, see Coupry (1954, 1964, 1981).
63 By analogy, during the Ionian revolt the entire Ionian fleet placed itself under a specialist, Dionysios the Phokaian, who commanded merely three ships: Hdt. 6.8, 6.11–12.
64 Hodge (1998), p. 138.
65 See references in Hornblower (2008), p. 293 (but replace his quotation "a blend of Chalkidic and Ionian" with "a blend of Chalkidic and Dorian" in Thuc. 6.5.1).

based on literary evidence that consists mostly of late geographical accounts, modern assessments of material evidence, and essentializing ethnic assumptions. It does not help scholarly research that the Phokaian pottery from Asia Minor was rather mediocre and that Phokaians seem to have specialized in carrying trade rather than exporting their own products, thus making it more difficult to identify them by their pottery.[66]

The multiethnic appearance of the early *emporia* in southern France points to a variety of Greeks, who arrived probably as individuals or in small groups, some perhaps intending just to trade and depart, and others choosing to trade and stay. Most of the sixth- and early-fifth-century settlements appear not as the result of foundational acts that involved both intention and a critical mass of polis settlers but as unplanned *emporia* that involved local elites, traders, and immigrants.[67]

Let us note, too, that the term "foundational colony" itself requires qualification. At Massalia, only Phokaians initially settled the promontory, whereas the surrounding area also yielded Etruscan material.[68] From rescue excavation in the center of Massalia it seems that between 600 and 575 the imported fineware was Greek (mostly east Greek and Corinthian), which seems plausible if it belonged to the first generation of settlers. Following that there is a change in the next quarter-century, when both fineware and imported wine amphorae are predominantly Etruscan. After the middle of the sixth century, we note a dramatic decline in Etruscan imports.[69] Before the influx of Phokaians, following the Persian conquest of 545, Massalia appears therefore as a commercial mediator *together* with Etruscans. Once the critical mass changed with the apparent arrival of more Phokaians, both Etruscans and Phoenicians seemed to disappear, and the shift from a middle-ground network to a homogenizing hub network becomes apparent.

Mediterranean networks did not function on a Euclidian plane, as Jean-Paul Morel seems to portray them.[70] The networks were complex, multidimensional, and multidirectional. Posing the question of "Phokaian or Massaliot?" or even "Etruscan?" places exclusive stress on the concept of "actor." Indeed, one of the trends in the current theoretical study of networks, called actor network theory,[71] diminishes the role of the "subjective actor" and stresses instead the "bundle" of factors that operate simultaneously, turning the actor into subject and object at the same time. Thus, in spite of the tendency of our later sources to point out a single "actor" (as in "this city was founded by Massalia"), perhaps the concept of a "bundle" or "cluster network" would be more appropriate. These are sociological terms

66 Boardman (1999), pp. 216–19.
67 Bats (1992).
68 Shefton (1994), p. 63.
69 Shefton (1994), p. 63.
70 Morel (1995); cf. Morel (1992), p. 16, and see pp. 12; 208.
71 Law and Hassard (1999). Cf. Mizruchi and Potts (1998).

that are partially equivalent to the historical middle ground. They suggest an alternative approach to an "actor-dominated" history (as in "it was in Massalia's interest that . . .") in favor of the more enmeshed historical circumstances in the western Mediterranean during the Archaic period.

Coastal Middle Grounds

Specific regions of settlement, such as the coastal areas of southern France, functioned as "clusters" by connecting to the major networks via local hubs. In historical terms, these clusters functioned as middle-ground networks that involved Greeks and non-Greek populations, some of whom were also immigrants, apparently stimulated by Greek presence. It seems likely that the storage facilities (silos, granaries) found in several native sites close to Phokaian settlements served for an exchange of commodities, compensating for a usually small *chôra*.[72] However, Brian Shefton and particularly Michel Bats call for an approach that is more sophisticated than a simple exchange among people.[73] In terms of our discussion, we note that the edges of the regional network produced new neighborhoods with a guarded outlook, marking their difference and serving as a vehicle of cultural and material transmission. This is perhaps more typical of the early situation than the later image of fortified sites (*teichismata*) such as those mentioned by Strabo: Agathe, Taroeis, Olbia, Antipolis, Nikaia, and some unnamed ones in Iberia.[74]

Agathe (Agde) is a case in point, as it is a foundation that followed long periods of middle-ground contacts. The first Greek discovery is in the native necropolis of Peyrou, which consists of four Greek vases that date to the third quarter of the seventh century (although there is nothing that marks them as particularly Phokaian). During the last third of the sixth century some Phokaians settled by the Bessan River, some fifteen kilometers from the sea, at La Monédière. They were also frequenting the site of Agathe (five kilometers from the sea), where they finally settled around the end of the fifth century. Morel remarks that the site is somewhat similar to Emporion: a small, similar rectangular plan, with a wall whose position changed several times.[75]

The actual site of Greek Antipolis (Antibes), probably founded during the last quarter of the sixth century, has not been found; it is apparently opposite (the name signifies "the city opposite") a native village with prominent Greek influence in its material culture.[76] This "dance" of Greek and native settlements, "talking" to each other at close distances, is a consistent pattern that is

72 By Emporion, Agathe, at Martigues near Marseille, and at Mont-Garou by Toulon. Morel (2006), p. 383.
73 Shefton (1994), pp. 65–66; Bats (1992).
74 Strabo 4.1.5 C180. Morel (1992), p. 17, sees these as defining the regional *réseau*. Cf. Bats (2009).
75 Morel (2006), pp. 389–90.
76 Bats (1994), p.146.

seen also in Massalia's later foundations. Yet this is a middle-ground dance: The "Greek" is not entirely Greek, and the "native settlement" seems mixed. Olbia (founded ca. 340) seems to have been oriented more to the sea, specifically to the passage among the islands of Hyères; similarly, Rhodanousa, identified with the "Petit Rhône" is oriented to the sea. It is not clear how Greek it was, beginning with material from the late sixth century with a significant increase after 475. Nice (Nikaia) was founded sometime between the third and the second centuries by a native village with a long history of exchanges with Phokaians.[77]

To further illustrate the partners' dance: About the time of Massalia's foundation we find at the site of Baou de Saint Marcel evidence for a native site that was settled and fortified ca. 575. It lies inland only seven kilometers from Massalia, and although it contains much Greek material, the place seems to have been non-Greek and newly established *in relation to* the Greek presence—all this within the first generation of Greek settlement.[78] The phenomenon of "antipolis" foundations is familiar in the history of colonization in various periods and areas. As Robert Bartlett has shown with the medieval colonization of Europe, as well as Walter Hawthorne for the upper Guinea coast,[79] settlement creates a new economic niche and attracts people from the hinterland who work and produce for the newcomers and trade with them. Sometimes, as Kenneth Kelly shows with regard to the history of seventeenth-century Dahomei in Africa, an entire "nation kingdom" can be set up on a European model to face those landing on the shore. The shore itself was a middle ground in the sense that neither Europeans nor Dahomeians had been there before.[80] Such observations should seriously modify some of the simplistic Orientalist notions current in postcolonial theory.[81] With Europeans arriving from the sea and natives advancing from the hinterland, both met on the shore. Colonization, then, stimulates or provokes what may be called "antithetical imitations." A new culture emerges in which the Dahomeians invent what they think is something similar to a European state, and European culture penetrates along lines that are very different from those known to contemporary Europeans.

The site of Baou de Saint Marcel is particularly symptomatic. As Michel Bats notes, the appearance of *emporia*, some independent, some promoted by Massalia, created a line of indigenous settlements along the coast, parallel to the Greek ones.[82] As mentioned, in the fourth century Massalia established a series of colonies, notably Olbia ca. 350, which increased the number of "parallel" indigenous settlements twofold. Thus, in a perspective of about two centuries,

77 Bats and Mouchot (1990).
78 Shefton (1994), pp. 66–69.
79 Bartlett (1993); Hawthorne (2001).
80 Kelly (2002).
81 Malkin (2004).
82 Bats (1992).

we observe the dynamics of population attraction, a familiar phenomenon in social geography.[83] These dynamics produced mediating coastal areas, with Greek and native settlements facing each other and probably *interdependent* in commerce, produce, and labor. The degree of dependency, specifically on Massalia, is sadly unclear because of the hindsight perspective of the late sources. For Strabo, cities such as Agathe, Taroeis, Olbia, and Antipolis were the *teichismata* of Massalia, but the term need not signify constant hostilities, and it probably reflects the later history of Massalia in the second and first centuries.[84]

Michel Bats, one of the best scholars dealing with these issues, applies the term "gateway communities" to the string of native communities that were created parallel to the Phokaian-Massaliot ones. The image of the two-way gate indicates a mediated two-way traffic of culture, yet in a measured way. It is borrowed from central-place theory and applied specifically by Barry Cunliffe to southern France in relation to central Europe.[85] The concepts of central-place theory may be useful on a microregional level to see the relationships between new, native gateway communities, set up almost in conjunction with shore settlements, and Massalia.[86] I prefer to remain with the term "middle-ground networks," forming local clusters that undergo fluctuating connections, for the simple reason that there was no center.

The "center" was the entire Archaic Mediterranean, free from any *mare nostrum* claims. It was multiethnic, multicultural, and, most important, multidirectional. "Greece" was no central place radiating outward. The perspective needs to be reversed: The "Greece" of our own abstraction had evolved from the network, the result of both outward *and* backward currents along the network lines.

Emporion

Iberian Emporion illustrates additional limitations of applying central-place-theory concepts. It is perhaps the most interesting site to illustrate the complexities of colonial middle grounds and maritime regions. Emporion lies on the other side of the Gulf of Lion, facing Massalia. Rhode, a little north of Emporion, is considered by Strabo as belonging to Emporion; its first archaeological traces point to the fifth century, and, like Emporion, it possesses a temple to Artemis of Ephesos.[87] We need, of course, to side-step the modern cognitive

83 Portugali (1993).
84 Strabo 4.1.5 C180.
85 For central-place theory, see Christaller (1933), also published in English in partial translation as Christaller (1966). Also Christaller (1972). On Christaller's work, see Preston (1983); see King (1984) for more on central-place theory and Kosso and Kosso (1995), who focus on Minoan Crete.
86 Barry Cunliffe's attempt to apply the central-place model is successful with some aspects concerning the relation to northern Europe and the domino effects of what was reaching it from the Mediterranean. However, I am interested rather in what happens *to* the network that causes the domino effect. See Cunliffe (1988).
87 *Polichnon Emporiton*: Strabo 3.4.3. Domínguez (2006), p. 445. For Artemis see chapter 6.

division between France and Spain: Whereas the hinterlands of both were geographically and ethnically fragmented, in maritime terms, from a ship-to-shore
perspective, the Gulf of Lion constituted a single region of connectivity.

How was Emporion settled? Late literary sources, notably geographers
such as Ps. Skylax, Ps. Skymnos, or Strabo, specify Massalia as the mother city
of Emporion, although some modern scholars prefer to see this as being at first
a Phokaian settlement that acquired its Massaliot attributes only later on. The
archaeological date of its beginnings revolves around 575 and applies to the little offshore island Palaiapolis (old town), with the settlement extending to the
mainland (as, for example, at Sicilian Syracuse or Thracian Thasos) within a
generation (ca. 550). In the modern literature it is called Neapolis. As a site
abandoned since the Middle Ages, it could be excavated extensively.[88] The concentration and proportion of the Greek material, mostly east Greek pottery, is
high in comparison with other Greek material found in either Phoenician or
Iberian contexts.[89] The Archaic pottery, with a strong presence of commercial
amphorae, is a mélange of Iberian, Chiote, Corinthian, Athenian, east Greek,
Phoenician, Lakonian, Massaliot, and Etruscan.[90]

In spite of denials that early Emporion existed as a civic-ethnic entity,[91] a
study by Denise Demetriou (2005) rightly stresses the fact that the term "Emporitai" (implying precisely such an entity) appears in a lead tablet from the mid-
sixth century at Emporion and another from the fifth at Pech Maho, indicating,
together with the fifth-century coinage bearing the legend *EMP*, that Emporion
was a polis (see later discussion). Also, as the same evidence demonstrates,
commercial activities involving local populations were predominant from the
start, hence perhaps the origins of the name Emporion. In general, there are
several settlements called "Emporion," such as in Macedonia, Sicily, and Campania,[92] Emporion on Chios, and Tanais in the Black Sea ("Emporion" was an
alternative name). A city's harbor could also be called Emporion, as Strabo says
of the harbor of Medma, a Lokrian city in Italy.[93] The Spartans were disap-
pointed when they lost the African *emporia*, mentioned in conjunction with
Dorieus's failed attempts to colonize there.[94]

The lead tablets just mentioned illustrate the commercial character of
Emporion, pointing to the microregional networks of commerce. In a lead tablet from (Neapolis) Emporion,[95] dating to the mid-sixth century, someone is

---

88 Almagro (1966), p. 14. Contra Plana-Mallart (1994a), p. 23. Her suggestions: 600 for the foundation of
Palaipolis and 580–75 for Neapolis.

89 Richard J. Harrison (1988), p. 74.

90 Bats (1998), p. 623. Cabrera Bonet (1996).

91 Hansen (1997a). Cf. Hansen (1996); Wilson (1997).

92 Stephanos of Byzantium, s.v. *Emporion.*

93 Strabo 6.1.5 C256.

94 Hdt 7.158; Malkin (1994b), ch. 7, especially pp. 201–203. Cf. Strabo 17.3.2 C825–26 for the Phoenician
emporia of north Africa.

95 Sanmartí and Santiago (1987, 1988); Sanmartí and Santiago (1988); Santiago (1990a, 1990b); Musso
(1986–1989).

asked to tell Basped, who is perhaps an Iberian, to transport his merchandise in exchange for half a share. Basped is encouraged to suggest his own price (if unhappy with the arrangement), getting first refusal before the sender can search for an alternative.

The second, a lead tablet from Pech Maho (today in France),[96] dating to about the second third of the fifth century (480–60?), has two inscriptions on its sides. One is inscribed in Etruscan. It is fragmentary and undeciphered, yet the name "Massalia" is readable,[97] thus testifying to the regional aspects of the local networks, which involved Greeks from Emporion and Massalia, natives and Etruscans. The other side is inscribed in Greek, constituting a legal document that describes a sophisticated sale of boat(s) at Emporion. The person buying the boat(s) sold a share of the profits to the person writing the document; he then paid his debt in installments in front of witnesses.[98] The boats were probably used not in long-distance trading but within the microregion of the Gulf of Lion or the inland river routes.

The lead tablet of Pech Maho provides an excellent illustration of an early multiethnic middle ground. Written in Ionian Greek, it deals with buying boats, and the witnesses to the agreement—Basigerros, Bleruas, Golo.biur and Sedegon—are clearly not Greek. Significantly, the tablet deals with a person who bought boats from the Emporitans, and it is possible that the boat was bought at Emporion itself.

The lead tablet reveals a multilingual world,[99] a middle ground of commerce where ethnicity seems to play no role and where people deal with each other equally, as if all are *sui iuris* (not as colonial masters and humble natives), with non-Greek witnesses testifying to a transaction in Greek language among (apparently) Greeks and on which, if connected, there is also an Etruscan text that mentions Massalia. This is perhaps analogous to the mention of Emporion on the Greek side of the tablet. This is an illustration of the extent of the networks of commerce: a Greek (possibly a Cypriote) buying boats at Emporion with a complicated deal of payments and installments that implied a trust in *future* transactions, namely in the continuing existence of the network. It spans Etruscans, possibly Cypriotes, Greeks who are probably "Phokaians" (or Ionians), residents of the western Mediterranean, and non-Greeks, who apparently

---

96 Chadwick (1990). See also Lejeune and Pouilloux (1988); Lejeune, Pouilloux, and Solier (1988); Pouilloux (1988); Ampolo and Caruso (1990–1991); Lejeune (1991–1992); Effenterre and Vélissaropoulos-Karakostas (1991); Rodríguez Somolinos (1996).

97 Colonna (1988).

98 "So-and-so (*perhaps* Kyprios) bought a boat [from the] Emporitans. He also bought [three(?) more] (i.e., from elsewhere). He passed over to me a half share at the price of 2.5 *hektai* (each). I paid 2.5 *hektai* in cash and two days later personally gave a guarantee. The former (i.e., the money) he received on the river. The pledge I handed over where the boats are moored. Witness(es): Basigerros and Bleruas and Golo.biur and Sedegon; these (were) witnesses when I handed over the pledge. But when I paid the money, the 2.5 hektai,.auaras, Nalb..n." Trans. Chadwick (1990), p. 165; cf. Demetriou (2005).

99 One awaits the full publication of a lead tablet from Lattes with two Greek names, Kleanax and Keosthenes (Michel Bats, oral communication).

understood what the document was saying in Greek. They probably also knew Etruscan. The personal microregional level of the middle ground thus joins with the grand context of the Mediterranean network.

What about the hinterlands? A dominant paradigm espoused, for example, by Ettore Lepore considers *emporia* as settlements with no agricultural hinterlands,[100] especially the Phokaian "outposts."[101] In contrast, a more varied picture now emerges involving labor and agriculture, cooperation with native populations, natural resources, and types of control.[102] Emporion, according to the previous paradigm, knew two phases. Palaiapolis was strictly commercial; "Neapolis" became a *polis* with a *chôra* in the fifth century.[103] However, according to Plana Mallart, Emporion, right from the start, extended its influence in a complicated web of relations with native populations and *oppida* that marked a type of Greek-native territory.[104]

Emporion thus illustrates how our perspective of what constitutes a Greek colony can be revised and nuanced according to circles of interacting functions and identities: first the offshore Palaiopolis, then Neapolis growing into a settlement with a Greek and native quarter, and a *chôra* comprising something like native *perioikoi*, all facing other, hinterland natives. The result was that Greek and natives together, all somehow Emporitai, faced other non-Greek populations. It is likely that the non-Greeks who testified to the commercial transaction in the Pech Maho tablet belonged to this category of Greek-native Emporitai or some other class of bilingual (or, more likely, multilingual) mediation. Perhaps these were non-Greeks residing in a gateway community. In short, Emporion illustrates that while a Greek-native divide did exist, its modalities were different from simplistic models of antagonism or enslavement.[105] This is how Strabo describes its development:

> The Emporitai formerly lived on a small island that is now called the "old polis" (*Palaiaopolis*) but now live on the mainland (*epeiros*). The city is a "double city" (*dipolis*), divided by a wall because in the past it had some Indiketans as neighbors, who, although they had their own regime (or "constitution" *idia*[i] *politeuomenoi*), they also wished to have [a] walled enclosure together with the Greeks for the sake of security. This is a double enclosure, divided in its middle by a wall. In time, they came together under the same regime (*politeuma*), mixing barbarian and Greek customs (*nomima*), as has happened in many other cases.[106]

100 For example, Lepore (1968), especially p. 34; Vallet (1968), p. 72.
101 Vallet (1968), pp. 136–40, especially p. 137.
102 Bats (1982); Benoit (1985); Nickels (1982, 1983), especially pp. 418–21, 423–25; Clavel-Lévêque (1983, 1999).
103 Sanmartí (1982).
104 Plana-Mallart (1994a, 1994b, 1999).
105 Examples of these may indeed be found at places such as Sicilian Syracuse and its Kyllyrioi or at Black Sea Herakleia Pontike and the enslaved, native Maryandinoi.
106 Strabo 3.4.8 C160.

The mention of a *dipolis* is striking as an articulation of the complexities of colonial middle grounds. As Demetriou notes, for ancient geographers, such as Ps. Skylax, it is a technical term that indicates, for example, islands with two poleis such as Mykonos, Ikaros, Ikos, and Skiathos.[107] In contrast, Strabo uses it in the sense of a "twin city," which for some reason, either natural or constructed, is divided into two parts, as he does in relation to Knidos and Nysa.[108] Livy, in his similar description of Emporion, also illustrates the difference between Greeks and *Hispani* in terms of maritime perspective:

> Even at that time Emporiae consisted of two towns divided by a wall. One of the towns was inhabited by Greeks from Phocaea (which was also the original home of the Massilians), the other by Spaniards. The Greek town was open to the sea, and the whole extent of its wall was less than four hundred yards in length; whereas the Spaniards, who were further removed from the sea, had a wall with a circumference of three miles. Roman colonists later formed a third class of inhabitants; these were added by the divine Caesar after the final defeat of Pompey's sons, and at the present time all the inhabitants have been amalgamated into one body, after the granting of Roman citizenship, first to the Spaniards and finally to the Greeks.[109]

By Livy's time, the name of the settlement had changed from the singular Emporion to the plural Emporiae, the result, apparently, of the union of Greek "Neapolis" with the Roman city (to its west), founded in the first century BCE.[110] Emporion allows us then to observe a *longue durée* of the colonial middle ground, from the time of Emporion's first settlement in the early sixth century through the maritime-hinterland, Greek-barbarian *dipolis*, and up to the foundation of the Roman city with the emergence of a kind of a *tripolis*, a "triple city."

The Emporion middle ground is an excellent illustration of what might constitute the "edges" of the networks. This is significant because in network theory *nodes* are perceived as "points." In contrast, the colonial middle grounds allowed for both points, such as Massalia, as well as less clearly delineated contact zones, with their own, regional dynamics. The network, therefore, should not be perceived as a fishing net tied to protruding poles at the edges since there never were clear-cut edges. It is precisely because the edges constitute a middle ground that the network can reach it and have some of its nodes exist *within* it. It is the constant ripple at the edges, the ripple of commercial and migratory mediation that was both regional and Mediterranean, that stabilized the overall network.

---

107 Ps. Skylax *Periplus*, 58. See Demetriou (2005). On "*dipolis*" in Ps. Skylax, see Flensted-Jensen and Hansen (1996), pp. 148–49.
108 Strabo, 14.2.15 C656 and 14.1.43 C649.
109 Livy 34.9.1–2. Translation by Bettenson (1976).
110 Peña (1985), especially pp. 71–76.

The Greek-Phokaian presence in the wider geographical dimensions of the western Mediterranean, between Italy and Spain, has led us mostly to the sixth century BCE, involving middle grounds of Greeks, Etruscans, and Phoenicians. All three belonged to maritime civilizations, and to all we can apply the maritime perspective, from ship to shore, that involves similar typologies of settlement sites, microregional activities, and long-distance voyages.

The concept of middle ground qualifies the type of network involved and seems particularly useful in understanding the role of networks and their shifting balances, with a trend toward the enlargement and homogenization of zones yet denying the a-priori modernist interpretation of monopolized sea lanes and clear-cut zones of trade and colonization. It also allows us to view, in spatial terms, the overlap between short-, mid-, and long-distance connectivity in the ancient Mediterranean. In temporal terms it explains the various overlaps between the primitivist and the modernist approaches to the history of the ancient economy and society. It allows a healthy perspective when criticizing teleological interpretations, according to which everything was leading to Massaliot, Carthaginian, and eventually Roman foundations and zones of influences. Yet it also permits us to accept some intentional foundations. We need to retain, as at Massalia or Alalia, the notion of foundational colonies, noting the role of a critical mass of immigrants that could fundamentally change the equilibrium of a network.

Just as Shlomo Dov Goitein has successfully illustrated in his *Mediterranean Society* the kind of connectivity in the Middle Ages that, according to Henri Pirenne, should have disappeared from the Mediterranean after the Muslim conquests, so does the study of settlement patterns and rare documents (like the Pech Maho tablet) reveal a multiethnic and multilingual complex world of Mediterranean connectivity, pointing at once to the regional and the long-distance categories of maritime connections.

The Greek-barbarian divide has also been shown to consist of a far more complex picture of enclave and other types of *emporia*, as well as gateway communities with natives migrating from the hinterlands and settling in coastal regions *because* of the arrival of new settlers coming from the sea, thus seriously questioning some current postcolonial approaches to ancient colonization. A middle-ground culture developed along the shores, and its influences stretched to the hinterlands, often along the river routes. But there was no central place behind the coasts—and no empire. The center consisted of diffusion and diversity. When we speak of "*the* Phokaians or *the* Greeks" in the west, we may need to delete the definite article in favor of a more nuanced network approach.

6

Cult and Identity in the Far West: Phokaians, Ionians, and Hellenes

Greeks were not always aware of the networks discussed in this book. However, some of the networks were quite expressive, as we have seen with the common altar of Apollo Archêgetês and its Sikeliote *theôria*. Cult functioned in Greek society as an expression of commonalities and communities and often defined principles of inclusion or exclusion. Within the new networks of the central and western Mediterranean, the geographical dimensions were extended. Sicily witnessed the rise of a regional network, expressive of the new, regional Sikeliote identity. The western Mediterranean cults, deliberately instituted and exported, functioned as expressions of the five major interrelating circles of Greek identity: the polis (Massalia, Emporion); the "Phokaian" (only loosely connected to the actual mother city of Phokaia); the regional (especially in southern France and Spain); the subethnic "Ionian," and the Greek, or Panhellenic.

By means of a network perspective we can better observe how these collective identities were either enhanced or defined and how they interacted with one another, including an observation of the Phokaian network with its (self-aware) similarity of cults and institutions (*nomima*). These also functioned on the discrete level of the polis, sometimes expressing Massaliot identity. Phokaian *nomima*, those sets of customs that regulated the sacred calendar, social divisions, magistracies, and more, provide a more positivistic aspect to the Phokaian network, freer of inventions and the manipulations of ancient literary traditions.

FIGURE 6.1. A visual perspective from the sea: the Phokaian Far West. After Google Earth (2010).

I place special emphasis on the Phokaian form of the cult of "Artemis of Ephesos," deliberately spread by Phokaians in the Mediterranean between Rome and Spain (for the "Phokaian Mediterranean" see figure 5-1).The goddess not only expressed Phokaian identity but also contextualized Phokaia and its associated projects of migration and colonization within a pan-Ionian context. Facing the non-Greek hinterlands, Artemis of Ephesos also mediated among the regional networks of Greeks and non-Greek populations, with a probable back-ripple effect on a generalized Greek identity. Pan-Ionian identity, revitalized in the face of external enemies (Lydians, Persians), was expressed by Ionians (other than Phokaians) in terms of potential or actual colonization overseas, west of Italy. The Phokaians, the only Ionians to do this, expressed the "Ionian project" with cults to Apollo Delphinios, together with some aspects of Artemis Ephesia. Finally, Phokaians, especially Massaliots, made special efforts to enhance their connection with the Panhellenic oracle of Delphi.

We can thus observe Greek networks, as articulated by Greeks in terms of cult and *nomima*, that express the "emic" (self-perception) rather than the "etic" (the external observer's perspective) point of view. To the extent possible, we may also apply terms of network theory to assess such networks in order to see how their dynamics contributed to the regional middle grounds (Greeks and non-Greeks in the western Mediterranean) and to the emergence and functioning of Greek collective identities.

Phokaians were considered Ionian Greeks, and what is remarkable about Phokaia's involvement in the western Mediterranean, as far away as Iberia, is that it was closely connected with a revitalization of an overarching Ionian identity in Asia Minor. It would be wrong to observe the eastern and western Mediterranean in isolation from each other or to treat sixth-century visions of Ionian migrations to the west as merely fanciful. A richer understanding of what it meant to be an Ionian Greek can be obtained through the prism of Archaic networks that connected the east and west by means of (mostly Phokaian) trade and colonization.

Greeks in Asia Minor (see figure 2-1) had been living in a colonial situation since the Dark Ages.[1] Their traditions followed the *ktisis* pattern of colonization with the motifs of founders, consultations at Delphi, migration, and wars,[2] although this apparent continuity was probably a later development, following the models of Archaic colonization. However, the sites chosen for settlement indicate genuine continuity between the Dark Ages (eleventh to mid-eighth century BCE) and the Archaic period (ca. 750 BCE–480 BCE). They demonstrate a remarkable consistency and similarity in the choice of settlement sites (see pp. 48–49), namely islands, promontories, and river mouths. Unlike the Greeks in islands such as Ionian Samos or Aiolian Lesbos, Greeks living in cities on the Anatolian mainland, such as Ephesos or Phokaia, were facing a huge non-Greek hinterland that could sometimes coalesce against them. This is what took place, particularly during the sixth century, first with the Lydians and then with the Persians. It was under these threats that a unifying sense of common Ionian identity and fate came into play. In Jonathan Hall's apt terminology, this is a case of "oppositional identity," a collective identity born from or enhanced by external threat and the compacting, objectifying vision of the enemy.

During the Archaic period Phokaia was an Ionian polis, and the Phokaians probably shared images of the Ionian migration to Aegean Anatolia and the adjacent islands with other Ionians.[3] The Ionian *ktisis*, a mixture of foundation stories and migration lore, had many variants but shared in the notion of migration over the water and the foundation of new cities.[4] Now, Ionians from Phokaia were about to embark on a new migration. To the Ionians in Asia Minor, the world around 600 must have appeared to be in momentous transition. Phrygia had fallen. A series of cataclysms involving invasions and conquests by Kimmerians, Assyrians, Babylonians, Lydians, Medes, and finally Persians all must have seemed to be part of a huge, escalating turbulence. Nineveh, for example, had fallen to the Babylonians in 612 and Ascalon in 604. Nebuchadnezzar besieged Tyre at the beginning of the sixth century,

---

1 Vanschoonwinkel (2006).

2 Schmid (1947); Prinz (1979).

3 Specifically, it may be possible that the Phokaians were (or saw themselves as) originally Aiolians who transformed into Ionians, Vanschoonwinkel (2006), p. 127.

4 See Sakellariou (1958) with Pearson (1975) and Vanschoonwinkel (2006).

a siege that lasted some thirteen years. This was also when the Greeks were hard pressed by the Lydians. Miletos almost fell to the Lydians, who were pursuing an aggressive policy of conquest in Asia Minor, resulting, among other things, in the destruction of Smyrna. When the Persians arrived, the citizens of two Ionian cities, Phokaia and Teos, relocated elsewhere.

Mass relocation to the west was apparently on the minds of Ionians even before the Persian conquest. King Arganthonios urged the Phokaians to abandon their homeland and settle at Tartessos; facing the Lydians, the people of Kolophon fled and founded Siris in Italy.[5] Specifically, Phokaia, too, around 565 seems to have considered this option, which is why it no doubt chose the fertile lands of Alalia in Corsica for settlement. In maritime terms Alalia is atypical when compared to Phokaian sites and is definitely inferior to other sites in Corsica (e.g., Bonifacio Bay). However, as Michel Gras demonstrates, Phokaia was preparing an alternative site for relocation (see chapter 5)

Some scholars also support the idea that Lydian aggression was the background for the pronounced Ionian colonization in the Black Sea:

> The constant armed incursions by the Lydian kings against the Greek cities of Asia Minor, on which they embarked not long before the end of the 7th century, had the most disastrous consequences for the Greeks. Their cities . . . were not only robbed of a chance to extend their territory but had also lost part of their *chôra* . . . There is no doubt that at critical moments in their history many Ionian *poleis* had to resolve to take the one remaining step open to them which could provide a fundamental solution to their problem—to leave their homeland and to settle elsewhere.[6]

Finally, it is perhaps no wonder that a myth was born that it was the Lydians themselves who had once migrated to the west to become the Etruscan nation.[7] This context of Lydian aggression (not long before the Persian arrival) is also the backdrop for Thales' famous suggestion that the Ionians amalgamates into a megapolis with a common *bouleouterion* (council house) at Teos (discussed later).

The Persian invasion in the mid-sixth century, which brought about the evacuation of Phokaia, thus appears as the culmination of mainlanders' attacks

---

5 Hdt. 1.168 (Phokaians); cf. chapter 5, note 4. Strabo 6.1.14 C264 speaks of the colonists as "Ionians . . . in flight from the dominion of the Lydians"; specifically, Teians (aside from those who went to Abdera?) founded Phanagoreia in the Black Sea. See Demand (1990), pp. 39–41. For the exceptional circumstances of naming a city after a living founder (Phanagoras) see Malkin (1986b). Kolophonians: Aristotle fr. 584 (Rose); Timaios *FGrHist* 566 F 51 (= Ahenae. 523c)

6 Tsetskhladze (1994), pp. 125–26. Cf. Akurgal (1962), p. 373; Kocybala (1978), p. 132; Balcer (1984), p. 49; Greaves (2002), pp. 107–108; Solovyov (1999), pp. 29–30; Tsetskhladze (1998, 2002). This view is contested by Alexander Fantalkin (2008), who puts forth a strong case for Ionian colonization resulting from cooperation between mostly Lydia and Miletos.

7 Hdt. 1.94; cf. (contra: a case for Etruscan autochthony) Dion. Hal. *Ant. Rom.* I. 25–30. See Briquel (1991); Drews (1992); Beekes (2002).

against coastal cities, both Greek and Phoenician. Around 600 the Phokaians could not have known that the situation would worsen, but it probably seemed harmful enough at the time. Ionian Greeks believed that they had once lived elsewhere and then were forcibly driven out and immigrated to Asia Minor. Now, around 600, when the world must have seemed on the brink of catastrophe, it seemed to be the appropriate time to pack up and once again create an overseas option. It was a realistic option based on the dynamism of a "colonial" network, on its lines of connectivity, and on the accumulated experience of creating new nodes and expanding the network.

Let us begin with some issues that Strabo mentions in a passage that recounts the Phokaian foundation of Massalia (with figures 5-2 and 5-3):

> Massilia was founded by the Phokaians, and it is situated on a rocky place . . . It is on the headland . . . that the Ephesion (i.e., the temple of Artemis of Ephesos) and also the temple of Apollo Delphinios were consecrated and founded (*hidrutai*). The latter is shared in common (*koinon*) by all Ionians, whereas the Ephesion is a temple dedicated solely to the Ephesian Artemis: for when the Phokaians were setting sail from their homeland an oracle was delivered to them, it is said, to use for their sailing voyage a guide (*hegemôn tou plou*) received from the Ephesian Artemis; accordingly, some of them put in at Ephesos and inquired in what way they might procure from the goddess what had been enjoined upon them. Now the goddess, in a dream, it is said, had stood beside Aristarcha, one of the women held in very high honour, and commanded her to sail away with the Phokaians, taking with her some *aphidruma* (a sacred object, here probably a cult statue) from the temples. This done and the colony finally settled, they not only established the temple but also did Aristarcha the exceptional honour of appointing her priestess; further, in all the daughter *poleis* (*en . . . apoikois polesi*, either those of Massalia or other Phokaian cities) the people everywhere do this goddess honours of the first rank, and they maintain the same shape of the *xoanon* and otherwise adhere to the same *nomima*, which were traditional (*nenomisthai*) in the metropolis.[8]

Apollo Delphinios and the Ionians

Unlike Artemis Ephesia, the temple of Apollo Delphinios at Massalia was meant to serve "all Ionians." The statement is sufficiently curious to be credible, for it is difficult to understand what Strabo could have meant by this if

---

8 Strabo 4.1.4 C179, trans. Horace L. Jones (1917), LCL (heavily modified).

it did not come to him from an ancient source.[9] It is clearly not a statement of hindsight, as the temple obviously never became a pan-Ionian temple. Nor is it a statement of contemporary fact, as in "Ionian cities worship Apollo Delphinios, but not all worship Artemis of Ephesos." In fact, non-Ionians worshipped him, too, and many Ionians, particularly in the west, did worship Artemis of Ephesos, as Strabo himself indicates. Moreover, as we will see, Artemis of Ephesos herself had pan-Ionian functions as an Ionian *hegemônê (hegemôniê)*. It thus seems that Strabo, within the context of recounting the Phokaian purpose, speaks of the temple of Apollo Delphinios in Massalia in terms of what it was intended to be. Strabo's statement that the Ephesian Artemis belonged only to Massalia, whereas that of Apollo Delphinios belonged to all Ionians, exemplifies the reversal between what may have been the planned and the eventual historical outcome. Subsequently the Apollo Delphinios of Massalia had no more pan-Ionian status than Apollo Delphinios at the mother city, Phokaia,[10] whereas the cult of Artemis Ephesia is the one that became common to the Greeks in the west but never expressly as pan-Ionian.[11]

Why was the Apollo of Massalia worshipped as Delphinios? There is much to say about Apollo as Delphinios, such as his dolphin epithet and Apollo's maritime attributes, which include the dolphin as a "guide" at sea—a parallel to Apollo Aigyeus and Archêgetês on land, and Apollo *embasios* and *ekbasios*, god of embarkations and disembarkations from ships.[12] The title Delphinios is also associated with Delphi and the *Homeric Hymn to Apollo*. Having landed with the shipload of bewildered Cretans whom Apollo had abducted to serve as his priests and before setting out for the first time to the site of the oracle up on the mountain, the newly appointed priests disembarked and sacrificed on the beach to Apollo as Delphinios.[13] This act seems to signify a special moment, celebrating an arrival at a new land for the purpose of a new foundation.[14]

Unlike Apollo Karneios, a salient Dorian god, Apollo Delphinios was more universal,[15] sharing a Delphic (Panhellenic) association, yet in terms of the

---

9 Strabo 4.1.3–4 C179. For a short review of Strabo's sources, see Dueck (2000), pp. 180–86. Lasserre (1966), pp. 4–11, and (1969), pp. xxxiv–xlii, attributes Strabo's sources for Massalia to Poseidonius. His view is dismissed by Dirkzwager (1975), pp. 3–13, 28, 38f, 43, 62, 66, 86.

10 Graf (1985), pp. 401–23. Apollo and Artemis: pp. 410–17.

11 The statement in Strabo should be read in relation to what Phokaian settlers intended and to the results of those intentions. This is, after all, the theme of the entire excursus. I need to stress this because a literary reading of the sentence is possible, signifying merely a general description: "Apollo Delphinios is a cult which is common to all the Ionians (or perhaps, 'to the cities of Ionia'?), but the other temple is a temple of the Artemis of [just one of them] Ephesos." However, this makes little sense. In the *Homeric Hymn to Apollo*, for example, he is not "Ionian" and is rather associated with Cretans. The erudite Strabo must have known that he was a god also of non-Ionian Greeks. Strabo is providing a description of the constitutive acts of the new polis, not a general lecture on Greek cult. One major result of these constitutive acts had been the spread of the cult of Artemis of Ephesos by Phokaians, to which Strabo keeps referring because it was a cult peculiar to them in the west. I believe that the historical circumstances I analyze here explain why there was no comparable result with the cult of Apollo Delphinios.

12 See chapter 3, note 23.

13 *Homeric Hymn to Apollo*, 487–96.

14 For echoes of Greek colonization practices in the *Homeric Hymn*, see Malkin (2000).

reality of his cult he was prominently present in Ionian cities. At Miletos his sanctuary was located in the agora at the port, and the god is found in Milesian colonies, notably at Black Sea Olbia.[16] In myths found in late sources, Apollo is presumed to have arrived at Didyma from Delos, riding a Dolphin.[17] The Sacred Harbor (*hieros limen*) of Oropos, facing Eretria, was called Delphinion.[18] Phokaia, too, had a Delphinion, and at Chios the Delphinios was the name of the harbor, some fifteen kilometers north of the capital of Chios.[19]

Pan-Ionianism was a relevant, early sixth-century discourse, especially in view of the rise of the Persians. But it began earlier. When Lydian power was still prominent, Thales suggested founding a common Ionian Bouleuterion at Teos, suppressing the political autonomy of each Ionian polis. Herodotus mentions Thales specifically as the antecedent to Bias of Priene, who, just after the Persian invasion, suggested fleeing and creating a single Ionian state in Sardinia.[20] It is not clear from the context in Herodotus's writings when precisely these pan-Ionian meetings were taking place.[21] Thales is said to have given his advice "before the destruction," leaving the chronology obscure, although the solar eclipse he is said to have predicted anchors him in 585 BCE.[22] Thales was probably aware that Lydia had been confronting other powers, notably the Medes, before the Persians. Although Kroisos ended his war with the Medes in a draw and a diplomatic marriage,[23] there was probably good reason to imagine

---

15 On Apollo Delphinios, see Farnell (1896), vol. 4, pp. 145–48, who supports the identification of Apollo Delphinios with maritime activity and with the dolphin; also Fontenrose (1988), pp. 121–22. His prominent political and social functions might overshadow, but were not exclusive to, his maritime roles. See Gorman (2001), pp. 168–74, who dismisses for such reasons the association made between Apollo Delphinios, seafaring, and colonization. Detienne (1998), pp. 19–39; see also Graf (1979) and Graf (1985), pp. 56–57.

16 On the importance of Apollo Delphinios in Miletos and the Delphinion temple, see Greaves (2002), pp. 109–30, especially 123, 126–27; Herda (2008). Greaves examines the oracle of Apollo at Didyma and its relations with Miletos. The central role of Didyma and Apollo in the religious life of the Miletos no doubt enhanced the significance of the cult of Apollo Delphinios in the city and of the deity's main sanctuary, the Delphinion, as in the case of oracular responses from Didyma, recorded on inscriptions from the Delphinion. Gorman (2001), p. 196:

> Didyma was a tremendously important Panhellenic center. Control over it gave the Milesians considerable honor and prestige, and the various cults of Apollo at Miletos gained all that much more distinction as a result of their connection with Didyma. This was especially true of Delphinios, whose special connection was noted through the annual procession from the one sanctuary to the other. Thus the famous oracular shrine was inextricably linked to the worship of the patron of Miletos on the Lion Harbor.

On the excavations in the Delphinion, see Kawerau and Rehm (1914). Also Gorman (2001), pp. 152–53, on the Delphinion in the context of the orthogonal city plan. See also Belin de Ballu (1972), pp. 44–45, 76, on Apollo Delphinios in Olbia in the Archaic and Classical periods and note 100, this chapter.

17 Conon *Narr.* 33 with Fontenrose (1988), p. 107.

18 Strabo 9.2.6 C. 403.

19 See note 10. Chios: Thuc. 8.32.2. Cf. Graf (1985), p. 56.

20 Hdt. 1.170.

21 Asheri (1999a), p. 362.

22 Hdt. 1.170. On Thales' prediction and its dating, see Hartner (1969); Mosshammer (1981); Panchenko (1994); Worthen (1997); Couprie (2004).

23 Hdt. 1.74.

24 Hdt. 1.75. However, stories about Thales must have abounded. Herodotus, too, is unreliable here. The chronology of his life seems unrealistic and needs to be taken with caution.

that this was not the end of the threat. At some point Thales also became aware of the ascendancy of the Persians. He is said to have aided Kroisos's army to cross the River Halys during his military campaign against Cyrus.[24] The distance between the two proponents of pan-Ionianism, Thales and Bias, may not have been all that significant.

After the Persian invasion, Bias of Priene suggested moving en masse to Sardinia.[25] Bias, too, apparently had experienced Lydian aggression and was aware of the difference between maritime and terrestrial civilizations. He is said to have convinced the Lydian Kroisos that, although Kroisos had conquered the Greek mainlanders, he should desist from attempting to conquer the Greek islands because, unlike cavalry, ships were not his *forte*.[26]

Apparently the idea of Ionians somehow having designs on Sardinia or generally on the west was in the air for quite some time. Histiaios promised the Persian king to fix matters in Ionia and then deliver Sardinia to him.[27] Aristagoras also promised the Ionian rebels a place of refuge in Sardinia to which he would lead them himself.[28] When Kolophonians fled the Lydians to found Siris in Italy (mentioned earlier), Strabo in fact spoke more generally of Ionians: "Ionians . . . in flight from the dominion of the Lydians."[29] The idea of a mass Ionian migration to the west was still around after 493. When the Persians won the naval battle of Lade, Sicilian Zankle offered the defeated Ionians an opportunity to colonize Kale Akte in Sicily. The Samians, "together with other Ionians" (mostly Milesians) came, although Anaxilas of Rhegion persuaded them to take over Zankle itself.[30]

Finally, even at the moment of victory over the Persians, the triumphant Greeks assembled in Samos to decide on the future of the Ionian Greeks, debating whether or not, in spite of their success, to evacuate the lot:

> They debated concerning the *anastasis* (depopulation, uprooting) of Ionia and in what Greek lands under their power it were best to settle the Ionians, abandoning the country itself to the Barbarians, for it seemed to them impossible to stand on guard between the Ionians and their enemies forever. Yet, if they should not so stand, they had no hope that the Persians would allow the Ionians to go unpunished. . . . But the Athenians did not like the plan of the evacuation of Ionia, nor were they happy that the Peloponnesians (who had suggested this) should decide concerning their own colonies.[31]

---

25 Hdt. 1.170.
26 Hdt.1.27 (however, the story may refer to Pittakos, says Herodotus).
27 Hdt. 5.106; 6.2.
28 Hdt. 5.124. Cf. Thuc. 104.4.2, where Aristagoras finally failed to colonize Amphipolis.
29 Strabo 6.1.14 C264.
30 Later he expelled them. Hdt. 6.22 with Thuc. 6.4.5; cf. Hdt. 7.164.
31 Hdt. 9.106.
32 Asheri (1999b). Generally on *metoikesis*, "relocation," in this context see the comprehensive discussion of Demand (1990), pp. 34–44.

This passage is a sober reminder of the consistently precarious geopolitical situation of the Ionians in Asia Minor, where they inhabited a relatively narrow stretch of coastal areas and faced the powers of a non-Greek hinterland. As David Asheri reminds us, "decolonization" was always there as a realistic, albeit traumatic, option.[32]

Since the beginning of the sixth century, the pan-Ionian project was perceived as intimately linked with overseas colonization. In their collective *imaginaire* the Ionians had originally colonized in Asia Minor. Now, since around 600, some were redirecting their gaze westward. The Kolophonians had settled Siris. The disparate Ionian cities therefore had the option of either founding a new Ionian state at Teos (Thales), migrating and doing the same in Sardinia (Bias), emigrating under stress to Sicily and settling *together* at Kale Akte (Zankle's offer), or emigrating en masse to an unspecified place (postwar suggestions). More significantly, the pan-Ionian project indicates how, on the contemporary horizon of Greek expectations, colonization and new foundations could result in the political and ethnic homogenization of the discrete Ionian poleis.[33]

In authentic Greek terms, what erases differences and consolidates identities is not permanence but movement and distance. As we have seen, that was also the point of Alkibiades' slander against the hodgepodge of Greeks in Sicily, already echoed in Archilochos's own slander against his fellow settlers at Thasos: "[T]he misery of all the Greeks (*panhellénôn*) has rushed together (*sunedramen*) to Thasos!" he exclaims.[34] The "misery of all the Greeks" is apparently all those who did not come from his home island of Paros, but very soon *all* Thasians were considered originally Parians. Aside from Teos, two of the options involved moving across a great distance to Sardinia or Sicily. This is precisely the point I wish to emphasize: Greater distance and movement result in the creation of new nodes and links, thus expanding notions of the collective identity. We see that far from being an observation of a modern scholar, the idea also truly belonged to the mental map of contemporary Ionians, expressed in specific and practical terms of relocation (*metoikesis*) and settlement.[35] The networks are dynamic: The Ionian cities of Asia Minor, interconnected in a loose network, would amalgamate to a single cluster through the kind of immigration that was itself dependent on the already existing networks in the western Mediterranean.

Perceptions of what it meant to be an Ionian were not airtight, as Herodotus seems to tell us. Whatever we may think of his unsympathetic slandering of the Ionians,[36] he appears to testify to traditions about how Greeks first came

---

33 The case is different from other relocations en masse as a single polis, as Themistocles famously threatened to do before the battle of Salamis; Hdt. 7.143.

34 Archilochos frg. 102 = Strabo 8.6.6 C370. Trans. Gerber (1999b), LCL (modified). See pp. 56; 108.

35 Cf. Demand (1990), pp. 34–36.

36 Hdt. 1.146. See How and Wells (1912), p. 122; Asheri (1999a), p. 350.

37 Hdt. 1.146.2.

38 See Jonathan Hall (1997), pp. 51–56, and Jonathan Hall (2002), pp. 67–73.

to colonize Asia Minor: Some started out from Athens as being "pure Ionians,"[37] whereas others *became* Ionians through processes of co-optation. It may be possible that since the Phokaians were originally considered Aiolian (earlier), this may explain their enthusiastic Ionianism. It was Dionysios the Phokaian, after all, who commanded the combined Ionian fleets against Persians and Phoenicians at the battle of Lade. Earlier still, around the time the Phokaians were ready to sail to Alalia, they were officially recognized as "Ionians" at Naukratis, where Phokaia was one of the four "Ionian poleis" sharing the Hellênion (see chapter 2).

The "impure Ionians" of the quasi-historical accounts of the migration to Asia Minor were a jumble of settlers. Their "ethnic" Ionian identity was consolidated later on in the new colonial terrain of Asia Minor. It soon transcended even that. For the non-Greek peoples of the Near East, all Greeks became "Ionians" (e.g., Egyptian *Wynn*, Hebrew *Yavan*, Turkish *Yunan*) regardless of whether they were Dorians, Aiolians, or Ionians in the Greek sense.[38]

The circles of Greek identities integrated. For Bias, contemporary circumstances might have seemed to be a replay of the circumstances of the original Ionian migration to Asia Minor, when they were expelled from their homeland. What had happened in the primordial past was about to repeat itself: Ionians' finding freedom by means of migration and colonization. They had also found self-definition as Ionians because of the colonial circumstances. The "Sardinia" of Bias would have taken this one step further: Ionians would no longer retain their discrete political communities. Their collective identity secured, they would create one Ionian state. In the end only Teos, Thales' candidate for the center of the Ionian state, and Phokaia, actually attempted relocation, but we need to distinguish what really happened from the "ideology" of relocation. It was closely associated both with the idea of freedom and ethnic blending and probably kept echoing within a pan-Ionian framework. If the temple of Apollo Delphinios at Massalia had been established around 600, I suspect that its pan-Ionian attributes were more firmly attached to it after Phokaia's abandonment in 545. This is why I believe that the cult to Apollo Delphinios was established at Massalia as a pan-Ionian cult. It was a cult of expectation, perhaps anticipating a mass Ionian migration to the west, possibly replacing the Sardinia of Bias with southern France. The Phokaians and Massaliots were to become the hub of a new pan-Ionian network in the western Mediterranean.

The Phokaians instituted Apollo Delphinios, as the Naxians had done earlier with Apollo Archêgetês in Sicily, in a "new" land. This ritual action, specifically with Apollo Delphinios, has a literary parallel. We noted how, in the *Homeric Hymn to Apollo*, once the "colonists" disembarked in their new land, they first set up an altar to Apollo Delphinios. The imagined situation is comparable with that

39 Lohmann (2004).

of Sicily (Apollo Archêgetês), Cyrenaica (Apollo Karneios, Zeus Ammon), and possibly the Black Sea (Achilles Pontarches). As with Delphi, Apollo Delphinios opened up the land of Massalia, this hitherto non-Greek land, to Greek coloniza-tion. Before ca. 600 that land had known Greeks as traders and perhaps settlers in mixed *emporia* but without a Greek polis. The Phokaians seem to have taken note of this inasmuch as they imbued their constitutive acts with implications of collective identity that transcended any particular group of settlers. The contrast between a land with a Greek settlement and one without seems to have been sufficiently apparent to require its own overarching, ritual symbolism for an all-encompassing Hellenic identity, here defined as "Ionian." As noted, based on the experience of previous colonization elsewhere, the Phokaians were probably expecting more Greeks to come. In Cyrenaica we saw (see pp. 55; 80) that the second foundation oracle encouraged "all Greeks" to join in the settlement of Libya. More specifically, in their particular historical circumstances, the terms of collective identity of the Phokaian were probably more "Ionian" than "Greek." With the fall of the Assyrians, the pressure of the Lydians, and eventually the rise of the Persians, many other Ionians might have been expected to rush to the west.

Apollo Delphinios has led us to an interesting overlap. On the one hand, "oppositional" identity was proclaimed with regard both to the enemy in the east and to the newness of the land settled—"new" because no Greeks had ever before founded a polis there. On the other hand, we are also on the "aggregative" side of identity formation: Positive foci for Ionian identity, while loosely expressed in the Panionion,[39] were now to find a stronger Ionian focus overseas. These processes of identity formation may be seen in network terms both metaphorically and heuristically. Just as a network may compensate for the loss of some nodes by enhancing the role of others, so could the loss of "Ionia" be compensated for by a relocation of Ionians to other nodes of the network. This is what the Kolopho-nian fugitives from the Lydians did when founding Siris. Similarly, when Themis-tokles threatened to relocate the Athenians to Siris, he was implying that it "belonged" to "Athenians" because it was Kolophonian and Ionian, and Athens—as everybody supposedly knew—was the mother city of all Ionians.[40]

A network of Mediterranean nodes would be an apt articulation of the mental maps of contemporary Greeks. The assumption of relocation as a via-ble option for entire populations could arise only because of the existence of the network and its dynamic mode. It is the old network of coming and going among seaboard towns, as articulated by Odysseus's imagined ships with "symmetrical trim hulls to cross the sea / and visit all the seaboard towns, as

---

40 Hdt. 8.62; cf. Plut. *Them.* 32.2. For traditions relating to Siris, see Moscati Castelnuovo (1989) with Malkin (1998), pp. 226–31.

41 Homer *Odyssey* 9.116ff.

42 Malkin (1991). See also Rolley (1997); Anguissola (2006a, 2006b).

men do / who go and come in commerce over water."[41] That such "coming and going" could easily lead to colonization was also an old, viable option, as Odysseus goes on to say: "This island—seagoing folk would have annexed it and built their homestead on it, all good land, fertile." In terms of Greek perceptions, around 600 BCE that option has been practiced for centuries, beginning with the Ionian migrations to the islands and seaboard of Asia Minor through the Greek colonization of the eighth and seventh centuries, creating the transfer points, the settlement nodes, and the maritime links of the Archaic Mediterranean.

Artemis of Ephesos

What Strabo found remarkable about the cult transfer of Artemis was the duplication of the cult of the Ephesian Artemis and the duplication of both its status and its statue. The result would be an "Ephesian Artemis" network, foreshortening connectivity among the nodes and extending to Greek settlements, to regional middle grounds, and to "international" links with non-Greeks (Rome). In Strabo's text the relevant term is *aphidruma*. Elsewhere I have presented a lexicographic study of the term *aphidruma* within the context of cult transfers and have also commented on the particular role of priestesses in such contexts.[42] The relevant conclusion is, first, that Greek colonists needed Greek women for particular religious functions, such as the washing of a cult statue. Hence, the presence of Greek women among the first generation of colonists should not be surprising.[43] Second, while *aphidruma* may mean things as different from each other as cinders and ashes taken from an altar, cult statues, or model reproductions of temples, essentially it refers to sacred objects with which to found a new cult. Brunel designates the new cult a *succursale*, a "subsidiary branch," an obvious misnomer that follows the "arborist" semantic field of centers and peripheries, the trunk of the tree and its offshoots.[44] However, cults in Greek colonies were never "subsidiary branches" but central polis cults. In the Phokaian-Massaliot case the *aphidruma* in question was indeed a cult statue, and both Greek and Latin authors kept insisting that its form remained the same for centuries.[45]

The goddess was from Ephesos, not Phokaia, and therefore must have possessed some quality that transcended her role as a polis deity. Artemis was an Ionian *hegemônê*, "leader," and *sôteira* (*sôtêria*) [savior]. To illustrate from a late fifth-century case: When the mercenary army of the Ten Thousand, which had

---

43 Graham (1984); For intermarriage between colonists and native women, see Coldstream (1993); Hodos (1999).
44 Brunel (1953).
45 Pliny *NH* 16.79. For a good review of the goddess in the Greco-Roman world see LiDonnici (1992).
46 Xen. *Anab.* 5.3.7.

set out in the service of a Persian pretender, returned, it dedicated part of the spoils to Apollo and in particular to the Ephesian Artemis. On a more personal level, the Athenian Xenophon left a sum of money in the hands of the Ephesian Megabyzos with the instruction that, should he not return safely from his adventures, Megabyzos would make a dedication at Ephesos, probably of a statue. Later, when Xenophon finally retired to an estate he was given by the Spartans, the money from Megabyzos was returned to him, and he consecrated a sacred precinct (temenos) to the Ephesian goddess, whose grounds were happily similar, he says, to the precinct at Ephesos. He chose the "place which Apollo's oracle appointed."[46] Moreover, he built a reduced copy of the naos (temple) of Artemis at Ephesos and established in it a xoanon of the goddess, both as close as possible to the xoanon and naos in Ephesos.[47] For Xenophon, Artemis of Ephesos was clearly meant to protect his departure and return. Had he become a founder of a city (he is quite explicit about his wish to have become one),[48] he would have probably founded her cult at the new polis. As it turned out, he founded not a city but a new estate, where he let Artemis of Ephesos stamp its mark.

Xenophon's reconnaissance points to those attributes of the goddess that made her attractive to him and the army in terms of safety, leadership, and colonization. These attributes had a special role in the Ionian context. In the Hymn to Artemis, Callimachus calls Artemis a "resident" (epidême) of Miletos, a term sometimes used for foreigners arriving in a city to live there.[49] She is the leader and guide of Neleus, the legendary Ionian founder, and is explicitly called hegemônê, the "guide who shows the way:[50] "Lady of many shrines, of many cities, hail! Goddess of the Tunic, resident in Miletos; for Neleus made you his Guide (hegemônê) when he set out with his ships from the land of Kekrops." Note that in Strabo's passage, "hegemôn for the sailing voyage" is precisely what the Phokaians, about to sail from Asia Minor, were supposed to receive from the Ephesian Artemis.

A parallel motif concerns Boiai, in Lakonia: Pausanias says that when the inhabitants of Etis, Aphdodisias, and Side were expelled, they received an oracle prophesying that Artemis would tell them where to settle.[51] When the refugees landed with their ship, a hare acted as their hegemôna, stopping at a myrtle

47 Xen. Anab. 5.3.7–13.

48 Xen. Anab. 5.6.15ff, 6.4.13–14.

49 LSJ s.v. ἐπιδημεύω iii.

50 Callimachus, Hymn to Artemis, 225–27, trans. Mair and Mair (1977) (modified). For hegemôn in Greek colonization, see Malkin (1987), pp. 246–47 and later.

51 Pausanias 3.22.12–13. Cf. 8.37. I wish to thank Denise Demetriou for drawing my attention to this passage and some of the later references. See Demetriou (2005).

52 Artemis sometimes has the epithet hegemôn when performing as sôteira from tyranny: She freed Ambracia from a tyrant and received a cult in the name of Artemis hegemônê: Antoninus Liberalis, Metamorphoseon Synagoge 4.5. Artemis also directed someone called Chronius to kill the tyrant Aristomelidas of Orchomenos. He then built a temple in her honor and dedicated it to Artemis hegemônê. Cf. Pausanias, 8.47.6.

53 Pherecydes FGrHist 3 F 154, 155 (Strabo 14.1.3 C633). See Fowler (2000), p. 355, no. 155.

tree. There the refugees built the city of Boiai and set up the worship of Artemis *sôteira*, their savior.[52]

Ephesos in particular seems to have played a prominent role in the Ionian *ktisis*. According to Pherecydes it was Androklos, the son of Kodros, who founded Ephesos and "for this reason . . . the royal seat of the Ionians was established there."[53] Moreover, there is a tradition that Phokaia was not admitted into the Panionion before she agreed to accept the Kodridai princes from Teos and Erythrai, namely, the family that was led by Artemis *hegemônê*.[54]

However, Callimachus makes a distinction between Artemis *hegemônê*, the goddess leading the Ionian migration, and her cult statue at Ephesos, which had already been there, it seems, when the Ionians arrived. It was the Amazons, he says, who had set up her image (*bretas*) under an oak, accompanied by a ritual war dance.[55] The orientation of the Amazons' ritual is toward the hinterland, not the sea: The echo of their dance reaches (Lydian) Sardis. Finally, although the poetic chronology is imprecise, sometime before the Kimmerian invasions (i.e., after the Ionians had settled at Ephesos) (verse 228), "around that image was raised a shrine of broad foundations." In other words, according to Callimachus, Artemis was clearly the *hegemônê* of Neleus, leader of the Ionians. Specifically for Ephesos, Callimachus says that her cult image had already been there when the Ionians arrived, yet the poet seems to imply that the temple housing the statue was the later work of the Ionian settlers (interestingly, the actual temple had a western orientation). Callimachus thus expresses the duality of the Ephesian Artemis: an Anatolian, Cybele-like goddess with an orientation to Sardis, who was then identified with Artemis *hegemônê* when some Ionians established themselves at Ephesos. She was *hegemônê* for the immigration travel, and she was *ephesia* in terms of arrival and settlement, particularly at Ephesos. From this point on these attributes would coalesce. Artemis not only *led* them to the site of settlement but also mediated their presence in Anatolia as an *epichorios theos*, a local divinity found already holding the land (see p. 131).[56]

Anticipating a similar role in the far west, it appears that, especially under Lydian domination, Artemis of Ephesos mediated the coastal Ionian Greeks of Anatolia with the hinterland. Mark Munn has studied the Anatolian aspects, presenting a full and convincing picture of her Lydian connection and the overlap with aspects of the Anatolian mother of the gods.[57] With Callimachus we noted that the echo of the Amazons' dance reached

---

54 Paus. 7.3.10; cf. Roebuck (1961), p. 501.

55 Cf. Pausanias 4. 31. 7; 7. 2. 6: "The cult of Artemis Ephesia is far more ancient still than the coming of the Ionians."

56 Cf. Xen. *Hell.* 1.2.6 (with Thuc. 8.109.1), where Tissafernes calls the Ionians to rally for the defense of Ephesos.

57 Munn (2006), pp. 163–69; cf. Kerschner (2008).

58 Borgeaud (1996), p. 28, with Munn (2006), p. 168.

Lydian Sardis (i.e., a hinterland orientation). Callimachus seems to echo an older tradition in connection with the Anatolian mother of the gods: Philippe Borgeaud notes that both the Homeric hymn to Artemis and the one to the mother of the gods end with the same formula, "to you and all the Goddesses together," arguing that the *Hymn to Artemis* places her in an Ionian setting, whereas the mother is a hinterland goddess.[58] Moreover, her connections with Sardis are explicit and significant. Kroisos is said to have appealed to Artemis of Ephesos before becoming king and vowed to offer dedications to her.[59] There had been intermarriage between the Basilids of Ephesos and the Lydian Mermnad dynasty.[60] When Kroisos, at the start of his rule, besieged Ephesos, its ruler was Pindar, his sister's son.[61] Kroisos contributed significantly to the temple of Artemis of Ephesos, and Munn convincingly argues that, in conjunction with Cybele at Sardis, Kroisos adopted Artemis of Ephesos as an embodiment of Lydian sovereignty. In fact, the links between Sardis and Ephesos, articulated in terms of cult to Artemis Ephesia, are impressive. An inscription dating to the fourth century speaks of a customary procession linking the sanctuary at Ephesos with that of Artemis in Sardis. There had been a monumental altar to Artemis Ephesia in Sardis since the sixth century, the site of the major temple in the Hellenistic era. Lydian inscriptions, between the late sixth century and the fourth, mention Artemis (*Artimús*) of Ephesos, once with the epithet "of Sardis" and several times "of Ephesos," and bilingual Lydian-Aramaic inscriptions mention Artemis of Ephesos as a protector of graves.[62] Finally, illustrating her role of protector of voyages, a Phrygian in the play *Persians* by Timotheus prays to Artemis of Ephesos for a safe return to Sardis.[63]

The Ionian *ktisis*, telling of the Ionians' arrival in Asia Minor, implies a primordial cult transfer of Artemis to the east that is similar to the historical cult transfer that the Phokaians were effecting in the west. In both, Artemis functions as a *hegemônê* of Ionian colonization, and in both, sacred objects, *hiera* or *aphidrumata*, were brought along with which to establish the cult of Artemis of Ephesos. A similar notion of an Ionian cult transfer is implied in cults that expressly pertain to the Ionians as a collective. Both relate not to Artemis but to Poseidon Helikonios and Ephesos. The chronology is uncertain, but it seems that at some point Ionians concentrated their common cults at Ephesos, having ceased to celebrate as Ionians at Delos and having removed the Panionia (the

59 Nic. Dam. *FGrHist* 90 F 65.
60 Georges (1994), pp. 29–32.
61 Ael. *VH* 3.26 with Hdt. 1.26 (on which more later).
62 Munn (2006), pp. 166–67; cf. Schaber (1982); Bammer (1984), pp. 74–78, 212–29; Hanfmann (1975), pp. 10–13, (1983), pp. 221–22 (= 1983a, p. 91), discusses Sardis-Ephesos.
63 Timotheus *Persians* 97–173 (Edmonds *LG*).

pan-Ionian festival) from the Panionion at Cape Mykale to Ephesos. Thucydides remarks that the common Ionian festival is no longer celebrated at Delos but is celebrated as "Ephesia," and Diodorus and Strabo suggest that at some point the Panionia had also moved from the Panionion to Ephesos.[64]

In that context, namely the move to Ephesos, the Ionians were told by the Delphic oracle to take *aphidrumata* from the altars of their ancestors at the sanctuary of Poseidon Heikonios (also the god of the Panionion at Cape Mykale) in Peloponnesian Achaia. Here the *aphidruma* probably represented ashes and sacrificial remains from the altar, which could be mixed with the foundations of a new altar established elsewhere. The people of Achaian Helike opposed this. In 373 BCE a great earthquake submerged Helike, and it was later believed that this was Poseidon's revenge for their refusal.

By the Augustan period (Diodorus, then Strabo), the earthquake and the cultic transfer seem to have grown into causal relation and become close in time. In fact, as Simon Hornblower has convincingly argued, the date of the move to Ephesos should precede Thucydides, possibly in the 440s or considerably earlier, sometime during the Persian conquest. The *Ephesia* was not identical with the *Artemisia*, as Martin Nilsson thought, but they are mentioned together in an inscription. A fourth-century inscription, mentioning both a "King of the Ephesians" (a cult title), as well as Panionian altars and sacrifices, probably reflects the time before the move back from Ephesos to Mykale, the site of the Panionion.[65] Thus, Ephesos appears to have articulated pan-Ionian identity for a substantial period and was involved with ritual transfer of *aphidrumata* of various kinds, essentially linked with pan-Ionian identity.

The *aphidruma* is at the heart of the stories of both the Panionion and the transformation of the Panionia into the Ephesia, as well as of the transfer of Artemis of Ephesos to the west. This ritual practice of cult transfer in a pan-Ionian context, revolving around a story of migration and settlement, may clarify the mindset of those Phokaians who, when migrating westward, took an *aphidruma* not from their own city but rather from Ephesos and its sanctuary with common Ionian associations.[66] This may have been the historical frame of reference for action at the time. The request for *aphidrumata* from Helike was possibly cast as a repeat ritual action that had once taken place during the primordial migration of the Ionians to the east. They were, after all, asking to sacrifice on the altars of *their ancestors*, on which Androklos, the leader of the

64 Thuc. 3.104.3 with Hornblower (1982); Diod. *Sic.* 15.49.1; Strabo 14.1.3 C633; cf. 8.7.2 and 4; cf. Hdt. 1. 148. Note that around 409 BCE Tissaphernes called upon (mostly) Ionians to rally at Ephesos "for the sake of the protection of Artemis." Xen. *Hell.* 1.2.6 with Thucydides (8.109), who mentions Tissaphernes sacrificing at Ephesos.

65 For discussion and references, see Hornblower (1991) on Thuc. 3.104.1.

66 Strabo 8.7.2 C385. Perhaps one may use this episode to date the Ionian request for *aphidrumata* from Helike to at least before 545 and thus place the context of the removal of the Panionion even to the time of Kroisos.

67 Pherekydes *FGrHist* 3 F 154, 155; Strabo 14.1.3 Alternatively: Neleus as the Ionian leader; for discussion and sources see Vanschoonwinkel (2006), p. 118.

Ionian migration, perhaps had sacrificed before setting out to Asia Minor and becoming the founder of no other city than Ephesos.[67] It is precisely because what we have here is an Ionian *ktisis* and because the Ionians at the time of the Phokaian cult transfer would have believed in its veracity that we should take the ritual seriously. Facing first the Lydians, then the Persians, the Ionians considered a new migration a realistic option, and yet again a significant *aphidruma* was to be brought along.

The title *hegemôn* in relation to Artemis had a specific function within the context of colonization, as it appears in Herodotus to be the Ionian equivalent of *archêgetês* (and sometimes *oikistês*), a leader and founder of a colony.[68] For example, when Herodotus paraphrases the formula "*archêgetês* and *basileus*" of the decree of the people of Thera to send out a colony to Cyrene in Libya, written in the Cyrenaian Dorian dialect, he says that the founder, Battos, was to be a "*hegemôn* and a *basileus*."[69] When describing Pentathlos and the foundation of Lipara, Antiochos also uses *hegemôn* as "founder of a colony."[70] Dionysius of Halikarnassos, relying on various authors, uses *oikistês* and *hegemôn* interchangeably.[71] Plutarch is rather explicit: While describing the "foundation" of Lesbos he says that "the *archêgetai* were seven in number, all kings (*basileis*), and the eighth was Echelaos, designated by the oracle at Delphi to be the *hegemôn* of the colony."[72] In this instance, *hegemôn* is the equivalent of *oikistês* and is further differentiated by the Delphic designation. Similarly, Menekrates says that Theseus founded Pythopolis according to an oracle that he had once received at Delphi; the hero left some of his followers there as *hegemônes* with clear functions of oikists: presiding and law making.[73]

A series of Hellenistic and Roman inscriptions from both Ephesos and Magnesia link Artemis with colonization, calling her *archêgetis tês poleôs*, city leader/founder.[74] The inscriptions from Magnesia emphasize also the *asylia* aspect of Artemis Leukophryene,[75] the institution of games and sacrifices in honor of the goddess,[76] and the consecration of a new temple to Artemis Leukophryene.[77] This seems to express continuities of attitudes from earlier periods. Anakreon, for example, speaks of Artemis as watching over the city of

---

68 For a discussion and analysis of the relevant terms and sources, see Malkin (1987) pp. 241–50, to which add Isocrates *Archidamos* 22 (*oikistês* = founder, *archêgetês* = leader, commander).

69 Hdt. 4.153 with Meiggs and Lewis (1989), no. 5, lines 25–26.

70 *FGrHist.* 555 F 1 = Paus. 10.11.3.

71 Dion. Hal. *Ant. Rom.* 1. 72.

72 Plut. *Mor.* 163 b–c (trans. Frank Cole Babbitt, LCL).

73 *FGrHist.* 701 F 1 = Plut. *Theseus* 26.

74 Ephesos: *Die Inschriften von Ephesos* (Wankel 1979) iv. Ia 27; iv. IV 1387, 1398. Magnesia: *Syll.*³ 557, 560, 562, 695; *Die Inschriften von Magnesia am Maeander* (Kern 1900) iv. 37, 41, 53, 54, 56, 60, 63, 64, 79, 85, 89; *OGIS* 231, 232, 233, 319.

75 *Syll.*³ 557, 560, 562; Iv. Magn. 37, 53, 54, 56, 62, 63, 79, 85.

76 Iv. Magn. 41, 60, 64; OGIS 231, 232, 233, 319.

77 *Syll.*³ 695.

78 Anakreon, fr. 348 in Campbell (1988), pp. 46–49.

79 Strabo 14.1.20 C640.

Magnesia.[78] Finally, add to all this the alternative myth of the birth of Artemis not on Delos but at Ephesos,[79] and the explicit statements of our sources that what used to be the pan-Ionian festival at Delos had been replaced by the Ephesia festival in Ionia,[80] and that the Panionia had moved to Ephesos. We then have a full spectrum that demonstrates the importance of Artemis of Ephesos as an Ionian goddess, with specific connections to notions of migration and colonization.

An Ionian sôteira and hegemônê, Artemis of Ephesos played a direct role in the particular historical contexts that preceded the evacuation of Phokaia. Merely fifteen years before the flight of the Phokaians (545 BCE), Ephesos surrendered to the Lydian Kroisos, and Herodotus recounts how the Ephesians had attached their city to the temple of Artemis with a cord, thus placing the entire city under the protection of the goddess and threatening sacrilege to anyone who might hurt them.[81] In a later period the Persian Xerxes would demonstrate the same clemency to Apollo's temple, also at Ephesos.[82] The strategy proved a happy one. Kroisos achieved what he wanted, an honorable surrender, and, for its part, Ephesos prospered.

During those fifteen years between the Lydian conquest of Ephesos and the Persian invasion, the city of Ephesos was removed to a less defensive site on the plain below. While the new site was less easy to defend, it was closer to the temple of Artemis, which was itself being rebuilt. All of this did not happen at once, and it is quite probable that when the Persians arrived there was still much activity, as the evacuation of a site and the relocation of an entire Ionian city (Ephesos) was no doubt still ongoing, and again, all of this occurred under the protection of the Ephesian Artemis. This protective aspect is consistent with the Ionian ktisis. When Androklos, the quasi-historical Ionian founder of Ephesos, conquered the land, he expelled all the inhabitants. However, those who "dwelt around the sanctuary for the sake of its hikesia had nothing to fear . . . they exchanged oaths of friendship with the Ionians and escaped warfare."[83] This, too, sits well with Callimachus's claim, noted earlier, that the Amazons had set up the bretas of Artemis of Ephesos, and hence it preceded the Ionian arrival.

Phokaia was likewise an Ionian state and part of the Ionian network, particularly in Asia Minor. During the sixth century this network expressed itself not only in Panionian festivals but also overseas: Being "Ionian" was the criterion for inclusion among the four Ionian poleis represented at the Hellênion at

---

80 Thuc. 3.104.3. Cf. Farnell (1896), p. 466, also for her title, Delphinia, and her role as a goddess of harbors and maritime life. On the court at Delphinion, see Boegehold (1995), pp. 120–21, 35–39.

81 Hdt. 1.26, Aelian Varia Historia 3.26; Polyaenus Stratagemata 6.50. Similarly, by 399 BCE, under Persian domination, the inhabitants of Magnesia moved their city higher up in order to be closer to the temple of Artemis Leukophryene. Diod. Sic. 14.36.3.

82 Strabo 14. 1. 5.

83 Pausanias 7.2.8; cf. Strabo 14.1.21 C640 on the expulsion.

Naukratis (chapter 2). Moreover, some contemporary Ionians were contemplating an Ionian migration to Sardinia. In immediate terms, Phokaia was close enough to Ephesos to observe how the Ephesian Artemis had protected it from Kroisos, how Ephesos prospered, and how other Ionian states declined in comparison. Now history seemed to be repeating itself. After the Lydian pressure, the Persians arrived, and this time Phokaia was the first city standing in the path of the formidable barbarian enemy. It decided to evacuate. However, why not attach itself to the Ephesian Artemis, whose virtues as *sôteira* and *hegemônê* were so eminently conspicuous both in Ionian historical lore and in such similar circumstances within contemporary memory? The answer seems that this attachment redefined its purpose as *sôteira* in terms of her function as the Ionian *hegemônê*. The Ionian symbolic frame of reference, together with the protective Artemis of Ephesos of recent memory, seems to have coalesced.[84]

Nomima

The prominent Phokaian cults of Artemis of Ephesos and Apollo Delphinios belong, as Strabo says, to the set of *nomima* disseminated especially by Massalia.[85] In general, *nomima* constituted a set of practical, organizing data for society, such as names and numbers of tribal divisions or magistracies and their terminology. They also regulated society's relations with the gods through sacred calendars, festivals, and the constitution of a polis pantheon. Before turning more specifically to the Phokaian case, let us illustrate the usefulness of *nomima* as expressing patterns and networks in the world of Greek colonization.

Dorian, Aiolian, and Ionian *nomima* varied greatly among them, but there was also a wide variety among cities of supposedly the same subethnic identity. Because of their comprehensive nature, sets of *nomima* must have been chosen deliberately as close to the time of foundation as possible and "assigned" (*tithemi*) to a colony. A community simply needed a consistent set of *nomima*. Thucydides is explicit: *Nomima* are "assigned" (presumably by the founder) or "given," implying a comprehensive act that is rather similar to the way ancient

84 Xenophon recounts that Tissaphernes rallied his (Ionian) allies to gather at Ephesos "for the protection of Artemis," which they did (Xen. *Hell.* 1.2.6–8; cf. Thuc. 8.109.1, where Tissaphernes goes to Ephesos and sacrifices to Artemis).

85 Strabo 4.1.4 C179. On Phokaian *nomima* in the context of colonization in general see Bilabel (1920), pp. 238–46. The following few paragraphs recapitulate passages on *nomima* from Malkin (2003b). See also chapter 2, pp. 73–74; 92; 104.

86 Thucydides uses the verb *tithemi* for Gela (6.4.3), a verb laden with legal implications (e.g., *themis*, with Ostwald [1969] and *didômi* for Akragas [6.4.4]). In the case of Himera, where an exiled Dorian group of settlers joined the original Chalkidian nucleus, Thucydides says that the Chalkidian *nomima* "prevailed" (see later mention). Hornblower (2008), p. 291, thinks this may signify "the opposite of a single-moment imposition," but surely Thucydides assumes that the Chalkidian *nomima* that had been given prevailed. In 6.5.1 he is describing the process that followed Himera's foundation (e.g., the language that *became* a mixed Ionian-Doric dialect), not the initial event. Cf. Pindar *Pyth.* 1.64 on Dorian institutions in the context of colonization, and see p. 113. For the common denominator of oikists, reformers, and tyrants, see Malkin (1989); cf. McGlew (1993).

"lawmakers" (and sometimes tyrants) applied comprehensive reforms to their communities.[86]

We hardly hear of their choice as being created expressly for symbolic values, although we may assume that in terms of collective identity the choice as such was meaningful during the first generation of settlement. As we will immediately see, *nomima* were used to identify a city, say, as "Chalkidian." For the most part, *nomima* were established because they were necessary, and they existed as long as they were common and comprehensive. There is an analogy to be drawn between social architecture and city planning and *nomima*. It is well known that, unlike "Old Greece," the territories of Greek colonies were more clearly organized and divided into private and public spaces. For example, the first generation of settlers at Megara Hyblaia organized public, sacred, and private spaces, with an apparently strong egalitarian principle (see p. 150). The agricultural countryside, the *chôra*, was also divided into demarcated plots, often traceable through aerial photography. In other words, probably for practical reasons that also mirrored social realities (equality within the first generation of settlers), the founders of Greek colonies needed to practice some second-order thinking: reflecting and making abstractions of society, defining its categories, and giving all this a visible expression. Now, just as people arrived in their new world from unplanned settlements but suddenly needed to translate social and religious needs into formal planning on the ground, they needed to do the same for their new society and its relationships with the gods. This seems evident from the result, the sets of *nomima* that existed in practically every Greek polis. Settlers abstracted and formalized *nomima* to apply them to the new polities they were founding.

As to religion, especially festivals and sacrifices, and the right of colonists to participate in sacrifices of the mother city (and vice versa), *nomima* would express a network of reciprocity, always potentially actualized, although one suspects this was not a frequent occurrence. Such a framework of reciprocity could exist only if one assumed similarity between mother city and colonies or among colonies *tout court*. There was no need for a citizen of one city to share in unfamiliar rites in an unfamiliar month to an unfamiliar deity-cum-local-epithet with whom the citizen had nothing in common. The similarity between *nomima* of mother cities and colonies is hardly noticed these days, when trends in research tend to emphasize the *imaginaire* at the expense of facts, without noticing that such facts were also employed in antiquity precisely to construct the *imaginaire*.

In time, such *nomima* could serve as the salient identifiers of a city. An external observer, Thucydides, emphasized them as one of the four defining factors of a colony: its mother city, date of foundation, name of the founder, and its *nomima*. We noted (see pp. 74–75), for example, how Thucydides pays particular attention to the Dorian *nomima* of Sicilian Gela (comprised of Rhodian and Cretan settlers, both Dorian) vs. the specifically "Geloan" *nomima* of Gela's own colony, Akragas.

Choices about *nomima* were not neutral, and were symbolic of collective identity. Because of their comprehensive nature (especially with regard to the sacred calendar with its social and religious implications), copying the *nomima* of a mother city was accomplished mostly during foundation, but not always. For example, the similarity between the *nomima* of both Sparta and Taras (a Spartan colony in southern Italy, founded ca. 706 BCE) is well known. What is striking is that both had Ephors, an institution that probably did not exist at Sparta in the eighth century.[87] This indicates that at some point, perhaps in the sixth century, either Taras "copied" an institution from its mother city or perhaps it was Sparta that adopted the Ephorate from its colony. In either case, adopting the Ephorate must have also involved adopting some of its implications, notably the "overseeing" aspect and limitations imposed on authority. It also indicates that a close relationship between Sparta and Taras was ongoing, an aspect of a network that we usually overlook because of the nature of our sources. As noted (see pp. 34–35), the "silent" network of mother cities and colonies, persisting for centuries, came to the foreground only in extreme cases, as when Sparta sent generals to aid Taras in the fourth century. The two, Sparta and Taras, were too far away from each other for the existence of any "colonial" relations in the modern sense. It is precisely here that the decentralized aspect of the network is apparent, not merely as a matter of observation but also in terms of explaining the dynamics of interaction. Both opted for the shortest link. Taras (or Sparta) were free to choose whatever *nomima* they wanted, but they chose instead to replicate from each other a major institution of their political order.

Aside from the choice of *nomima*, which must have been deliberate and symbolically significant, for the modern scholar *nomima* can and should be used to pose questions of verifying traditions about mother cities. For example, was Megara really the mother city of Byzantion? In that sense, namely in identifying similarities among sets of *nomima*, these do have a positivistic, "neutral" quality that reveals connections that are not dependent on foundation myths, fabricated prophecies, or quasi-historical accounts. On the one hand, *nomima* were dependent on subjective choice and selected with an awareness of their implications for collective identity and practice. By the fifth century (see p. 192) Thucydides is using *nomima* as a yardstick for identifying a colony, for example, as "Chalkidian." Yet very early on, once in place and apart from particular changes and adaptations (such as the Ephorate at Taras and Sparta), *nomima* can serve the same purpose for the modern historian that they did for Thucydides: an objective set of data for observing a network aspect of ancient Greek networks. Moreover, as *nomima* involved actual practice by entire communities, what we are told about them is less prone to suspicion of literary

---

87 See Nafissi (1999). Ephors existed in Herakleia, a colony of Taras; hence the direct implication they also existed in Taras. See also Richer (1998), p. 137n17.

manipulation (unlike, say, genealogies in Archaic poetry). *Nomima* were usually not used to invent kinship relationships (myths of kinship, *syngeneia*, and eponymous heroes would serve that purpose quite well).[88] They reveal patterns of religious, social, and political life that underlie a very Greek experience of identity and connectedness.

A colony's founder must have made active, deliberate choices in mediating a social and religious order for the new collective, an order without which people simply could not live together for very long without incurring the anger of the gods or losing the semblance of social cohesion. *Nomima* were also a powerful assimilative force when settlers of varied origins would join a nucleus of founders and co-opt their identity by being absorbed in the social order, itself largely determined by *nomima*. Incidentally, they also provide a good explanation for the great numbers of "Milesian" or "Chalkidian" colonists, when Miletos or Chalkis could not have possibly provided the resources of population to settle so many colonies in the Black Sea and in the west.[89]

Greek colonization could be expressed in terms of chains and links. Thucydides, for example, speaks of the chain of Chalkis, Zankle, and Himera. Zankle, on the tip of Sicily facing the Italian "boot," was initially settled by Greeks ("pirates") from Kyme (a Greek city in Campania, in the Bay of Naples). It became a political community with the joint foundation of people from Kyme (itself a Chalkidian colony) and Chalkis in Euboia, now with *two* respective oikists, one from Kyme (Perieres) and the other from Chalkis (Krataimenes), whose cult is evidenced in the *Aetia* of Callimachus.[90] Thucydides also comments that this was a *nomos*: to have an oikist come from the mother city when its "daughter" founded a colony.[91]

Himera, on the northeastern shore of Sicily, was founded by Zankle, probably in 648 BC, and now, with this third link of the colonial chain, three oikists are mentioned (Eukleides, Simos, Sakon). But it was a mixed colony: Aside from the many Chalkidians who were Ionian Greeks, the exiled Myletidai from Syracuse, a Dorian city, also came to settle.[92] An interesting change now occurs: The language of Himera resulted in a mixture of "Doric and Chalkidic," says Thucydides, but the *nomima* that prevailed (*ekratesan*) were Chalkidian.[93] The implication is significant. The colonial situation produced a linguistic mixture because language was neutral, not an object of symbolic and formal decision (unlike certain cases of modern nationalism). In contrast, since one needed, from the outset, to have common, interdependent *nomima*, to have

---

88 Curty (1995); Jones (1999); Erskine (2001). Also Elwyn (1991, 1993).

89 Cf. Malkin (2009). Scheidel (2003) estimates the number of immigrants from the Aegean during this period as thirty thousand.

90 Callimachus *Aetia* II frg. 43 with Malkin (1987), pp. 75–76, 108–109, 197–200.

91 Thuc. 1.24.2.

92 Knoepfler (2007), p. 95, considers that Sakon (whose name is found also in Selinous and Gela, both Dorian poleis) was one of the Myletidai; Eukleides and Simos were apparently "Chalkidians."

93 Thuc. 6.5.1.with note 86, this chapter.

magistrates, and live according to a common sacred calendar and social divisions, no one could wait for an evolutionist mixture to emerge, as in the case of the language. Rather, deliberate selection and exclusion were necessary.

For further illustration, let us briefly look at two other examples of city-state networks based on mother city and colony connections; Samos and its colonies Perinthos, Bisanthe, and Heraion on the north shore of the Propontis and on the island Amorgos.[94] Similarities of cults between Samos and its Propontid colonies have been noted. About a generation after the foundation of Perinthos we find two Perinthians at Samos dedicating a *dekate* to Hera in the form of a gold Gorgon and a silver Siren.[95] The inscription recording this is variously interpreted either as a formal Perinthian dedication or that of returning citizens or simply a private dedication. In any event, the two are called *oikêioi*, revealing close ties between the two cities. Another inscription, this time from Perinthos, indicates the prominence of Hera, probably at a site twenty-four kilometers west of Perinthos, at Heraion. The goddess, perhaps the most prominent in the Samian pantheon, also appears on Perinthian coins.[96] Finally, at the political level, we find Perinthos at the beginning of the sixth century as the point of departure for the Samians against their oligarchs, the Geomoroi.[97]

Another aspect of *nomima* is calendars, the basis of which was religious, with the names of the months often following a prominent cult. If a colony adopted the same theophoric month names, it is legitimate to assume that it also adopted the associated cult, as the case of Paros (mother city) and Thasos seems to illustrate.[98] We have the order of Samian months and can observe that Samos and Perinthos had at least seven months in common. Sometimes colonial *nomima* reveal the situation at a mother city before it underwent certain reforms, as seems to be the case with the calendar of Amorgos.[99] In his studies of Greek chronology, Samuel could do no more than guess that the calendars of Miletos and her Black Sea colony, Olbia, were the same, and he was right. We now have a spiral inscription on a bottom of a vase of ca. 450 from Olbia, which gives a full list of Olbian months, and it happily corresponds to those of Miletos.[100] Moreover, it has a dedication to "Apollo Delphinios, Iatros, Thargelios." As noted, Apollo Delphinios was worshipped in the agora of Miletos.

The copying, or rather transfer, of *nomima*, particularly those concerned with the sacred calendar, point to the role of religion (aside from Delphi) in forming and intensifying Greek networks. In general, whereas the Greek Gods

94 Loukopoulou (1989), pp. 96–97.
95 *SEG* 12 (1955), no. 391.
96 Graham (1964); Loukopoulou (1989), pp. 101–102.
97 Plutarch, *QG* 57 (= *Moralia* 303e–304c). Loukopoulou (1989), pp. 54–55, 97.
98 Samuel (1972), p. 130; Pouilloux (1954), p. 457.
99 Loukopoulou (1989), pp. 110, 113–17.
100 See Dubois (1996), pp. 160–64; Samuel (1972), pp. 114–18; Gorman (2001), pp. 37–38.

were "universal," cult was political and specific to a polis—apart from the regional or Panhellenic cults. By creating a new settlement, Greeks were also forming a new node of religious practice, expressed in cult that was shared by their citizens. If we were to direct an imaginary ray of light from a divine "node," say, Hera "up there," to each of her new cult places (e.g., Poseidonia in Italy), with the colonizing movement we would receive numerous projections lighting up more and more nodes at sections of the seaboard. So far the "link" is heavenly, as it were. But what happens when we connect the nodes among themselves on the Eukleidian, human plane?

The result, for example, could be the "Achaian League," with its center at the temple of Hera at Cape Lakinion. In that respect, the affinity of *nomima* among Achaian cities identified them as Achaian, and, when searching for an all-embracing regional identity, they chose Hera as their goddess.[101] The tension between ad hoc reasons for creating a suprapolis organization (a "league") and the mental background that allowed for such a response is always difficult to assess. However, as I have demonstrated with Apollo Archêgetês in Sicily, it seems probable that regional network dynamics were prominent in forming that mindset.

The initial copying of institutions, especially when the organizing nucleus was consistently, say, "Chalkidian," was perhaps ideological to the extent that it declared a focus of identity. Colonies were usually sovereign states, not dominions of their mother cities. That is probably why colonies did not object to making changes when *nomima* in the mother city would be reformed. For example, contrary to Taras (discussed earlier), the Amorgos calendar remained independent of developments in the mother city. This is particularly evident with the division of a society into tribes. The tribes of Perinthos continued to follow the traditional Ionian names even when, at Samos, a reform in the citizen body replaced the Ionian kinship tribes with two, region-related tribes, the "river area," Chesia, and the "old city," the Astypalaia.[102]

To date, the best-researched *nomima* of colonial cities are those of Megara.[103] A list of Megarian colonies and subcolonies includes Megara Hyblaia in eastern Sicily (founded in 728 BCE) and its daughter colony Selinous (Selinunte) in western Sicily (628 BCE); Chalkedon and Astakos on the Asian side of the Bosporos and Byzantion and Selymbria on the European; Herakleia Pontike and its own colonies, Mesembria, Apollonia, Kallatis, and (the Tauric) Chersonesos in the Black Sea.

The pantheon of Selinous is similar to that of Megara (Nisaia) in mainland Greece. We note, too, that, when founded, an *oikistês* was invited to come from

---

101 For the nature of the "Achaians" in Italy and the "direction" of their relations with "homeland" Achaia, see Morgan and Hall (1996). Contra Walbank (2000). For the sanctuary, see Spadea (1996).

102 Samuel (1972), pp. 105–106; on Amorgos, see Reger (2004), p. 734ff; Loukopoulou (1989), pp. 116–19. See Jones (1987), pp. 197–98, for the Samian reform; Rubinstein (2004), p. 1096 (Samos); Loukopoulou and Laitar (2004), p. 920 (Perinthos).

103 Hanell (1934); Antonetti (1997a), p. 82 and passim; Loukopoulou (1989), pp. 103–109; Adrian Robu (2007, forthcoming–a). On Megara's colonial expansion, see Legon (1981), pp. 71–84.

the *metropolis*, which probably received a founder's cult at Selinous, thus expressing the colonial chain of grandmother, mother, and daughter cities.[104] At Byzantion we also find prominent Megarian cults, such as that of Pythian Apollo; Demetra Malophoros, a cult exclusive to Megara and her colonies; Artemis Orthosia; the diviner Polyeidos; and Ajax, son of Telamon. Apollo Archêgetês and Daphnêphoros were also prominent at Selymbria.[105]

In contrast to the full cycle of Byzantion, we have no information about the calendar of Megara. Nonetheless, there are distinct similarities between the calendar of Byzantion and of Selymbria and that of the subcolonies of Herakleia Pontike, Kallatis, and Tauric Chersonesos. All these point to a common, Megarian source.[106]

Megara possessed the three customary, kinship-based, Dorian tribes. However, a Megarian citizen was called by his name, a patronymic, and the name of his *hekatostys*. This middle term of social and probably military division related not to the fictional kinship tribes but to a regional division, the five *komai* (*pente mere*), from which the main magistrates, the five archons and the five *strategoi* were drawn up. In mainland Greece the *hekatostys* is found only in Megara. The unit (based on the figure of one hundred) served various reforms, allowing for the inclusion of new citizens, as it did also in Byzantion. The names of the magistracies, too, are indicative: an annual, eponymous, *basileus* at Megara and the board of five *aisymnatai*. These, including the *proaisymnon* (analogous to the chair, the *epistates*, of the Athenian councilors, or Prytaneis), are found in all the colonies apart from Byzantion: Selymbria, Chalkedon, Herakleia Pontike, the Tauric Chersonesos, Kallatis, and Selinous in Sicily, thus probably also implying Megara Hyblaia. If the *aisymnatai* are an innovation of the Classical period, as Adrian Robu suggests, then we have another case of "adjustments" made among *nomima* within the colonial network, similar to the Ephors in the world of Sparta's colonies.[107]

These examples should be sufficient to establish that *nomima*: (a) were vital to the social, political, and religious organization of a Greek polis; (b) were considered as comprehensive sets and formally recognized as such; and (c) served as identifiers of a city as, for example, "Chalkidian." Detailed studies are still needed to establish connections between mother cities and colonies (in the vein of the work done by Denis Knoepfler for Euboian-associated colonies,[108] Catherine Hadzis for the

---

104 Cf. note 91; Thuc.6.4.2. For the foundation of Selinous, see Bérard (1957), pp. 244–46; Fischer-Hansen, Nielsen, and Ampolo (2004b), p. 220–24; De Angelis 2003; on the sanctuaries at Selinous, see Fischer-Hansen, Nielsen, and Ampolo (2004b), pp. 223–24.

105 For the religious institutions of Byzantion, see Isaac (1986), pp. 234–36; Loukopoulou (1989), pp. 103–109.

106 Hanell (1934), p. 192; Loukopoulou (1989), pp. 120–22. See Samuel (1972), pp. 87–88, 89, with bibliography for the calendar of Byzantion and those of Kallatis, Tauric Chersonesos, and Megara. On the Megarian influence on Byzantion, see also Loukopoulou and Laitar (2004), pp. 915–16, no. 647. For Selymbria, see Loukopoulou and Laitar (2004), p. 921, no. 679.

107 Loukopoulou (1989), pp. 138–42; Adrian Robu (in press; forthcoming–a; forthcoming–b). I thank Adrian Robu for allowing me to consult his work.

108 Knoepfler (1989, 1990).

calendars of Corinthian colonies, and Petra Reichert-Südbeck on the cults of Corinth and Syracuse).[109] *Nomima* were also co-optative on the intra-Greek, subethnic level, marking differences among Dorians, Ionians, and Aiolians. "Having the same *nomima*" placed communities in mental networks of affinity. In regional terms such affinities could be articulated into a regional identity, as in Greek Phokis or Italian "Achaia," relying on an image of coherent similarity among cities. Still, such regional development could also be interpreted in a reverse order: By means of a kind of "centripetal" development, people who live long enough in the same region may eventually develop similar habits, which they later interpret as ancient *nomima* and translate into a notion of affinity. However, as we will see with Artemis of Ephesos in the western Mediterranean, the spread of *nomima* could also be "centrifugal," involving no contiguous territorial spaces. The nodes of Artemis cults and associated *nomima* became widely spread out and yet, precisely because of the huge distances and the speeding up of the links among them, such *nomima* functioned effectively in forming a "Phokaian identity."

Phokaians shared both Ionian *nomima* and specific Phokaian ones. Once in the west, Artemis of Ephesos became one of the defining features of collective identity among Phokaians, while presenting a more general, "Greek" face, to the non-Greek world. She was also a mediator with other civilizations that, in turn, also helped define what "Phokaians" in the west represented. The Phokaians taught the particulars of the cult of Artemis of Ephesos and transferred her image to people as different from each other as the Iberians in Spain and the Romans in Italy. However, with regard to the Phokaian settlements in the West, which Strabo understood as colonies specifically of Massalia, the cult of Artemis of Ephesos was one element, albeit the major one, of entire sets of *nomima*:

> [I]n all the daughter *poleis* (*en . . . apoikois polesi* [either those of
> Massalia or other Phokaian cities]) the people everywhere do this god-
> dess honours of the first rank, and they maintain the same shape of
> the *xoanon* and otherwise adhere to the same *nomima*, which were
> traditional (*nenomisthai*) in the metropolis.[110]

What might have been considered Phokaian *nomima*? An overview of Phokaian-associated cities indicates that it is possible to treat their *nomima* as constituting a network of affinity. Once deliberate choices about *nomima* were made, probably around the time of the foundations, Phokaian *nomima* spread along the network lines, while enhancing their salient feature as Phokaian. Here we have a combination of "centralized" networks (those colonies settled close to Massalia) and decentralized ones: "Phokaian" colonies and *emporia*, non- or partially Massaliot foundations. Some *nomima* spread from Phokaia in Asia Minor, and some from Massalia, Emporion, and other settlements. Others

---

109 Hadzis (1995); Reichert-Südbeck (2002).
110 Strabo 4.1.4 C179.

probably spread among the mixed settlements and the gateway communities, adopted probably from neighboring Phokaian sites rather than from the mother city in Asia Minor (or from Massalia).

We can, for example, compare the calendars of Massalia, Lampsakos, and Phokaia. We do not have a full list of the Massaliot months, but epigraphic evidence reveals the existence of the Anthesteria and Thargelia at Massalia with corresponding month names in Phokaia and Lampsakos in the Hellespont. Lampsakos in the east is important as it signifies the extension of the Phokaian network regardless of the western geographical "zones." Noteworthy is the Apatouria festival that Herodotus uses as the salient mark of those who claim to be pure Ionians.[111] A lead tablet from Massalia, dating to the third century, has someone called Leukon setting up as deadline "the Apatouria," confirming its existence in Massalia. An altar to Zeus Partroos was also found in Massalia.[112]

Phokaian Elea shared the cult of Leukothea with Massalia, a cult that Maurizio Giangiulio sees as characteristic of Tyrrhenian, Phokaian *emporia*. Perhaps, as Morel thinks, Leukothea is to be identified with the Siren Leukosia, whose body reached the island of Licosa (Leukosia) between Poseidonia and Velia. In Lampsakos, Leukothea was a name of a month, implying a major role and probably some festival.[113]

The most celebrated Phokaian *nomima* in the west concerned the major cults of Apollo Delphinios and especially that of Artemis Ephesia. Artemis of Ephesos accompanied the Phokaian founders of Massalia, and the colonists honored her with a prominent temple on the promontory of what is today the Vieux Port of Marseilles. In the Far West the Phokaians founded her temples in many locations: at Emporion, Rhode, Hemeroskopeion, and other, more minor, sites, copying her cult statue and transmitting and teaching rites to non-Greeks. The goddess is particularly illustrative of the role of *nomima* and their place in the context of colonial networks, looking to mediation with non-Greeks and affirming commonalities and collective identities within Greek communities that belonged to the same network.

The Expressive Network of Artemis Ephesia in the West

The horizons of the Ephesian Artemis in the west are impressive: When describing the area of Hemeroskopeion (Dianum), on the southeastern coast of Iberia, Strabo says there are "Three small Massaliot cities. Of these, the best

---

111 Hdt. 1.147.

112 Ghiron-Bistagne (1992).

113 Giangiulio (1986), p. 109. Morel (2000), p. 37 (together with Tocco Sciarelli [2000] in the same volume). See also Morel (2006), p. 407n206. "Leukothea" is conventional, although the name may be found with varying orthography (e.g., "Leukotheia"). For the multidirectional ripples of the spread of her cult see the excellent article by Finkelberg (2006).

known is Hemeroskopeion, a place held in very great esteem since it has on its promontory a temple of the Ephesian Artemis."[114] Similarly, with regard to both Rhode and Emporion, Strabo says, "Here, too, is Rhode, a small town belonging to the Emporitans, though some say it was founded by Rhodians. Both in Rhode and in Emporion they worship Artemis of the Ephesians, and I shall tell the reason for this in my account of Massalia."[115]

Both Massalia and Hemeroskopeion built their Artemis temple on the promontory that marked the entrance to the port. A promontory temple "speaks" to those seeing it from the sea.[116] It is a widespread phenomenon, and the temple serves as daytime lighthouse (Hemeroskopeion, for example, means "day watch") since it is conspicuous from the sea. The deity responsible for the sanctuary suggests familiarity and hoped-for benevolence for those arriving from afar. Such temples proffer *epiphaneia*, one of the criteria in our ancient sources for choosing a temple site: a "clearly seen" expression of the deity's presence on the liminal area between sea and coast. It hints at invitation and it promises protection.[117] It is, however, not an anonymous *epichorios theos*, such as the anonymous deities to whom the Argonauts pour libations upon arrival in Kolchis,[118] but distinctly identified with the community that established it, particularly when the deity in question is the titular goddess of the polis.

Yet Artemis of Ephesos transcended the idea of a *poliouchos* (guardian deity, who "holds the polis") of a single city, in being common to all western Phokaians and disseminated by all of them. In terms of the Mediterranean shoreline of what is today France and Spain, this "Artemis of Ephesos of the Phokaians" both belonged to and expressed the Phokaian network of the coasts of France and Spain. Massalia may have had a special role in disseminating the cult, but there is no a priori reason to exclude other Phokaian agents, such as Emporion, which may also be inferred from Strabo's words quoted earlier. Mediterranean ports imply each other by their mutual connectivity. When this connectivity is formally expressed in having the same goddess, situated in the same maritime, promontory position and welcoming the "same" sailors in the same region, we can say that the participants have become aware of the network as such (figure 6-1). We may perhaps examine this even further: In the case of the deliberate dissemination of Artemis's

114 Strabo 3.4.6 C159, trans. Jones (1917), LCL. Further study is needed for Artemis of Ephesos in the Black Sea area, especially in relation to Miltetos's role as a dominant colonial hub. Note the work in progress by Immacolata Balena (Lecce), whom I wish to thank for her advice on the dossier of inscriptions she has collected and for pointing out some of the relevant references. See especially Ehrhardt (1983), p. 155; Guldager Bilde (2009); Treister (1999); and Tokhtas'ev (2010).

115 Strabo 3.4.8 C160, trans. Jones (1917), LCL. For the cults of Emporion see Morel (2006), p. 400, and Peña (2000).

116 Semple (1932), ch. 21.

117 Malkin (1987), ch. 4, especially pp. 147–48.

118 Apollonius Rhodius, *Arg.* 2. 1271–75 with Malkin (1987), ch. 4, especially p. 150.

cult, it appears that Phokaians *expected* some type of these dynamics within the growing Phokaian network even though this is not articulated in network theory terminology. The "sameness" of the cult both colored the network of settlements as Phokaian and mediated all non-Greeks who adopted the cult and its statue to the entire Phokaian network and, in special cases, particularly to Massalia.

Artemis of Ephesos was also exceptional because she looked toward non-Greek peoples and mediated a middle ground between Phokaians and various groups of non-Greeks, notably Ligurians, Celts, Iberians, and Romans. What is noteworthy is the Massaliot investment, possibly at the end of the first century BCE, in the dangerous coasts at the Rhône (Rhodanos) delta, when the Massaliots' role seems to have become more aggressive. Here Artemis of Ephesos appears to have become an instrument of appropriation:

> The Massaliots set up towers as beacons because they were in every way appropriating the country (*exoikeioumenoi . . . tên chôran*) as their own; and for that purpose they also founded there a temple of the Ephesian Artemis, after first annexing (*apolabontes*) a portion of land which is made an island by the mouths of the river.[119]

Again, as with the promontories, Massalia built the towers and the temple with a maritime perspective: how the shore would be seen from the sea and how the river might be navigated. The temple, at least according to Strabo, also seems to "speak" toward the hinterland in terms of territorial annexation of the symbol of Artemis of Ephesos.

Toward the west, aside from the major temples mentioned, Strabo describes the Massaliot cities in Iberia as "strongholds against the Iberians" and says:

> Later, however, their valour enabled them to take in some of the surrounding plains, thanks to the same military strength by which they founded their cities, I mean their stronghold cities (*epiteichismata*), namely, first, those which they founded in Iberia as strongholds against the Iberians. They even handed down to the Iberians the customary rites (*hiera*) of the Ephesian Artemis, so that they sacrificed in the Greek manner (*Hellenisti*).[120]

Strabo goes on to speak of Massaliot cities Rhoë and Agathe, which faced the barbarians around the River Rhône; and Tauroention, Olbia, Antipolis, and Nikaia, which faced the Sallyoi and the Ligurians around the Alps.

---

119 Strabo 4.1.8 C184, trans. Jones (1917), LCL (modified), with Morel 2006: 393 infra, arguing for a late period.

120 Strabo 4.1.5 C180: οἷς καὶ τὰ ἱερὰ τῆς Ἐφεσίας Ἀρτέμιδος παρέδοσαν τὰ πάτρια, ὥστε Ἑλληνιστὶ θύειν. Trans. Jones (1917), LCL (heavily modified). For the use of *ta patria* in a ritual context of mother city and colony (Miletos and Olbia), see Gorman (2002), pp. 187–90.

This is a summary of colonial activities during a few centuries, and the term *epiteichismata* clearly relates to defense. Strabo is probably reflecting a later situation, perhaps relevant more to the second and first centuries BCE than to the era of peaceful commerce, which is reflected in the lead tablets discussed earlier (see pp. 165–167). It is noteworthy that these strongholds also seem to be the gates through which Greek-style rituals were taught to non-Greeks. Curiously, Strabo seems to confine the "missionary" aspects of Artemis of Ephesos to Spain, perhaps reflecting a historical period earlier than the time of Roman influence.[121]

What are the customary rites (*hiera*) of the Ephesian Artemis that were taught to the Iberians? We have already noted that Aristarcha was told to take "some *aphidruma* from among the *hiera*." *Hiera* constitutes the category to which the *aphidruma* belongs. When the Phokaians fled in the face of the Persians, they also took with them *agalmata* (statues) from among the *hiera*,[122] and what the Phokaians are said to have transferred to the Iberians are also *hiera*. These may translate again as "sacred objects" or, less concretely, as "their collective rites." Probably both are implied, with the former indicating the latter (that is, teaching the Iberians the use of the rites that involve the sacred objects). In comparison, the sacred gifts of the Hyperborean Maidens, sent each year to Delos, the birthplace of Apollo and Artemis and sacred especially to the Ionians, were also called *hiera* by Herodotos.[123]

What Strabo finds remarkable is the duplication not only of the cult of the Ephesian Artemis but also of both its status and its statue. This emphasis on precise copying of statue, cult, and position among Greek colonies is paralleled by the deliberate teaching to the Iberians of the *hiera* and sacrificial practices specific to that goddess. Having translated the text as "They even handed down to the Iberians the customary rites (*hiera*) of the Ephesian Artemis," a more literal translation provides a concrete sense: "They also transferred to the Iberians sacred objects of the Ephesian Artemis [such as] they had in their fatherland so that the Iberians sacrifice according to Greek rites." Since the cult statue was one of the *hiera* taken from Asia Minor, it is reasonable to assume that a cult statue as a sacred object was what had been transferred to the non-Greeks.

Strabo makes two explicit claims, both of which contradict the notion of confrontation: the first about teaching the Iberians the customary rites of the Ephesian Artemis and the second about teaching Greek-style sacrifice, *Hellenisti*. Out of 283 times that the word *Hellenisti* is mentioned in Greek sources it invariably refers to language and writing, as Denise Demetriou has observed.[124] This

121 A mediating function in relation to natives is also made explicit in the Ionian *ktisis* about the settlement in Asia Minor. Androkles, son of Kodros, reaches a compromise with the natives residing in the area of the temple of the goddess, whereas he expelled the other Lydians and Leleges. Pherecydes *FGrHist* 3 F 155.

122 Hdt. 1.164.3.

123 Hdt. 4.33.

124 Demetriou (2005), p. 77n141.

is the only place where a Greek text uses *Hellenisti* in terms of cult, signifying particular attention by Strabo or his source. It seems authentic as a curious reflection of the interplay of what colonization can do to ancient perceptions of collective Greek identity. Strabo may simply be referring to some salient features of sacrifice, common to many Greek communities, or he may be reversing the perspective to demonstrate how non-Greeks, who were on the receiving end of the teaching, viewed this. We are again reminded that the term "Phokaians" might have come to mean all Greeks in the far west, where no other mother city apart from Phokaia was active. From a native perspective, what they therefore learned from the Phokaians was both "Greek" sacrifice and, more specifically, the particularities of the cults of the Phokaian Artemis Ephesia. In other words, for native populations, Phokaian cult came to signify Greek cult. This is a case where the external, generalizing perspective of "Greeks" developed from middle grounds of religious influences that belonged to the Greek-barbarian colonial exchange. These appear very different from the conventional scholarly image of the Greek/barbarian divide.

Strabo pays particular attention to the conventional form of the statue. "[I]n all the daughter *poleis* (*en . . . apoikois polesi*, either those of Massalia or other Phokaian cities)," says Strabo, "the people everywhere do this goddess honours of the first rank, and they maintain the same shape of the *xoanon* and otherwise adhere to the same *nomima*, which were traditional (*nenom-isthai*) in the metropolis."[125] As noted, Strabo counts the worship of Artemis as integral to the set of *nomima* with an explicit insistence on the similarity between those of Massalia and her mother city.

Strabo finds not only the degree of adherence to the form of the statue and to its position in the divine hierarchy to be exceptional but also the prominence of the titular deity. Entire pantheons were often copied in colonies, but the hierarchies within them fluctuated and often depended on local circumstances and developments. Note the position, for example, of Demeter and Persephone in Sicily, which was more prominent than in many poleis in the Greek main-land.[126] Aside from Artemis, a special connection seems to have existed between Phokaia and Massalia with regard to other cult statues. Elsewhere Strabo says that "There are to be seen many of the ancient wooden images of Athena in a sitting posture, as, for example, in Phokaia, Massalia, Rome, Chios, and several other places."[127]

Unlike other Greeks in the Black Sea and Italy, the Phokaians were engaged in explicit and intentional teaching and transfer of their salient cult as an integral part of their colonizing policy, not unlike what the Tyrian Phoenicians were doing with Melqart (chapter 4). This did not involve forceful conversion, characteristic

125 Strabo 4.1.4 C179.
126 Zuntz (1971).
127 Strabo 13.1.41 C601. Cf. Paus. 2.31.6, 7.5.4.

of truth-exclusive monotheism. The result was rather a middle ground, where a mutual, dynamic double play seems to have taken place along regional network lines. Phokaians were teaching a "Greek" cult to non-Greeks; these in turn would expect the prominence, statue form, and customs to adhere to precisely the same patterns as among those who transmitted these teachings to them.

A stabilizing, conservative dynamic of networks now becomes apparent: While in other colonies and *poleis* emphasis and form could vary greatly, the reverse was true in the far west. It is precisely the "missionary," mediating function of the cult that kept the prominence, form, and customs associated with the goddess as conservative as possible. This conservatism is to be found among Greeks, who would then feel less free to make changes precisely because the cult now belonged to a multifaceted network. In other words, it is the network that solidifies the cult, a dynamic characteristic of decentralized networks in general.

By the sixth century, when the Romans, too, had their cult image of Diana on the Aventine made "on the same artistic design as the *xoanon* which the Massaliots have,"[128] the Massaliot cult was solidifying into a larger framework, not just Phokaian- or Massaliot-style but Greek. The loss of independence is usually the most opportune time to compensate with symbols of identity. The newly struck Massaliot coins bore the image of the Archaic *xoanon* of the goddess. It was a conservative cult statue, replicated in 48 BCE on Massaliot coins after Julius Caesar conquered Massalia.[129]

The framework, as we see, is much larger than the specific case of Massalia. It was the result of currents that ran multidirectionally among the expanding nodes of the Phokaian network. The concept of "network" is thus both illustrative and explanatory. It is useful for the understanding of these dynamics since such currents kept increasing their volume because of the continuous multiple action of Phokaians and non-Greeks worshipping an Artemis of Ephesos. Because of its network characteristics, at the outreaches of the colonization networks, at least in the far west, we observe degrees of crystallization and homogenization of the cult that are found nowhere else. What is noteworthy is that the process by which this took place involved Phokaian self-affirmation through the founding of Artemis sanctuaries, functioning within the regional middle ground networks of cult transfer with non-Greeks.

The Roman dedications at Delphi were made at Massalia's treasury.[130] This illustrates the interlinking of networks up to the explicit level of the Panhellenic sanctuary. Massalia's own relations with Delphi are relevant. By about 525 BCE,

---

128 Strabo 4.1.5 C180, trans. Jones (1917), LCL. It is noteworthy, perhaps, that Strabo uses the exact same words (τὴν αὐτὴν διάθεσιν ἔχον) to define both the similarity between the *xoana* of Artemis at Massalia and at Rome as between those in Massalia and in her daughter colonies. On the alliance between the Phokaians and the Romans, see Justin 43.3.4. See also Ampolo (1970); Gras (1987). Cf. Malkin (1990), p. 45, with Trotta (2005), pp. 120–22.

129 Malkin (1990), p. 49 and notes 29, 30. Image: Fleischer (1973), pl. 60b. Generally for images of Artemis Ephesia: *LIMC* II.1–2, II.1 pp. 618–21, 755–63; II.2 564–73, especially nos. 15–133.

130 Appian *Italica* frg. 8; Diod. *Sic.* 14.93.3; Livy 5.28.1–5. Cf. Mari (2006).

approximately two generations after its foundation, Massalia became one of the few states at that time to build a treasury at Delphi.[131] We have noted Massalia's magnificent dedications of statues of Athena and Apollo following its victory over the Carthaginians. In contrast to this investment in Delphi, nobody from Massalia had ever won an Olympic victory.[132] Clearly, Massalia maintained an agenda different from that of the Sikeliote Greeks, who loved nothing better than to show off at Olympia. Gillian Shepherd[133] convincingly claims they were using Olympia not just to integrate themselves into a Panhellenic network but also to compete with each other. In contrast to Sicily, there were no other Greeks in the west to compete with except other Phokaians, and there was not much point for Hemeroskopeion, for example, to compete with Massalia.

Delphi is another story. Arriving from the west, the route to the site of the Delphic oracle is much longer than the one to Olympia, so convenience and distance could not have been the overriding considerations for Massalia to prefer Delphi. Perhaps Phokaians would visit Delphi en route to Asia Minor and back. But Delphi had a special meaning for the Massaliots. In matters of colonization Phokaia, the mother city, consulted the Delphic oracle and not the oracle closer to home, at Didyma. We can be certain about Phokaia consulting Delphi with regard to Alalia since we are told that its foundation oracle came specifically from the Pythia.[134] We are less certain about Massalia's own foundation oracle as all we have is an anonymous oracle that Strabo mentions, telling the Phokaians to take for themselves a *hegemôn* from Artemis of Ephesos. Scholars sometimes take it for granted that Phokaia consulted the oracle at Didyma, but the case of Alalia seems decisive in pointing to Delphi.[135] In terms of prestige, Delphi was more distant than Didyma and hence more challenging, with distance contributing to prestige.[136] Moreover, by 600 Didyma was identified mainly with Miletos and its colonies, whereas Delphi had become the true seat of Apollo Archêgetês. The Ionian revolt put an end to Didyma's oracle after the first decade of the fifth century. It would seem, therefore, that Massalia chose to emphasize her integration in the Panhellenic world at Delphi because, more than any other point in the Greek world, Delphi was its "virtual center," its *omphalos*. From a Delphic point of view, Massalia had the advantage of providing it with a wider Panhellenic network that reached all the way to the coasts of France and Spain. Traditionally, the Delphic oracle was at the very

131 Diod. *Sic.* 14.93.4; Appian *Italica* 8.1.3; Lawrence (1996), pp. 95–97; Arafat and Morgan (1994), p. 127; Villard (1960), pp. 90–91. For the excavation report, see pp. 43–78 in Daux's "Les deux trésors" in Demangel and Daux (1923).

132 Hodge (1998), p. 221.

133 Shepherd (2000), pp. 68–69.

134 Hdt. 1.167.4; Malkin (1987), p. 72.

135 Salviat (2000), p. 29, with reference to (Malkin 1987, pp. 69–70), claims that I have invented the consultation at Delphi. However, he overlooks the basic fact that the Pythia (i.e., Delphi) is explicitly mentioned by Herodotus. See (also overlooked by Salviat) Malkin (1987), p. 73, with Hdt. 1.167.4.

136 On Didyma, see Fontenrose (1988) and Parke (1985, 1986).

origin of many Greek cities, thus "chartering" their singular, discrete autonomy. Yet it was also Delphi that provided the link to the wider Greek web.

Conclusion

Between intention and realization, between the Phokaian Artemis Ephesia,
which was meant to be local but became Panhellenic, and Apollo Delphinios,
which was meant to be pan-Ionian but remained Massaliot, was the network
cast. The wider Mediterranean horizons, the Phokaian "long-voyage" category,
which connected *emporia* such as Gravisca and cities such as Elea, Massalia,
Emporion, Rhode, Hemeroskopeion, and perhaps Mainake, was deliberately
expressed by cult foundation and dissemination. The several sanctuaries of
Artemis Ephesia were observed from the sea on promontories and delta islands,
thereby providing a visual unity to the Greek maritime "hinterlands." On a local
level they functioned as central polis cults, possibly attracting the hinterland
and certainly radiating toward it in the form of "conversion," namely, teaching
of "Greek" rites and copying cult statues. In the process, the network evolved
while conserving uniform attributes of the cult. Internationally, Diana at the
Aventine in Rome had some of her origins in this cult, and her cult statue followed a Massaliot model. And it was in the Massaliot treasury at the Panhellenic
Delphi that Rome placed its dedications, the spoils of Veii, just as Kroisos had
placed his in the treasury of the Corinthians. In terms of midrange networks,
the Phokaian Elea (with Neapolis, modern Naples) sent a priestess of Demeter
to Rome.[137] We are reminded that Elea was in the midst of "Massaliot Italy"
(*Italia massalitokē*).[138]

The networks multiply and "intermesh": Panhellenism and Delphi; pan-
Ionianism and the cults of Artemis of Ephesos and Apollo Delphinios; pan-
Phokaianism with the new functions of the cult of Artemis of Ephesos as
expressing *nomima* for all of the western Mediterranean; the regional networks,
which consisted of the "middle grounds" of Greeks and non-Greeks along the
coastal strips of France and Spain. It is perhaps ironic that the cult of Artemis
of Ephesos, a goddess whose special attributes are often deemed "oriental,"
was perhaps taught to the Greeks when they had migrated during the Dark
Age(s) to the eastern Mediterranean and now came to be taught *à la grecque* to
barbarians in the Mediterranean far west.

137 Cic. *Pro Balbo* 24.55 with Val. *Max.* 1.1.1 (Valerius mentions Velia alone). See Morel (2000), pp. 36–37.
138 Eustathius ad *Il.* 2.561. Cf. Steph. Byz. s.v. Troizen.

Conclusions

My purpose in this book has been to present a network perspective for studying the history of the Archaic Mediterranean, especially that of the ancient Greeks. I have been looking for an explanatory link between two uncontested phenomena: (a) by ca. 500 BCE we can recognize (as did ancient Greeks) something we may call "Greek civilization," which had converged and crystallized during the earlier centuries, and (b) the fact that during the Dark Ages and after, especially between ca. 750 and 500 BCE, Greeks were spreading away from each other, founding new settlements, and establishing their cities and *emporia* on shores that were getting more and more distant from each other. Thus, on the one hand, we observe the convergence and crystallization of the commonalities of a civilization and, on the other, the physical dispersal among its members, which might have hindered their appearance. Is this a historical oxymoron? Should we admire the Greeks for having achieved their civilization and a sense of collective identity in spite of their territorial discontinuity? My suggested answer has been to replace "in spite of" with "because": It was distance and network dynamics that created the virtual Greek center and enhanced both the practice and the awareness of Greek commonalities.

What we see here is the self-organization of a complex system through the formation and rapid dynamics of decentralized, accessible, nonhierarchical, multidirectional, expansive, and interactive networks. Network connectivity became faster and more efficient because, as is often the case with such networks, it was enough for several random links to appear among distant nodes for the overall system to be connected. This connectivity had little to do with geographical distance but rather with the decreasing degree of separation among the nodes. The result, familiar from other disciplines (physics, biology, sociology) is the creation of a "small world" or, in our case, of a Greek civilization.

The tautology implied in the claim that networks explain networks is apparent since the evolving and expanding networks are the "same" only in the sense of their architecture and patterns of connectivity, not in the dynamics of their increasing number of flows (contents) and their persistence through time. It is precisely the point that, with the proliferation of new nodes and clusters (*emporia*, colonies, subcolonies, and colonial middle grounds) and with the small world attributes of rapid connectivity and diminishing distance (again that of degree, not of kilometers), these, too, began "behaving" in a network mode, with the nodes serving as links and hubs and allowing for a greater variety of flows of cultural content among them.

The small-world phenomenon of decrease in degrees of separation, together with the increase in material and cultural flows, has direct bearing on the issue of collective Greek identity and ethnicity. The elements that constitute collective identity are not a zero-sum game, and the network approach offered here does not come to replace or to suggest a hierarchy among other criteria of ethnicity and identity (e.g., genealogy and notional kinship, common cults, common historical or quasi-historical experiences, common language, common poetry). It is another way to understand how such criteria could emerge and become widely accepted with the crystallization of commonalities that were in their turn mutually recognized as "Greek."

The opening up of new horizons and the shrinking of vast spaces through improvement in overall connectivity also reshaped mental maps of identity because collective identities acquired new perspectives and underwent swift realignments. There was never any territorial dimension (in the modern sense of an overlap between a nation and its territory) to Greek identity. The new Mediterranean network necessarily involved refiguring the common five circles of a person's collective identity (beyond those of the family and various civic and ritualistic groups of belonging): the polis, the locality (or region), the origins, the subethnic, and the ethnic. It was not territory but the Mediterranean network that linked those intertwining circles, enhancing the self-awareness of their commonalities in the process.

Connecting the Dots?

Identifying networks, "connecting the dots," has been one major task of the book. Nonetheless, to claim that everything is connected is of little significance unless "connections" are presented with a meaningful qualification. This is because "connection," like "influence," is an obscurantist concept (everything *is* connected in some way); it is not an answer but a question. Thus, aside from *identifying* specific networks (in the case studies presented here), my purpose has been to identify those problems that can be better served by a network approach. The identification of connections and particular networks falls within the historian's search for "what was there" (the factual, or the truth level); the suggestion that network dynamics formed the Greek "small world" is by contrast an interpretation, but to my mind it is one that has a high probability of being right.

Networks and Historical Contingency

Ancient Mediterranean networks were historically contingent. They had their cutoff areas at the nodes and regional clusters or middle grounds on the hinterlands of the Mediterranean coasts. In physics, network dynamics are rarely studied with regard for time; nor do mathematical nodes have a contingent identity. Among sociologists, too, perhaps because they are less used to working with *longue-durée* perspectives, time and change have a lesser role to play. But that is not the case for historians, and I have pointed out a process of "network homogenization" that lasted about two and a half centuries (or more, if one starts the count earlier). By 500 BCE we have noted that the increase in the number of the networks was accompanied by a decreased variety in the agents of exchange.

Starting as "many-to-many" networks involving especially Greeks, Phoenicians, and Etruscans, Mediterranean networks transformed during the period between about 750 and 500 BCE. Their growth involved processes of preferential attachment, familiar from much shorter "behavior spans" of complex systems (such as the World Wide Web): New nodes prefer to link up with the existing nodes (or hubs) that already have more links (here: major poleis, such as Massalia, Carthage, or Syracuse). It is a process that led, by the end of the sixth century (especially after the battle of Alalia), to more homogenized Phoenician-Carthaginian, Etruscan, and Greek subareas in the Mediterranean. In the centuries to come Rome would awaken to a Mediterranean of zones of influence, notably (for the West) those of Carthage and Rome's ally, Massalia.

The Spatial Turn

Traditionally, space (geography) is seen as static, whereas history (time and change) is considered dynamic. It has long been recognized that space has its effects on what exists within it. However, the traditional use of geography by historians has been "background" chapters comparable to what one finds in guidebooks for tourists: the climate, flora, fauna, and the layout of a country;

having gone through this tedious detail we can then move to real "history." When geography has been used less neutrally, there was apprehension that we might be raising the phantom of "geographical determinism." For example, it was often claimed that since the topography of Greece is so split up by mountains, the land was less prone to centralized royal rule; hence, too, the emergence of the individual polis. Yet similar topography does not create similar history; for example, a city-state culture did not develop in Nepal, which lies among mountains that are somewhat more forbidding than those of Greece.

The spatial turn has changed all that, and space is no longer considered a mere "container." Geography and history now mix in exciting new ways that are more fluid and mutual. We have seen how geographical space, especially when it shrinks into a small world, does not allow for a simple application of Euclidian geometry and criteria of topographical distances. That is also the problem with the brilliant legacy of Fernand Braudel: He emphasized the Mediterranean as the arena for exchange and "movement in space," where "towns are like electric transformers,"[1] but the networks (*réseaux*) he identified were Euclidian and representational, not multidimensional and explanatory in terms of their own dynamics.

For Fernand Braudel, the claim about Mediterranean *réseaux* is a statement about historical truth: Networks existed and need to be pointed out by historians. In this book, that indeed has been a goal in itself, as were analyzing and suggesting new interpretations of specific issues of Archaic history. While Braudel apparently had the feel for the implications of the Mediterranean networks, he did not yet have the explanatory framework to appreciate the network dynamics of his *échanges* within the *structures* of the *longue durée* as a significant historical category. This study, too, has shifted the emphasis from cellular history (e.g., a discrete "history of Syracuse") to relational models of fluidity and connectivity, paralleling the shift in geographical thought from discrete categories of scale (local, regional, national, or global) to scalar continuity, where local spaces and "global" processes continuously interact. This has been a history observed through a wide-angle lens that is at the same time capable of zooming in on regional middle grounds and local clusters while observing the single sea from the River Phasis to the Pillars of Herakles (the Mediterranean and Black seas) in order to provide a synoptic vision of civilizational connectivity.

At the end of this work I hope it has become clear that my approach is the reverse of geographical determinism: To regard the Mediterranean as the active space of the small world is to reject its essentialization. What I have taken from Mediterranean historiography has been the existence of networks of exchange and the *longue durée* (Braudel), the functioning of networks as connecting shores split up by supposedly antagonistic civilizations (Goitein), the fractal aspects of the microregions and their connectivity as clusters, as well as other

---

1 Braudel (1981), vol. 1, p. 479.

aspects of connectivity and visual perceptions (Horden and Purcell). The networks presented in this book belong to the discourse of the spatial turn since they were both informed by geographical space (e.g., location of natural ports, river mouths, maritime straits, prehistorical routes) and shaped it (rendering coasts significant and connected), turning the Mediterranean into a small world of city-state culture (and not only Greek). In short, network theory has taken networks beyond the representational and the descriptive and has given them a creative and explanatory role but never in any deterministic fashion: "Chaotic" behavior, fractal patterns, and random links appear ubiquitous, yet directly relate to patterns of self-organization and the emergence of the Greek small world.

Why Colonization?

The detailed case studies in the previous chapters all relate to Greek colonization. I have deliberately chosen to emphasize particular phenomena of Mediterranean networks in each chapter, yet to each area (e.g., Rhodes, Sicily, southern France) I might have applied the same questions concerning gods and heroes, settlement patterns, Panhellenic rituals, polytheistic matrix and syncretism, foundational practices, relations with non-Greeks, *nomima*, and the like. What this means is that whereas each network phenomenon that may be observed separately (e.g., commerce in amphorae) and represented as a distinct network, what matters is that all of these discrete networks were basically using the same links. Eventually (rather quickly) the distinct networks would overlap or intermesh to create the matrix that formed the basis for collective Greek identity and civilization.

Network dynamics may explain the speed with which this process of self-organization of the "Greek-Mediterranean complex system" occurred and may be equally applicable for Phoenician and possibly Etruscan studies. The network dynamics were stimulated by the foreshortening of distances and the bringing together of the whole system into a coherent, self-aware civilization or, in network parlance, a Greek Wide Web.

The choice of "colonization" (as noted, a conventional yet misleading modern term that stands for the founding of mostly independent city-states and the creation of *emporia*) for the subject matter of my detailed examination has proven to be important for the study of the Greek small world. Primarily this is because the fact of the colonies' existence across wide geographical horizons is incontrovertible, and no other phenomenon in Archaic history has such a spatial dimension. Moreover, it seems that mobility and colonization expressly encouraged the formation of overarching identities among Greeks. We have seen, for example, how Ialysians, Kameirians, and Lindians became "Rhodians" at Egyptian Naukratis and eventually, through a back-ripple effect, became

Rhodians also at "home." Surprisingly early we saw Archilochos referring to *panhellenes* arriving *together* at Thasos to join the nucleus of the foundation by Paros.[2] Similarly, although Cyrene was settled, specifically, by Therans, Delphi addressed its second immigration oracle to "*all* the Greeks." Moreover, at Egyptian Naukratis the *emporion* shared by several Greek poleis was expressly centered on the Hellênion, the only explicitly "Greek" temple of the Archaic period. The network dynamics encouraging the link between colonization and "Hellenicity" thus worked in several directions.

Movement, migration, and the foundation of new political communities appear as an authentic Greek framework for the articulation of collective identity, whether poetically, by referring to some past (e.g., the return of the Herakleidai, the Ionian migrations), or as actual settlement (e.g., Syracuse, Massalia), or as a program for future action (e.g., Sardinia), or as utopia (Plato's *Laws*, Aristophanes' *Birds*). Dorians in the Peloponnese and Ionians in Asia Minor emphasized common migration in a quasi-historical past as a common point for their positive, "we" identity ("we" as subject, as contrasted with "us"—the compacted object as viewed by an outsider). Being young and on the move appears to have been a salient characteristic of Greek self-perception.

Another major reason for choosing colonization has been that an increased volume of commerce, the founding of cities, and human mobility from the eighth through the seventh centuries correspond to a "phase transition" or a "tipping point," where local interactions lead to the global emergence of an entire system. The proliferation of new settlements and regional clusters, concurrent with the increase of volume in mobility and trade along both new and ancient routes, may have appeared to the participants as a series of discrete and random events. However, the result—through network dynamics, where the addition of a small number of random links drastically reduces the distance between any two nodes—was a "globalized" Mediterranean. To return to Duncan Watts: "[O]ne of the great mysteries of large distributed systems—from communities and organizations to the brain and ecosystems—is how globally coherent activity can emerge in the absence of centralized authority or control."[3]

The Archaic network dynamics of convergence and dispersal in the context of colonization, forcing people into larger "Greek" categories, appear to have been consistent until eventually, during the Hellenistic era, there were no poleis that functioned as discrete mother cities, only "Greek settlers." At the end of the fifth century the Athenian Xenophon found himself as one of the generals of the Ten Thousand, successfully cutting their way through the Persian Empire to the coasts of the Black Sea, where he wished to settle the remains of the army and found a new city. The mercenaries were not convinced. Xenophon was just a little too early for such a venture, yet he foreshadowed typical

---

2 Archilochos frg. 102 = Strabo 8.6.6 C370 with chapter 1, note 167; chapter 2, note 48; chapter 3, note 44.
3 Watts (2003), p. 64.

Hellenistic colonization, when all kinds of "Greeks" would come as settlers to the Hellenistic *katoikiai* (colonies founded within an empire's territory) with no identifiable mother city.[4] At Ai Khanoum in Afghanistan inscriptions bearing Delphic maxims were publicly set up, but it had no *metropolis* of the kind we know in Archaic colonization. It is as if Apollo, although he first prophesied to Thera that it should found Cyrene and only later called on "all the Greeks" to join in, now skipped the first phase altogether. Hellenistic colonization and Hellenistic Greek ("common language," *koinê dialektos*) went hand in hand.

The Greek "colony," *apoikia*, belongs to a semantic field of "away from home" and sometimes relates also to exiles (*apoikoi*).[5] Since *oikos* may signify both a "house" and a "household," it would seem that the early signification of the *oikos* compounds with *ap-* has more to do with "individual" migration (implying also accompanying households or clans) than with state enterprises.[6] *Apoikos-apoikia* originally seems to have emphasized not immigration and destination but *emigration*, denoting a clear notion of origins—yet not necessarily from any "city" as such (in fact, *metro-polis* appears to be somewhat of an anachronism). Saying "far away" naturally implies a point of origin from which one is distant. Hence, too, practices that we find in both domestic and collective life, practices that stress symbolic and ritual links between nodes: specification of an exile's rights for returning to his home community; a bride taking fire from the hearth at home to the hearth of her new husband; a military commander taking fire from the hearth at the home city to ignite sacrificial fire en route; an *oikistês* taking fire from the *koinê Hestia* (common hearth) to initiate the fire in the new collective home, the colony. With many sites far away from each other, the web of individual homes and new homes and of mother cities and colonies seems to have provided the mental maps of Archaic Greeks with definite network characteristics.

If we look for the "origins" of the Mediterranean network (network theorists may not like issues of origins, but historians still do), we may need to look for them in terms of the Mediterranean mobility of various *apoikoi*. In my opinion eighth-century colonization happened roughly along the lines reported by the ancient sources when telling of the beginnings of the colonization movement. Those are represented not as well-organized state projects, as some modern scholars insist on misrepresenting them in order to argue against that very point. Rather, they speak of leaders and their own followers, who resemble Odysseus the Liar, taking his private band to Egypt, or Philippos of Kroton (chapter 4), who joined Dorieus with his own ship and followers. As we have seen (chapter

---

4 Ma (2004).

5 For the Greek emphasis on the point of origin "*apo-*" for travel, immigration, and colonization see Montiglio (2005), p. 2; Baslez (1984), p. 49. This is a subject of a forthcoming study following my Triennial Address (2009) at Oxford University. Cf. Casevitz (1985) on *apoikia* and related terms.

6 Even the Homeric *oikos* signifies something more like *familia* in early Latin, involving a master and "all that is his," including slaves.

3), this is precisely how Thucydides (6.3.1, apparently following Antiochos) describes Theokles, the earliest Greek founder in Sicily: "[S]ome Chalkidians from Euboia sailed with Theokles as oikist" (not "Chalkis was the mother city"). However, as early as the lifetime of Theokles, when the residents of the third city he founded, Katane, rebelled in order to choose their own *oikistês*, the bands of *apoikoi* and their new settlements were acquiring formal aspects.

This "Thoukles effect" seems typical: The open-ended colonial frontiers evened out the personal prominence of founders (see later on the effect of the "frontier"). None (except for the Battiads at Cyrene) became dynastic rulers, and their direct descendants do not seem to have had any special status. After Thoukles it quickly became conventional that a founder could found only one colony. Moreover, a *nomos* appeared, whereby a colony founding a city would request a cofounder from the mother city. By the Classical period there were already several founders per city.

Historical founders became heroes after death, and their cult became a ritualized focus of collective identity. But they never became *eponymous* heroes (with the exception of Phanagoreia).[7] Fictional genealogies of heroes (e.g., Doros-Dorians) could always serve to express origins and kinship. What is fascinating in the new cities of the Archaic world is that their kinship relations were perceived as mostly communal (e.g., between Corinthians and Syracusans) rather than among heroic families. This is the precedent of communal *syngeneia* relationships, which became so prominent in the Hellenistic era. Networks of Mediterranean colonization revolutionized perceptions of collective identity since now these became laterally defined in geographical and social space (Corinth-Syracuse) rather than in terms of vertical lines reaching to an ancient past of specific mythical ancestors. Colonization, then, contributed to the historicization of the collective *imaginaire* in spatial terms.

The quick standardization of *nomos* relating to the founding of cities applied both to their physical aspects of spatial divisions and to the social aspects of *nomima*. These *nomima* still afford the best evidence (with a few exceptions, sadly neglected in current research) for direct similarities among mother cities and colonies, and we have seen their use by Greeks as identifying markers of collective identity and origins. Having the same *nomima* placed communities in mental networks of affinity. Perhaps the very phenomenon of copying comprehensive sets of *nomima* (as well as sometimes mutually adjusting some of their elements in later periods) was encouraged by the connectivity among cities; the vehicles for this standardization seem to have been the decentralized and mutually emulating nodes of the colonial network.

Networks that result from colonization provide a good illustration of how colonial patterns were being formed, copied, and quickly asserted. Archaic colonization is a fast-pace history of foundations linked to wide-ranging Mediterranean

7 Malkin (1986b).

nodes. It presents a situation of *complexity*, where individual and local action determined global patterns and interactions. It was a process of *self-organization* through mutual emulation of foundational patterns, as well as quick solidification of mutual practices, together with the civilizational values attached to them.

An entire system of poleis, both mother cities and colonies, emerged, soon to be followed by narratives of how the cities in the older Greek mainland, too, had once been "founded" along the lines of the later, historical, Archaic foundations (complete with oracular prophecies from Delphi given to a founder). This is another *back-ripple effect*, to be observed with the wide-angle lens of Mediterranean history: Almost the entire Greek world of poleis came to adhere to the same narratological scheme—and the collective identity resulting from it—of the network of "foundations."

Stories of migration, movement, and settlement are important for notions of origins and identity. They are equivalent in some way to the role of the biblical Exodus as the formative experience that forged a nation's identity. However, unlike the Exodus, there were as many *ktiseis* as there were polities; Greeks reached not one but plenty of promised lands, with each community eager to remember its own *ktisis*, yet not to forget its overall connection to the entire movement of colonization and the role of Delphi. In a famous passage Plato has Hippias telling Socrates about his success at Sparta, where "They are very fond of hearing about the genealogies of heroes and men . . . and the foundations of cities in ancient times."[8] The patterns and themes of Greek *ktiseis* (foundation stories) often follow the same themes, and that similarity itself mattered for shaping Greek awareness of commonalities. In short, it was not concerted action but divergence through colonial networks that brought to the foreground the similarity of the *ktisis* outlook, as well as some of the salient features of the living experiences of Greek civilization.

A "Hellas" somehow emerged from all this. In his introduction Thucydides, searching for the first-ever common project of Hellas, identified it with the siege of Troy, where Greeks (the Danaans, Argives, and Achaians of Homer) came together for a common campaign. However, once at Troy, all we hear about are the differences among the heroes and what makes each so special in terms of his honor and *kleos* (renown). In contrast, I think that it is rather the *Odyssey* and other "return stories" (*nostoi*) of the heroes who dispersed around the Mediterranean area, founding cities and dynasties, that are closer in spirit to the formation of "Hellas." For in contrast to the quasi-historical *imaginaire* of the *Iliad*, Greeks in the Archaic period set out not to converge on a "Troy" but to spread out, with figures such as Odysseus as their protocolonial heroes. In other words, it was the lived experience of dispersal (*nostoi*-like) that shaped their outlook.

8 Plato *Hipp. Major* 285d. Cf. Schmid (1947); Prinz (1979).

The Dimension of Space

Apollo's gaze is panoptic, from above, encompassing all geography, seeing the grains of sand, as well as the vast contours of the seas, and contracting the human cosmos into a relational web of habitable sites. "If you know Libya, nurse of sheep, better than I," says Apollo to the exasperated Therans, "[t]hough I have been there and you have not, then I am very much astonished at your knowledge."[9] As noted in my earlier work, it is no accident that the most prominent aspect of foundation prophecies was their divine geographical and topographical knowledge expressed as (mostly maritime) travel directions: how to get "there" and how to identify a site once you do.[10] In contrast, human mobility could be described as "hodological" (hodos = the way, the route), following itineraries and routes, observing space from the inside.[11]

But "Apollo's gaze," too, was a human construction. Greeks certainly possessed such a panoptic vision long before Aristagoras of Miletos carried around with him a map of the world. For example, an expression of a broad panoptic vision that comprehends the entire Mediterranean and the Black Sea would be the physical placement of colonies in relation to long-distance routes and at strategic maritime straits (more later on the maritime perspective). On a more immediate scale, it is enough to look at archaeological spatial plans of "polis and chôra," whether in the Black Sea or in southern Italy, to note that Greeks knew, concretely, how to perceive space as a whole: Sometimes the lines of a city's streets continue into the countryside to form the baselines of field divisions. No wonder: Modern aerial and space photography are not the only means to observe the ground from above; sometimes simply climbing a hill or a tree could be just as useful.

The network approach offered here requires a major revision of our cognitive maps of "ancient Greece," basically eliminating the hierarchy implied in a center-periphery vision or between "Greeks at home" (center) and "Greeks overseas" (periphery). Contemporary processes of state formation ripple back and forth, with "mother cities" being formed by sending out "colonies" (and not always across the water) and with colonies more advanced than their mother cities in terms of urbanization and the codification of the social order. As for Hellas, never a name of a country in antiquity, it was a dynamic term that extended with Greek settlement. One may adopt the view attributed to Demokedes of Kroton, who is said to have convinced the Persian king to send him as a spy to Italy with the intention of conquering that part of "Hellas." The network perspective of Greek nodes constituting Hellas seems to provide a more accurate vision, one that is closer to both the perspectives and the lived experience of the Archaic period.

9 Hdt. 1.47.3; Hdt. 4.157.2.
10 Malkin (1987, ch. 1. "To which land I should go to settle?" seems to have been the normative question (Hdt. 4.42.2).
11 On *spazio odologico* see Janni (1984), part II, with the excellent discussion by Purves (2010), pp. 144–50.

Middle Grounds

The colonial experience of the "middle ground" refers to what emerges from the encounters among colonies and between colonists and "local populations." It is the "third space" of accommodation and cultural negotiation that depends on the inability of any one side to apply full control or hegemony. We are now in a position to state that during the Archaic period the entire Mediterranean region, with its emergent city-state culture and commercial connectivity was a vast middle ground. Nobody controlled the Mediterranean, and, although Near Eastern powers might have wished to become lords of the sea, they failed.

In a more restricted sense we have traced middle grounds in particular colonial regions where the degree of control of certain powers was contingent on the specific conditions of the area. Middle grounds functioned also as "clusters" with locally based, centralized networks and their major hubs. Links through such hubs (e.g., Syracuse, Massalia, Cyrene) connected clusters to the overarching Mediterranean networks.

Where, strictly speaking, is the colonial middle ground to be located? We have seen it both as a territorial *chôra* and beyond. For example, within the Massaliot *chôra* the position of Massalia was hegemonic. However, what about, for example, Basigerros, Bleruas, Golo.biur, and Sedegon, as well as the other people involved in the Pech Maho transaction? The people concerned were apparently Greeks, "natives" who spoke Greek, and possibly Etruscans. They do not appear to depend on a hegemonic, tax-controlling network. Still, even where Massalia was hegemonic, for about six centuries the *chôra* extended into the hinterland to no more than between five and fifteen kilometers. When his time came, Julius Caesar would not think in such terms when conquering all of Gaul.

Immigration from the hinterland toward the Greek foundations sometimes resulted in newly founded, non-Greek, gateway communities. These transformed the coastal areas into spaces of mediation and provided an imprecise "edge," or cutoff point to the Mediterranean networks. Such phenomena are in need of further study since the binary model of "colonists vs. natives" seems widely off the mark in many areas where colonization either stimulated migration from the hinterlands toward the coasts or when coastal activity by locals encouraged colonization or at sites where Greeks and non-Greeks cohabited.

Let me conclude this point with an evocative passage that illustrates the middle grounds as the "edges of the networks." Herodotus (4.108) recounts the story of Gelonos, a city among the Budini in the Black Sea area. The edges are indeed blurry and relate to issues such as lifestyle, the coast vs. the hinterland, language, religion, city dwelling, ethnic contrasts, and collective naming. It describes Greeks who had left the coastal *emporia* to settle among non-Greeks inland: Unlike other Greek cities Gelonos is built entirely of wood, even its temples "of the Greek gods (*hellenikôn theôn*) and are furnished in the Greek way (*Hellenikôs*) with images, altars, and shrines of wood." "These people were originally Greeks (*Hellenes*), who, being driven out of the [coastal] *emporia*, came to the Budini . . . They speak a language half Greek, half Scythian" (4.109). "[W]hereas . . . the Budini are nomads . . . [t]he Gelonoi are tillers of the soil, they eat bread and use gardens; they are wholly unlike the Budini in form and in complexion. Yet the Greeks call the Budini, too, Gelonoi." "But," added Herodotus, "this is wrong."

The Maritime Perspective

Both the Greek language and locations of Greek settlements reveal a visual perception of the world from ship to the shore. The regional name "Epeiros," for example, signifies "the mainland," thus revealing whence it was observed. This perspective fits well with the contrast (Horden and Purcell) between the visual continuum of the coasts, when seen from the sea, and their fragmented nature, when observed from the hinterland. The importance of the maritime perspective is mostly revealed by the choice of sites for settlement (islands, promontories, river mouths) and in particular in the colonies founded on both sides of maritime straits that were established by the same mother city (Greeks at the Crimean Bosporus, the Bosporus at the entrance to the Dardanelles, the Straits of Messina; Phoenicians at Gibraltar, etc.). This pattern of settlement sites implies a periodization of the history of Greek settlements that is different from the customary division into the Dark Ages (ca. 1200–800) and the Archaic period. In both eras, Greeks consistently preferred to settle on offshore islands, on promontories, and at river mouths. From a maritime perspective what we see is continuity rather than rupture.

It is this consistent settlement pattern, with its accumulated experience, that following the eighth century shaped connectivity, commerce, and the choice of new locations for settlement. We have seen this pattern turn into a network in the early Archaic period at the time of the "phase transition," when the intensity of human mobility and settlement activity along more distant coasts jumped up the scale.

With discontinuous coastal territories, relatively small hinterlands, and orientations to the sea, Greek cities and large sections of the Mediterranean coasts functioned effectively as "islands." This was a factor that greatly enhanced the network effect. Whether we observe long-distance voyaging or the long-distance effect through *cabotage* (short hops) sailing, the "island" character of Mediterranean connectivity seems prominent. It is in this context, too, that we may understand the notion of "routes": That there was no central power in the Mediterranean also meant no monopoly over maritime routes. In any case, "maritime routes" is a problematic term since, unlike rivers, the sea affords alternatives (aside from very few narrow straits). The Archaic Mediterranean could not be easily controlled by a central power, as

were the great rivers of the ancient Near East, China, and India.[12] The resulting relative freedom of access and movement seems to have encouraged the
development of a decentralized network with nodes in the form of *emporia*
and city-states together with their regional clusters.

The Mediterranean Frontier

In the *Laws* Plato imagined his utopia as a new colony (in the sense of an independent, new foundation). Should it fail, however, a disaffected group may split
off to found yet another city. This is a Greek way of expressing an aspect of
Fredrick Jackson Turner's "frontier theory" of American expansion and formation of social attributes: When in need, there was always a frontier where one
could found a new community, relatively distant from and free of central
authority. The Mediterranean and the Black Sea were such a frontier for the
Greeks, again enhancing the decentralized character of their resulting network.[13] In extreme cases what applies to segments of a city's population depart-
ing as *apoikiai* might apply to entire poleis: Whole cities could be relocated,
borne on ships to new frontiers, as we have seen in the cases of Phokaia, Teos,
and, optionally, the Athenians before Salamis, and the Ionians of Asia Minor,
who might have immigrated to Sardinia. No such relocations would have been
conceivable without relying on established network lines and recognized nodes
of affinity across the water.[14]

The factor of physical distance (as distinct from "degrees of separation")
has direct bearing on the notion of frontier and on whether a network becomes
hierarchical or decentralized. Syracuse and its close-range subcolonies (Akrai
and Kasmenai) or Massalia and its foundations in Gaul created clusters with
central hierarchical points. However, once distance was sufficiently large there
would be no more question of control. "Distance," of course, is relative to the
technology that aims to overcome it (note the attempts by Corinth and its
advanced ships to intervene in its colonies). However, for the most part, this
was not the case in the Archaic period: Our best candidate, Massalia, so predominant in the seas west of Italy, does not seem to have attempted an empire
(beyond its immediate vicinity), in contrast to Carthage and, later on, Rome.

There had been a precedent to Rome: At the height of the Classical period,
during the fifth century BCE, there emerged an intellectual interest in thalas-
socracies, empires of the sea, an interest that appears to have been kindled by
the formation of the Athenian maritime empire. Athens broke the pattern of
decentralized networks by attempting a centralized maritime control first in

12 Cf. Wittfogel (1963).
13 Purcell (2005), pp. 121–22 (following Ettore Lepore). See Turner ([1921] 1962).
14 Cf. Demand (1990).

the eastern Mediterranean and then, with much grander visions, in the west. In the early Archaic period we saw in the Mediterranean a decentralized, many-to-many network that transformed, by the end of the sixth century, into a network of hubs. However, Athens tried to be an exclusive hub, a thalassocracy, thus replacing the horizontal network model with a hierarchical one (ostensibly justified by the threat of the Persian Empire). It lasted just a few decades before collapsing. At least where the sea was concerned, before the Hellenistic empires, before Rome, the decentralized dynamics of the Greek web, where emphasis on "freedom" for each node was meaningful, were as yet too strong for a lasting thalassocracy.

Networks and "Others"

Much has been written by sociologists, anthropologists, and historians about ethnic identity being defined in terms of a binary contrast with the "Other": Greeks were Greeks because they were "not barbarians" or because barbarians saw them collectively as Greeks. That such a contrast had a role to play may be taken as self-evident, although we need to be careful not to project to the Archaic period views about barbarians that were articulated, especially by Aristotle, in the fourth century. The network approach to collective identity offered here regards the notion of difference from barbarians during the Archaic period (Greeks looking away from each other, toward the terrestrial hinterland of their new foundations) as of relatively minor importance in relation to the much more important phenomenon of commonalities resulting from colonization (Greeks looking at each other across the sea). When Greeks were reaching extended and ethnically varied geographical horizons, common colonial experiences and mutually copied solutions (e.g., criteria for organizing space, codification of *nomima*, standardization of pantheons, the functions and cult of the oikist, Delphi's oracles, ways of accommodation with local populations) probably taught Greeks that the overall differences and variety among themselves were far less significant than the differences they could observe among the populations in Italy, France, north Africa, and the Ukraine.

Another conclusion would be that the Greek-barbarian "difference" consists not in a binary contrast with "barbarians" as such but rather in the multipolar differences *among* barbarians that Greeks could observe, which seems to have been contrasted with what was recognizable, acceptable, and commonly Greek. In other words, because of the intensive time frame and the great number of settlements and subsettlements across widening geographical horizons, connectivity and network dynamics speeded up the spread of mutual patterns and the awareness of their common significance, as well as perhaps their overall coherent similarity in relation to the varied and distinct identities of non-Greeks.

For their part, the "Others" did not seem to bother with fine distinctions among subethnic Greek identities. We know little, but it seems significant that of the three common names for Greeks—Hellenes (self appellation), Graeci (a western name), and "Ionians" (Yavan, Wynn, Yanuna, etc.)—the latter two represent an all-encompassing outsider's perspective formed at the margins of the areas of Greek settlement. As for the *Graeci* in the west, opinions vary, but my own view (as I have argued elsewhere) is that commercial contacts, migration, and settlement probably via the Otranto Straits extended the name of the people living around the oracle of Dodona, the Graikoi, to all *graeci*.[15] In the east during the Dark Ages, migration and settlement gave Greeks a generalized "Ionian" name. Traditionally, "Ionians" had been an ethnic name of a dominant subethnic group that migrated from the Peloponnese via Athens to the Aegean islands and the coasts of Asia Minor. Conversely, Ionia (itself not a Greek word) may have been the name of the region in Asia Minor in which Greeks settled and from which they eventually got their common collective, "ethnic" name.[16] According to this scenario the "Ionian migration" foreshadowed the role of regionalism during the Archaic colonization.

Regionalism, Back-Ripples, and Collective Identity

Given time and different circumstances, the "Sikeliôtai" (Greeks living in Sicily), too, might have become a subethnic "kinship" category with some invented eponym.[17] Something similar may have been happening in Italy, where the regional identity of Italiotes (Greeks living in Italy) was also emerging: Thucydides notes, for example, that when the Athenians asked Rhegion to help Leontinoi in the name of their "Chalkidian" kinship, they preferred to wait for what other "Italiotes" had to say.[18]

I have also noted the possibility that all Greeks in the far west came to be known as "Phokaians," an appellation similar to that of the "Chalkidian" Greeks of Sicily, which comprehended all Euboians and was characterized by Chalkidian (Ionian) *nomima*. In sum, overseas settlement extended network lines and made identities more inclusive and all-encompassing both on the regional basis, on the self-expressive (emic) level of collective identities throughout the Mediterranean and the Black Sea regions, and from the (etic) point of view of outsiders (whether barbarians in antiquity or modern scholars). In authentic Greek terms, it seems that what erases differences and consolidates identity are not nearness and permanence but rather movement, distance, and connectivity. However,

15 Malkin (1998), pp. 147–50.
16 Hall (2002), pp. 67–71.
17 Cf. McInerney (1999), who argues for the evolving regional identity of Phokis and the invention of the eponym Phokos.
18 Thuc. 6.54.3.

once in a new region or in a new land, local settlers were creating regional networks that came into play, articulating new, collective circles of identity.

Regionalism is also linked to the ritual articulation of *new* lands (i.e., lands that are new for Greeks in the collective sense of the term). We noted earlier that the dynamics of colonization quickly extended the notion of access to new foundations to settlers *not* from the mother city but to "Greeks" as such. It appears that new lands came to be seen as open to "Greeks," which may be inferred from the cults of Apollo Archêgetês in Sicily, which were shared by all Sikeliôtai Greeks (whether "Chalkidian" or "Dorian"), the expectation of a pan-Ionian cult of Apollo Delphinios at Massalia, the worship of Zeus Ammon in Libya, and the cult of Achilles Pontarches in the Black Sea. The latter, expressing the "tying-in" of the coasts with the sea as a virtual center, is in need of further study. Terrestrial regions functioned also as clusters with their own network dynamics. The Sikeliote *theôria* in particular illustrates this: Setting out as *Sikeliôtai* from the altar of Apollo Archegetes, entire Sikeliote (Greek) Sicily functioned as a "cluster" with the altar of Apollo and the *theôria* as the link to the Panhellenic sanctuaries.

The concept of "region" emerges therefore as highly significant and multilayered. As such it may appear dull and "merely" geographical. However, when attached to the concept of human networks, with their nodes of settlement and the mobility among them, it directly bears on the formation of collective identities. The interplay between region and network appears multidirectional inasmuch as it involves expanding and shrinking categories of inclusion and exclusion, as well as contracting or expanding regional notions. Greeks were happily applying narrower or wider categories of belonging according to context and the direction of movement of trade and colonization. This flexibility is especially relevant when we consider the back-ripple effect of ancient networks.

Processes of compacting and expanding identities seem to pervade the network experience of the Archaic Mediterranean, characterized by what I have termed a "back-ripple effect" of the network, namely when the "waves" wash back to flood their point of departure. Rhodes has served as a case in point; we have already noted processes of compacting and expanding identities: Being "Rhodians" overseas made them Rhodians at home. Rhodes was "compacted" by common activities of "Rhodians" across the water: Tlepolemos at Troy (quasi-historical); the port of Vroulia; Rhodians colonized at Phaselis, Gela, and Akragas; Rhodians probably settled in the Adriatic, joined Pentathlos of Knidos to conquer Lilybaion in western Sicily and immigrated to Cyrene; individual victors from the island were proclaimed as *Rhodioi* at Olympia, and the three Rhodian poleis shared in the Hellênion at Naukratis as a single "Dorian" polis called "Rhodes"—about a century and a half before the *synoikismos* at home. Rhodes became a major hub in Mediterranean networks, and its position also made it more "Greek," especially when Rhodians "at home" were observed from various points within the Mediterranean network by both Greeks and non-Greeks (especially Phoenicians and Egyptians).

The multidirectional ripple effects also reveal aspects of network dynamics that are fractal in nature. The three cities of Rhodes in relation to Vroulia show the same pattern as all of Rhodes in relation to the Mediterranean. The synoptic vision, especially when islands are concerned, thus reveals parallel processes that defy the traditional categories of "home and abroad" and emphasize ripples and back ripples, as we also noted for Paros, where processes of abandonment and new foundations on the island were contemporary with Parians' founding Thasos, together with plenty of other "Greeks." In network-fractal terminology, what was happening to Lindos, Kameiros, and Ialysos, converging into "Rhodes" for the purpose of partnership in the *Hellênion* of Naukratis, was also happening to the "Dorians, Aiolians, and Ionians," who converged there simply as Greeks.

Through the Hellênion and its religious convergence, Greeks of all kinds, Dorians, Ionians, and Aiolians, coming from a variety of poleis, dedicated together and agreed upon some common *nomima* if only for the sake of calendar, cults, and divinely ensured communal existence. The Hellênion indicates a self-assertive content, formed through network dynamics, which Greeks expressly gave to their settlement. Naukratis in Egypt has thus revealed an apparent paradox: It is the most "diasporic" of Greek sites in the Archaic period, and, *because* it was diasporic (our constant point), it was also the most expressly Hellenic. Naukratis's Hellenicity was an articulated accommodation of Greek identity among Greeks of varying origins, with a generalized, self-referential, Greek identity in relation to Egyptians.

Polis Civilization

Previously I suggested something like the phenomenon of ripples and back ripples with regard to the rise of the polis, namely that the colonial experience was not only contemporary with the rise of the polis but also significantly responsible for it.[19] Rather than thinking that colonists sailed away from home with a definite idea of what a polis was all about and then implanting the model overseas, we should ask whether the rapid pace of colonization, as well as the swift crystallization of models for spatial organization and even urbanism that are apparent in colonies sometimes before their own metropoleis, was not to a large extent responsible for mutual copying and implementation of colonial models in the older Greek world. Moreover, when sending out some distinct groups to colonize elsewhere, the reason is often told in terms of allowing the home society to homogenize and emerge as a polis; was colonization, therefore, also responsible for the "foundation" of the mother city?[20]

19 On "polis civilization" see Hansen (2006).
20 Malkin (1994a).

The dissemination of colonies along the Mediterranean and Black Sea shores brought about, it seems, a back-ripple effect of crystallizing major aspects of polis civilization. On the formal level it is easy to detect priority for the colonies as innovators in urbanism (e.g., Syracuse's urbanization preceding its mother city, Corinth). However, urbanization involves not only housing but also the conceptualization and division of space according to the polis's functional and symbolic institutions. It is likely, for example, that settlers had a notion of a common public space, an *agora*, when they set out even if we cannot detect it on the ground in a mother city. On the other hand, the clearer distinctions between the private, the public, the sacred, and the agricultural spaces in the world of new settlements must have refined or even created a new, self-aware category or "model" for a polis. It is otherwise very difficult to explain the model's overall uniformity, with similar elements and spatial divisions that are apparent from Olbia in the Black Sea to Metapontion in Italy. The contribution of multidirectional networks (with their ripples and back ripples) for the evolvement of the Mediterranean polis civilization is therefore important.

One implication of the rise of the polis is that it is a phenomenon to be observed, like many others suggested in this book, with a wide-angle lens. It is a concurrent development where the precedence of "origins" (such as coming from Corinth) signifies little for the simultaneous aspects of the emergence of polis civilization. Corinth, for example, probably learned not only from its specific colonies of Corcyra and Syracuse but more likely from what was happening in the wide-ranging Mediterranean networks of new foundations and mother cities.

Actors and Connectors

For this process of abstracting and implementing the polis, the role of "actors" or "connectors" must have been significant. These may include major aristocratic figures, such as the Corinthian Demaratos, who migrated to Italy to become an ancestor of a king of Rome, or experts moving along the network lines, such as urban and territorial planners, lawmakers, architects, sculptors, *manteis* (seers) and other cult experts, and poets (such as Aristophanes satirizes in the *Birds*). What is important to note is that network dynamics of foreshortening distances and making links function rapidly should probably be seen as the key to understanding why such connectors could link and influence so swiftly—something for which a satisfactory direction of explanation has not been available.

An example from the Classical period may be illustrative of the agency of connectors and the enrichment of "flows" (here: of both cultural and material content) moving along the same links: Just picture a cargo ship with several travelers on board, such as the Athenian orator Lysias (son of Kephalos of Syracuse), the Athenian seer Lampon, the philosopher Protagoras of Abdera, the town planner and author of utopias Hippodamos of Miletos, the historian

Herodotus of Halikarnassos, as well as some city founders. They were all settlers of the ostensibly Panhellenic (yet Athenian-founded) Thourioi in Italy. Aside from its material cargo the ship thus carried various cultural agents who were all employing the same link, all contributing to the overlap of cultural traits.

Further Implications

Let me note a few aspects that directly relate to what I have been doing yet may need further investigation, starting with a specific issue and moving to more general questions. We may need to return to Delphi: The Delphic oracle, itself a virtual *omphalos* (the "navel of the earth"), grew in influence and enhanced its status as a Panhellenic institution because of its ever-growing horizons of colonization (Olympia, too, is known for the special ritual investment by the western Greeks). This growth may be understood in terms of intermeshing networks: that of colonies and mother cities, that of Delphi and the mother cities, and that of Delphi, the colonies, and the subcolonies. Delphi provided foundation prophecies for new cities and encouraged further immigration to those foundations of individual "Greeks" (not specific members of a mother city). It was the center of ongoing consultations by Greek poleis at its oracle, the site of periodic Panhellenic games, and the focus of Greek *theôria* networks. It most probably functioned also as a mediating hub among Greeks, on both a practical level (while converging on the sanctuary they would share information) and a symbolic one. We need to remember that each colony had not a single but a double origin: in the mother city and in Apollo's oracle, whose prophecies of colonization were not addressed to a mother city as such but to a human founder who was leading an *apoikia* (in the sense of a group of colonists) away from a *metropolis* to found an *apoikia* (in the sense of a new settlement), usually on a distant shore.

Applying network concepts to the history of the Archaic Mediterranean seems to hold much promise for future research. When reaching the conclusion of this book I find that the potential for the network approach for relational, wide-angle historical questions within a *longue-durée* perspective is impressive. Outside of ancient history one could think offhand of obvious areas of investigation where network theory might be useful, such as diaspora studies, commerce and colonialism, religious conversion, Atlantic studies, and so much more. For ancient historians and archaeologists there is much more to do, especially while fine-tuning aspects of Greek civilization that seem clearly worthy of network analysis. Religion, for example: In this book I have emphasized the polytheistic matrix of ancient Mediterranean religions, which made possible the intricate interplay between the "Greek" Herakles and the "Phoenician" Melqart, as well as the mediating role of Artemis of Ephesos. But how did the major aspects of religion become *Greek* commonalities? Here is James Davidson, writing on "time and Greek religion":

[T]hat so many fiercely independent poleis, acknowledging no overarching religious authority, managed, nevertheless, quietly to keep their "moons" and festivals more or less in step with each other over long periods is itself quite remarkable, and it gives us a tangible illustration of how there is an "ancient Greek religion" to speak of, without there being a unitary "ancient Greece."[21]

I suggest that applying a network approach would provide Davidson's impressionistic "quite remarkable" with a heuristic concept with which to approach the question of how "they managed" and perhaps as to how the religion of all those fifteen hundred poleis, according to the latest count, formed, shared, and maintained their religion as "Greek."

There is, of course, room for more such studies pertaining to various aspects of Greek colonization and other maritime regions (the Black Sea in particular has not been represented here). Beyond colonization, I can think of other areas of study in Greek history where networks may prove particularly good to think with, such as the spread of maritime knowledge among both Greeks and Phoenicians; the dissemination Greek poetry, dance, and music; the spread of tyranny and networks of tyrants; leagues and amphiktyonies; *ethnos* formations; interaction inside states such as Athens and Attica; island connectivity; synoikistic formations; networks of sanctuaries and festivals; trading contacts and emporia; *xenia* relations and aristocracies; the spread of literacy; the creation of a common visual language (art and architecture); intellectual networks; the transfer of technology; the conventions of warfare, the hoplite system, and the growing role of mercenaries; law codes and *nomima*; the spread of new cults; human mobility (traders, mercenaries, teachers, artisans, etc.), and so on.

A Small World

At a time when our mindset has become attuned to the idea of networks and while the Internet and the World Wide Web have become a "space" unto themselves, we are perhaps more open to a different positioning of historical questions in network terms. Small world dynamics and evolving network structures are noted today for fields as far apart as biology, chemistry, sociology, and physics, and I see no reason that history, too, should not be a fertile field for network perspectives. As a historian not only of ancient Greece but also of the Mediterranean, with its *réseaux* that transcend traditional periodization, I have been somewhat prepared for a network perspective but not to where it led me. Research is like travel, but the travel book you eventually write presents the sites in a different order and may arrive at surprising connections and implications. So let me return to Cicero's picturing Hellas as stretched across the sea with its "hems stitched onto the lands of barbarian peoples." The "Hellas" he was observing had evolved as a small world.

---

21 Davidson (2010), p. 205. See especially Clarke (2008), pp. 1–56.

Bibliography

Akurgal, Ekrem (1956). "Les fouilles de Phocée et les sondages de Kymé," *Anatolia*, 1, pp. 3–14.

––––––– (1962). "The Early Period and the Golden Age of Ionia," *AJA*, 66, pp. 369–79.

Alberro, Solange (1992). *Les Espagnols dans le Mexique colonial: Histoire d'une acculturation*. Cahiers des annales 43. Paris: Armand Colin.

Alcock, Susan E. (2005). "Alphabet Soup in the Mediterranean Basin: The Emergence of the Mediterranean Serial," in Harris (2005b), pp. 314–38.

Alfonso, Corral Martin (2002). *Ezekiel's Oracles against Tyre: Historical Reality and Motivations*. Rome: Istituto Pontifico Biblico.

Almagro Basch, Martín (1966). *Ampurias: Guide to the Excavations and Museum*. Barcelona: Casa provincial de Caridad.

Alty, John (1982). "Dorians and Ionians," *JHS*, 102, pp. 1–14.

Amitay, Ory (2008). "Why Did Alexander the Great Besiege Tyre?" *Athenaeum*, 96, pp. 91–102.

Ampolo, Carmine (1970). "L'Artemide di Marsiglia e la Diana del Aventino," *PP*, 25, pp. 130–33, 200–10.

––––––– (1977). "Demarato. Osservazioni sulla mobilità sociale arcaica," *Dialoghi di archeologia*, 9, pp. 333–45.

––––––– and Teres Caruso (1990–1991). "I greci e gli altri nel Mediterraneo occidentale. Le iscrizioni greca ed etrusca di Pech-Maho: Circolazione di beni, di uomini, di istituti," *Opus*, 9–10, pp. 28–57.

Anderson, Benedict R. (1991). *Imagined Communities: Reflections on the Origin and Spread of Nationalism*. Rev. edn. London: Verso.

Andreau, Jean and Catherine Virlouvet (eds.) (2002). *L'information et la mer dans le monde antique*. Collection de l'École française de Rome 297. Rome: École française de Rome.

Anguissola, Anna (2006a). "Note on Aphidruma 1: Statues and Their Function," *CQ*, 56(2), pp. 641–43.

———— (2006b). "Note on Aphidruma 2: Strabo on the Transfer of Cults," *CQ*, 56(2), pp. 643–46.

Antonaccio, Carla Maria (1995). *An Archaeology of Ancestors*. Lanham, Md.: Rowman and Littlefield.

———— (2001). "Ethnicity and Colonization," in Malkin (2001c), pp. 113–57.

———— (2007). "Elite Mobility in the West," in Simon Hornblower and Catherine Morgan (eds.). *Pindar's Poetry, Patrons, and Festivals: From Archaic Greece to the Roman Empire*. Oxford: Oxford University Press, pp. 265–85.

Antonelli, Luca (2008). *Traffici focei di età arcaica*. Hesperia 23. Rome: "L'Erma" di Bretschneider.

Antonetti, Claudia (1997a). "Megara e le sue colonie: Un'unità storico-culturale?" in Claudia Antonetti (ed.). Il dinamismo della colonizzazione greca-Atti della tavola rotonda Espansione e colonizzazione greca d'età arcaica: Metodologie e problemi a confronto (Venezia, 10–11/11/95). Napoli: Loffredo, pp. 83–94.

———— (ed.) (1997b). Il dinamismo della colonizzazione greca. Atti della tavola rotonda "Espansione e colonizzazione greca d'età arcaica: Metodologie e problemi a confronto" (Venezia, 10–11/11/1995). Napoli: Loffredo.

Appadurai, Arjun (ed.) (1986). *The Social Life of Things: Commodities in Cultural Perspective*. Cambridge: Cambridge University Press.

Arafat, Karim and Catherine Morgan (1994). "Athens, Etruria, and the Heuneburg: Mutual Misconceptions in the Study of Greek-Barbarian Relations," in Ian Morris (ed.). *Classical Greece: Ancient Histories and Modern Archaeologies*. New Directions in Archaeology. Cambridge: Cambridge University Press, pp. 108–34.

Arcelin, Patrice (1995). "Arles protohistorique, centre d'échanges économiques et culturels," in Patrice Arcelin (ed.). *Sur les pas des Grecs en occident: Hommages à André Nickels*. Études massaliètes 4. Lattes-Paris: A.D.A.M.-Errance, pp. 325–38.

Arnold, Irene Ringwood (1936). "Festivals of Rhodes," *AJA*, 40(4), pp. 432–36.

Asheri, David (1988). "Carthaginians and Greeks," in John Boardman, N. G. L. Hammond, D. M. Lewis, and M. Ostwald (eds.). *Cambridge Ancient History*. 2nd edn. Vol. 4: *Persia, Greece, and the Western Mediterranean c. 525 to 479 B.C.* Cambridge: Cambridge University Press, pp. 739–80.

———— (1999a). *Erodoto: Le storie*. 5th edn. Vol. 1: *A Lidia e la Persia*. Scrittori greci e latini. Milano: Fondazione Lorenzo Valla.

———— (1999b). "Processi di 'decolonizzazione' in Magna Grecia: Il caso di Poseidonia Lucana," in *La colonization grecque en Méditerranée occidentale: Actes de la rencontre scientifique en homage à Georges Vallet organisé par le Centre Jean Bérard, l'École française de Rome, l'Istituto universitario orientale, et l'Università degli studi di Napoli 'Frederico II' (Rome-Naples, 15–18 novembre 1995)*, pp. 361–70.

Aubet, María Eugenia (2001). *The Phoenicians and the West: Politics, Colonies, and Trade*. 2nd edn. Cambridge: Cambridge University Press.

———— (2008). "Political and Economic Implications of the New Phoenician Chronologies," in C. Sagona (ed.). *Beyond the Homeland: Markers in Phoenician Chronology*. Ancient Near Eastern Studies Suppl. Series 28. Leuven: Peeters, pp. 247–59.

Austin, M. M. (1970). "Greece and Egypt in the Archaic Age," *PCPhS*, Suppl. 2.

———— (2004). "From Syria to the Pillars of Herakles." In Hansen and Nielsen (2004), pp. 1232–49.

Bachelard, Gaston (1994). *The Poetics of Space*. Translated by Maria Jolas. Boston: Beacon.

Bagnall, Roger S. and Peter S. Derow (2004). *The Hellenistic Period: Historical Sources in Translation*. Oxford: Blackwell.

Balcer, J. M. (1984). *Sparda by the Bitter Sea: Imperial Interaction in Western Anatolia*. Brown Judaic Studies. Chico, Calif.: Scholars Press.

Bammer, Anton (1984). *Das Heiligtum der Artemis von Ephesos*. Graz: Akademische Druck- und Verlagsanstalt.

Barabási, Albert-Lásló ó (2003). *Linked: How Everything Is Connected to Everything Else and What It Means for Business, Science, and Everyday Life*. New York: Plume.

Barney, Darin David (2004). *The Network Society*. Cambridge: Polity.

Barth, Fredrik (ed.) (1969). Ethnic Groups and Boundaries: The Social Organization of Culture Difference. London: Allen and Unwin.

Bartlett, Robert (1993). *The Making of Europe: Conquest, Colonization, and Cultural Change, 950–1350*. Princeton, N.J.: Princeton University Press.

Baslez, M.-F. (1984). *L'étranger dans la Grèce antique*. Paris: Belles Lettres.

———— (1986). "Cultes et dévotions des Phéniciens en Grèce: Les divinités marines," in Corinne Bonnet, Edward Lipiński, and P. Marchetti (eds.). *Religio Phoenicia (= Studia Phoenicia 4)*. Namur: Société des Études Classiques, pp. 289–305.

Bats, Michel (1982). "Commerce et politiques massaliètes aux IVe et IIIe siècles av. J.-C.: Essai d'interprétation du faciès céramiques d'Olbia de Provence (Hyères, Var)," *PP*, 204–208, pp. 256–67.

———— (1988). "La logique de l'écriture d'une société à l'autre en Gaule méridionale protohistorique," *Revue archéologique de Narbonnaise*, 21, pp. 121–48.

———— (1990). "Nice," in *Voyage en Massalie: 100 ans d'archéologie en Gaule du Sud*, Marseille: Édisud, pp. 222–25.

———— (1992). "Marseille, les colonies massaliètes et les relais indigènes dans le trafic le long du littoral méditerranéen gaulois (VIe–Ier s.v. J.-C.)," in Michel Bats et al. (1992), pp. 263–78.

———— (1994). "Les silences d'Hérodote ou Marseille, Alalia, et les Phocéens en occident jusqu'à la fondation de Vélia," in David Ridgway and Bruno D'Agostino (eds.). *Apoikia: Scritti in onore di Giorgio Buchner, AION ArchStAnt* n.s. 1. Naples: Istituto universitario orientale, pp. 133–48.

———— (1998). "Marseille archaïque: Étrusques et Phocéens en Méditerranée nord-occidental," *MEFRA*, 110(2), pp. 609–33.

———— (2009). "Le colonie di Massalia," in Lombardo and Frisone (2009), pp. 203–208.

————, Guy Bertucchi, Gaétan Conges, and Henri Tréziny (eds.). (1992). *Marseille grecque et la Gaule*. Études massaliètes 3, Aix-en-Provence: ADAM and Université de Provence.

———— and D. Mouchot (1990). "Nice," in *Voyage en Massalie: 100 ans d'archéologie en Gaule du Sud*. Marseille: Édisud, pp. 222–25.

Beekes, Robert S. P. (2002). "The Prehistory of the Lydians, the Origin of the Etruscans, Troy, and Aeneas," *Bibliotheca Orientalis*, 59(3–4), pp. 205–41.

Belin de Ballu, Eugène (1972). *Olbia: Cité antique du littoral nord de la Mer Noire*. Leiden: Brill.

Bell, Malcolm (1995). "The Motya Charioteer and Pindar's Isthmian 2," in *Memoirs of the American Academy in Rome*, 40, pp. 1–42.

Ben Ami, Shlomo (1990). "L'image de l'Espagne en France," in Irad Malkin (ed.). *La France et la Méditerranée: Vingt-sept siècles d'interdépendance*. Leiden: Brill, pp. 363–88.

Ben Artzi, Yossi (2004). "The Idea of a Mediterranean Region in Nineteenth- to Mid-Twentieth-Century German Geography," *MHR*, 19(2), pp. 2–15.

Ben-Dov, Yoav (1995). *Invitation à la physique*. Paris: Seuil.

—— (1997). *Quantum Mechanics: Reality and Mystery* (in Hebrew). Tel Aviv: Dvir.

Benoit, J. (1985). "L'étude des cadastres antiques: À propos d'Olbia de Provence," *Documents d'Archéologie Méridionale*, 8, pp. 25–48.

Bérard, Jean (1957). *La colonisation grecque de l'Italie méridionale et de la Sicile dans l'antiquité: L'histoire et la légende*. 2nd edn. Bibliothèque des Écoles françaises d'Athènes et de Rome 150. Paris: De Boccard.

—— (1960). *L'expansion et la colonization grecques jusqu'aux guerres médiques*. Paris: Aubier.

Bergquist, Birgitta (1973). *Herakles on Thasos: The Archaeological, Literary, and Epigraphic Evidence for his Sanctuary, Status, and Cult Reconsidered*. Acta Universitatis Upsaliensis, Boreas 5. Uppsala: University of Uppsala.

Bernand, André (1970). *Le delta égyptien d'après les textes grecques, I: Les confins libyques*. Mémoires publiés par les membres de l'Institut Français d'Archéologie Orientale du Caire. Cairo.

—— and Olivier Masson (1957). "Les inscriptions grecques d'Abou-Simbel," *REG*, 70, pp. 1–46.

Bernard, Paul (1973). *Fouilles d'Ai Khanoum I: Campagnes 1965, 1966, 1967, 1968*. Mémoires de la Délégation archéologique française en Afghanistan (= MDAFA) 21. Paris: Klincksieck.

—— (1985). *Fouilles d'Ai Khanoum IV: Les monnaies hors trésors*. Questions d'histoire gréco-bactrienne. Mémoires de la Délégation archéologique française en Afghanistan (= MDAFA) 28. Paris: Klincksieck.

Berranger, Danièle (1992). *Recherches sur l'histoire et la prosopographie de Paros à l'époque archaïque*. Clermont-Ferrand: Association des Publications de la Faculté des Lettres et Sciences Humaines.

Berthold, R. M. (1984). *Rhodes in the Hellenistic Age*. Ithaca, N.Y.: Cornell University Press.

Berti, Fede and Piero Giovanni Guzzo (eds.) (1993). *Spina: Storia di una città tra Greci ed Etruschi* (Exhibition Catalog). Ferrara: Ferrara Arte.

Bétant, Elie-Ami (1969). *Lexicon Thucidideum*. Hildesheim: Olms.

Bettenson, Henry Scowcroft (1976). *Livy: Rome and the Mediterranean. Books XXXI–XLV of the History of Rome from its Foundation*. Penguin Classics. Harmondsworth: Penguin.

Bilabel, Friedrich (1920). *Die ionische Kolonisation*. Philologus Suppl. 14(1). Leipzig: Dieterich.

Bistolfi, Robert (1995). *Euro-méditerranée, une région à construire*. Collection "Espaces méditerranées." Paris: Publisud.

Blackman, David J. (2004). "The Ports of the Two Cities of Naxos," in M. C. Lentini (ed.). *Le due città di Naxos: Atti del Seminario di Studi Giardini Naxos 29–31 Ottobre 2000.* Giardini Naxos: Comune di Giardini Naxos, pp. 51–58.

———— and M. C. Lentini (2003). "The Shipsheds of Sicilian Naxos: Researches 1998–2001. A Preliminary Report." *Annual of the British School at Athens,* 98, pp. 387–435.

Blakely, Sandra (1998). "Daimones, Metallurgy, and Cult." PhD diss., University of Southern California–Los Angeles.

———— (2006). *Myth, Ritual, and Metallurgy in Ancient Greece and Recent Africa.* Cambridge: Cambridge University Press.

Blinkenberg, Chr. (1941). *Lindos: Fouilles de l'acropole 1902–1914.* Vol. 2: *Inscriptions.* Berlin: de Gruyter.

Boardman, John (1999). *The Greeks Overseas.* 4th edn. London: Thames and Hudson.

———— and J. W. Hayes (1966). *Excavations at Tocra: 1963–1965.* 2 vols. BSA Suppl. 196. London: Thames and Hudson.

Boegehold, Alan L. (1995). *The Lawcourts at Athens: Sites, Buildings, Equipment, Procedure, and Testimonia.* Athenian Agora 28. Princeton, N.J.: American School of Classical Studies at Athens.

Boesch, Paul (1908). *Theoros: Untersuchung zur Epangelie griechischer Feste.* Berlin: Mayer and Muller.

Boissevain, Jeremy (1974). *Friends of Friends: Networks, Manipulators, and Coalitions.* Oxford: Blackwell.

———— and J. Clyde Mitchell (eds.) (1973). *Network Analysis: Studies in Human Interaction.* The Hague: Mouton.

Bommelaer, Jean-François (1991). *Guide de Delphes: Le site.* Athens: École Française d'Athènes.

Bonacasa, Nicola and Antonino Buttitta (eds.) (1988). *La statua marmorea di Mozia e la scultura di stile severo in Sicilia: Atti della giornata di studio, Marsala, 1 giugno 1986.* Roma: "L'Erma" di Bretschneider.

Bonnet, Corinne (1988). *Melqart: Cultes et mythes de l'Héraclès tyrien en Méditerranée.* Studia Phoenicia 8. Namur: Presses Universitaires.

———— (2009). "Appréhender les Phéniciens en Sicile: Pour une lecture de l'archéologie sicilienne de Thucydide (vi 1.1–2)," *Pallas,* 79, pp. 27–40.

———— (2011). "On Gods and Earth: The Tophet and the Construction of a New Identity in Punic Carthage," in Gruen (2011), pp. 373–87.

Bono, Salvatore (1999). *Il Mediterraneo: Da Lepanto a Barcellona.* Perugia: Morlacchi.

Bopearachchi, Osmund (2003). *De l'Indus à l'Oxus: Archéologie de l'Asie Centrale.* Catalogue de l'exposition. Lattes: Association imago-musée de Lattes.

Borgatti, Stephen Peter, Martin G. Everett, and Lin C. Freeman (2002). *Ucinet for Windows: Software for Social Network Analysis.* Harvard, Mass.: Analytic Technologies.

Borgeaud, Philippe (1996). *La mère des dieux: De Cybèle à la vierge Marie.* Paris: Seuil.

Bouloumié, Bernard (1979). "Saint-Blaise: Note sommaire sur cinq années de fouilles et de recherches (1974–1978)," *Gallia,* 37, pp. 229–36.

———— (1982a). *Recherches stratigraphiques sur l'oppidum de Saint-Blaise (B.d.R.).* Revue archéologique Sites. Hors série, no. 15. Avignon: Revue archéologique Sites.

———— (1982b). "Saint-Blaise et Marseille au VIe siècle avant J.-C.: L'hypothèse étrusque," *Latomus,* 41, pp. 74–91.

———— (ed.) (1984). "Saint-Blaise: Oppidum du sel," special issue, *Histoire et Archéolo-gie*, 84.

———— (1992). *Saint-Blaise: L'habitat protohistorique, les céramiques grecques.* Travaux du Centre Camille Jullian 13. Aix-en-Provence: Université de Provence.

Bowden, Hugh (1996). "The Greek Settlement and Sanctuaries at Naukratis: Herodotus and Archaeology," in Hansen and Raaflaub (1996), pp. 17–37.

———— (2003). "The Functions of the Delphic Amphictyony before 346 BCE," *SCI*, 22, pp. 67–83.

Bowersock, Glen W. (2005). "The East-West Orientation of Mediterranean Studies and the Meaning of North and South in Antiquity," in Harris (2005b), pp. 167–78.

Brauch, Hans Günter (2000). *Euro-Mediterranean Partnership for the 21st Century.* Collection Strademed 8. New York: Macmillan Press/St. Martin's Press.

Braudel, Fernand (1972). *The Mediterranean and the Mediterranean World in the Age of Philip II.* Translated by Sîan Reynolds. 2 vols. Glasgow: Collins.

———— (1981). *Civilization and Capitalism, 15th–18th Century.* 3 vols. London: Collins.

———— (1994). *A History of Civilizations.* Translated by Richard Mayne. New York: Allen Lane/Penguin Press.

Braun, T. F. R. G. (1982). "The Greeks in Egypt," in John Boardman and N. G. L. Hammond (eds.). *The Cambridge Ancient History.* 2nd edn. Vol. 3, Part 3: *The Expansion of the Greek World, 8th to 6th Century B.C.* New York: Cambridge University Press, pp. 32–56.

Braund, D. (1998). "Writing and Re-Inventing Colonial Origins: Problems from Colchis and the Bosporus," in Gocha R. Tsetskhladze (ed.). *The Greek Colonisation of the Black Sea Area: Historical Interpretation of Archaeology.* Stuttgart: Steiner, pp. 287–96.

Brenk, P. E. 1998. "Artemis of Ephesos: An Avante Garde Goddess." *Kernos* 11, pp. 157–71.

Bresciani, Edda (1984). "Egypt, Persian Satrapy," in W. D. Davies and Louis Finkelstein (eds.). *The Cambridge History of Judaism.* Vol. 1. Cambridge: Cambridge University Press, pp. 358–72.

Bresson, Alain (1986). "Deux légendes rhodiennes," in *Les grandes figures religieuses: Fonctionnement pratique et symbolique dans l'antiquité: Besançon, 25–26 avril 1984.* Annales Littéraires de l'Université de Besançon 329. Paris: Belles Lettres, pp. 411–21.

———— (1991). "Le fils de Pytheas, Egyptien de Naucratis," in N. Fick and J.-C. Carriere (eds.). *Mélanges Étienne Bernard.* Paris: Belles Lettres, pp. 37–42.

———— (2000a). "La dynamique des cités de Lesbos," in *La cité marchande.* Paris: De Boccard, pp. 101–109. Originally published in *Cahiers Radet* (Université de Bordeaux III), 3, 1983.

———— (2000b). "Retour a Naucratis," in *La cité marchande.* Paris: De Boccard, pp. 64–84.

———— (2000c). "Rhodes, l'Hellénion, et le statut de Naucratis," in *La cité marchande.* Paris: De Boccard, pp. 13–63. Originally published in *DHA*, 6 (1980): 291–349.

———— (2000d). *La cité marchande.* Paris: De Boccard.

———— (2005). "Naucratis: De l'emporion à la cité." *Topoi* 12–13, pp. 133–55.

———— and P. Rouillard (eds.) (1993). *L'Emporion.* Paris: De Boccard.

Briant, Pierre and Raymond Descat (1998). "Un registre douanier de la satrapie d'Égypte à l'époque achéménide (TAD C3, 7)," in Bernadette Menu and Nicolas-Christophe Grimal (eds.). *Le commerce en Égypte ancienne*. Bibliothèque d'étude 121. Cairo: IFAO, pp. 59–104.

Briquel, Dominique (1991). *L'origine lydienne des Étrusques: Histoire de la doctrine dans l'antiquité*. Paris: École française de Rome.

Brody, Aaron Jed (1998). *"Each Man Cried Out to His God": The Specialized Religion of Canaanite and Phoenician Seafarers*. Harvard Semitic Museum Publications 58. Atlanta: Scholars Press.

Brommer, Frank (1986). *Heracles: The Twelve Labors of the Hero in Ancient Art and Literature*. Translated by Shirley J. Schwarz. New Rochelle, N.Y.: Caratzas.

Brughmans, Tom (2010). "Connecting the Dots: Toward Archaeological Network Analysis," *OJA*, 29, pp. 277–303.

Brun, Cristophe (2007 [1997]). "Presentation," in David Cosandey, *Le secret de l'Occident: Vers une théorie générale du progrès scientifique*. Paris: Flammarion, pp. 11–94.

Brunel, J. (1953). "Apropos de transferts de cultes: Un sens méconnu du mot ἀφίδρυμα," *Revue de philologie*, 27, pp. 21–33.

Brunet, Michèle (1999). *Territoires des cités grecques: Actes de la table ronde internationale organisée par l'École française d'Athènes, 31 octobre–3 novembre 1991*. BCH Suppl. 34. Paris: De Boccard.

Buchanan, Mark (2002). *Nexus: Small Worlds and the Groundbreaking Theory of Networks*. New York: Norton.

Bunnens, Guy (1983). "Tyr et la mer," in E. Gubel, E. Lipiński, and B. Servais-Soyez (eds.). *Studia Phoenicia I–II*. Orientalia Lovaniensia Analecta 15. Leuven: Peeters, pp. 7–21.

Burgers, Gert-Jan and Jan Paul Crielaard (2007). "Greek Colonists and Indigenous Populations at l'Amastuola, Southern Italy," *Bulletin Antieke Beschaving*, 82, pp. 87–124.

Burkert, Walter (1979). *Structure and History in Greek Mythology and Ritual*. Sather Classical Lectures, vol. 47. Berkeley: University of California Press.

——— (1983). "Itinerant Diviners and Magicians: A Neglected Element in Cultural Contact," in Robin Hägg (ed.). *The Greek Renaissance of the Eight Century BC: Tradition and Innovation*. Stockholm: Svenska institutet i Athen, pp. 115–19.

Burr, Viktor (1932). *Nostrum mare: Ursprung und Geschichte der Namen des Mittelmeeres und seiner Teilmeere im Altertum*. Würzburger Studien zur Altertumswissenschaft 4. Stuttgart: Kohlhammer.

Bury, J. B. (1895). "The History of the Names Hellas, Hellenes," *JHS*, 15, pp. 217–38.

Buskikh, B. Sergei (2005). "Les sanctuaires extra-urbains à l'époque de la colonisation grecque dans le Bug méridional," in Darejan Kacharava, Murielle Faudot, and Evelyne Geny (eds.). *Pont-Euxin et polis: Polis hellenis et polis barbaron. Actes du Xe symposium de Vani, 23–26 septembre 2002: Homage à Otar Lordkipanidzé et Pierre Lévêque*. Besançon: Presses universitaires franc-comtoises, pp. 181–202.

Buxton, A. H. (2002). "Lydian Royal Dedications in Greek Sanctuaries." PhD diss., University of California–Berkeley.

Cabanes, Pierre (2008). "Greek Colonisation in the Adriatic," in Gocha R. Tsetskhladze (ed.). *Greek Colonisation: An Account of Greek Colonies and Other Settlements Overseas*. Vol. 2. Leiden: Brill, pp. 155–86.

Cabrera Bonet, Paloma (1996). "Emporion y el comercio griego arcaico en el nordeste de la Península Ibérica," in Ricardo Olmos and Pierre Rouillard (eds.). *Formes archaïques et arts ibériques*. Vol. 59. Collection de la casa de Velázquez. Madrid: Casa de Velázquez, pp. 43–54.

Campbell, David A. (ed.) (1988). *Greek Lyric*. Reprinted with corrections. Vol. 2: *Anacreon, Anacreontea: Choral Lyric from Olympus to Alcman*. Loeb Classical Library. Cambridge, Mass.: Harvard University Press.

———— (ed.) (1990). *Greek Lyric*. Reprinted with corrections. Vol. 1: *Sappho and Alcaeus*. Loeb Classical Library. Cambridge, Mass.: Harvard University Press.

Carpez-Csornay, B. (2006). *A Relationship in Flux: Egypt and Cyprus during the Iron Age*. Report of the Department of Antiquities, Cyprus, pp. 213–22.

Cartledge, Paul (2001). "The Spartan Kingship: Doubly Odd?" in Paul Cartledge (ed.). *Spartan Reflections*. Berkeley: University of California Press and Duckworth, pp. 55–67.

————, Edward E. Cohen, and Lin Foxhall (eds.) (2002). *Money, Labour, and Land: Approaches to the Economies of Ancient Greece*. London: Routledge.

Casevitz, Michel (1985). *Le vocabulaire de la colonisation en grec ancien: Étude lexicologique. Les familles de ktizō et de oikeō-oikizō*. Études et commentaires 97. Paris: Klincksieck.

Castagnino Berlinghieri, Elena Flavia (2003). *The Aiolian Islands: Crossroads of Mediterranean Maritime Routes: A Survey on Their Maritime Archaeology and Topography from the Prehistoric to the Roman Periods*. BAR International Series 1181. Oxford: Archaeopress.

Castells, Manuel (1996). *The Rise of the Network Society*. The Information Age: Economy, Society and Culture. Vol. 1. Malden, Mass.: Blackwell.

Caven, Brian (1990). *Dionysius I: War-Lord of Sicily*. New Haven, Conn.: Yale University Press.

Chadwick, John (1990). "The Pech-Maho Lead," *ZPE*, 82, pp. 161–66.

Chamoux, François (1953). *Cyrène sous la monarchie des Battiades*. Bibliothèque des Écoles françaises d'Athènes et de Rome, fasc. 177. Paris: De Boccard.

Chausserie-Laprée, J. (1990). "Martigue," in *Voyage en Massalie: 100 ans d'archéologie en Gaule du Sud*. Marseille: Édisud, pp. 54–71.

Christaller, Walter (1933). *Die zentralen Orte in Süddeutschland*. Jena, Germany: Fischer.

———— (1966). *Central Places in Southern Germany*. Translated by Carlisle Whiteford Baskin. Englewood Cliffs, N.J.: Prentice-Hall.

———— (1972). "How I Discovered the Theory of Central Places: A Report about the Origin of Central Places," in Paul Ward English and Robert C. Mayfield (eds.). *Man, Space, and Environment: Concepts in Contemporary Human Geography*. New York: Oxford University Press, pp. 601–10.

Ciaceri, Emanuele (1911). *Culti e miti nella storia dell'antica Sicilia*. Catania, Sicily: Battiato.

Clark, M. (1999). "Thucydides in Olympia," in Ronald Mellor and Lawrence A. Tritle (eds.). *Text and Tradition: Studies in Greek History and Historiography in Honor of Mortimer Chambers*. Claremont, Calif.: Regina, pp. 115–34.

Clarke, Katherine (1999). *Between Geography and History: Hellenistic Constructions of the Roman World*. Oxford: Clarendon.

———— (2008). *Making Time for the Past: Local History and the Polis*. New York: Oxford University Press.

Clavel-Lévêque, Monique (1983). "Cadastres, centuriations, et problèmes d'occupation du sol," in Monique Clavel-Lévêque (ed.). *Cadastres et Espace Rural: Approches et réalités antiques.* Table ronde de Besançon mai 1980. Paris: Éditions du Centre national de la Recherche scientifique, pp. 207–58.

———— (1999). "Le territoire d'Agde grecque: Histoire et structures," in Michèle Brunet (ed.). *Territoires des cités grecques. BCH* Suppl. 34, pp. 177–97.

Clay, Diskin (2004). *Archilochos Heros: The Cult of Poets in the Greek Polis.* Washington, D.C.: Center for Hellenic Studies; Cambridge, Mass.: Harvard University Press.

Cline, Eric H. (1994). *Sailing the Wine-Dark Sea: International Trade and the Late Bronze Age Aegean.* BAR International Series 591. Oxford: Tempus Reparatum.

Clogg, Richard (2002). *A Concise History of Greece.* 2nd edn. Cambridge Concise Histories. Cambridge: Cambridge University Press.

Cohen, Getzel M. (1978). *The Seleucid Colonies: Studies in Founding, Administration, and Organization.* Wiesbaden: Steiner.

———— (1995). *The Hellenistic Settlements in Europe, the Islands, and Asia Minor.* Berkeley: University of California Press.

———— (2006). *The Hellenistic Settlements in Syria, the Red Sea Basin, and North Africa.* Berkeley: University of California Press.

Coldstream, John Nicolas (1969). "The Phoenicians of Ialysos," *Bulletin of the Institute of Classical Studies,* 16, pp. 1–8.

———— (1982). "Greeks and Phoenicians in the Aegean," in Hans Georg Niemeyer (ed.). *Phönizier im Westen: Die Beiträge des Internationalen Symposiums über 'Die phönizische Expansion im westlichen Mittelmeerraum' in Köln vom 24 bis 27 April 1979.* Madrider Beiträge 8. Mainz am Rhein: Zabern, pp. 261–75.

———— (1993). "Mixed Marriages at the Frontiers of the Early Greek World," *OJA,* 12, pp. 89–107.

———— (2003). *Geometric Greece: 900–700 BC.* 2nd edn. New York: Routledge.

———— (2004). "The Various Aegean Affinities of the Early Pottery from Sicilian Naxos," in M. C. Lentini (ed.). *Le due città di Naxos: Atti del Seminario di Studi Giardini Naxos 29–31 Ottobre 2000.* Giardini Naxos: Comune di Giardini Naxos, pp. 40–50.

Collar, Anna (2007). "Network Theory and Religious Innovation," *MHR,* 22(1), pp. 149–62.

Colonna, Giovanni (1988). "L'iscrizione etrusca del piombo di Linguadoca," *Scienze dell'antichità: Storia, archeologia, antropologia,* 2, pp. 547–55.

———— (1993). "Doni di Etruschi e di altri barbari occidentali nei santuari panellenici," in Mastrocinque (1993b), pp. 43–67.

Constans, Léopold Albert (1921). *Arles antique.* Bibliothèque des Écoles françaises d'Athènes et de Rome 119. Paris: De Boccard.

Constantakopoulou, Christy (2005). "Proud to Be an Islander: Island Identity in Multi-Polis Islands in the Classical and Hellenistic Aegean," *MHR,* 20(1), pp. 1–34.

———— (2007). *The Dance of the Islands: Insularity, Networks, the Athenian Empire, and the Aegean World.* Oxford: Oxford University Press.

Corral, Martin Alonso (2002). *Ezekiel's Oracles against Tyre: Historical Reality and Motivations.* Rome: Istituto Pontificio Biblico.

Cosandey, David (2007 [1997]). *Le secret de l'Occident: Vers une théorie générale du progrès scientifique.* Paris: Flammarion.

Cosgrove, D. (2004). "Landscape and *Landschaft*." Lecture delivered at the "Spatial Turn in History" Symposium, German Historical Institute, Washington, D.C., February 19, 2004. *German Historical Institute Bulletin*, 35, pp. 57–58.

Couprie, Dirk L. (2004). "How Thales Was Able to 'Predict' a Solar Eclipse without the Help of Alleged Mesopotamian Wisdom," *Early Science and Medicine*, 9, pp. 321–37.

Coupry, Jacques (1954). "Fouilles à Olbia," *Gallia*, 12, pp. 3–33.

———— (1964). "Les fouilles d'Olbia, à Hyères," *CRAI*, 1964, pp. 313–21.

———— (1981). "Olbia 'la fortunée,' " *Dossiers d'Archéologie*, 57, pp. 29–31.

Courbin, Paul (1966). *La céramique géométrique de l'Argolide*. Bibliothèque des Écoles françaises d'Athènes et de Rome 208. Paris: De Boccard.

Craik, Elizabeth M. (1980). *The Dorian Aegean: States and Cities of Ancient Greece*. London: Routledge and Kegan Paul.

Crielaard, Jan Paul (2000). "Honour and Value as Discourse for Early Greek Colonialism (8th–7th Centuries BC)," in Friedrich Krinzinger (ed.). *Die Ägäis und das westliche Mittelmeer: Akten des Symposions Wien 1999*. Vienna: Verlag der Österreichischen Akademie der Wissenschaften, pp. 499–520.

Cunliffe, Barry W. (1988). *Greeks, Romans, and Barbarians: Spheres of Interaction*. London: Batsford.

Curtin, Philip D. (1984). *Cross-Cultural Trade in World History*. Cambridge: Cambridge University Press.

Curty, Olivier (1995). *Les parentés légendaires entre cités grecques: Catalogue raisonné des inscriptions contenant le terme syngeneia et analyse critique*. Hautes études du monde gréco-romain 20. Geneva: Librairie Droz.

D'Alessio, Giovan Battista (2009). "Defining Identities in Greek Lyric Poetry," in Hunter and Rutherford (2009), pp. 137–67.

Cusumano, Nicola (1994). *Una terra splendida e facile da possedere: I Greci e la Sicilia*. Rome: Bretschneider.

D'Andria, Francesco (1988). "Messapi e Peuceti," in G. Pugliese Carratelli (ed.). *Italia: omnium terrarum alumna: La civiltà dei Veneti, Reti, Liguri, Celti, Piceni, Umbri, Latini, Campani, e Iapigi*. Milan: Scheiwiller, pp. 653–751.

D'Asaro, Leonardo (1991). *Minosse e Cocalo: Mito e storia nella Sicilia occidentale*. Khora 1. Palermo: Augustinus.

D'Ercole, Maria Cecilia (2005). "Identités, mobilités, et frontières dans la Méditerranée antique: L'Italie adriatique, VIIIe–Ve siècle avant J.-C.," *Annales: Histoire, sciences sociales*, 60, pp. 165–81.

———— (2007). "Mobilité et colonisation dans la Méditerrannée archaïque et classique," in Pierre Rouillard, Catherine Perlès, and Emmanuel Grimaud (eds.). *Mobilité, immobilismes: L'emprunt et son refus*. Paris: De Boccard, pp. 45–54.

———— (2010). " 'Oublier Paros': Départ, retours et conquêtes imaginaires dans la colonization grecque archaïque et classique," in Rouillard (2010), pp. 71–90.

———— (2011). "Sharing New Worlds: Mixed Identities around the Adriatic (6th–4th Century B.C.)," in Gruen (2011), pp. 428–51.

Dakhlia, Jocelyne (2008). *Lingua franca: Histoire d'une langue métisse en Mediterranée*. Paris: Acte Sud.

Danowski, Alexander M. (1990). "Analysis of Ancient Networks: Personal Communication and the Study of Social Structure in a Past Society." *Social Networks* 12, pp. 313–35.

Davidson, James (2010). "Time and Greek Religion," in Daniel Ogden (ed.). *A Companion to Greek Religion*. Malden, Mass.: Wiley Blackwell, pp. 205–18.

Davis, Whitney M. (1979). "Ancient Naukratis and the Cypriotes in Egypt," *Göttinger Miszellen*, 35, pp. 13–23.

———— (1980). "The Cypriotes at Naukratis," *Göttinger Miszellen*, 41, pp. 7–19.

De Angelis, Franco (2003). *Megara Hyblaia and Selinous: Two Greek City-States in Archaic Sicily*. Oxford: Oxbow Press for Oxford University School of Archaeology.

———— (2010). "Re-assessing the Earliest Social and Economic Developments in Greek Sicily." *Mitteilungen des deutschen archäologischen Instituts, Römische Abteilung*, 116, pp. 21–53.

de la Genière, Juliette (1978). "Ségeste et l'hellénisme," *MEFRA*, 90, pp. 33–48.

———— (2000). "Quelques reflexions sur la religion grecque d'est en ouest," in Friedriech Krinzinger (ed.). *Die Ägäis und das westliche Mittelmeer: Akten des Symposions Wien 1999*. Vienna: Verlag der Österreichischen Akademie der Wissenschaften, pp. 133–41.

De Vido, Stefania (1997). *Gli Elimi: Storie di contatti e di rappresentazioni*. Pisa: Scuola Normale Superiore.

de Vries, Keith (2000). "The Nearly Other: The Attic Vision of Phrygians and Lydians," in Beth Cohen (ed.). *Not the Classical Ideal: Athens and the Construction of the Other in Greek Art*. Leiden: Brill, pp. 338–63.

De Wever, Josette (1968). "Thucydide et la puissance maritime de Massalia," *L'antiquité classique*, 37, pp. 37–58.

Degenne, Alain and Michel Forsé (eds.) (1999). *Introducing Social Networks*. London: Sage.

———— (2010). *Les réseaux sociaux*. 2nd edn. Paris: Collection U. Colin.

Deleuze, Gilles and Félix Guattari (1987). *A Thousand Plateaus: Capitalism and Schizophrenia*. Translated by Brian Massumi. Minneapolis: University of Minnesota Press.

Demand, Nancy H. (1990). *Urban Relocation in Archaic and Classical Greece: Flight and Consolidation*. Oklahoma Series in Classical Culture. Vol. 6. Norman: University of Oklahoma Press.

Demangel, R. and Georges Daux (1923). *Le sanctuaire d'Athéna Pronaia*. Fouilles de Delphes. Vol. 2: *Topographie et architecture*. Paris: De Boccard.

Demetriou, Andreas (2001). "Phoenicians in Cyprus and Their Hellenization: The Case of Kition," *Archaeologia Cypria*, 4, pp. 135–44.

Demetriou, Denise (2005). "Negotiating Identity: Greek Emporia in the Archaic and Classical World." PhD diss., Johns Hopkins University, Baltimore.

Dening, Greg (1980). *Islands and Beaches: Discourse on a Silent Land, Marquesas, 1774–1880*. Honolulu: University Press of Hawaii.

des Courtils, Jacques, Tony Koželj, and Arthur Muller (1982). "Des mines d'or à Thasos," *BCH*, 106, pp. 409–17.

Descœudres, Jean-Paul (ed.) (1990). *Greek Colonists and Native Populations: Proceedings of the First Australian Congress of Classical Archaeology Held in Honour of Emeritus Professor A. D. Trendall, Sydney, 9–14 July 1985*. Oxford: Clarendon.

———— (2008). "Central Greece on the Eve of the Colonization Movement," in Gocha R. Tsetskhladze (ed.). *Greek Colonisation: An Account of Greek Colonies and Other Settlements Overseas*. Vol. 2. Leiden: Brill, pp. 289–382.

Detienne, Marcel (1998). *Apollon le couteau à la main: Une approche expérimentale du polythéisme grec.* Bibliothèque des sciences humaines. Paris: Gallimard.

Dietler, Michael (1997). "The Iron Age in Mediterranean France: Colonial Encounters, Entanglements, and Transformations," *Journal of World Prehistory*, 11, pp. 269–358.

——— (1998). "Consumption, Agency, and Cultural Entanglement: Theoretical Implications of a Mediterranean Colonial Encounter," in J. Cusick (ed.). Studies in Culture Contact: Interaction, Culture Change, and Archaeology. Carbondale: Southern Illinois University Press, pp. 288–315.

——— (2005). *Consumption and Colonial Interaction in the Rhône Basin of France: A Study of Early Iron Age Political Economy.* Lattes, France: Monographies d'Archéologie Meditéranéenne.

Dillon, Matthew (1997). *Pilgrims and Pilgrimage in Ancient Greece.* London: Routledge.

Dion, Roger (1962). "La voie Héracléenne et l'itinéraire transalpin d'Hannibal," in Marcel Renard (ed.). *Hommages à A. Grenier.* Vol. 1. Collection Latomus, vol. 58. Bruxelles-Berchem: Latomus, Revue d'Études Latines, pp. 527–43.

Dirkzwager, A. (1975). *Strabo über Gallia Narbonensis.* Studies of the Dutch Archaeological and Historical Society 6. Leiden: Brill.

Dobbin, Frank (1994). *Forging Industrial Policy: The United States, Britain, and France in the Railway Age.* Cambridge: Cambridge University Press.

Docter, Roald F., Fehti Chelbi, and B. M. Telmini (2003). "Carthage Bir Massouda: Preliminary Report on the First Bilateral Excavations of Ghent University and the Institut national du patrimoine (2002–2003)." *Bulletin Antieke Beschaving*, 78, pp. 43–71.

Docter, Roald F. and H. G. Niemeyer (1994). "Pithekoussai: The Carthaginian Connection. On the Archaeological Evidence of Eubeo-Phoenician Partnership in the 8th and 7th Centuries BC," *AION ArchStAnt* n.s., 1, pp. 101–15.

———, A. J. Nijboer, and J. van der Plicht (2005). "Radiocarbon Dates of Animal Bones in the Earliest Levels of Carthage," in G. Bartoloni and F. Delpino (eds.) (2005). *Oriente e Occidente: Metodi e discipline a confronto. Riflessioni sulla cronologia dell'età del ferro in Italia. Atti dell'incontro di studi, Roma, 30–31 ottobre 2003.* Pisa: Istituti Editoriali e Poligrafici Internazionali = Mediterranea: Quaderni annuali dell'Istituto di studi sulle civiltà italiche e del Mediterraneo antico del Consiglio nazionale delle ricerche, 1 (2004), pp. 557–77.

Domínguez, Adolfo J. (1989). *La colonización griega en Sicilia: Griegos, indígenas, y púnicos en la Sicilia arcaica: Interacción y aculturación.* BAR international series 549. Oxford: BAR.

——— (2006). "Greeks in Sicily," in Tsetskhladze (2006b), pp. 253–357.

Dougherty, Carol (1993). *The Poetics of Colonization: From City to Text in Archaic Greece.* New York: Oxford University Press.

Doumet-Serhal, Claude (ed.) (2008). Networking Patterns of the Bronze Age and Iron Age Levant: The Lebanon and Its Mediterranean Connections. Beirut: ACCP.

Drachmann, A. B. (1903). *Scholia vetera in Pindari carmina.* Vol. 1: *Scholia in Olympionicas.* Leipzig: Teubner.

Dressler, H. (1900). "Altgriechischer Münzfund aus Ägypten," *Zeitschrift für Numismatik*, 22, pp. 231–58.

Drews, Robert (1979). "Phoenicians, Carthage, and the Spartan Eunomia," *American Journal of Philology*, 100, pp. 45–58.

—— (1992). "Herodotus 1.94, the Drought ca. 1200 BC, and the Origin of the Etruscans," *Historia*, 41, pp. 14–39.

Dubois, Laurent (1989). *Inscriptions grecques dialectales de Sicile: Contribution à l'étude du vocabulaire grec colonial.* Rome: École française de Rome.

—— (1996). *Inscriptions grecques dialectales d'Olbia du Pont.* Geneva: Librairie Droz.

Dueck, Daniela (2000). *Strabo of Amasia: A Greek Man of Letters in Augustan Rome.* London: Routledge.

Dunbabin, Thomas James (1948a). *The Western Greeks: The History of Sicily and South Italy from the Foundation of the Greek Colonies to 480 B.C.* Oxford: Clarendon.

—— (1948b). "Minos and Daidalos in Sicily," *BSR*, 16, pp. 1–18.

Effenterre, Henri and J. Vélissaropoulos-Karakostas (1991). "Une affaire d'affrètement à propos du 'plomb de Pech Maho,'" *Revue historique de droit français et étranger*, 69(2), pp. 217–25.

Ehrhardt, Norbert (1983). Milet und seine Kolonien: Vergleichende Untersuchung der kultischen und politischen Einrichtungen. *Europäische Hochschulschriften* 3, 206. New York: Lang.

Elayi, Josette (1986). "Le roi et la religion dans les cités phéniciennes à l'époque perse," in Corinne Bonnet, Edward Lipiński, and P. Marchetti (eds.). Religio Phoenicia (= Studia Phoenicia 4). Namur: Société des Études Classiques, pp. 249–61.

—— (2000). "Les sites phéniciens de la Syrie," in Guy Bunnens (ed.). *Essays on Syria in the Iron Age.* Ancient Near Eastern Studies. Suppl. 7, Leuven: Peeters, pp. 327–48.

Elsner, Jas and Ian Rutherford (2005a). "Introduction," in Jas Elsner and Ian Rutherford (eds.). *Pilgrimage in Graeco-Roman and Early Christian Antiquity: Seeing the Gods.* Oxford: Oxford University Press, pp. 1–38.

—— (eds.) (2005b). *Pilgrimage in Graeco-Roman and Early Christian Antiquity: Seeing the Gods.* Oxford: Oxford University Press.

Elwyn, Susan F. (1991). "The Use of Kinship Terminology in Hellenistic Diplomatic Documents: An Epigraphical Study." PhD diss., University of Pennsylvania.

—— (1993). "Interstate Kinship and Roman Foreign Policy," *TAPhA*, 123, pp. 261–86.

Eriksen, Thomas Hylland (1993). *Ethnicity and Nationalism: Anthropological Perspectives.* Anthropology, Culture, and Society. London: Pluto.

Erskine, Andrew (2001). *Troy between Greece and Rome: Local Tradition and Imperial Power.* Oxford: Oxford University Press.

Etherington, Norman (2001). *The Great Treks: The Transformation of Southern Africa, 1815–1854.* London: Longman.

Ethington, P. J. (2007). "Placing the Past: 'Groundwork' for a Spatial Theory of History." *Rethinking History*, 11(4), pp. 465–93.

Études thasiennes (1944–). Paris: De Boccard.

Evelyn-White, Hugh G. (ed.) (1936). *Hesiod: The Homeric Hymns and Homerica.* Rev. edn. Loeb Classical Library. Cambridge, Mass.: Heinemann and Harvard University Press.

Fabre, Thierry (2002). "Metaphors for the Mediterranean: Creolization or Polyphony?" *MHR*, 17, pp. 15–24.

Falsone, G. (1988). "The Bronze Age occupation and Phoenician Foundation at Motya," *Bulletin of the Institute of Archeology*, University of London, 25, pp. 31–53.

Fantalkin, Alexander (2006). "Identity in the Making: Greeks in the Eastern Mediterranean during the Iron Age," in Alexandra Villing and Udo Schlotzhauer (eds.). *Naukratis: Greek Diversity in Egypt. Studies on East Greek Pottery and Exchange in the Eastern Mediterranean.* London: British Museum, pp. 199–208.

────── (2008). "Contacts between the Greek World and the Southern Levant during the Seventh–Sixth Centuries BCE." PhD diss., Tel Aviv University.

Farnell, Lewis Richard (1896). *The Cults of the Greek States.* Oxford: Clarendon.

Fentress, James and Elizabeth Fentress (2001). "Review Article of *The Corrupting Sea*: The Hole in the Doughnut," *Past and Present,* 173(1), pp. 203–19.

Ferjaoui, Ahmed (1993). *Recherches sur les relations entre l'Orient phénicien et Carthage. Orbis Biblicus et Orientalis* 124. Fribourg: Editions universitaires de Fribourg, Vandenhoeck, and Ruprecht.

Figueira, Thomas J. (1981). *Aegina: Society and Politics.* Monographs in Classical Studies. Salem, N.H: Ayer.

────── (1984). "Karl Polanyi and Ancient Greek Trade: The Port of Trade," *Ancient World,* 10, pp. 15–30.

────── (1988). "Four Notes on the Aiginetans in Exile," *Athenaeum,* 66, pp. 523–51.

────── (ed.) (2004). *Spartan Society.* Swansea: Classical Press of Wales.

Finkelberg, Margalit (2005). *Greeks and Pre-Greeks: Aegean Prehistory and Greek Heroic Tradition.* Cambridge: Cambridge University Press.

────── (2006). "Ino-Leukothea between East and West." *Journal of Ancient Near Eastern Religions,* 6(1), pp. 105–21.

Finley, M. I. (1975). *The Use and Abuse of History.* Edinburgh: University of Edinburgh Press.

────── (1983). *Economy and Society in Ancient Greece.* Harmondsworth: Penguin.

────── (1999 [1973]). *The Ancient Economy.* Updated edn. Berkeley: University of California Press.

Fischer, Theobald (1877). *Beiträge zur physischen Geographie der Mittelmeerländer besonders Siciliens.* Leipzig: Fues's Verlag.

────── (1882). "Die Kustenländer Nordafrikas in ihren Beziehungen und in ihrer Bedeutung für Europa," *Deutschen Revue,* 7.

Fischer-Hansen, Tobias, Thomas Heine Nielsen, and Carmine Ampolo (2004a). "Italia and Kampania," in Hansen and Nielsen (2004), pp. 249–320.

────── (2004b). "Sikelia," in Hansen and Nielsen (2004), pp. 172–248.

Fleischer, Robert (1973). *Artemis von Ephesos und verwandte Kultstatuen aus Anatolien und Syrien.* Études préliminaires aux religions orientales dans l'Empire romain 35. Leiden: Brill.

Flensted-Jensen, Pernille and Mogens Herman Hansen (1996). "Pseudo-Skylax' Use of the Term 'Polis,'" in Hansen and Raaflaub (1996), pp. 137–67.

Fletcher, R. (2004). "Sidonians, Tyrians, and Greeks in the Mediterranean: The Evidence from Egyptianizing Amulets," *Ancient West and East,* 3(1), pp. 51–77.

Flower, Michael (2008). *The Seer in Ancient Greece.* Berkeley: University of California Press.

Fontenrose, Joseph Eddy (1988). *Didyma: Apollo's Oracle, Cult, and Companions.* Berkeley: University of California Press.

Forrest, W. G. (1957). "Colonization and the Rise of Delphi," *Historia,* 6, pp. 160–75.

Fowler, Robert. L. (1998). "Genealogical Thinking, Hesiod's Catalogue, and the Creation of the Hellenes," *PCPhS*, 44, pp. 1–19.

———— (2000). *Early Greek Mythography*. Oxford: Oxford University Press.

Foxlee, Neil (2006). "Mediterranean Humanism or Colonialism with a Human Face? Contextualizing Albert Camus' 'The New Mediterranean Culture,'" *MHR*, 21(1), pp. 77–97.

Francfort, Henri-Paul (1984). *Fouilles d'Ai Khanoum III: 1. Le sanctuaire du temple a niches indentes 2. Les trouvailles*. Mémoires de la délégation archéologique française en Afghanistan (= MDAFA) 27. Paris: Klincksieck.

Frasca, Massimo (1997). "E anonima la città siculo-greca di Monte San Mauro di Caltagirone?" *PP*, 52(295–97), pp. 407–17.

Frau, Benvenuto (1982). "Graviscae: Porto Greco di Tarquinia," in Benvenuto Frau (ed.). *Gli antichi porti di Tarquinia*. Rome: Gruppo Archeologico Romano, pp. 1–81.

Frazer, James George (1898). *Pausanias's Description of Greece*. Vol. 4. London: Macmillan.

Freeman, Edward Augustus (1891). *The History of Sicily from the Earliest Times*. Oxford: Clarendon.

Freeman, Linton C. (2004). *The Development of Social Network Analysis: A Study in the Sociology of Science*. Vancouver, BC: Empirical; North Charleston, S.C.: BookSurge.

Frisch, P. (1978). *Die Inschriften von Lampsakos*. IGSK 6. Bonn: Habelt.

Frödin, Otto Vilhelm Anders, Axel W. Persson, and Alfred Westholm (1938). *Asine: Results of the Swedish Excavations, 1922–1930*. Stockholm: Generalstabens litografiska anstalts förlag i distribution.

Frontisi-Ducroux, Françoise (1975). *Dédale: Mythologie de l'artisan en Grèce ancienne*. Paris: Maspero.

Gabrielsen, Vincent (ed.) (1999). *Hellenistic Rhodes: Politics, Culture, and Society*. Aarhus, Denmark: Aarhus University Press.

———— (2000). "The Synoikized Polis of Rhodes," in Pernille Flensted-Jensen, Thomas Heine Nielsen, and Lene Rubinstein (eds.). *Polis and Politics: Studies in Ancient Greek History. Presented to Mogens Herman Hansen on His Sixtieth Birthday, August 20, 2000*. Copenhagen: Museum Tusculanum Press, pp. 175–205.

Gagarin, Michael (1986). *Early Greek Law*. Berkeley: University of California Press.

Gaifman, Milette (2006). "Statue, Cult, and Reproduction," *Art History*, 29, pp. 258–79.

Gale, N. H. (ed.) (1991). *Bronze Age Trade in the Mediterranean: Papers Presented at the Conference Held at Rewley House, Oxford, in December 1989*. Studies in Mediterranean Archaeology 90. Jonsered: Åström.

Gantès, Lucien-François (1992). "La topographie de Marseille grecque: Bilan des recherches (1829–1991)," in Bats et al. (1992), pp. 71–88.

Gantz, Timothy (1993). *Early Greek Myth: A Guide to Literary and Artistic Sources*. Baltimore: Johns Hopkins University Press.

Garnsey, Peter, Keith Hopkins, and C. R. Whittaker (1983). *Trade in the Ancient Economy*. London: Chatto and Windus.

Gentili, Bruno and Carlo Prato (1988). *Poetarum elegiacorum testimonia et fragmenta*. Rev. 2nd edn. Bibliotheca scriptorum Graecorum et Romanorum Teubneriana. Leipzig: Teubner.

Gentili, Bruno and Antonino Pinzone (eds.) (2002). *Messina e Reggio nell'antichità, storia, società, cultura: Atti del Convegno della S.I.S.A.C. (Messina-Reggio Calabria 24–26 maggio 1999)*. Messina: Dipartimento di scienze dell'antichità dell'Università di Messina.

Georges, Pericles B. (1994). *Barbarian Asia and the Greek Experience: From the Archaic Period to the Age of Xenophon.* Ancient Society and History. Baltimore: Johns Hopkins University Press.

Gerber, Douglas E. (1999a). *Greek Elegiac Poetry: From the Seventh to the Fifth Centuries B.C.* Loeb Classical Library. Cambridge, Mass.: Harvard University Press.

—— (1999b). *Greek Iambic Poetry: From the Seventh to the Fifth Centuries BC.* Loeb Classical Library. Cambridge, Mass.: Harvard University Press.

Ghiron-Bistagne, Paulette (1992). "Un autel massaliote de Zeus Patrôos," in Bats et al. (1992), pp. 151–54.

Giangiulio, Maurizio (1983). "Greci e non Greci in Sicilia alla luce dei culti e della legende di Eracle," in *Modes de contacts et processus de transformation dans les sociétés anciennes: Actes du colloque de Crotone (24–30 Mai 1981).* Collection de l'École française de Rome 67. Pisa: Scuola Normale Superiore, pp. 785–846.

—— (1986). "Appunti di storia dei culti," *Neapolis,* pp. 101–54.

—— (1989). *Ricerche su Crotone arcaica.* Pubblicazioni della Classe di lettere e filosofia, Scuola Normale Superiore. Pisa: Scuola Normale Superiore.

—— (1996). "Avventurieri, mercanti, coloni, mercenari: Mobilità umana e circolazione di risorse nel Mediterraneo antico," in Salvatore Settis (ed.). *I Greci: Storia, cultura, arte, società.* Vol. 2.1, *Una storia greca: Formazione.* Turin: Einaudi, pp. 497–525.

—— (2009). "Bricolage coloniale: Fondazioni greche in Cirenaica." In Lombardo and Frisone (2009), pp. 87–98.

Giovannini, Adalberto (1969). *Étude historique sur les origines du Catalogue des vaisseaux.* Berne: Francke.

Gladwell, Malcolm (2000). *The Tipping Point: How Little Things Can Make a Big Difference.* London: Little, Brown.

Glotz, Gustave (1948). *Histoire grecque.* 4th edn. Paris: Les Presses Universitaires de France.

Godley, A. D. (1926). *Herodotus.* Rev. edn. 4 vols. Loeb Classical Library. Cambridge, Mass.: Harvard University Press and Heinemann.

Goitein, S. D. (1967–1993). *A Mediterranean Society: The Jewish Communities of the Arab World as Portrayed by the Documents of the Cairo Geniza.* 6 vols. Berkeley: University of California Press.

Gomme, Arnold Wycombe, Antony Andrewes, and Kenneth James Dover (1970). *A Historical Commentary on Thucydides.* Vol. 4: *Books V(25)–VII.* Oxford: Clarendon.

Gorman, Vanessa B. (2001). *Miletos, the Ornament of Ionia: A History of the City to 400 B.C.E.* Ann Arbor: University of Michigan Press.

—— (2002). "Milesian Decrees of *Isopoliteia* and the Refoundation of the City, ca. 479 BCE," in Gorman and Robinson (2002), pp. 181–93.

—— and Eric W. Robinson (eds.) (2002). Oikistes: Studies in Constitutions, Colonies, and Military Power in the Ancient World, Offered in Honor of A. J. Graham. *Mnemosyne* Suppl. 234. Leiden: Brill.

Graf, Fritz (1979). "Apollon Delphinios," *Museum Helveticum,* 36, pp. 2–22.

—— (1985). *Nordionische Kulte: Religionsgeschichtliche und epigraphische Untersuchungen zu den Kulten von Chios, Erythrai, Klazomenai, und Phokaia.* Bibliotheca Helvetica Romana, 21. Rome: Swiss Institute in Rome.

Graham, A. J. (1964). "OIKHIOI ΠEPINΘIOI," *JHS*, 84, pp. 73–75. Reprinted in Graham (2001), pp. 257–62.

—— (1971). "Patterns in Early Greek Colonisation," *JHS*, 91, pp. 35–47. Reprinted in Graham (2001), pp. 1–24.

—— (1978). "The Foundation of Thasos," *Annual of the British School at Athens*, 73, pp. 61–98. Reprinted in Graham (2001), pp. 165–229.

—— (1982a). "The Colonial Expansion of Greece," in John Boardman and N. G. L. Hammond (eds.). *The Cambridge Ancient History*. 2nd edn. Vol. 3, Part 3: *The Expansion of the Greek World, 8th to 6th Century B.C.* New York: Cambridge University Press, pp. 83–162.

—— (1982b). "The Western Greeks," in John Boardman and N. G. L. Hammond (eds.). *The Cambridge Ancient History*. 2nd edn. Vol. 3, Part 3: *The Expansion of the Greek World, 8th to 6th Century B.C.* New York: Cambridge University Press, pp. 163–95.

—— (1983). *Colony and Mother City in Ancient Greece*. 2nd edn. Chicago.

—— (1984). "Religion, Women, and Greek Colonization," in *Religione e città nel mondo antico: Atti del convegno internazionale. Bressanone (Brixen) 1981, 24–27 Ottobre. Atti del Centro Ricerche e Documentazione sull'antichità classica*, 11. Rome: L'Erma di Bretschneider, pp. 115–36. Reprinted in Graham (2001), pp. 327–48.

—— (1990). "Pre-Colonial Contacts: Questions and Problems," in Descœudres (1990), pp. 45–60. Reprinted in Graham (2001), pp. 25–44.

—— (2001). *Collected Papers on Greek Colonization*. Leiden: Brill.

Graham, Shawn and Giovanni Ruffini (2007). "Network Analysis and Greco-Roman Prosopography," in K. S. B. Keats-Rohan (ed.). *Prosopography: Approaches and Applications. A Handbook. Prosopographica et Genealogica*, vol. 13. Oxford: Linacre College, Unit for Prosopographical Research, University of Oxford, pp. 325–36.

Granovetter, Mark (1973). "The Strength of Weak Ties," *American Journal of Sociology*, 78(6), pp. 1360–80.

—— (1983). "The Strength of Weak Ties: A Network Theory Revisited," *Sociological Theory*, 1, pp. 201–33.

Gras, Michel (1985). *Trafics tyrrhéniens archaïques*. École française de Rome 258. Paris: De Boccard.

—— (1987). "Le temple de Diane sur l'Aventin," *REA*, 89, pp. 47–61.

—— (1995a). *La Méditerranée archaïque*. Cursus, Série "Histoire." Paris: Colin.

—— (1995b). "La Méditerranée occidentale, milieux d'échanges: Un regard historiographique," in Georges Vallet (ed.). *Les Grecs et l'Occident: Actes du Colloque de la Villa "Kérylos" (1991)*. Collection de l'École française de Rome 208. Rome: L'École française de Rome, pp. 109–21.

——, Pierre Rouillard, and Javier Teixidor (1989). *L'univers phénicien*. Paris: Arthaud.

Gras, Michel, Henri Tréziny, and Henri Broise (2004). *Mégara Hyblaea*. Vol. 5: *La ville archaïque*. Paris: École française de Rome.

Graux, Charles (1881). "Notes paléographiques 1: Une olympique de Pindare écrite à l'encre d'or," *Revue de philologie, de literature, et d'histoire anciennes*, 5, pp. 117–21. Reprinted in his *Notices bibliographiques et autres articles publiés dans les revues critique, historique de philologie et internationale de l'enseignement*. Paris: F. Vieweg, 1884, pp. 302–307.

Greaves, Alan M. (2002). *Miletos: A History*. London: Routledge.

———— (2007). "Milesians in the Black Sea: Trade, Settlement, and Religion," in V. Gabrielsen and J. Lund (eds.). *The Black Sea in Antiquity: Regional and Interregional Economic Exchanges*. Aarhus: Aarhus University Press, pp. 9–22.

Greene, Kevin (2000). "Technological Innovation and Economic Progress in the Ancient World: M. I. Finley Re-Considered," *Economic History Review*, 53, pp. 29–59.

Greenewalt, C. H., Jr. (1992). "When a Mighty Empire Was Destroyed: The Common Man at the Fall of Sardis, ca. 546 BC," *PAPhS*, 136, pp. 247–71.

Gruen, Erich S. (ed.) (2011). *Cultural Identity in the Ancient Mediterranean*. Los Angeles: Getty Research Institute.

Guarducci, Margherita (1967). *Epigrafia greca*. 4 vols. Rome: Istituto Poligrafico dello Stato Libreria dello Stato.

Guenzel, S. (2005). "Einführung: Spatial Turn, Topographical Turn," in *"Topologie: Weltraum Denken" Symposium, Weimar 10.11.2005*. Weimar. http://www.stephan-guenzel.de/ Material/Guenzel_Topologie-Einfuehrung.pdf; http://www.stephan-guenzel.de/.

Guillaume, Olivier (1983). *Fouilles d'Ai Khanoum II: Les propylées de la rue principale*. Mémoires de la délégation archéologique française en Afghanistan (= MDAFA) 26. Paris: Klincksieck.

Guldager Bilde P. (2009). "Quantifying Black Sea Artemis: Some Methodological Reflections," in Thomas Fischer-Hansen and B. Poulsen (eds.), *From Artemis to Diana: The Goddess of Man and Beast. Acta Hyperborea* vol. 12. Copenhagen: Museum Tusculanum, pp. 303–32.

Guyot-Rougemont, C. and Georges Rougemont (1992). "Marseille antique: Les textes littéraires grecs et latins," in Bats et al. (1992), pp. 45–50.

Hadzis, Catherine (1995). "Fêtes et cultes à Corcyre et à Corinthe: Calendrier d'Épire, calendriers des cités coloniales de l'Ouest, et calendrier de Corinthe," *Corinto e l'Occidente: Atti del trentaquattresimo convegno di studi sulla Magna Grecia, Taranto, 7–11 ottobre 1994*. Taranto: Istituto per la storia e l'archeologia della Magna Grecia, pp. 445–52.

Hall, Edith (1989). *Inventing the Barbarian: Greek Self-Definition through Tragedy*. Oxford Classical Monographs. Oxford: Oxford University Press.

Hall, Jonathan M. (1997). *Ethnic Identity in Greek Antiquity*. Cambridge: Cambridge University Press.

———— (2001). "Contested Ethnicities: Perceptions of Macedonia within Evolving Definitions of Greek Identity," in Malkin (2001c), pp. 159–86.

———— (2002). *Hellenicity: Between Ethnicity and Culture*. Chicago: University of Chicago Press.

———— (2004). "Culture, Cultures, and Acculturation," in Robert Rollinger and Christoph Ulf (eds.). *Griechische Archaik: Interne Entwicklungen, externe Impulse*. Berlin: Akademie, pp. 35–50.

Hanell, Krister (1934). *Megarische Studien*. Lund: Lindstedts Universitetsbokhandel.

Hanfmann, George Maxim Anossov (1975). *From Croesus to Constantine: The Cities of Western Asia Minor and Their Arts in Greek and Roman Times*. Ann Arbor: University of Michigan Press.

———— (1983). "On the Gods of Lydian Sardis," in R. M. Boehmer and H. Hauptmann (eds.). *Beiträge zur Altertumskunde Kleinasiens: Festschrift für Kurt Bittel*. Mainz am Rhein: Von Zabern, pp. 219–31.

Hans, Linda-Marie (1983). *Karthago und Sizilien: Die Entstehung und Gestaltung der Epikratie auf dem Hintergrund der Beziehungen der Karthager zu den Griechen und den nichtgriechischen Völken Siziliens (VI.–III. Jahrhundert v. Chr.).* Historische Texte und Studien 7. New York: Olms.

Hansen, Mogens Herman (1996). "City Ethnics as Evidence for Polis Identity," in Hansen and Raaflaub (1996), pp. 169–96.

———— (1997a). "Emporion: A Study of the Use and Meaning of the Term in the Archaic and Classical Periods," in Thomas Heine Nielsen (ed.). *Yet More Studies in the Ancient Greek Polis: Papers from the Copenhagen Polis Centre 4.* Stuttgart: Steiner, pp. 83–105.

———— (1997b). "A Typology of Dependent Poleis," in Thomas Heine Nielsen (ed.). *Yet More Studies in the Ancient Greek Polis. Papers from the Copenhagen Polis Centre 4.* Stuttgart: Steiner, pp. 29–37.

———— (2004). "Attica," in Hansen and Nielsen (2004), pp. 624–42.

———— (2006). *Polis: An Introduction to the Ancient Greek City-State.* Oxford: Oxford University Press.

———— and Thomas Heine Nielsen (eds.) (2004). *An Inventory of Archaic and Classical Poleis: An Investigation Conducted by the Copenhagen Polis Centre for the Danish National Research Foundation.* New York: Oxford University Press.

Hansen, Mogens Herman and Kurt Raaflaub (eds.) (1996). *More Studies in the Ancient Greek Polis: Historia.* Stuttgart: Steiner.

Harris, William V. (2005a). "The Mediterranean and Ancient History," in Harris (2005b), pp. 1–42.

———— (ed.) (2005b). *Rethinking the Mediterranean.* New York: Oxford University Press.

Harrison, Ann B. and Nigel Spencer (1998). "After the Palace: The Early 'History' of Messenia," in Jack L. Davis (ed.). *Sandy Pylos: An Archaeological History from Nestor to Navarino.* Austin: University of Texas Press, pp. 147–62.

Harrison, Richard J. (1988). *Spain at the Dawn of History: Iberians, Phoenicians, and Greeks.* London: Thames and Hudson.

Hartner, W. (1969). "Eclipse Periods and Thales' Prediction of a Solar Eclipse," *Centaurus,* 14, pp. 60–71.

Hasebroek, Johannes (1965). *Trade and Politics in Ancient Greece.* Translated by L. M. Fraser and D. C. Macgregor. Reprint edn. New York: Biblo and Tannen.

Hawthorne, Walter (2001). "Nourishing a Stateless Society during the Slave Trade: The Rise of Balanta Paddy-Rice Production in Guinea-Bissau." *Journal of African History* 42: 1–24.

Head, Barclay Vincent (1886). "Coins Discovered on the Site of Naukratis," *Numismatic Chronicle and Journal of the Numismatic Society.* 3rd Series, 6, pp. 1–18, pl. 1.

———— (1897). *Catalogue of the Greek Coins of Caria, Cos, Rhodes, etc.* London: British Museum.

———— (1911). *Historia Numorum: A Manual of Greek Numismatics.* New and enlarged edn. Oxford: Clarendon.

Hedreen, Guy Michael (1991). "The Cult of Achilles in the Euxine," *Hesperia,* 60(3), pp. 313–30.

Heikell, Rod (2006). *Greek Waters Pilot: A Yachtsman's Guide to the Coasts and Islands of Greece.* 9th rev. edn. St. Ives, Cambridgeshire: Imray, Laurie, Norie, and Wilson.

Herda, A. (2008). "Apollon Delphinios—Apollon Didymeus: Zwei Gesichter eines mile-sischen Gottes und ihr Bezug zur Kolonisation Milets in archaischer Zeit." In R. Bol, U. Höckmann, and P. Schollmeyer (eds.). *Kult(ur)kontakte: Apollon in Milet/ Didyma, Histria, Myus, Naukratis, und auf Zypern*. Rhaden, Germany: Leidorf, pp. 13–86.

Hermary, Antoine, Antoinette Hesnard, and Henri Tréziny (1999). *Marseille grecque: La cité phocéenne (600–49 av. J.-C.)*. Collection Hauts lieux de l'histoire. Paris: Éditions Errance.

Hermary, Antoine and Henri Tréziny (eds.) (2000). *Les cultes des cités phocéennes: Actes du colloque international, Aix-en-Provence/Marseille, 4–5 juin 1999*. Études massal-iètes 6, Aix-en-Provence: Édisud and Centre Camille-Jullian.

Herring, Edward (1991). "Socio-Political Change in the South Italian Iron Age and Clas-sical Periods: An Application of the Peer Polity Interaction Model," *Accordia Research Papers*, 2, pp. 31–54.

——— (2005). "'Sleeping with the Enemy': Mixed Residency Patterns in Pre-Roman South Italy," in Peter Attema, Albert Nijboer, Andrea Zifferero et al. (eds.). *Papers in Italian Archaeology VI: Communities and Settlements from the Neolithic to the Early Medieval Period*. Proceedings of the 6th Conference of Italian Archaeology held at the University of Groningen, Groningen Institute of Archaeology, the Netherlands, April 15–17, 2003. Bar International Series 1452. Oxford: Archaeopress, pp. 292–301.

Heubeck, Alfred, Stephanie West, and J. B. Hainsworth (1988). *A Commentary on Hom-er's Odyssey*. Vol. 1: *Introduction and Books I–VIII*. Oxford: Clarendon.

Hezser, Catherine (1997). *The Social Structure of the Rabbinic Movement in Roman Pales-tine*. Texte und Studien zum antiken Judentum 66. Tübingen: Mohr Siebeck.

Higbie, Carolyn (2003). *The Lindian Chronicle and the Greek Creation of Their Past*. Oxford: Oxford University Press.

Höckmann, Ursula and Astrid Möller (2006). "The Hellênion at Naukratis: Questions and Observations," in Alexandra Villing and Udo Schlotzhauer (eds.). *Naukratis: Greek Diversity in Egypt*. Studies on East Greek Pottery and Exchange in the Eastern Mediterranean. London: British Museum, pp. 11–22.

Hodge, A. Trevor (1998). *Ancient Greek France*. London: Duckworth.

Hodos, Tamar (1999). "Intermarriage in the Western Greek Colonies," *OJA*, 18, pp. 61–78.

——— (2006). *Local Responses to Colonization in the Iron Age Mediterranean*. London: Routledge.

Hogarth, David George, Hilda L. Lorimer, and C. C. Edgar (1905). "Naukratis, 1903," *JHS*, 25, pp. 105–36.

Holtzmann, Bernard (1979). "Des mines d'or à Thasos?" in *Thasiaca*. BCH Suppl. 5, Paris: École française d'Athènes and De Boccard, pp. 345–49.

Hommel, Hildebrecht (1980). *Der Gott Achilleus*. Heidelberger Akademie der Wissen-schaften, Philosophisch-historische Klasse. Sitzungsberichte Abh. 1. Heidelberg: Winter.

Hooker, J. T. (1988). "The Cults of Achilles," *Rheinisches Museum für Philologie*, 131, pp. 1–7.

Horden, Peregrine and Nicholas Purcell (2000). *The Corrupting Sea: A Study of Mediter-ranean History*. Oxford: Blackwell.

Hornblower, Simon (1982). "Thucydides, the Panionian Festival, and the Ephesia (III 104)," *Historia* 31, pp. 241–45.

———— (1991). *A Commentary on Thucydides*. Vol. 1: *Books I–III*. Oxford: Clarendon.

———— (1997). "Thucydides and Chalkidic Torone," *OJA*, 16, pp. 177–86.

———— (2004). *Thucydides and Pindar: Historical Narrative and the World of Epinikian Poetry*. Oxford: Oxford University Press.

———— (2008). *A Commentary on Thucydides*. Vol. 3: *Books 5.25–8.109*. Oxford: Clarendon.

———— and Elaine Matthews (2000) (eds). *Greek Personal Names: Their Value as Evidence*. Proceedings of the British Academy 104. New York: Oxford University Press for the British Academy.

Hornblower, Simon and Catherine Morgan (eds.) (2007). *Pindar's Poetry, Patrons, and Festivals: From Archaic Greece to the Roman Empire*. Oxford: Oxford University Press.

How, W. W. and J. Wells (1912). *A Commentary on Herodotus*. Oxford: Clarendon.

Hunter, Richard and Ian Rutherford (eds.) (2009). *Wandering Poets in Ancient Greek Culture*. Cambridge: Cambridge University Press.

Hurst, H. R. and Sara Owen (eds.) (2005). *Ancient Colonizations: Analogy, Similarity, and Difference*. London: Duckworth.

Isaac, Benjamin (1986). *The Greek Settlements in Thrace until the Macedonian Conquest*. Leiden: Brill.

Jacob, Christian (1991). *Géographie et ethnographie en Grèce ancienne*. Paris: Colin.

———— (2006). *The Sovereign Map: Theoretical Approaches in Cartography throughout History*. Translated by Tom Conley. Chicago: University of Chicago Press.

Jacopi, Giulio (1932–1941). *Esplorazione archeologica di Camiro*. Clara Rhodos 6–7. Rhodes: Istituto storico-archeologico.

Jacquemin, Anne (1993). "Oikiste et tyran: Fondateur-monarque et monarque-fondateur dans l'Occident grec," *Ktema*, 18, pp. 19–27.

Janni, Pietro (1984). *La mappa e il periplo: Cartografia antica e spazio odologico*. Rome: Bretschneider.

Jehasse, Jean and Laurence Jehasse (1991). *Aléria antique*. 2nd edn. Lyon: Les amis d'Aléria.

Jones, Christopher P. (1999). *Kinship Diplomacy in the Ancient World*. Revealing Antiquity 12. Cambridge, Mass.: Harvard University Press.

Jones, Horace Leonard (1917). *The Geography of Strabo*. 8 vols. Loeb Classical Library. Cambridge, Mass.: Heinemann and Harvard University Press.

Jones, Nicholas F. (1987). *Public Organization in Ancient Greece: A Documentary Study*. Memoirs of the American Philosophical Society 176. Philadelphia: American Philosophical Society.

Jones, Roger S. (1983). *Physics as Metaphor: A Mind-Expanding Exploration of the Human Side of Science*. New York: Times Mirror.

Jourdain-Annequin, Colette (1989a). "De l'espace de la cité à l'espace symbolique: Héraclès en Occident," *DHA*, 15(1), pp. 31–48.

———— (1989b). *Héraclès aux portes du soir: Mythe et histoire*. Annales littéraires de l'Université de Besançon. Paris: Belles Lettres.

Just, R. (1989). "Triumph of the Ethnos," in Elizabeth Tonkin, Maryon McDonald, and Malcolm Chapman (eds.). *History and Ethnicity*. ASA Monographs 27. London: Routledge, pp. 71–88.

Kaplan, Philip (2002). "The Social Status of the Mercenary in Archaic Greece," in Gorman and Robinson (2002), pp. 229–43.

——— (2003). "Cross-Cultural Contacts among Mercenary Communities in Saite and Persian Egypt," *MHR*, 18, pp. 1–31.

Kasher, Rimon (2004). *Yehezkel: Im mavo u-ferush* (= *Ezekiel: Introduction and Commentary: Hebrew*). Tel Aviv: Am Oved and Magnes.

Katzenstein, H. Jacob (1997). *The History of Tyre: From the Beginning of the Second Millennium B.C.E. until the Fall of the Neo-Babylonian Empire in 538 B.C.E.* 2nd edn. Jerusalem: Bialik Institute.

Kawerau, Georg and Albert Rehm (eds.) (1914). *Milet 1.3: Das Delphinion in Milet*. Berlin: Reimer.

Keating, Michael (ed.) (2004). *Regions and Regionalism in Europe*. Cheltenham, UK: Elgar.

Kelly, Kenneth (2002). "Indigenous Responses to Colonial Encounters on the West African Coast: Hueda and Dahomei from the Seventeenth through the Nineteenth Century," in Lyons and Papadopoulos (2001), pp. 96–120.

Kelly, Thomas (1967). "The Argive Destruction of Asine," *Historia*, 16, pp. 422–31.

Kern, Otto (1900). *Die Inschriften von Magnesia am Maeander*. Berlin: Spemann.

Kerschner, M. (2008). "Die Lyder und das Artemision von Ephesos," in Ulrike Muss (ed.). *Die Archäologie der ephesischen Artemis: Gestalt und Ritual eines Heiligtums*. Vienna: Phoibos, pp. 223–33.

Khondker, Habibul Haque (2004). "Glocalization as Globalization: Evolution of a Sociological Concept," *Bangladesh e-Journal of Sociology*, 1(2), pp. 1–9.

Kinch, Karl Frederik (1905). *Explorations archéologiques de Rhodes, IIIe Rapport*. Bulletin de l'Académie Royale des Sciences et des Lettres de Danemark 2. Copenhagen: Lunos.

——— (1914). *Vroulia*. Berlin: Reimer.

Kindt, J. (2006). "Delphic Oracle Stories and the Beginning of Historiography: Herodotus' *Croesus Logos*," *CPh*, 101, pp. 34–51.

King, Leslie J. (1984). *Central Place Theory*. Scientific Geography Series 1. Beverly Hills: Sage.

Knoepfler, Denis (1988). "Communication sur les traces de l'Artémision d'Amarynthos près d'Erétrie," *CRAI*, pp. 382–421.

——— (1989). "Le calendrier des Chalcidiens et de Thrace: Essai de mise au point sur la liste et l'ordre des mois eubéens," *Journal des Savants*, pp. 23–59.

——— (1990). "The Calendar of Olynthus and the Origin of the Chalkidians in Thrace," in Jean-Paul Descoeudres (ed.). *Greek Colonists and Native Populations: Proceedings of the First Australian Congress of Classical Archaeology Held in Honour of Emeritus Professor A. D. Trendall, Sydney, 9–14 July 1985*. Oxford: Clarendon, pp. 99–115.

——— (2007). "Was there an Anthroponymy of Euboian Origin in the Chalkid-Eretrian Colonies of the West and of Thrace?," in Elaine Matthews (ed.). *Old and New Worlds in Greek Onomastics*. Proceedings of the British Academy 148. Oxford: Oxford University Press for the British Academy, pp. 87–119.

Kocybala, A. K. (1978). "Greek Colonization of the North Shore of the Black Sea in the Archaic Period." PhD diss., University of Pennsylvania.

Koldewey, Robert (1890). *Die antiken Baureste der Insel Lesbos*. Berlin: Reimer.

Kolodny, Emile Y. (1974). *La population des îles de la Grèce: Essai de géographie insulaire en Méditerranée orientale*. Aix-en-Provence: Édisud.

—— (1976). "Aspects d'ensemble de l'insularité méditerranéenne," *Bulletin de l'Association de Géographes Français*, 435–36, pp. 191–95.

Koshelenko, G. A. and V. D. Kuznetsov (1992). "The Greek Colonization of the Bosporus (in Connection with Certain General Problems of Colonization)," in G. A. Koshelenko (ed.). *Essays on the Archaeology and History of the Bosporus*. Moscow [in Russian], pp. 6–28.

Kosso, Peter and Cynthia Kosso (1995). "Central Place Theory and the Reciprocity between Theory and Evidence," *Philosophy of Science*, 62(4), pp. 581–98.

Kowalzig, Barbara (2002). "Singing for the Gods: Aetiological Myth, Ritual, and Locality in Greek Choral Poetry of the Late Archaic Period." DPhil thesis, University of Oxford, 2003, Faculty of Classics, St. John's College.

—— (2005). "Mapping Out Communitas: Performances of Theoria in Their Sacred and Political Context," in Jas Elsner and Ian Rutherford (eds.). *Pilgrimage in Graeco-Roman and Early Christian Antiquity: Seeing the Gods*. Oxford: Oxford University Press, pp. 41–72.

—— (2007). *Singing for the Gods: Performance of Myth and Ritual in Archaic and Classical Greece*. Oxford: Oxford University Press.

Kraay, Colin M. (1976). *Archaic and Classical Greek Coins*. Library of Numismatics. London: Methuen.

Kraemer, Joel L. (1990). "Goitein and His Mediterranean Society," *Zmanim*, 34–35, pp. 6–17 [in Hebrew].

Krebs, S. A. (1997). "Greek Colonization and Agriculture in Dobrudja," in John M. Fossey (ed.). *Antiquitates proponticae et Caucasicae II: Proceedings of the First International Conference on the Archaeology and History of the Black Sea* (McGill University, November 22–24, 1994). Amsterdam: Giesen, pp. 47–65.

Krinzinger, Friedriech (ed.) (2000). *Die Ägäis und das westliche Mittelmeer: Akten des Symposions Wien 1999*. Vienna: Verlag der Österreichischen Akademie der Wissenschaften.

Kurke, Leslie (1991). *The Traffic in Praise: Pindar and the Poetics of Social Economy*. Ithaca, N.Y.: Cornell University Press.

Labarre, Guy (1994). "ΚΟΙΝΟΝ ΛΕΣΒΩΣ," *REA*, 96, pp. 415–63.

—— (1996). *Les cités de Lesbos aux époques hellénistique et impériale*. Collection de l'Institut d'Archéologie et d'Histoire de l'Antiquité, Université Lumière, Lyon 2. Vol. 1. Paris: De Boccard.

Lacroix, Léon (1974). "Héraclès héros voyageur et civilisateur," *Bulletin de l'Académie Royale de Belgique* 60, pp. 34–59.

Lambert, Pierre-Yves (1992). "La diffusion de l'écriture gallo-grecque en milieu indigène," in Bats et al. (1992), pp. 289–94.

Lancel, Serge (1995). *Carthage: A History*. Oxford: Blackwell.

Lane Fox, Robin (ed.) (2004). *The Long March: Xenophon and the Ten Thousand*. New Haven, Conn.: Yale University Press.

Lasserre, François (1966). *Strabon: Géographie*. Vol. 2. Paris: Belles Lettres.

—— (1969). "Introduction," in François Lasserre (1969). *Strabon: Géographie*. Vol. 1. Paris: Belles Lettres, pp. xxxiv–xlii.

Latour, Bruno (2005). *Reassembling the Social: An Introduction to Actor-Network Theory.* Oxford: Oxford University Press.

Lattimore, Richmond Alexander (1961). *The Iliad of Homer.* Chicago: University of Chicago Press.

Launey, Marcel (1944). *Le sanctuaire et le culte d'Héraklès à Thasos.* Études thasiennes 1. Paris: De Boccard.

Law, John and John Hassard (1999). *Actor Network Theory and After.* Oxford: Blackwell.

Lawrence, A. W. (1996). *Greek Architecture.* 5th edn. rev. by R. A. Tomlinson. Pelican History of Art. New Haven, Conn.: Yale University Press.

Leclerc, Stéphane (ed.) (2003). *L'Europe et les régions: Quinze ans de cohésion économique et social.* Troisièmes rencontres européennes de Caen. Brussels: Bruylant.

Lefebvre, Henri (1991). *The Production of Space.* Translated by Donald Nicholson-Smith. Cambridge, Mass.: Wiley-Blackwell.

Legon, Ronald P. (1981). *Megara: The Political History of a Greek City-State to 336 B.C.* Ithaca, N.Y.: Cornell University Press.

Lejeune, Michel (1991–1992). "Ambiguïtés du texte de Pech-Maho," *REG,* 104, pp. 311–29.

———— and Jean Pouilloux (1988). "Une transaction commerciale ionienne au Ve siècle à Pech-Maho," *CRAI,* pp. 526–36.

———— and Yves Solier (1988). "Étrusque et ionien archaïques sur un plomb de Pech Maho (Aude)," *Revue Archéologique de Narbonnaise,* 21, pp. 18–59.

Lentini, M. C. (ed.) (2009). *Naxos di Sicilia: L'abitato coloniale e l'arsenale navale. Scavi 2003–2006.* With David Blackman. Messina: Sicania.

Leontis, Artemis (1995). *Topographies of Hellenism: Mapping the Homeland.* Ithaca, N.Y.: Cornell University Press.

Lepore, Ettore (1968). "Per una fenomenologia storica del rapporto città-territorio in Magna Grecia," in *Atti dal VII Convegno di Studi sulla Magna Grecia.* Naples: L'arte tipografica, pp. 29–66.

———— (1970). "Strutture della colonizzazione focea in Occidente," *PP,* 25, pp. 19–54.

Leriche, Pierre (1986). *Fouilles d'Ai Khanoum V: Les ramparts et les monuments associés.* Mémoires de la délégation archéologique française en Afghanistan (= MDAFA) 29. Paris: Klincksieck.

Lévy, E. (1991). "Apparition des notions de Grèce et de grecs," in Saïd (1991), pp. 49–69.

Liakos, Antonis (2001). "The Construction of National Time: The Making of the Modern Greek National Imagination," *MHR,* 16(1), pp. 27–42. Reprinted in Jacques Revel and Giovanni Levi (2002). *Political Uses of the Past: The Recent Mediterranean Experience.* Special issue of *MHR* 16(1), June. London: Cass, pp. 27–42.

LiDonnici, Lynn R. (1992). "The Images of Artemis Ephesia and Greco-Roman Worship: A Reconsideration." *Harvard Theological Review* 85, pp. 389–415.

Lipiński, Edward (1995). *Dieux et déesses de l'univers phénicien et punique.* Studia Phoenicia 14. Leuven: Peeters.

Lloyd, Alan B. (1975a). *Herodotus: Book II.* Vol. 1: *Introduction.* Leiden: Brill.

———— (1975b). *Herodotus: Book II.* 3 vols. Leiden: Brill.

Lloyd-Jones, Hugh (1996). *Sophocles: Fragments.* Loeb Classical Library. Cambridge, Mass.: Harvard University Press.

Lobel, Edgar and Denys Lionel Page (1955). *Poetarum Lesbiorum fragmenta*. Oxford: Clarendon.

Lobel, Edgar, C. H. Roberts, and E. P. Wegener (eds.) (1941). *The Oxyrhynchus Papyri*. Vol. 18. London: Egypt Exploration Society.

Lohmann, H. (2004). "Mélia, le Panionion, et le culte de Poséidon Héliconios," in Guy Labarre (ed.). *Les cultes locaux dans les mondes grec et romain: Actes du colloque de Lyon, 7–8 Juin 2001*. Collection de l'Institut d'archéologie et d'histoire de l'antiquité, vol. 7. Paris: De Boccard, pp. 31–49.

Lomas, Kathryn (ed.) (2004). *Greek Identity in the Western Mediterranean: Papers in Honour of Brian Shefton*. Mnemosyne Suppl. 246. Leiden: Brill.

Lombardo, Mario and Flavia Frisone (eds.) (2009). *Colonie di colonie: Le fondazioni subcoloniali greche tra colonizzazione e colonialismo*. Atti del Convegno Internazionale (Lecce, 22–24 giugno 2006). Galatina, Lecce: Congendo Editore.

Longo, A. (1999). *Mozia: Crocevia di cultura nel Mediterraneo*. Messina: Società Messinese di Storia Patria.

Loukopoulou, Louisa D. (1989). *Contribution à l'histoire de la Thrace propontique durant la période archaïque*. Meletemata 9. Athens: Centre de Recherches de l'antiquité grecque et romaine, Fondation nationale de la recherche scientifique.

———— and Adam Laitar (2004). "Propontic Thrace," in Hansen and Nielsen (2004), pp. 912–23.

Luraghi, Nino (1991). "Fonti e tradizioni nella archaiologia siciliana (per una rilettura di Thuc. 6, 2–5)," *Hesperia*, 2 (Studi sulla grecità di Occidente), pp. 41–62.

———— (1994). *Tirannidi arcaiche in Sicilia e Magna Grecia: Da Panezio di Leontini alla caduta dei Dinomenidi*. Florence: Olschki.

———— (2000). "Author and Audience in Thucydides' *Archaeology*. Some Reflections," *HSCP*, 100, pp. 227–39.

———— (2008). *The Ancient Messenians: Constructions of Ethnicity and Memory*. Cambridge: Cambridge University Press.

Lyons Claire L., and John K. Papadopoulos (eds.). *The Archaeology of Colonialism*. Los Angeles: Getty Information Institute.

Ma, John (2003). "Peer Polity Interaction in the Hellenistic Age," *Past and Present*, 180, pp. 9–39.

———— (2004). "You Can't Go Home Again: Displacement and Identity in Xenophon's *Anabasis*," in Lane Fox (2004), pp. 330–45.

Mair, A. W. and G. R. Mair (1977). *Callimachus: Hymns and Epigrams, Lycophron and Aratus*. Cambridge, Mass.: Harvard University Press and Heinemann.

Malkin, Irad (1984). "What Were the Sacred Precincts of Brea? (*IG* I³ no. 46)," *Chiron*, 14, pp. 43–48.

———— (1986a). "Apollo Archêgetês and Sicily," *Annali della Scuola Normale Superiore di Pisa*, 16(4), pp. 959–72.

———— (1986b). "What's in a Name? The Eponymous Founders of Greek Colonies," *Athenaeum*, 63, pp. 115–30.

———— (1987). *Religion and Colonization in Ancient Greece. Studies in Greek and Roman Religion 3*. Leiden: Brill.

———— (1989). "Delphoi and the Founding of Social Order in Archaic Greece," *Métis*, 4(1), pp. 129–53.

—— (1990). "Missionaires païens dans la Gaule grecque," in Irad Malkin (ed.). *La France et la Méditerranée: Vingt-sept siècles d'interdépendance*. New York: Brill, pp. 42–52.

—— (1991). "What Is an 'Aphidruma'?" *Classical Antiquity*, 10(1), pp. 77–96.

—— (1994a). "Inside and Outside: Colonisation and the Formation of the Mother City," *Apoikia: Studi in onore di G. Buchner = AION Annali di archeologia e storia antica*, n.s. 1, pp. 1–9.

—— (1994b). *Myth and Territory in the Spartan Mediterranean*. Cambridge: Cambridge University Press.

—— (1996a). "The Polis between Myths of Land and Territory," in Robin Hägg (ed.). *The Role of Religion in the Early Greek Polis*. Proceedings of the Third International Seminar on Ancient Greek Cult, organized by the Swedish Institute at Athens, October 16–18, 1992. Stockholm: Swedish Institute at Athens, pp. 9–19.

—— (1996b). "Rhodes and Sicily: Dorian Colonization in Two Islands," in *Proceedings of the International Scientific Symposium Rhodes: 24 Centuries*, October 1–5, 1992. Athens: Greek Academy, pp. 188–98.

—— (1998). *The Returns of Odysseus: Colonization and Ethnicity*. Berkeley: University of California Press.

—— (2000). "La fondation d'une colonie apollonienne: Delphes et l'Hymne homérique à Apollon," in Anne Jacquemin (ed.). *Delphes cent ans après la grande fouille. Essai de bilan. Actes du Colloque international organisé par l'École française d'Athènes, Athènes-Delphes, 17–20 septembre 1992. BCH* Suppl. 36. Athens: École française d'Athènes, pp. 69–77.

—— (2001a). "Greek Ambiguities: Between 'Ancient Hellas' and 'Barbarian Epirus,' " in Malkin (2001c), pp. 187–212.

—— (2001b). "Introduction," in Malkin (2001c), pp. 1–28.

—— (ed.) (2001c). *Ancient Perceptions of Greek Ethnicity*. Center for Hellenic Studies Colloquia 5. Washington, D.C.: Center for Hellenic Studies.

—— (2002a). "A Colonial Middle Ground: Greek, Etruscan, and Local Elites in the Bay of Naples," in Lyons and Papadopoulos (2001), pp. 151–81.

—— (2002b). "Exploring the Validity of the Concept of 'Foundation': A Visit to Megara Hyblaia," in Gorman and Robinson (2002), pp. 195–224.

—— (2003a). *Ethnicity and Identity in Ancient Greece*. [in Hebrew]. Tel Aviv: Misrad Habitachon.

—— (2003b). "Networks and the Emergence of Greek Identity," *MHR*, 18(2), pp. 56–74. Reprinted in Malkin (2005), pp. 56–74.

—— (2003c). " 'Tradition' in Herodotus: The Foundation of Cyrene," in Peter Derow and Robert Parker (eds.). *Herodotus and His World: Essays from a Conference in Memory of George Forrest*. Oxford: Oxford University Press, pp. 153–70.

—— (2004). "Postcolonial Concepts and Ancient Greek Colonization," *Modern Language Quarterly* (special issue on "Postcolonialism and the Past," eds. Barbara Fuchs and David J. Baker), 65(3), pp. 341–64.

—— (ed.) (2005). *Mediterranean Paradigms and Classical Antiquity*. Special issue of *MHR* 18 (2003). London: Routledge.

—— (2009). "Foundations," in Kurt Raaflaub and Hans van Wees (eds.). *A Companion to Archaic Greece*. Malden, Mass.: Wiley-Blackwell, pp. 373–94.

Malkin, Irad, Christy Constantakopoulou, and Katerina Panagopoulou (eds.) (2009). *Greek and Roman Networks in the Mediterranean*. London: Routledge.

Mandelbrot, Benoit B. (1967). "How Long Is the Coast of Britain? Statistical Self-Similarity and Fractional Dimension," *Science*, 156(3775), pp. 636–38.

——— (1983). *The Fractal Geometry of Nature*. Rev. edn. New York: Freeman.

——— (2004). *Fractals and Chaos: The Mandelbrot Set and Beyond*. New York: Springer.

Maniscalco, Laura and Brian E. McConnell (2003). "The Sanctuary of the Divine Palikoi (Rocchicella di Mineo, Sicily): Fieldwork from 1995 to 2001," *AJA*, 107(2), pp. 145–80.

Manni-Piraino, M. T. (1959). "Inscrizione inedita da Poggioreale," *Kokalos*, 5, pp. 159–73.

Manning, Joseph Gilbert and Ian Morris (eds.) (2005). *The Ancient Economy: Evidence and Models*. Stanford, Calif.: Stanford University Press.

Marconi, Clemente (2007). *Temple Decoration and Cultural Identity in the Archaic Greek World: The Metopes of Selinus*. New York: Cambridge University Press.

Mari, Manuela (2006). "Sulle tracce di antichi ricchezze: La tradizione letteraria sui *thesauroí* di Delfi e di Olimpia," in Alessandro Naso (ed.) (2006). *Stranieri e non cittadini nei santuari greci*. Florence: Le Monnier Università, pp. 36–70.

Markoe, Glenn (1996). "The Emergence of Orientalizing in Greek Art: Some Observations on the Interchange between Greeks and Phoenicians in the Eighth and Seventh Centuries B.C.," *BASOR*, 301, pp. 47–67.

——— (2000). *The Phoenicians*. London: British Museum Press.

Martin, Roland (1979). "Introduction à l'étude du culte d'Héraclès en Sicile," in *Recherches sur les cultes grecs et l'Occident*. Vol. 1. Cahiers du Centre Jean Bérard 5, Naples: Centre Jean Bérard, pp. 11–18.

Marzoli, Dirce (2000). "Emproion und sein Hinterland: Ergebnisse einer interdisziplinären Untersuchung," in Friedriech Krinzinger (ed.). *Die Ägäis und das westliche Mittelmeer. Akten des Symposions Wien 1999*. Vienna: Österreichischen Akademie der Wissenschaften, pp. 117–27.

Masala, Carlo (2000). *Die Euro-Mediterrane Partnerschaft: Geschichte Struktur, Prozess*. ZEI Discussion Paper 68. Reinische Friedrich-Wilhelms-Universität Bonn. http://www.zei.de/download/zei_dp/dp_c68_masala.pdf.

Masson, Olivier and Maurice Sznycer (1972). *Recherches sur les Phéniciens à Chypre*. Hautes études orientales 3. Paris: Droz.

Mastrocinque, Attilio (ed.) (1993a). *Ercole in occidente: Atti del colloquio internazionale, Trento, 7 marzo 1990*. Labirinti 2. Trento: Dipartimento di scienze filologiche e storiche, Università degli studi di Trento.

——— (ed.) (1993b). *I grandi santuari della Grecia e l'occidente: Atti del Convegno, Trento, marzo 1991*. Labirinti 3. Trento: Dipartimento di scienze filologiche e storiche, Università degli studi di Trento.

Matvejevitch, Predrag (1998). *La Méditerranée et l'Europe. Leçons au Collège de France*. Paris: Stock.

Mazzarino, Santo (1947). *Fra Oriente e Occidente: Ricerche di storia greca arcaica*. Florence: La Nuova Italia.

McGlew, James F. (1993). *Tyranny and Political Culture in Ancient Greece*. Ithaca, N.Y.: Cornell University Press.

McInerney, Jeremy (1999). *The Folds of Parnassos: Land and Ethnicity in Ancient Phokis*. Austin: University of Texas Press.

Meiggs, Russell and David M. Lewis (1989). *A Selection of Greek Historical Inscriptions to the End of the Fifth Century B.C.* Rev. edn. Oxford: Clarendon.

Mertens, Dieter (1990). "Some Principal Features in West Greek Colonial Architecture," in Descœudres (1990), pp. 373–83.

——— (1996). "Greek Architecture in the West," in Giovanni Pugliese Carratelli (ed.). *The Western Greeks: Classical Civilization in the Western Mediterranean.* London: Thames and Hudson, pp. 315–416.

Milgram, Stanley (1967). "The Small World Problem," *Psychology Today,* 2, pp. 60–67.

Mizruchi, M. S. and Blyden B. Potts (1998). "Centrality and Power Revisited: Actor Success in Group Decision Making," *Social Networks,* 20, pp. 353–87.

Moggi, Mauro (1976). *I sinecismi interstatali greci.* Relazioni interstatali nel mondo antico. Fonti e studî 2. Pisa: Marlin.

——— (2009). "L'area ethea: Le colonie di Thoukles." In Lombardo and Frisone (2009), pp. 37–47.

Mollat du Jourdin, Michel (1993). *L'Europe et la mer.* Paris: Seuil.

Möller, Astrid (2000). *Naukratis: Trade in Archaic Greece.* New York: Oxford University Press.

——— (2005). "Naukratis as a Port of Trade Revisited," *Topoi,* 12–13, pp. 183–92.

Momigliano, Arnaldo (1975). "Note sulla storia di Rodi," in Arnaldo Momigliano (ed.). *Quinto contributo alla storia degli studi classici e del mondo antico.* Vol. 1. Rome: Edizioni di storia e letteratura, pp. 511–29.

Montiglio, Sylvia (2005). *Wandering in Ancient Greek Culture.* Chicago: University of Chicago Press.

Moore-Gilbert, B. J. (1997). *Postcolonial Theory: Contexts, Practices, Politics.* London: Verso.

Morel, Jean-Paul (1984). "Greek Colonization in Italy and in the West: Problems of Evidence and Interpretation," in Tony Hackens, Nancy D. Holloway, and R. Ross Holloway (eds.). *Crossroads of the Mediterranean: Papers Delivered at the International Conference on the Archaeology of Early Italy, Haffenreffer Museum, Brown University, May 8–10, 1981.* Publications d'Histoire de l'Art et d'Archéologie de l'Université catholique de Louvain 38. Providence, R.I.: Brown University Center for Old World Archaeology and Art and Institut Supérieur d'Archéologie et d'Histoire de l'Art, Collège Erasme, pp. 123–61.

——— (1992). "Marseille dans la colonisation phocéenne," in Bats et al. (1992), pp. 15–25.

——— (1995). "Les grecs et la Gaule," in *Les grecs et l'occident: Actes du colloque de la villa "Kérylos" (1991).* Rome: École française de Rome, pp. 41–69.

——— (1997). "Problématique de la colonisation grecque en Méditerranée occidentale: L'exemple des réseaux," in Claudia Antonetti (ed.). *Il dinamismo della colonizzazione greca: Atti della tavola rotonda "Espansione e colonizzazione greca d'età arcaica: Metodologie e problemi a confronto" (Venezia, 10–11/11/1995).* Naples: Loffredo, pp. 59–70.

——— (2000). "Observations sur les cultes de Velia," in Hermary and Tréziny (2000), pp. 33–49.

——— (2006). "Phocaean Colonisation," in Tsetskhladze (2006b), pp. 358–428.

Morelli, Donato (1959). *I culti in Rodi.* Studi Classici e Orientali 8. Pisa: Libreria Goliardica.

Morgan, Catherine (1988). "Corinth, the Corinthian Gulf, and Western Greece during the 8th Century BC." *Annual of the British School at Athens* 83, pp. 313–38.

———— (1990). *Athletes and Oracles: The Transformation of Olympia and Delphi in the Eighth Century BC*. New York: Cambridge University Press.

———— (1999). "The Archeology of Ethnicity in the Colonial World of the Eighth to Sixth Centuries BC: Approaches and Prospects," in *Frontieri e Confini: Atti della 370 Convegno internazionale di studi sulla Magna Grecia, Taranto Ott. 1997*. Taranto: Istituto per la Storia e l'Archeologia della Magna Grecia, pp. 85–145.

———— (2003). *Early Greek States beyond the Polis*. London: Routledge.

———— and Jonathan Hall, M. (1996). "Achaian Poleis and Achaian Colonisation," in Mogens Herman Hansen (ed.). *Introduction to an Inventory of Poleis: Acts of the Copenhagen Polis Centre 3*. Copenhagen: KDVS, pp. 164–232.

Morgan, Catherine and Gocha R. Tsetskhladze (eds.) (2001). *Art and Myth in the Colonial World*. Leiden: Brill.

Morris, Ian (1987). *Burial and Ancient Society: The Rise of the Greek City-State*. New Studies in Archaeology. Cambridge: Cambridge University Press.

———— (1992). *Death-Ritual and Social Structure in Classical Antiquity. Key Themes in Ancient History*. Cambridge: Cambridge University Press.

———— (2005). "Mediterraneanization," in Malkin (2005), pp. 30–55.

———— (2009). "The Eighth-Century Revolution." In Kurt Raaflaub and Hans van Wees (eds.), *A Companion to Archaic Greece*. Malden, Mass.: Wiley-Blackwell, pp. 64–80.

Morris, Sarah P. (1992). *Daidalos and the Origins of Greek Art*. Princeton, N.J.: Princeton University Press.

Moscati Castelnuovo, Luisa (1989). *Siris: Tradizione storiografica e momenti della storia di una città della Magna Grecia*. Collection Latomus. Brussels: Latomus.

Moscati, Sabatino (1984–1985). "Fenici e Greci in Sicilia: Alle origini di un confronto," *Kokalos*, 30–31, pp. 1–19.

———— (1985). "Thucidide e i Fenici," *RFIC*, 113, pp. 129–33.

Mosshammer, Alden A. (1981). "Thales' Eclipse," *TAPhA*, 111, pp. 145–55.

Muller, A. (1979). "La mine de l'acropole de Thasos," in *Thasiaca*. BCH Suppl. 5, Paris: École française d'Athènes: De Boccard, pp. 315–44.

Munn, Mark Henderson (2006). *The Mother of the Gods, Athens, and the Tyranny of Asia: A Study of Sovereignty in Ancient Religion*. Berkeley: University of California Press.

Murphy, John P. (1977). *Avienus, Rufius Festus: Ora Maritima: A Description of the Seacoast from Brittany to Marseilles [Massilia]*. Translated by John P. Murphy. Chicago: Ares.

Muss, Ulrike (2000). "Das Artemision von Ephesos-Wege von und nach Westen," in Friedriech Krinzinger (ed.). *Die Ägäis und das westliche Mittelmeer: Akten des Symposions Wien 1999*. Vienna: Österreichischen Akademie der Wissenschaften, pp. 149–55.

Musso, Olimpio (1986–1989). "Il piombo inscritto di Ampurias: Note linguistiche e datazione," *Empúries*, 48–50(2), pp. 156–59.

Nafissi, Massimo (1999). "From Sparta to Taras: *Nomima, Ktiseis*, and Relationships between Colony and Mother City," in Stephen Hodkinson and Anton Powell (eds.). *Sparta: New Perspectives*. London: Duckworth, pp. 245–72.

Naso, Alessandro (2006). "Etruschi (e Italici) nei santuari greci," in Alessandro Naso (ed.) (2006). *Stranieri e non cittadini nei santuari greci*. Florence: Le Monnier Università, pp. 341–46.

Negbi, Ora (1992). "Early Phoenician Presence in the Mediterranean Islands: A Reappraisal," *AJA*, 96, pp. 599–615.

Nenci, Giuseppe, Sebastiano Tusa, and Vincenzo Tusa (eds.) (1988–1889). *Gli Elimi e l'area elima fino all'inizio della prima guerra punica: Atti del seminario di studi Palermo, Contessa Entellina, 25–28 Maggio 1989*. Archivo Storico Siciliano ser. IV, vols. 14–15. Palermo: Società siciliana per la storia patria.

Netz, Reviel (1997). "Classical Mathematics in the Classical Mediterranean," *MHR*, 12(2), pp. 1–24.

Nickels, André (1982). "Agde grecques: Les recherches récentes," *PP*, 204–208, pp. 267–79.

——— (1983). "Les Grecs en Gaule: L'exemple du Languedoc," in *Modes de contact et processus de transformation dans les sociétés anciennes: Actes du Colloque de Cortone (24–30 mai 1981)*. Rome: Scuola normale superiore and l'École française de Rome, pp. 405–28.

Niemeyer, Hans-Georg (1990). "The Phoenicians in the Mediterranean: A Non-Greek Model for Expansion and Settlement in Antiquity," in Descoeudres (1990), pp. 469–89.

Nijboer, A. J. (2008). "A Phoenician Family Tomb, Lefkandi, Huelva, and the Tenth Century BC in the Mediterranean," in C. Sagona (ed.). *Beyond the Homeland: Markers in Phoenician Chronology*. Ancient Near Eastern Studies, Suppl. 28. Leuven: Peeters, pp. 365–77.

Nordman, Daniel (1998). "La Méditerranée dans la pensée géographique française (vers 1800–vers 1950)," in Claude Guillot, Denys Lombard, and Roderich Ptak (eds.). *From the Mediterranean to the China Sea: Miscellaneous Notes*. South China and Maritime Asia 7, Wiesbaden: Harrassowitz, pp. 1–20.

Ohana, David (2003). "Mediterranean Humanism," *MHR*, 18(1), pp. 59–75.

Oliver, James H. (1960). *Demokratia, the Gods, and the Free World*. Baltimore: Johns Hopkins University Press.

O'Neill, Eugene (1938). "Aristophanes," in Whitney J. Oates and Eugene O'Neill Jr. (eds.). *The Complete Greek Drama*, vol. 2. New York: Random House.

Orsi, Paolo (1900). "L'Heroon di Antifemo," *Notizie degli scavi di antichità*, pp. 272–77.

——— (1906). *Gela, scavi del 1900–1905*. Monumenti Antichi, Pubblicati per cura della Reale Accademia dei Lincei, vol. 17. Milan: Ulrico Hoepli.

Osanna, Massimo, Luisa Prandi, and Aldo Siciliano (eds.) (2008). *Eraclea. Culti greci in Occidente II*. Taranto: Istituto per la storia e l'archeologia della Magna Grecia.

Osborne, Robin (1998). "Early Greek Colonization," in Nick Fisher and Hans van Wees (eds.). *Archaic Greece: New Approaches and New Evidence*. London: Duckworth and Classical Press of Wales, pp. 251–69.

Ostwald, Martin (1969). *Nomos and the Beginnings of the Athenian Democracy*. Oxford: Clarendon.

Owen, Sara (2003). "Of Dogs and Men: Archilochos, Archaeology, and the Greek Settlement of Thasos," *PCPhS*, 49, pp. 1–18.

——— (Forthcoming). *Archaic Greek Colonization: A Study of Thrace and Thasos*. Cambridge: Cambridge University Press.

Özyigit, Ömer (1994). "The City Walls of Phokaia," *REA*, 96(1), pp. 77–109.

Panchenko, D. (1994). "Thales's Prediction of a Solar Eclipse," *JHA*, 25, pp. 275–88.

Parke, Herbert William (1985). *The Oracles of Apollo in Asia Minor*. London: Croom Helm.

—— (1986). "The Temple of Apollo at Didyma: The Building and Its Function," *JHS*, 106, pp. 121–31.

—— and D. E. W. Wormell (1956). *The Delphic Oracle*. Vol. 1. Oxford: Blackwell.

Parker, Robert (1989). "Spartan Religion," in Anton Powell (ed.). *Classical Sparta: Techniques behind Her Success*. London: Routledge, pp. 142–72.

—— (1998). *Cleomenes on the Acropolis: Inaugural Lecture, University of Oxford, 12 May 1997*. Oxford: Clarendon.

Pearson, Lionel (1975). *Early Ionian Historians*. Westport, Conn.: Greenwood.

Pébarthe, C. (2005). "Lindos, l'Hellénion, et Naucratis: Réflexions sur l'administration de l'emporion." *Topoi* 12–13, pp. 157–81.

Peitgen, Heinz-Otto, Hartmut Jürgens, and Dietmar Saupe (2004). *Chaos and Fractals: New Frontiers of Science*. 2nd edn. New York: Springer.

Pelagatti, Paola (2004). "Le due Naxos: Un gemellaggio dalle origini," in M. C. Lentini (ed.). *Le due città di Naxos: Atti del Seminario di Studi Giardini Naxos 29–31 Ottobre 2000*. Giardini Naxos: Comune di Giardini Naxos, pp. 22–27.

Peña, María-José (1985). "Le problème de la supposée ville indigene à côté d'Emporion: Nouvelles hypotheses," *DHA*, 11, pp. 69–83.

—— (2000). "Les cultes d'Emporion," in Hermary and Tréziny (2000), pp. 59–68.

Perlman, Paula Jean (2000). *City and Sanctuary in Ancient Greece: The Theorodokia in the Peloponnese*. Hypomnemata 121. Göttingen: Vandenhoeck and Ruprecht.

Peserico, A. (1996). "L'interazione culturale Greco-fenicia: Dall'Egeo al Tirreno centro-meridionale," in E. Acquaro (ed.). *Alle soglie della classicità: Il Mediterraneo tra tradizione e inovazione*. Studi in onore di Sabatino Moscati. Rome: Istituti Editoriali e Poligrafici Internazionali, pp. 899–916.

Petrie, W. M. Flinders (1886). *Naukratis: Part I, 1884–5*. Egypt Exploration Fund Memoirs 3. London: Trübner.

Plana-Mallart, Rosa (1994a). *La chôra d'Emporion: Paysage et structures agraires dans le nord-est Catalan à la période pré-romaine*. Centre de Recherches d'Histoire Ancienne 137, Espaces et paysages 2. Paris: Belles Lettres.

—— (1994b). "La chôra de Emporion," in Julio Mangas and Jaime Alvar (eds.). *Homenaje a José Ma. Blázquez*. Madrid: Ediciones Clásicas, pp. 399–424.

—— (1999). "Cadastre et chôra ampuritaine," in Michèle Brunet (ed.). *Territoires des cités grecques*. Vol. 34. *BCH* Suppl., pp. 199–215.

Plommer, Hugh (1981). "The Temple of Messa on Lesbos," in Bluma L. Trell, Lionel Casson, and Martin Price (eds.). *Coins, Culture, and History in the Ancient World: Numismatic and Other Studies in Honor of Bluma L. Trell*. Detroit: Wayne State University Press, pp. 177–86.

Polanyi, Karl (1977). *The Livelihood of Man*. Studies in Social Discontinuity. New York: Academic Press.

Porten, Bezalel (1984). "The Jews in Egypt," in W. D. Davies and Louis Finkelstein (eds.). *The Cambridge History of Judaism*. Vol. 1. New York: Cambridge University Press, pp. 372–400.

—— and Ada Yardeni (1993). *Textbook of Aramaic Documents from Ancient Egypt*. Vol. 3: *Literature, Accounts, Lists: Texts and Studies for Students*. Jerusalem: Hebrew University, Department of the History of the Jewish People; Winona Lake, Ind.: Eisenbrauns.

Portugali, Juval (1993). *Implicate Relations: Society and Space in the Israeli-Palestinian Conflict.* GeoJournal Library 23. Dordrecht: Kluwer Academic.

———— (2000). *Self-Organization and the City.* Berlin: Springer.

———— (2004). "The Mediterranean as a Cognitive Map," *MHR,* 19(2), pp. 16–24.

Pouilloux, Jean (1954). *Recherches sur l'histoire et les cultes des Thasos, de la fondation de la cité à 196 av. J.-C.* Paris: De Boccard.

———— (1974). "Héraclès thasien," *RHR,* 76, pp. 305–16.

———— (1988). "Un texte commercial ionien trouvé en Languedoc et la colonisation ionienne," *Scienze dell'antichità: Storia, archeologia, antropologia,* 2, pp. 535–46.

Prato, Carlo (1968). *Tyrtaeus: Fragmenta.* Lyricorum Graecorum quae exstant 3. Rome: Athenaeum.

Pratt, Mary Louise (1992). *Imperial Eyes: Travel Writing and Transculturation.* London: Routledge.

Preston, R. E. (1983). "The Dynamic Component of Christaller's Central Place Theory and the Theme of Change in His Research," *Canadian Geographer,* 27, pp. 4–16.

Price, Martin and Nancy Waggoner (1975). *Archaic Greek Coinage: The Asyut Hoard.* London: Vecchi.

Prinz, Friedrich (1979). *Gründungsmythen und Sagenchronologie.* Zetemata 72. Munich: Beck.

Prontera, Francesco (1996a). "Sulla geografica nautica e sulla representazione litoreana della Magna Grecia," in Prontera (1996b), 281–98.

———— (ed.) (1996b). *La Magna Grecia e il mare: Studi di storia marittima.* Taranto: Istituto per la storia e l'archeologia della Magna Grecia.

Purcell, Nicholas (1990). "Mobility and the Polis," in Oswyn Murray and Simon Price (eds.). *The Greek City: From Homer to Alexander.* New York: Oxford University Press, pp. 29–58.

———— (2005). "Colonization and Mediterranean History," in Hurst and Owen (2005), pp. 115–40.

Purves, Alex C. (2010). *Space and Time in Ancient Greek Narrative.* Cambridge: Cambridge University Press.

Quinn, Josephine Crawley (2011). "The Cultures of the Tophet: Identification and Identity in the Phoenician Diaspora," in Gruen (2011), pp. 388–413.

Raaflaub, Kurt A. (2004). *The Discovery of Freedom in Ancient Greece.* 1st English edn. Rev. and updated from the German. Chicago: University of Chicago Press.

Race, William H. (1997a). *Pindar. Vol. 1: Olympian Odes, Pythian Odes.* Translated by William H. Race. Loeb Classical Library. Cambridge, Mass.: Harvard University Press.

———— (1997b). *Pindar. Vol. 2: Nemean Odes, Isthmian Odes, Fragments.* Translated by William H. Race. Loeb Classical Library. Cambridge, Mass.: Harvard University Press.

Raviola, Flavio (1986). "Temistocle e la Magna Grecia," in L. Braccesi (ed.). *Tre studi su Temistocle.* Padua: Editoriale Programma, pp. 13–112.

———— (2000). "La tradizione letteraria sulla fondazione di Massalia," in Braccesi (ed.), *Hesperìa,* 10 (Rome), pp. 74–82.

Ray, John D. (1988). "Egypt: 525–404 BC," in John Boardman, N. G. L. Hammond, David M. Lewis et al. (eds.). *The Cambridge Ancient History.* 2nd edn. Vol. 4: *Persia,*

Greece, and the Western Mediterranean. New York: Cambridge University Press, pp. 254–86.

Raymond, Eric S. (2001). *The Cathedral and the Bazaar: Musings on Linux and Open Source by an Accidental Revolutionary.* Rev. edn. Cambridge, Mass.: O'Reilly. http://catb.org/~esr/writings/cathedral-bazaar/cathedral-bazaar/.

Reger, Gary (1997). "Islands with One *Polis* versus Islands with Several *Poleis*," in Mogens Herman Hansen (ed.). *The Polis as an Urban Centre and as a Political Community: Symposium, August 29–31, 1996.* Acts of the Copenhagen Polis Centre 4, Copenhagen: Royal Danish Academy of Sciences and Letters, pp. 450–92.

———— (2004). "The Aegean," in Hansen and Nielsen (2004), pp. 732–93.

Reichert-Südbeck, Petra (2002). *Kulte von Korinth und Syrakus: Vergleich zwischen einer Metropolis und ihrer Apokia.* Dettelbach: Röll.

Renan, Ernest (1882). *Qu'est-ce qu'une nation? Conférence faite en Sorbonne, le 11 mars 1882.* Paris: Calmann-Lévy.

Renfrew, Colin and John F. Cherry (1986). *Peer Polity Interaction and Socio-Political Change.* Cambridge: Cambridge University Press.

Revel, Jacques and Giovanni Levi (2002). *Political Uses of the Past: The Recent Mediterranean Experience.* Special issue of *MHR* 16(1) (June 2001). London: Cass.

Rhodes, P. J. and Robin Osborne (2003). *Greek Historical Inscriptions, 404–323 BC.* Oxford: Oxford University Press.

Ribichini, Sergio (2001). "Beliefs and Religious Life," in Sabatino Moscati (ed.). *The Phoenicians.* London: Taurus, pp. 120–52.

Richer, Nicholas (1998). *Les Éphores: Études sur l'historie et sur l'image de Sparte, (VIIIe–IIIe siècles av. J.-C.).* Paris: Publications de la Sorbonne.

Ridgway, David (1973–1974). "Archaeology in Central Italy and Etruria, 1968–73," *Archaeological Reports,* 20, pp. 42–59.

———— (1992). *The First Western Greeks.* Cambridge: Cambridge University Press.

———— (2007). "Some Reflections on the Early Euboeans and Their Partners in the Central Mediterranean," in A. Mazarakis-Ainian (ed.). *Oropos and Euboea in the Early Iron Age: Acts of an International Round Table, University of Thessaly (June 18–20, 2004).* Volos: University of Thessaly Press, pp. 141–53.

Robert, Louis (1960). "Recherches épigraphiques," *REA,* 62, pp. 276–361.

Robertson, Roland (1992). *Globalization: Social Theory and Global Culture.* Theory, Culture, and Society. London: Sage.

———— (1995). "Glocalization: Time-Space and Homogeneity-Heterogeneity," in Mike Featherstone, Scott Lash, and Roland Robertson (eds.). *Global Modernities.* Theory, Culture, and Society, London: Sage, pp. 25–44.

———— (1997). "Comments on the 'Global Triad' and 'Glocalization,'" in Nobutaka Inoue (ed.). *Globalisation and Indigenous Culture.* Tokyo: Kokugakuin University, pp. 217–25.

———— (1998). "Glokalisierung, Homogenität, und Heterogenität in Raum und Zeit," in Ulrich Beck (ed.). *Perspektiven der Weltgesellschaft.* Frankfurt am Main: Suhrkamp, pp. 191–220.

Robu, Adrian (2007). "Le culte de Zeus Meilichios à Sélinonte et la place des groupements familiaux et pseudo-familiaux dans la colonisation mégarienne," in P. Brulé (ed.). *La norme en matière religieuse en Grèce ancienne, Actes du XIIe colloque international du CIERGA (Rennes, septembre 2007). Kernos* Suppl. 21, 2009, pp. 277–91.

—— (In press). "Traditions et innovations institutionnelles: L'organisation civique de Byzance et de Chalcédoine," *Il mar Nero*, 7 (2007–2009).

—— (Forthcoming) (a). *La cité de Mégare et les établissements mégariens de Sicile, de la Propontide, et du Pont-Euxin: Histoire et institutions.* Berne : Lang.

—— (In press) (b). "Traditions et innovations institutionnelles: L'organisation civique de Byzance et de Chalcédoine, " *Il mar Nero*, 7, 2007–2009.

Rodríguez Somolinos, Helena (1996). "The Commercial Transaction of the Pech-Maho Lead: A New Interpretation," *ZPE*, 111, pp. 74–78.

Roebuck, Carl (1961). "Tribal Organization in Ionia," *TAPhA*, 92, pp. 495–507.

Rolland, Henri (1951). *Fouilles de Saint-Blaise (Bouches-du-Rhone).* Paris: Centre national de la recherche scientifique.

—— (1956). *Fouilles de Saint-Blaise (1951–1956).* Paris: Centre national de la recherche scientifique.

Rolle, Renate, Karin Schmidt, and Roald F. Docter (eds.) (1998). *Archäologische Studien in Kontaktzonen der antiken Welt.* Göttingen: Vandenhoeck and Ruprecht.

Rolley, Claude (1997). "Encore sur les 'aphidrumata': Sur la fondation de Marseille, de Thasos, et de Rome," *AION ArchStAnt* n.s. 4, pp. 35–43.

Rougier-Blanc, S. (2008). "L'interprétation politique et sociale de l'oeuvre d'Archiloque: Bilan et perspectives," in *Archiloque poète dans l'histoire. Pallas* 77. Toulouse, pp. 15–32.

Rouillard, Pierre (1992). "La place de Marseille dans le commerce des vases attiques à figures rouges en Méditerranée occidentale (Ve–IVe siècles avant J.-C.)," in Bats et al. (1992), pp. 179–87.

—— (ed.) (2010). *Portraits de migrants, portraits de colons: Colloques de la Maison René-Ginouvès* 6. Paris: de Boccard.

Rouquette, Jean-Maurice and Claude Sintès (1989). *Arles antique: Monuments et sites.* Guides archéologiques de la France 17. Paris: Imprimerie Nationale.

Rubin, Zeev (1986). "The Mediterranean and the Dilemma of the Roman Empire in Late Antiquity," *MHR*, 1(1), pp. 13–62.

Rubinstein, Lene (2004). "Samos," in Hansen and Nielsen (2004), pp. 1094–98.

Ruffini, Giovanni (2004). "Late Antique Pagan Networks from Athens to the Thebaid," in W. V. Harris and Giovanni Ruffini (eds.). *Ancient Alexandria between Egypt and Greece.* Leiden: Brill, pp. 241–57.

—— (2008). *Social Networks in Byzantine Egypt.* New York: Cambridge University Press.

Rutherford, Ian (1998). "The Amphikleidai of Sicilian Naxos: Pilgrimage and Genos in the Temple Inventories of Hellenistic Delos," *ZPE*, 122, pp. 81–89.

—— (2002). "Theoria," in *Der Neue Pauly* 12/1. Stuttgart: Metzler, pp. 398–400.

—— (2007). "Network Theory and Theoric Networks," *MHR*, 22(1), pp. 23–37.

Saïd, Suzanne (2001). "The Discourse of Identity in Greek Rhetoric from Isocrates to Aristides," in Malkin (2001c), pp. 275–99.

—— (ed.) (1991). *Hellenismos: Quelques jalons pour une histoire de l'identité grecque: Actes du Colloque de Strasbourg, 25–27 octobre 1989.* Travaux du Centre de recherche sur le Proche-Orient et la Grèce antique 11. Leiden: Brill.

Sakellariou, Michel B. (1958). *La migration grecque en Ionie.* Athens: Institut français d'Athènes.

Salmon, J. B. (1984). *Wealthy Corinth: A History of the City to 338 BC.* Oxford: Oxford University Press.

Salviat, François (2000). "La source ionienne: Apatouria, Apollon Delphinios, et l'oracle, l'Aristarcheion," in Hermary and Tréziny (2000), pp. 25–31.

Samuel, Alan Edouard (1972). *Greek and Roman Chronology: Calendars and Years in Classical Antiquity.* Handbuch der Altertumswissenschaft 1.7. Munich: Beck.

Sánchez, Pierre (2001). *L'Amphictionie des Pyles et de Delphes: Recherches sur son rôle historique, des origines au IIe siècle de notre ère.* Historia Einzelschriften 148. Stuttgart: Steiner.

Sanmartí, Enric (1982). "Les influences méditerranéennes au nord-est de la Catalogne à l'époque archaïque et la réponse indigène," *PP*, 204–8, pp. 281–303.

——— (1988). "Notes additionnelles sur la lettre sur plomb d'Emporion," *ZPE*, 72, pp. 100–102.

——— and Rosa A. Santiago (1987). "Une lettre grecque sur plomb trouvée à Emporion (Fouilles 1985)," *ZPE*, 68(1987), pp. 119–27.

——— and Rosa A. Santiago (1988). "La lettre grecque d'Emporion et son contexte archéologique," *Revue archéologique de Narbonnaise*, 21, pp. 3–17.

Santiago, Rosa A. (1990a). "Encore une fois sur la lettre sur plomb d'Emporion (1985)," *ZPE*, 80, pp. 79–80.

——— (1990b). "Quelques corrections à *ZPE* 80, 1990, pp. 79–80," *ZPE*, 84, p. 14.

Sauneron, Serge and Jean Yoyotte (1952). "La campagne nubienne de Psammétique II et sa signification historique," *BIFAO*, pp. 157–207.

Schaber, Wilfried (1982). *Die archaischen Tempel der Artemis von Ephesos: Entwurfsprinzipien und Rekonstruktion.* Schriften aus dem Athenaion der Klassischen Archäologie Salzburg 2. Waldsassen-Bayern: Stiftland.

Scheidel, Walter (2003). "The Greek Demographic Expansion: Models and Comparisons," *JHS*, 123, pp. 120–40.

——— and Sitta von Reden (2002). *The Ancient Economy.* New York: Routledge.

Schengg, Michael (2006). "Reciprocity and the Emergence of Power Laws in Social Networks," *International Journal of Modern Physics C (Physics and Computers)*, 17(8), pp. 1067–76.

Schilardi, Demetrio (1973). "A Fortified Acropolis on the Oikonomos Island of Paros," *Archeologika Analekta ex Athenon*, 6, pp. 260–65.

——— (1975). "Paros, Report II: The 1973 Campaign," *Journal of Field Archaeology*, 2, pp. 83–96.

——— (1983). "The Decline of the Geometric Settlement of Koukounaries at Paros," in Robin Hägg (ed.). *The Greek Renaissance of the Eighth Century B.C.: Tradition and Innovation.* Stockholm: Svenska institutet i Athen and Åström, pp. 173–83.

——— (1988). "The Temple of Athena at Koukounaries: Observations on the Cult of Athena on Paros," in Robin Hägg, Nanno Marinatos, and Gullög Nordquist (eds.). *Early Greek Cult Practice.* Stockholm: Svenska institutet i Athen and Åström, pp. 41–48.

——— (1996). "Il culto di Atena a Koukounaries e considerazioni sulla topografia de Paros nel VII sec. A.C.," in Eugenio Lanzillotta and Demetrio Schilardi (eds.). *Le Cicladi ed il mondo egeo: Seminario internazionale di studi. Roma, 19–21 novembre 1992.* Rome: Università degli studi di Roma "Tor vergata," Dipartimento di storia, pp. 33–64.

Schmid, B. (1947). "Studien zu Griechischen Ktissisagen." PhD diss., University of Freiburg.

Schott, Carl (1977). "Die Mittelmeerforschung der deutschen Geographie vor dem zweiten Weltkrieg," in Klaus Rother (ed.). *Aktiv-und Passivräume im mediterranen Südeuropa: Symposium vom 24. bis 25. April 1976 im Geographischen Institut der Universität Düsseldorf.* Düsseldorfer Geographische Schriften 7. Düsseldorf: Selbstverlag des Institutes, pp. 7–20.

Schulten, Adolf (1928). "Mainake," in *RE*. Vol. 14, col. 575–76.

Segre, M. and Giovanni Pugliese Caratelli (1952). "Tituli Camirenses," *Annuario della Scuola archeologica di Atene e delle missioni italiane in Oriente*, 27–29, pp. 141–318.

Semple, Ellen Churchill (1932). *The Geography of the Mediterranean Region: Its Relation to Ancient History.* London: Constable.

Shaw, Brent (2004). "A Peculiar Island: Maghrib and Mediterranean," *MHR*, 18(2), pp. 93–125.

Shefton, B. B. (1994). "Massalia and Colonization in the North-Western Mediterranean," in Gocha R. Tsetskhladze and F. de Angelis (eds.). *The Archaeology of Greek Colonisation: Essays Dedicated to Sir John Boardman.* Oxford: Oxford University School of Archaeology, pp. 61–85.

Shepherd, Gillian (1995). "The Pride of Most Colonials: Burial and Religion in the Sicilian Greek Colonies," *Acta Hyperborea*, 6, pp. 51–82.

——— (2000). "Greeks Bearing Gifts: Religious Relationships between Sicily and Greece in the Archaic Period," in Christopher J. Smith and John Serrati (eds.). *Sicily from Aeneas to Augustus: New Approaches in Archaeology and History.* New Perspectives on the Ancient World. Edinburgh: Edinburgh University Press, pp. 55–70.

——— (2005). "Dead Men Tell No Tales: Ethnic Diversity in Sicilian Colonies and the Evidence of the Cemeteries," *OJA*, 24(2), pp. 115–36.

Sherwin-White, Susan M. (1978). *Ancient Cos: An Historical Study from the Dorian Settlement to the Imperial Period.* Hypomnemata 51. Göttingen: Vandenhoeck und Ruprecht.

Shipley, Graham (1987). *A History of Samos: 800–188 BC.* Oxford: Clarendon.

——— (1997). "'The Other Lakedaimonians': The Dependent Perioikic Poleis of Laconia and Messenia," in Mogens Herman Hansen (ed.). *The Polis as an Urban Centre and as a Political Community: Symposium, August 29–31, 1996.* Acts of the Copenhagen Polis Centre 4. Copenhagen: Royal Danish Academy of Sciences and Letters, pp. 189–281.

——— (2004). "Messenia," in Hansen and Nielsen (2004), pp. 547–68.

Silver, Morris (1995). *Economic Structures of Antiquity.* Contributions in Economics and Economic History 159. London: Greenwood.

Sintès, Claude (ed.) (1996). *Musée de l'Arles antique.* Arles: Actes Sud.

Sjöqvist, Erik (1973). *Sicily and the Greeks: Studies in the Interrelationship between the Indigenous Populations and the Greek Colonists.* Jerome Lectures, 9th series. Ann Arbor: University of Michigan Press.

Smith, Anthony D. (1986). *The Ethnic Origins of Nations.* Oxford: Blackwell.

——— (1991). *National Identity.* Ethnonationalism in Comparative Perspective. Reno: University of Nevada Press.

Smith, Charles F. (1921) *Thucydides.* Vol. 3. Translated by Charles Forster Smith. Loeb Classical Library. Cambridge, Mass.: Harvard University Press.

Snodgrass, Anthony M. (1980). *Archaic Greece: The Age of Experiment*. London: Dent.

Soja, Edward W. (1989). *Postmodern Geographies: The Reassertion of Space in Critical Social Theory*. London: Verso.

———— (1996). *Thirdspace: Journeys to Los Angeles and Other Real-and-Imagined Places*. Oxford: Blackwell.

Sokolowski, Franciszek (1969). *Lois sacrées des cités grecques*. Paris: De Boccard.

Solin, H. (1981). "Sulle dediche greche di Gravisca," *PP*, 36, pp. 185–87.

Solovyov, Sergei L. (1999). *Ancient Berezan: The Architecture, History, and Culture of the First Greek Colony in the Northern Black Sea*. Colloquia Pontica 4. Leiden: Brill.

Sommer, Michael (2000). *Europas Ahnen: Ursprünge des Politischen bei den Phönikern*. Darmstadt: Wissenschaftliche Buchgesellschaft.

Sourisseau, Jean-Christophe (1997). "Recherches sur les amphores de Provence et de la basse vallée du Rhône aux époques classique et archaïque (fin VIIe–début IVe s. av. J.-C.)." PhD diss., University of Provence.

———— (2003). "Saint-Blaise," in Christian Landes (ed.). *Les Étrusques en France: Archéologie et collections*. Catalogue de l'exposition, Lattes: Imago, pp. 61–80.

Sourvinou-Inwood, Christiane (2000). "What Is Polis Religion?" in R. G. A. Buxton (ed.). *Oxford Readings in Greek Religion*. Oxford: Oxford University Press, pp. 13–37. Originally published in Oswyn Murray and Simon Price (eds.). *The Greek City: From Homer to Alexander*. Oxford: Oxford University Press, 1990, pp. 295–322.

Spadea, Roberto (ed.) (1996). *Il tesoro di Hera: Scoperte nel santuario di Hera Lacinia a Capo Colonna di Crotone*. Milan: Edizioni ET.

Spencer, Nigel (1995). *A Gazetteer of Archaeological Sites in Lesbos*. BAR International Series 623. Oxford: Tempus Reparatum.

Stager, Lawrence E. (2001). "Port Power in the Early and the Middle Bronze Age: The Organization of Maritime Trade and Hinterland Production," in Samuel R. Wolff (ed.). *Studies in the Archaeology of Israel and Neighboring Lands: In Memory of Douglas L. Esse*. Studies in Ancient Oriental Civilization 59. Chicago: Oriental Institute of the University of Chicago, pp. 625–38.

Stahl, Frieda A. (1987). "Physics as Metaphor and Vice Versa," *Leonardo*, 20(1), pp. 57–64.

Stanford, William Bedell (1984). *The Odyssey of Homer*. Vol. 1: Books I–XII. 2nd edn. New York: Macmillan and St. Martin's Press.

Stobart, J. C. (1984). *The Glory That Was Greece*. 4th edn. London: Sidgwick and Jackson.

Stoneman, Richard and Richard Wallace (1989). *Classical Wall Maps: 1. Ancient Greece and the Aegean*. London: Routledge.

Strogatz, Steven H. (2003). *Sync: The Emerging Science of Spontaneous Order*. Harmondsworth: Penguin.

Styrenius, Carl-Gustaf (1998). *Asine: En svensk utgravningsplats i Grekland* [*Asine: A Swedish Excavation Site in Greece*]. Studies in Mediterranean Archaeology and Literature. Pocketbook 151. Stockholm: Museum of Mediterranean and Near Eastern Antiquities.

Swiderek, Anna (1961). "Hellénion de Memphis: La rencontre de deux mondes," *Eos*, 51, pp. 55–63.

Tammuz, Oded (2005). "Mare clausum? Sailing Seasons in the Mediterranean in Early Antiquity," *MHR*, 20(2), pp. 145–62.

Tandy, David (1997). *Warriors into Traders: The Power of the Market in Early Greece.* Berkeley: University of California Press.

—— (2004). "Trade and Commerce in Archilochos, Sappho, and Alkaios," in R. Rollinger and Ch. Ulf (eds.). *Commerce and Monetary Systems in the Ancient World: Means of Transmission and Cultural Interaction. Oriens et Occidens* 6. Stuttgart: Steiner, pp. 183–95.

Tausend, Klaus (1992). *Amphiktyonie und Symmachie: Formen zwischenstaatlicher Beziehungen im archaischen Griechenland.* Historia Einzelschriften 73. Stuttgart: Steiner.

Teixidor, Javier (1983). "L'interprétation phénicienne d'Héraclès et d'Apollon," *RHR,* 200, pp. 243–55.

Thomas, Rosalind (2001). "Ethnicity, Genealogy, and Hellenism in Herodotus," in Malkin (2001c), pp. 213–33.

Thompson, Dorothy J. (1988). *Memphis under the Ptolemies.* Princeton, N.J.: Princeton University Press.

Tocco Sciarelli, Giuliana (2000). "I culti di Velia; Scoperte recenti," in Hermary and Tréziny (2000), pp. 51–58.

Tod, Marcus Niebuhr (1946). *A Selection of Greek Historical Inscriptions to the End of the Fifth Century B.C.* Vol. 2. 2nd edn. Oxford: Clarendon.

Tokhtas'ev S. (2010). "Die Beziehungen zwischen Borysthenes, Olbia, und Bosporos in der archaischen Zeit nach den epigraphischen Quellen," in Sergei Solovyov (ed.). *Archaic Greek Culture: History, Archaeology, Art, and Museology: Proceedings of the International Round-Table Conference* [June 2005, St. Petersburg, Russia], BAR International Series 2061. Oxford: Archaeopress, pp. 103–108.

Torelli, Mario (1971a). "Gravisca (Tarquinia): Scavi nella città etrusca e romana. Campagne 1969 e 1970," *Notizie degli scavi di antichità,* ser. 8, 25, pp. 195–299.

—— (1971b). "Il santuario di Hera a Gravisca," *PP,* 26, pp. 44–67.

—— (1977). "Il santuario greco di Gravisca," *PP,* 32, pp. 398–458.

—— (1982). "Per la definizione del commercio greco-orientale: Il case di Gravisca," *PP,* 37, pp. 304–25.

—— (1988). "Riflessioni a margine dell'emporion di Gravisca," *PACT,* 20, pp. 181–90.

Torr, Cecil (1885). *Rhodes in Ancient Times.* Cambridge: Cambridge University Press.

Treister, M. Y. (1999). "Ephesos and the Northern Pontic Area in the Archaic and Classical Periods," in H. Friesinger and F. Krinzinger (eds.). *100 Jahre Österreichische Forschungen in Ephesos.* Vienna: Österreichische Akademie der Wissenschaften, pp. 81–86.

Tréziny, Henri (1997). "Marseille grecque à la lumière des fouilles récentes," *Revue archéologique,* 1, pp. 185–200.

Trotta, Francesco (2005). "The Foundations of the Greek Colonies and Their Main Features in Strabo: A Portrayal Lacking Homogeneity?" in Daniela Dueck, Hugh Lindsay, and Sarah Pothecary (eds.). *Strabo's Cultural Geography: The Making of a Kolossourgia.* New York: Cambridge University Press, pp. 118–25.

Trundle, Matthew (2004). *Greek Mercenaries: From the Late Archaic Period to Alexander.* London: Routledge.

Tsetskhladze, Gocha R. (1994). "Greek Penetration of the Black Sea," in Gocha R. Tsetskhladze and Franco De Angelis (eds.). *The Archaeology of Greek Colonisation: Essays*

Dedicated to Sir John Boardman. Oxford: Oxford University School of Archaeology, pp. 111–35.

———— (1998). "Greek Colonisation of the Black Sea Area: Stages, Models, and Native Population," in Gocha R. Tsetskhladze (ed.). *The Greek Colonisation of the Black Sea Area: Historical Interpretation of Archaeology.* Stuttgart: Steiner, pp. 9–68.

———— (2002). "Ionians Abroad," in Gocha R. Tsetskhladze and Anthony M. Snodgrass (eds.). *Greek Settlements in the Eastern Mediterranean and the Black Sea. BAR* International Series 1062. Oxford: Archaeopress, pp. 81–96.

———— (2006a). "Revisiting Ancient Greek Colonisation," in Tsetskhladze (2006b), pp. xxiii–lxxxiii.

———— (ed.) (2006b). *Greek Colonisation: An Account of Greek Colonies and Other Settlements Overseas.* Leiden: Brill.

———— (ed.) (2008). *Greek Colonisation: An Account of Greek Colonies and Other Settlements Overseas.* Vol. 2. Leiden: Brill.

Tuplin, Christopher (2004). "Xenophon, Artemis, and Scillus," in Thomas J. Figueira (ed.). *Spartan Society.* Swansea: Classical Press of Wales, pp. 251–81.

———— (2005) "Hellenicities: Marginal Notes on a Book and a Review," *Ancient West and East,* 4(2), pp. 421–29.

Turner, Frederick Jackson ([1921] 1962). *The Frontier in American History.* New York: Holt.

Tusa, Vincenzo (1986). "I Fenici e i Cartaginesi," in Giovanni Pugliese Carratelli (ed.). *Sikanie: Storia e civiltà della Sicilia greca.* Milan: Garzanti, pp. 577–631.

———— (1991). "Greci e Punici," in Georges Vallet (ed.). *Les Grecs et l'Occident: Actes du Colloque de la Villa "Kérylos"* (1991). Collection de l'École française de Rome 208. Rome: L'École française de Rome, pp. 19–28.

Urso, Gianpaolo (1998). *Taranto e gli xenikoi strategoi.* Rome: Istituto italiano per la storia antica.

Valavanis, Panos (2004). *Games and Sanctuaries in Ancient Greece: Olympia, Delphi, Isthmia, Nemea, Athens.* Translated by David Hardy. Los Angeles: Getty.

Vallet, Georges (1958). *Rhégion et Zancle: Histoire, commerce, et civilisation des cités chalcidiennes du détroit de Messine.* Bibliothèque des Écoles françaises d'Athènes et de Rome 189. Paris: De Boccard.

———— (1968). "La cité et son territoire dans les colonies grecques d'occident," *Atti dal VII Convegno di Studi sulla Magna Grecia.* Naples: L'arte tipografica, pp. 1–7, 67–142.

———— (1996). "Les cites chalcidiennes du Détroit de Sicile," in Georges Vallet (ed.). *Le monde grec colonial d'Italie du sud et de Sicile.* Collection de l'École française de Rome 218. Rome: École française de Rome, pp. 115–62.

———— and François Villard (1966). "Les Phocéens en Méditerranée occidentale à l'époque archaïque et la fondation de Hyélè," *PP,* 21, pp. 166–90.

———— and Paul Auberson (1976). *Mégara Hyblaea.* Vol. 1: *Le quartier de l'agora archaïque, avec la collaboration de Michel Gras et Henri Tréziny.* Paris: De Boccard.

Van Berchem, Denis (1967). "Sanctuaires à Hercule-Melquart: Contribution a l'étude de l'expansion phénicienne en Méditerranée," *Syria,* 44, pp. 73–109, 307–38.

Van Compernolle, Thierry (1985). "La colonization rhodienne en Apulie: Réalité historique ou légende?" *MEFRA,* 97, pp. 35–45.

Van Dommelen, Peter (1997). "Colonial Constructs: Colonialism and Archaeology in the Mediterranean," *World Archaeology,* 28(3), pp. 305–23.

———— (1998). *On Colonial Grounds: A Comparative Study of Colonialism and Rural Settlement in First Millennium BC West Central Sardinia*. Leiden: Faculty of Archaeology, Leiden University.

———— (2005). "Colonial Interactions and Hybrid Practices: Phoenician and Carthaginian Settlement in the Ancient Mediterranean," in Gil Stein (ed.). *The Archaeology of Colonial Encounters: Comparative Perspectives*. Santa Fe: School of American Research, pp. 109–42.

———— (2006a). "Colonial Matters: Material Culture and Postcolonial Theory in Colonial Situations," in C. Tilley, W. Keane, S. Kuechler et al. (eds.). *Handbook of Material Culture*. London: Sage, pp. 104–24.

———— (2006b). "The Orientalising Phenomenon: Hybridity and Material Culture in the Western Mediterranean," in C. Riva and N. Vella (eds.). *Debating Orientalisation*. Monographs in Mediterranean Archaeology 10. London: Equinox, pp. 135–52.

Vanschoonwinkel, Jacques (2006). "Greek Migrations to Aegean Anatolia in the Early Dark Age," in Tsetskhladze (2006b), pp. 115–41.

Vasconcelos, Alvaro and E. G. H. Joffé (2000). *The Barcelona Process: Building a Euro-Mediterranean Regional Community*. London: Cass.

Villard, François (1960). *La céramique grecque de Marseille, VIe–IVe siècle: Essai d'histoire économique*. Bibliothèque des Écoles françaises d'Athènes et de Rome 195. Paris: De Boccard.

Walbank, Frank W. (1999). *A Historical Commentary on Polybius*. Oxford: Clarendon.

———— (2000). "Hellenes and Achaians: Greek Nationality Revisited," in P. Flensted-Jensen (ed.). *Further Studies in the Ancient Greek Polis*. Papers from the Copenhagen Polis Centre 5. Historia Einzelschriften 138. Stuttgart: Steiner, pp. 19–33.

Walker, Keith G. (2004). *Archaic Eretria: A Political and Social History from the Earliest Times to 490 BC*. London: Routledge.

Wallinga, H. T. (1993). *Ships and Sea-Power before the Great Persian War: The Ancestry of the Ancient Trireme*. Mnemosyne Suppl. 121. Leiden: Brill.

Wankel, Hermann (ed.). (1979). *Die Inschriften von Ephesos: Inschriften griechischer Städte aus Kleinasien*, Bde. 11–17. Bonn: Habelt.

Warf, Barney and Santa Arias (eds.) (2008). The Spatial Turn: Interdisciplinary Perspectives. New York: Routledge.

Wasserman, Stanley and Katherine Faust (1994). *Social Network Analysis: Methods and Applications*. Structural Analysis in the Social Sciences. Cambridge: Cambridge University Press.

Watts, Duncan J. (1999). *Small Worlds: The Dynamics of Networks between Order and Randomness*. Princeton Studies in Complexity. Princeton, N.J.: Princeton University Press.

———— (2003). *Six Degrees: The Science of a Connected Age*. New York: Norton.

———— and Steven H. Strogatz (1998). "Collective Dynamics of 'Small World' Networks," *Nature*, 393, pp. 440–42.

Way, Arthur S. (1913). *Quintus Smyrnaeus: The Fall of Troy*. Loeb Classical Library. London: Heinemann.

Weatherill, Stephen and Ulf Bernitz (eds.) (2005). *The Role of Regions and Sub-National Actors in Europe*. Oxford: Hart.

West, Martin L. (1993). *Greek Lyric Poetry: The Poems and Fragments of the Greek Iambic, Elegiac, and Melic Poets (Excluding Pindar and Bacchylides) down to 450 B.C.* Oxford: Clarendon.

White, Edmund (2001). *The Flâneur: A Stroll through the Paradoxes of Paris.* London: Bloomsbury.

White, L. Michael (ed.) (1992). *Social Networks in the Early Christian Environment: Issues and Methods for Social History.* Semeia 56. Atlanta: Scholars Press.

White, Richard (1991). *The Middle Ground: Indians, Empires, and Republics in the Great Lakes Region, 1650–1815.* Cambridge Studies in North American Indian History. Cambridge: Cambridge University Press.

——— (2006). "Creative Misunderstandings and New Understandings," *William and Mary Quarterly*, 63(1), pp. 9–14.

Whitehead, David (1986). *The Demes of Attica, 508/7–ca. 250 B.C.: A Political and Social Study.* Princeton, N.J.: Princeton University Press.

Wilcken, Ulrich (1912). *Grundzüge und Chrestomathie der Papyruskunde.* Vol. 1, part 2. Leipzig: Teubner.

Williams, Charles Kaufman (1995). "Archaic and Classical Corinth," in *Corinto e l'Occidente: Atti del trentaquattresimo convegno di studi sulla Magna Grecia: Taranto, 7–11 ottobre 1994.* Taranto: Istituto per la storia e l'archeologia della Magna Grecia, pp. 31–45.

Wilson, John-Paul (1997). "The Nature of Greek Overseas Settlements in the Archaic Period: Emporion or Apoikia?" in Lynette G. Mitchell and P. J. Rhodes (eds.). *The Development of the Polis in Archaic Greece.* New York: Routledge, pp. 199–207.

Wittfogel, Karl August (1963). *Oriental Despotism: A Comparative Study of Total Power.* New Haven, Conn.: Yale University Press.

Woodbury, Leonard (1961). "Apollodorus, Xenophanes, and the Foundation of Massilia," *Phoenix* 15(3), pp. 134–55.

Worthen, Thomas (1997). "Herodotos's Report on Thales' Eclipse," Electronic Antiquity, 3(7). http://scholar.lib.vt.edu/ejournals/ElAnt/V3N7/worthen.html.

Yates, D. C. (2005). "The Archaic Treaties between the Spartans and Their Allies," *CQ*, 55, pp. 65–76.

Yntema, Douwe (2000). "Mental Landscapes of Colonization: The Ancient Written Sources and the Archeology of Early Colonial–Greek Southeastern Italy." *Bulletin antieke Beschavig* 75, pp. 1–50.

Zuntz, Günther (1971). *Persephone: Three Essays on Religion and Thought in Magna Graecia.* Oxford: Clarendon.

Index

decentralized network —

decentralized, network form, dynamism, divergence,
nodes, collective identity with commonalities &
continuities
distance, nonhierarchical, boundless

network = nodes, links, hub (nodes with numerous links)
clusters

CPSIA information can be obtained at www.ICGtesting.com
Printed in the USA
BVOW05s0401161215

430392BV00002B/5/P